FREE MONEY®
FOR GRADUATE SCHOOL

Fourth Edition

by Laurie Blum

☑®

Facts On File, Inc.

Free Money® for Graduate School: Fourth Edition

Checkmark Books
An imprint of Facts On File, Inc.
11 Penn Plaza
New York NY 10001

Library of Congress Cataloging-in-Publication Data

Blum, Laurie.
    Free money for graduate school / by Laurie Blum. —4th ed.
      p. cm.
    Includes bibliographical references and index.
    ISBN 0-8160-4278-0 (hc : acid-free paper)—ISBN 0-8160-4279-9 (pbk. : acid-free paper)
    1. Scholarships—United States—Directories.   2. Graduate students—Scholarships, fellowships, etc.—United States—Directories.   I. Title.
    LB2337.2.B58   2000
    378.3'025'73—dc21   00-026355

Cover design by Semadar Megged

Printed in the United States of America

MP Hermitage 10 9 8 7 6 5 4 3 2 1
    (pbk) 10 9 8 7 6 5 4 3 2 1

This book is printed on acid-free paper.

Contents

Introduction

Graduate education is a long, rigorous, expensive undertaking. The academic demands are enough of a challenge without having to worry about how to pay for it.

Fortunately, there is an enormous amount of money available in both low-cost loans and direct grants to fund advanced degrees. In many fields, graduate funding is more plentiful and accessible than undergraduate funding.

The hardest part has always been finding the sources of money, which is why I wrote this book. Sure there are many books that explain *how* students can attempt to locate sources to fund their education. There are a few extremely expensive and largely unavailable reference books one can try to find in the public library. And there are other books that have some student scholarship information, but they're combined with things like contests, awards, and prizes. This book provides you, the reader, with the actual sources of monies available.

Wherever possible, I have included the total amount of money awarded to students, the number of grants given, the average size of an award, the range of monies given, and the website address, which can be particularly useful in accessing information.

HOW TO APPLY

Applying for grants and scholarships is similar to applying for graduate school; it takes work, some thought, and organization, but at this stage in your life, you know what you have to do.

First comes the sorting-out process. Go through this book and mark off all of the listings that could give you money. Pay close attention to the restrictions, and eliminate the least likely foundations. Although very few of the foundations in this book require an application fee, the effort you will have to put in will probably limit you to no more than eight applications (if you are ambitious and want to apply to more than eight foundations, bravo, go right ahead). Write or call the most likely foundations for a copy of their guidelines. (In cases where the contact's name is not listed, begin your letter: "To Whom It May Concern.") If you call, simply request the guidelines; do not interrogate the person who answers the phone.

Grant applications take time to fill out. Often you will be required to write one or more essays. Proposals should be neatly typed and double-spaced. Be *sure* to make a copy for your records. Many applications require undergraduate transcripts. Often the tax returns of both the applicant (if you filed a return the previous year) and the applicant's parents are needed. You may be asked to include personal references (to avoid embarrassment, be sure to get permission from the people you are planning to use). Sometimes an interview is required. Remember, you have to sell yourself and persuade the grantors to give the money to you and not to someone else.

I divided this book into broad areas of study. The index lists more specific subject categories or academic disciplines (e.g., architecture, women's studies). Check all listings that pertain to your subject. Regardless of your field of study, you should qualify for at least some of the grants covered in this book.

FEDERAL MONEY

Federal aid has long been a funding mainstay for the graduate student. It remains one of the first sources of money to pursue. The process is not complicated, but you must fill out the applications to be considered. It is well worth your time and effort. Several billion dollars is available in this type of student aid.

OTHER SOURCES OF MONEY

Although you have probably been told this many times, you ought to check with the various organizations you have belonged to (professional organizations, fraternities, etc.), places of worship you attend, and employers you or your parents have worked for. Thousands of corporations have programs that will pay for all or part of their employees' or employees' children's university expenses. There is an enormous amount of unused employee tuition benefits. Your hobbies or talents may qualify you for prizes or awards. If you are a veteran or the child of a veteran, you probably qualify for another source of grant money.

As a graduate student, you will have opportunities to work within your department. Possibilities include reading assistantships, in which you grade examinations and papers for professors; teaching assistantships, in which you actually teach students on a limited basis; and research assistantships. Almost every department has a number of the latter available. Check with your department and with individual professors in your department.

Finally, be sure to request information on scholarships and other forms of aid from the financial aid office at each school to which you have applied.

Paying for graduate school isn't a one-year, one-shot deal. You must plan ahead to consider the costs of the entire program.

ONE FINAL NOTE

No reference book can be as up-to-date as the reader (or the author) would like. By the time this book is published, some of the information will have changed. Names, addresses, dollar amounts, telephone numbers, and other data are always in flux. Most of the information, however, will still be accurate.

Good luck!

Humanities and Social Sciences

Alpha Delta Kappa Foundation
Alpha Delta Kappa Fine Arts Grants
1615 West 92nd Street
Kansas City, MO 64114
(816) 363-5525

Description: Grants for the fine and performing arts; available at any academic level; recipients chosen on the basis of artistic skills and professional or advanced study plans.
Restrictions: Applicants may not have received grants from ADK within the past five years.
$ Given: Three grants per category; $5,000 for first place, $3,000 for second place, $1,000 for third place.
Application Information: Grants available every two years; categories change each two-year period.
Deadline: April 1 of even-numbered years.
Contact: Scholarship and Grants Secretary.

American Academy in Rome
Samuel H. Kress Foundation
Predoctoral Fellowships
7 East 60th Street
New York, NY 10022-1001
(212) 751-7200
www.aarome.org./
www.shkf.org

Description: Two two-year fellowships for independent study and research; one fellowship in classical art history, one fellowship in Italian art history; tenable at the American Academy in Rome; awarded to doctoral candidates who have completed coursework and are beginning the second year of dissertation work; recipients chosen on the basis of proposed research.
Restrictions: United States citizenship required.
$ Given: Two fellowships awarded annually; amount varies; travel allowance included.
Application Information: Write for details.
Deadline: November 30.
Contact: Fellowship Coordinator.

American Academy in Rome
Rome Prize Fellowships
School of Classical Studies
7 East 60th Street
New York, NY 10022-1001
(212) 751-7200
www.aarome.org

Description: One-year residential fellowships for doctoral candidates in classical studies, archaeology, classical art, history of art, postclassical humanistic studies, and Medieval and Renaissance studies; tenable at the American Academy in Rome.
Restrictions: Applicants must have completed all doctoral coursework and one year of dissertation work; recipients may not hold job or travel extensively during fellowship year. U.S. citizenship or three year residency in U.S. required.
$ Given: An unspecified number of fellowships of $15,000–$17,800 are awarded annually.
Application Information: Write for details.

Deadline: November 15.
Contact: Fellowships Coordinator.

American Academy in Rome
Rome Prize Fellowships
School of Fine Arts
7 East 60th Street
New York, NY 10022-1001
(212) 751-7200

Description: Several six month to one-year fellowships in architecture, historical preservation and conservation, landscape architecture, design art, painting, sculpture, visual arts, and musical compositions; tenable at the American Academy in Rome.
Restrictions: Painting, sculpture, and visual arts candidates need not hold a degree but must have three years professional commitment, clear ability, and current studio work; architecture and landscape architecture candidates need appropriate degree; other applicants need B.A. degree; recipients may not hold job or travel extensively during fellowship year. U.S. citizenship required.
$ Given: Fourteen fellowships of $9,000–$15,000 awarded annually.
Application Information: Write for details.
Deadline: November 15.
Contact: Fellowships Coordinator.

American Antiquarian
Society
Mellon Post-Dissertation
Fellowships
185 Salisbury Street
Worcester, MA 01609
(508) 755-5221

Description: Nine-month fellowships for graduate students in the fields of history, literature, American studies, political science, art history, music history, and others relating to America in the period of the Society's coverage to extend their research and/or revise their dissertation for publication.
Restrictions: Ph.D. must have been formally awarded before fellowship begins.
$ Given: An unspecified number of fellowships of varying amounts awarded annually.
Application Information: Write for details.
Deadline: N/A.
Contact: John Hench or Caroline Sloat.

American Antiquarian
Society
Visiting Academic Research
Fellowships
185 Salisbury Street
Worcester, MA 01609
(508) 755-5221

Description: One-to-twelve-month fellowships intended for scholars to pursue research in American history and culture through the year 1876 at the Society.
Restrictions: None.
$ Given: An unspecified number of fellowships of varying amounts awarded annually.
Application Information: Write for details.
Deadline: N/A.

American Architectural Foundation
RTKL Traveling Fellowship
129 Sibley Dome
Cornell University
Ithaca, NY 14853
(607) 255-9110

Description: Fellowship for student in second-to-last year of a bachelor or master of architecture program planning to travel outside the U.S. in an established program or accepted in a professional degree program and planning foreign travel that will have a beneficial and direct relationship to educational goals.
Restrictions: None.
$ Given: One fellowship awarded annually for $2,500.
Application Information: Write for details.
Deadline: N/A.
Contact: Director, AIA Scholarship and Career Programs.

American Association for the Advancement of Science
Mass Media Science and Engineering Fellows Program
1200 New York Avenue, N.W.
Washington, DC 20005
(202) 326-6760
www.aaas.org

Description: Ten-week summer fellowships for science graduate students to work as journalists (print, radio, or television) to increase their understanding of the news media; available to students at any graduate level of study in the natural and social sciences, mathematics, as well as engineering; recipients chosen on the basis of academic achievement and demonstrated commitment of conveying to the public a better understanding and appreciation of science and technology.
Restrictions: No funding to non-technical applicants; United States citizenship required; no concurrent funding allowed.
$ Given: Twenty fellowships awarded annually; weekly living stipend for 10 weeks plus travel costs.
Application Information: Write for details and application form; minorities and individuals with disabilities encouraged to apply.
Deadline: January 15.
Contact: Katrina Malloy, Program Manager.

American Association of University Women Educational Foundation
AAUW Selected Professions Fellowships
1111 Sixteenth Street, N.W.
Washington, DC 20036
(202) 728-7602
www.aauw.org.

Description: Fellowships for graduate students entering their final year of study in fields with traditionally low female representation, including architecture, business administration, computer science, dentistry, engineering, law, mathematics/statistics, medicine, and veterinary medicine; recipients chosen on the basis of academic achievement; tenable for full-time study at accredited United States institutions.
Restrictions: Limited to women who are members of minority groups; United States citizenship or permanent resident status required.
$ Given: An unspecified number of fellowships of $5,000–$12,000 each are awarded annually.
Application Information: Application forms available August 1 through December 20.
Deadline: January 10.

American Council of Learned Societies Eastern European Dissertation Fellowships
Office of Fellowships and Grants
228 East 45th Street
New York, NY 10017-3398
(212) 697-1505
www.acls.org.

Description: Fellowships for doctoral dissertation research related to Eastern Europe (Albania, Bulgaria, Czech Republic, Germany, Hungary, Poland, Romania, Slovakia, and (former) Yugoslavia); for research-related study at a university abroad, but not within Eastern Europe; for doctoral candidates in the humanities and social sciences; recipients chosen on the basis of academic achievement, financial need, and quality of proposed research.
Restrictions: United States citizenship or legal residency required.
$ Given: An unspecified number of fellowships awarded annually; each carries an annual stipend of up to $25,000, renewable for second year.
Application Information: Write for details.
Deadline: November 1.
Contact: Ruth Waters.

American Council of Learned Societies Fellowships for Dissertation Research Abroad Related to China
Office of Fellowships and Grants
228 East 45th Street
New York, NY 10017-3398
(212) 697-1505
www.acls.org

Description: Fellowships for doctoral dissertation research related to China; for research-related travel within the People's Republic of China; for doctoral candidates in the humanities and social sciences; recipients chosen on the basis of academic achievement, financial need, and quality of proposed research.
Restrictions: Foreign national applicants must be enrolled as full-time Ph.D. candidates at United States universities.
$ Given: An unspecified number of fellowships awarded annually; each carries an annual stipend of up to $15,000.
Application Information: Write for details.
Deadline: December 1.

American Council of Learned Societies Henry Luce Foundation Dissertation Fellowships in American Art
Office of Fellowships and Grants
228 East 45th Street
New York, NY 10017-3398
(212) 697-1505
www.acsl.org

Description: One-year fellowships for any stage of dissertation research or writing in the field of art history of the United States at any period.
Restrictions: U.S. Citizenship or Permanent Resident status required.
$ Given: Ten fellowships awarded annually, each with a stipend of $18,500.
Application Information: Write for details.
Deadline: November 15.

American Council of Learned Societies
International and Area Studies Fellowships
Office of Fellowships and Grants
228 East 45th Street
New York, NY 10017-3398
(212) 697-1505
www.acsl.org

Description: Six-to-twelve-month fellowships for post-doctoral research in all disciplines of the humanities and humanities-related social sciences on the societies and cultures of Asia, Africa, the Near and Middle East, Latin America, East Europe, and the former Soviet Union.
Restrictions: U.S. Citizenship or permanent resident status required.
$ Given: Approximately eight fellowships awarded annually, each for $25,000 (Junior Fellowships); to $40,000 (Senior Fellowships).
Application Information: Write for details.
Deadline: October 1.

American Council of Learned Societies
New York Public Library Fellowships
Office of Fellowships and Grants
228 East 45th Street
New York, NY 10017-3398
(212) 697-1505
www.acsl.org

Description: Residential fellowships for research at the New York Public Library's new Center for Scholars and Writers; granted to scholars whose projects will benefit from research in the NYPL Humanities and Social Sciences Library.
Restrictions: U.S. Citizenship or Permanent Resident status required.
$ Given: Up to five fellowships awarded annually; each with a maximum stipend of $50,000 plus, when necessary, a limited housing allowance for residency in New York during fellowship term.
Application Information: Contact the Center for Scholars Writers, The New York Public Library, Humanities and Social Sciences Library, Fifth Avenue and 42nd Street, New York, NY 10018-2788.
Deadline: October 1.

American Foundation for the Blind
Karen D. Carsel Memorial Scholarship
11 Pennsylvania Plaza
Suite 300
New York, NY 10001
(212) 502-7600
www.afb.org

Description: Funding to support full-time graduate studies; recipients chosen on the basis of financial need.
Restrictions: Limited to legally blind applicants only; United States citizenship required.
$ Given: One grant for $500 is awarded annually.
Application Information: Applications must include proof of legal blindness, proof of graduate school acceptance, evidence of financial need, personal statement, and letters of recommendation.
Deadline: April 30.
Contact: Julia Tucker, National Consultant in Low Vision.

American Geophysical Union Horton Research Grant in Hydrology and Water Resources
2000 Florida Avenue, N.W.
Washington, DC 20009
(202) 462-6900
www.agu.org

Description: Grants for doctoral candidates, to support research projects in hydrology and water resources; relevant disciplines include physical/chemical/biological aspects of hydrology, as well as water resources policy sciences (economy, sociology, and law).
Restrictions: None.
$ Given: One or more grants awarded annually; approximately $9,000 plus travel allowance to ensure attendance at awards luncheon.
Application Information: Proposal must be signed by faculty advisor; application forms required.
Deadline: March 1.
Contact: Wynelta Singhateh.

American Institute for Economic Research Summer Fellowship Program; In-Absentia Awards
P.O. Box 1000
Great Barrington, MA 01230
(413) 528-1217
www.aier.org

Description: Two-month summer fellowships for college seniors, graduate students, and professionals in economics; successful summer fellows eligible for In-Absentia Awards of partial to total tuition for the following academic year; recipients chosen on the basis of academic achievement and potential for success in graduate school.
Restrictions: United States citizens preferred.
$ Given: Ten to twelve two-month summer fellowships are awarded annually with a $250/week stipend plus room and board.
Application Information: Write for details.
Deadline: March 31.
Contact: Charles Murray, Director of Summer Fellowships.

American Institute of Architects AIA/AIAF Scholarships for First Professional Degree Candidates
1735 New York Avenue, N.W.
Washington, DC 20006
(202) 626-7511
www.aia.org

Description: Scholarships for master's candidates and undergraduates in the final two years of degree programs in architecture; recipients chosen on the basis of academic achievement and financial need; tenable at accredited United States and Canadian institutions.
Restrictions: For full-year study only.
$ Given: An unspecified number of grants of $500–$2,500 are awarded annually.
Application Information: Applications must be made through students' schools.
Deadline: February 1.
Contact: Mary Felber, Director, Scholarship Programs.

American Institute of Architects
AIA/AIAF Scholarships for Advanced Degree/Research Candidates
1735 New York Avenue, N.W.
Washington, DC 20006
(202) 626-7511
www.aia.org

Description: Scholarships for bachelor's and master's candidates in the final year of degree programs in architecture and related fields; recipients chosen on the basis of merits of proposed research/study; tenable for full academic year.
Restrictions: Limited to students enrolled in United States or Canadian universities.
$ Given: An unspecified number of grants of $500–$2,500 are awarded annually.
Application Information: Write for details.
Deadline: February 15.
Contact: Mary Felber, Director, Scholarship Programs.

American Institute of Certified Public Accountants
John L. Carey Scholarships in Accounting
1211 Avenue of the Americas
New York, NY 10036-8775
(212) 575-5504
www.aicpa.org

Description: Scholarships for college liberal arts majors to study accounting on the graduate level; tenable at United States graduate schools.
Restrictions: Applicants must have a liberal arts degree from a regionally accredited institution in the U.S., recipients must plan careers in accounting.
$ Given: Up to five scholarships awarded annually; each for $5,000/year; renewable for second year.
Application Information: Write for details.
Deadline: April 1.

American Institute of Indian Studies
1130 East 59th Street
Chicago, IL 60637
(773) 702-8638

Description: Postdoctoral and graduate fellowships to support research in all fields related to India.
Restrictions: U.S. Citizenship or resident alien status required.
$ Given: A varying number of fellowships of varying amounts awarded annually.
Application Information: Write for details.
Deadline: July 1.

American Institute of Pakistan Studies
American Institute of Pakistan Studies Fellowships
P.O. Box 7568
Wake Forest University
Winston-Salem, NC 27109
(336) 758-5453
www.wfu.edu

Description: Fellowships for doctoral candidates, postdoctoral scholars, and professional researchers to undertake study/research in Pakistan; for students of humanities and social sciences, especially rural development, agriculture, local government, economics, demography, history, and culture; recipients chosen on the basis of proposed research.
Restrictions: Doctoral candidates must have completed all preliminary Ph.D. requirements; United States citizenship required.
$ Given: An unspecified number of fellowships awarded annually; each to cover air travel, maintenance, rental allowance, research allowance, internal travel, and excess baggage allowance.
Application Information: Write for details.
Deadline: January 1.
Contact: Dr. Charles H. Kennedy, Director.

**American Jewish Archives
Lowenstein-Wiener Summer
Fellowship Awards in
American Jewish Studies**
3101 Clifton Avenue
Cincinnati, OH 45220-2488
(513) 221-1875
www.huc.edu/aja/

Description: Summer fellowships for ABDs and post-doctoral scholars studying American Jewish aspects of folklore, history, languages, literatures and linguistics, liberal studies, philosophy, religion, political science, public policy, sociology, anthropology, archaeology, women's studies, and interdisciplinary topics in the humanities and social sciences, education, and international affairs, recipients chosen on the basis of proposed research; tenable for one month of research and writing at the American Jewish Archives.
Restrictions: N/A.
$ Given: Five to eight grants are awarded annually; suitable to cover living expenses while in residence during the fellowship. No specific amounts given.
Application Information: Write for details.
Deadline: April 1.
Contact: Director of Fellowship program.

**American Library Association
David H. Clift Scholarship
Program**
50 East Huron Street
Chicago, IL 60611-2795
(312) 944-6780
www.ala.org

Description: Scholarships for master's candidates in library sciences; recipients chosen on the basis of academic achievement, leadership characteristics, and commitment to library career.
Restrictions: United States or Canadian citizenship required; tenable only for graduate program accredited by ALA.
$ Given: One grant of $3,000 is awarded annually.
Application Information: Write for details.
Deadline: April 1.
Contact: Pat Jackson.

**American Library Association
Frederick G. Melcher
Scholarships**
50 East Huron Street
Chicago, IL 60611-2795
(312) 944-6780
www.ala.org

Description: Scholarships for master's candidates specializing in children's library sciences; recipients chosen on the basis of academic achievement and career commitment/desire to work with children.
Restrictions: Tenable only for graduate program accredited by ALA.
$ Given: Two grants of $6,000 each are awarded annually.
Application Information: Write for details.
Deadline: April 1.
Contact: Pat Jackson.

American Philosophical Society
John Clarke Slater Fellowships
104 South Fifth Street
Philadelphia, PA 19106-3386
(215) 440-3403
www.amphilsoc.org

Description: Fellowships for doctoral candidates writing dissertations on the history of physical sciences in the twentieth century; recipients chosen on the basis of academic achievement and quality of proposed dissertation research.
Restrictions: Applicants must have completed all Ph.D degree requirements except dissertation.
$ Given: An unspecified number of fellowships of $12,000 are awarded annually.
Application Information: Write for details.
Deadline: December 1.

American Philosophical Society Library
Mellon Resident Research Fellowships
104 South Fifth Street
Philadelphia, PA 19106-3386
(215) 440-3400
www.amphilsoc.org

Description: One- to three-month residential fellowships for doctoral candidates at dissertation level and postdoctoral scholars studying the history of American science and technology, its European roots, and its relation to American history and culture; tenable at the Society Library for short-term research using the library's collections.
Restrictions: United States citizens as well as foreign nationals.
$ Given: An unspecified number of fellowships awarded annually; each for $1,900/month; tenable at Society for one to three months.
Application Information: Write for details.
Deadline: March 1.

American Philosophical Society Library
Phillips Fund Grants in North American Indian Linguistics and Ethnohistory
104 South Fifth Street
Philadelphia, PA 19106-3386
(215) 440-3400
www.amphilsoc.org

Description: Grants for graduate students, as well as postdoctoral scholars, studying North American Indian linguistics and ethnohistory; recipients chosen on the basis of proposed research.
Restrictions: N/A.
$ Given: A few grants for up to $1,500 each are awarded annually to cover expenses, not personal maintenance.
Application Information: Write for details.
Deadline: March 1.

American Philosophical Society
Sabbatical Fellowship in the Humanities and Social Sciences
104 South Fifth Street
Philadelphia, PA 19106
(215) 440-3429
www.amphilsoc.org

Description: One-year fellowship for mid-career faculty of universities and four-year colleges in the United States who have been granted a sabbatical year to pursue research.
Restrictions: None. Applicant's doctoral degree should have been awarded no fewer than five and no more than twenty-five years prior to date of application.
$ Given: One fellowship awarded annually, with a stipend of $40,000.
Application Information: Write for details.
Deadline: November 1.

American Planning Association
Charles Abrams Scholarship Program
122 So. Michigan Avenue
Suite 1600
Chicago, IL 60605
(312) 431-9100
www.planning.org

Description: Scholarships for master's candidates in urban planning; recipients chosen on the basis of financial need.
Restrictions: Applicants must attend and be nominated by one of these participating schools: Columbia University, Harvard University, MIT, New School for Social Research, or the University of Pennsylvania; United States citizenship required.
$ Given: One fellowship of $2,000 awarded annually.
Application Information: Application by school nomination only.
Deadline: April 30.
Contact: Margot Morrison.

American Planning Association
Minority Fellowships Program
122 So. Michigan Avenue
Suite 1600
Chicago, IL 60605
(312) 431-9100
www.planning.org

Description: Scholarships for master's candidates in urban planning; tenable for first year of graduate study (renewable for second year) at PAB-accredited institutions; recipients chosen on the basis of financial need.
Restrictions: Limited to African-American, Hispanic, and Native American applicants only; United States or Canadian citizenship required.
$ Given: An unspecified number of fellowships of $1,000–$4,000 per year are awarded annually.
Application Information: Write for details.
Deadline: May 15.
Contact: Margot Morrison.

American Political Science Association
Doctoral Dissertation Awards
1527 New Hampshire Avenue, N.W.
Washington, DC 20036
(202) 483-2512
www.apsanet.org

Description: Awards for outstanding dissertations written by doctoral candidates in various fields of political science; Almond Award for comparative politics, Anderson Award for general state and local politics, Corwin Award for public law and judicial process, Lasswell Award for policy studies, Reid Award for international relations/law/politics, Schattschneider Award for American government and politics, Strauss Award for political philosophy, and White Award for public administration.
Restrictions: Dissertation must have been completed within the last two calendar years.
$ Given: Eight prizes of $500 each are awarded annually.
Application Information: A copy of the dissertation and a letter of nomination from the department chair must be sent to each member of the award committee.
Deadline: January 15.
Contact: Sean Twombly.

American Psychological Association
APA Minority Fellowship Program in Psychology
750 First Street, N.E.
Washington, DC 20002-4242
(202) 336-6027
www.apa.org

Description: Fellowships for doctoral candidates in psychology; one program to support the training of clinicians, another program to support the training of researchers; recipients chosen on the basis of academic achievement and financial need.
Restrictions: Minorities and Caucasians eligible. Must be working with an ethnic minority clinic; United States citizenship or legal residency required; applicants must be planning career in psychology or neuroscience research.
$ Given: An unspecified number of fellowships awarded annually; $12,240 for 10 months; renewable for up to three years.
Application Information: Write for details.
Deadline: January 15.
Contact: Dr. James M. Jones, Director; or Ernesto Guerra, Minorities Fellowship Program.

American Research Center in Egypt
Fellowships for Research in Egypt
30 East 40th Street
Suite 401
New York, NY 10003
(212) 529-6661
www.arce.org

Description: Fellowships for doctoral candidates and post-doctoral scholars in archaeology, art, humanities, and social sciences in Egypt; recipients chosen on the basis of quality of proposed research; intended as maintenance support for research conducted in Egypt for three- to twelve-month period.
Restrictions: Proficiency in Arabic required; if applicable recipients may not hold outside employment during fellowship period; United States citizens only.
$ Given: Up to 20 fellowships awarded annually; each with stipend plus round-trip airfare and dependents' stipends, if needed.
Application Information: Write for details.
Deadline: November 1.
Contact: Catherine Klein, United States Director.

American Research Institute in Turkey
ARIT Fellowships
University Museum
33rd and Spruce Streets
Philadelphia, PA 19104-6324
(215) 898-3474

Description: Fellowships for doctoral candidates to conduct research concerning Turkey in ancient, medieval, and modern times in any field of the humanities or social sciences; recipients chosen on the basis of quality of proposed research; intended as maintenance support for dissertation research in Turkey over one- to twelve-month fellowship period.
Restrictions: Applicants must have satisfied all doctoral requirements except dissertation; recipients must obtain research permission from the Turkish government; applicants must be affiliated with United States or Canadian institutions.
$ Given: Six to 10 fellowships for $3,000–$10,000 per year are awarded annually.

Application Information: Write for details.
Deadline: November 15.
Contact: Nancy Leinwand.

**American Research Institute
in Turkey
Bosphorus University
Summer Turkish Language
Program**
University Museum
33rd and Spruce Streets
Philadelphia, PA 19104-6324
(215) 898-3474

Description: Fellowships for college graduates through
doctoral candidates; for the study of Turkish language in
an eight-week summer program at Bosphorus University
in Instanbul; recipients chosen on the basis of academic
achievement (minimum 3.0 GPA).
Restrictions: Preference for individuals planning career
in Turkish studies; two years of college-level Turkish language courses or equivalent required (written and oral
exam required); United States citizenship or permanent
resident status required.
$ Given: Ten to fifteen grants are awarded annually;
grant covers tuition, maintenance stipend, and round-trip
travel; nonrenewable.
Application Information: Write for details. ARIT
Summer Fellowship Program, Center for the Study of
Islamic Societies and Civilizations, Washington
University, Campus Box 1230, One Brookline Drive, St.
Louis, MO 63130-4899.
Deadline: February 15.
Contact: Sheila Andrew at (314) 935-5166.

**American School of
Classical Studies at Athens
Fellowships**
6-8 Charlton Street
Princeton, NJ 08540-5232
(609) 683-0800
www.ascsa.org

Description: Fellowships for graduate students to
engage in study/research in Greece for one academic
year; intended for students of archaeology, classical
studies, classical art history, and ancient Greece; named
fellowships include Thomas Day Seymour Fellowship,
John Williams White Fellowship, Samuel H. Kress
Fellowship, and James Rignall Wheeler Fellowship.
Restrictions: Applicants must be affiliated with United
States or Canadian institution; United States or Canadian
citizenship required; B.A. major in classics or classical
archaeology required.
$ Given: Four fellowships awarded annually; each for
$8,840 plus fees, room & partial board.
Application Information: Write for details. ASCSA
Committee on Admissions & Fellowships, State
University of New York at Buffalo, Department of
Classics, 338 Millard Fillmore Academic Center, Buffalo,
NY 14261.
Deadline: January 7.
Contact: Professor Carolyn Higbie, Chair.

American School of Classical Studies at Athens
Gennadeion Fellowship
6-8 Charlton Street
Princeton, NJ 08540-5232
(609) 683-0800
www.ascsa.org

Description: Fellowship for doctoral candidates at dissertation level to engage in study/research at the Gennadius Library in Athens for one academic year; intended for students of Byzantine and Greek studies; recipients chosen on the basis of academic achievement and quality of proposed research.
Restrictions: Applicants must be affiliated with a United States or Canadian institution; United States or Canadian citizenship required.
$ Given: One fellowship awarded annually for $8,840 plus fees, room, and partial board.
Application Information: Write for details.
Deadline: January 7.
Contact: Professor James McCredie.

American School of Classical Studies at Athens
Jacob Hirsch Fellowship
6-8 Charlton Street
Princeton, NJ 08540-5232
(609) 683-0800
www.ascsa.org

Description: Fellowship for doctoral candidates at dissertation level to engage in study/research in Greece; intended for students of archaeology; recipients chosen on the basis of academic achievement and quality of proposed research.
Restrictions: United States or Israeli citizenship required.
$ Given: One fellowship awarded annually for $8,840 plus room and partial board; non-renewable.
Application Information: Write for details. ASCSA Committee on Admissions & Fellowships, State University of New York at Buffalo, Department of Classics, 338 Millard Fillmore Academic Center, Buffalo, NY 14261.
Deadline: January 7.
Contact: Professor Carolyn Higbie, Chair.

American School of Classical Studies at Athens
Solow Summer Senior Research Fellowships
Solow Art and Architecture Foundation
9 West 57th Street
Suite 4500
New York, NY 10019
www.asor.org

Description: Postdoctoral scholars working toward publication of material from the school's excavations at the Athenian Agora or Ancient Corinth.
Restrictions: None.
$ Given: Several fellowships with maximum of $1,500/month.
Application Information: Write for details.
Deadline: January 7.
Contact: Rosalie Wolff.

American Schools of Oriental Research
George A. Barton Fellowship at the Albright Institute for Archaeological Research, Jerusalem
656 Beacon Street
5th Floor
Boston, MA 02215-2010
(617) 353-6570
www.asor.org

Description: Residential fellowships for doctoral study in near Eastern archeology, geography, history, and biblical studies; for one to five months of study/research at the Albright Institute in Jerusalem; recipients chosen on the basis of proposed research.
Restrictions: Fellowship may not be used for summer study.
$ Given: Award of $6,000 plus $2,650 stipend.
Application Information: Write for details.
Deadlines: September 15, October 15.
Contact: Dr. Rudolph H. Dornemann, Executive Director.

American Schools of Oriental Research
Samuel H. Kress Foundation Fellowship at the Albright Institute for Archaeological Research, Jerusalem
656 Beacon Street
5th Floor
Boston, MA 02215-2010
(617) 353-6570
www.asor.org

Description: Residential fellowships for doctoral candidates at dissertation level in art history, archaeology, and architecture; for nine to ten months of dissertation research at the Albright Institute in Jerusalem; recipients chosen on the basis of proposed research.
Restrictions: N/A.
$ Given: An unspecified number of fellowships of $16,500 awarded annually; each with $9,800 stipend plus room and half-board.
Application Information: Write for details.
Deadline: October 15.
Contact: Dr. Rudolph H. Dornemann, Executive Director.

American Schools of Oriental Research
Mesopotamian Fellowship
656 Beacon Street
5th Floor
Boston, MA 02215-2010
(617) 353-6570
www.asor.org

Description: Fellowship for doctoral candidates and postdoctoral scholars studying ancient Mesopotamian civilization and culture; recipients chosen on the basis of proposed research.
Restrictions: Membership in ASOR required; preference to projects affiliated with ASOR.
$ Given: One fellowship with $7,000 stipend is awarded annually.
Application Information: Write for details.
Deadline: February 1.
Contact: Dr. Rudolph H. Dornemann, Executive Director.

American Society for Eighteenth Century Studies
Folger Institute Fellowship
Folger Shakespeare Library
201 East Capitol Street, S.E.
Washington, DC 20003
(202) 675-0333

Description: Fellowship for graduate student or postdoctoral scholar conducting research in the period 1660 to 1815 to support independent research at the Folger Library.
Restrictions: Preference given to those candidates who are applying for a Folger Institute seminar.
$ Given: One fellowship awarded annually for $2,000.
Application Information: Write for details.
Deadline: September 1.

American Society for Eighteenth Century Studies Predoctoral Fellowships
William Andrews Clark
Memorial Library
UCLA
2520 Cimarron Street
Los Angeles, CA 90018
FAX (323) 731-8529
www.hum.net.ucla.edu

Description: Fellowships to support advanced doctoral students in study/research in any area represented in the Clark's collections or linked to programs supported by these or other collections at UCLA.
Restrictions: Open to advanced doctoral students.
$ Given: A variable number of fellowships offered annually; each for $6,000.
Application Information: Write for details.
Deadline: March 15.
Contact: Beverly Onley, Fellowship Coordinator.

American Sociological Association Minority Fellowship Program
1807 New York Avenue N.W., Suite 700
Washington, DC 20005-4701

Description: One-year fellowships for graduate students entering a doctoral program in sociology for the first time or for those who are in the early stages of their graduate programs. Institutions in which applicants are enrolled or to which they are applying must have strong mental health research programs. Recipients chosen on the basis of their commitment to research in mental health and mental illness, academic achievement, scholarship, writing ability, research potential, financial need, and racial/ethnic minority background.
Restrictions: U.S. Citizenship or permanent resident status required. Limited to one of the following ethnic/racial backgrounds: African Americans, Latinos, American Indians or Alaska Natives, Asians, or Pacific Islanders.
$ Given: An unspecified number of fellowships awarded annually; each with a stipend of $14,688 plus tuition. Renewable for up to three years.
Application Information: Write for details.
Deadline: December 31.

American Statistical Association
ASA/NSF Census Research Fellow and Associate Program
1429 Duke Street
Alexandria, VA 22314-3402
(703) 684-1221
www.amstat.org

Description: Fellowships/associateships for doctoral candidates and recent Ph.D.s in demography and population studies; for participation in research at the United States Bureau of Census; recipients chosen on the basis of academic achievement and quality of proposed research.
Restrictions: Significant computer experience required.
$ Given: An unspecified number of associateships are awarded annually; stipend is commensurate with qualifications and experience; fringe benefits and travel allowance also included.
Application Information: Write for details.
Deadline: December 10.
Contact: Carolyn Kesner, Fellowship Program Director.

American Statistical Association ASA/NSF/BLS Senior Research Fellow and Associate Program
1429 Duke Street
Alexandria, VA 22314-3402
(703) 684-1221
www.amstat.org

Description: Fellowships/associateships for doctoral candidates and recent Ph.D.s in economics, business, and labor studies; for participation in research at the Bureau of Labor Statistics; recipients chosen on the basis of academic achievement and quality of proposed research.
Restrictions: Significant computer experience required.
$ Given: An unspecified number of associateships are awarded annually; stipend is commensurate with qualifications and experience; fringe benefits and travel allowance also included.
Application Information: Write for details.
Deadline: December 10.
Contact: Carolyn Kesner, Fellowship Program Director.

Archaeological Institute of America Anna C. and Oliver C. Colburn Fellowship
656 Beacon Street
Boston, MA 02215-2010
(617) 353-9361
www.bu.edu

Description: One-year fellowship for doctoral candidates and postdoctoral scholars, for study/research in classical studies; tenable at the American School of Classical Studies in Athens.
Restrictions: United States or Canadian citizenship or legal residency required.
$ Given: One fellowship of $14,000 is awarded annually.
Application Information: Write for details.
Deadline: January 31.
Contact: Colburn Fellowship.

Archaeological Institute of America Olivia James Traveling Fellowships
656 Beacon Street
Boston, MA 02215-2010
(617) 353-9361
www.bu.edu

Description: Fellowships for doctoral candidates at dissertation level in architecture; for travel to Greece, the Aegean islands, Sicily, southern Italy, Asia Minor, and/or Mesopotamia; recipients chosen on the basis of proposed research/study.
Restrictions: Preference to project of at least six months duration; no funding for field excavation; United States citizenship or legal residency required.
$ Given: One fellowship of up to $22,000 is awarded annually.
Application Information: Write for details.
Deadline: November 1.
Contact: Olivia James Traveling Fellowship.

Archaeological Institute of America Harriet and Leon Pomerance Fellowship
656 Beacon Street
Boston, MA 02215-2010
(617) 353-9361
www.bu.edu

Description: Fellowship for doctoral candidates studying Aegean Bronze Age archaeology; for travel to the Mediterranean; recipients chosen on the basis of proposed research/study.
Restrictions: United States or Canadian citizenship required.
$ Given: One fellowship of $4,000 is awarded annually; non-renewable.

Application Information: Write for details.
Deadline: November 1.
Contact: Harriet Pomerance Fellowship.

Arctic Institute of North America
Grant-in-Aid Program
University of Calgary
2500 University Drive, N.W.
Calgary, Alberta T2N 1N4
Canada
(403) 220-7515
www.ucalgary.ca

Description: Grants for graduate students for natural/social sciences field work in the northern regions; recipients chosen on the basis of academic achievement and quality of proposed research.
Restrictions: N/A.
$ Given: An unspecified number of grants of up to $500 Canadian are awarded annually.
Application Information: Write for details.
Deadline: February 1.
Contact: Erich Follmann.

Armenian General Benevolent Union Graduate Scholarship Program
55 East 59th Street
New York, NY 10022
(212) 319-6383

Description: Scholarships for graduate students in law, medicine, international relations, and Armenian studies; recipients chosen on the basis of academic achievement, financial need, and involvement in the Armenian community.
Restrictions: Limited to individuals of Armenian descent who are enrolled in accredited United States institutions.
$ Given: Twenty grants of an average $5,000 are awarded annually; renewable.
Application Information: Write for details.
Deadline: April 1.

Association for Library and Information Science Education
Doctoral Students' Dissertation Competition Awards
P.O. Box 7640
Arlington, VA 22207
(703) 243-8040
www.alise.org

Description: Awards for outstanding doctoral dissertations in library and information sciences; recipients chosen on the basis of academic achievement and quality of doctoral dissertation.
Restrictions: Applicants must present summary of dissertation to ALISE annual conference and complete dissertation within the current calendar year.
$ Given: Two awards of $400 each are awarded annually; conference registration and one-year membership in ALISE also included.
Application Information: Write for details.
Deadline: July 1.
Contact: Prof. Delia Neuman, College of Library & Information Services, University of Maryland, 4105 College Park, MD 20742-4345, (301) 405-2054.

**Association for Library and
Information Science
Education
Research Grants**
P.O. Box 7640
Arlington, VA 22207
(703) 243-8040
www.alise.org

Description: Research grants for students in library and
information sciences; recipients chosen on the basis of
previous work and quality of proposed research.
Restrictions: membership in ALISE required; no fund-
ing for doctoral dissertation work.
$ Given: An unspecified number of grants totaling
$5,000 are awarded annually.
Application Information: Write for details.
Deadline: September 15.
Contact: Prof. Delia Neuman, College of Library &
Information Services, University of Maryland, 4105
College Park, MD 20742-4345, (301) 405-2054.

**Association for Library and
Information Science
Education
Research Paper Competition
Awards**
P.O. Box 7640
Arlington, VA 22207
(703) 243-8040
www.alise.org

Description: Awards for outstanding research papers on
library and information sciences.
Restrictions: Although master's and doctoral candidates
are eligible to submit original research papers, any papers
submitted for degree requirements cannot be considered
for awards; membership in ALISE required.
$ Given: A maximum of two awards of $500 each are
awarded annually.
Application Information: Write for details.
Deadline: September 15.
Contact: Prof. Delia Neuman, College of Library &
Information Services, University of Maryland, 4105
College Park, MD 20742-4345, (301) 405-2054.

**Association for Women in
Science Educational
Foundation
AWIS Predoctoral Award**
1200 New York Avenue, N.W.
Suite 650
Washington, DC 20005
(202) 326-8940
www.awis.org

Description: Awards for doctoral candidates in life sciences, physical sciences, social sciences, engineering,
mathematics, and behavioral sciences; recipients chosen
on the basis of academic achievement and quality of proposed research.
Restrictions: Limited to women only; United States citizenship or enrollment in United States institution
required.
$ Given: An unspecified number of grants of $1,000
each are awarded annually.
Application Information: Write for details.
Deadline: January 15.

**Association of American
Geographers
The Robert D. Hodgson Fund
Dissertation Research Grant**
1710 Sixteenth Street, N.W.
Washington, DC 20009-3198
(202) 234-1450
www.aag.org

Description: Research grants for doctoral candidates at
dissertation level in the field of geography, especially as
related to international cooperation; recipients chosen on
the basis of proposed research.
Restrictions: Applicants must complete all doctoral
requirements except dissertation by the term following the
date of the award; minimum one-year membership in
AAG required; funding for direct research expenses only.

$ **Given:**   An unspecified number of grants of up to $500 each are awarded annually.
Application Information: Write for application forms.
Deadline: December 31.
Contact: Ehsan Khater.

Association of American Geographers
The Otis Paul Starkey Fund Dissertation Research Grant
1710 Sixteenth Street, N.W.
Washington, DC 20009-3198
(202) 234-1450
www.aag.org

Description: Research grants for doctoral candidates at dissertation level in the field of regional geography, especially as related to a specific problem area in the United States or its possessions; recipients chosen on the basis of proposed research.
Restrictions: Applicants must complete all doctoral requirements except dissertation by the term following the date of the award; minimum one-year membership in AAG required; funding for direct research expenses only.
$ **Given:**   An unspecified number of grants of up to $500 each are awarded annually.
Application Information: Write for application forms.
Deadline: December 31.
Contact: Ehsan Khater.

Association of American Geographers
The Paul P. Vouras Fund Dissertation Research Grant
1710 Sixteenth Street, N.W.
Washington, DC 20009-3198
(202) 234-1450
www.aag.org

Description: Research grants for doctoral candidates at dissertation level in the field of geography; recipients chosen on the basis of proposed research.
Restrictions: Preference for applicants who are members of minority groups; applicants must complete all doctoral requirements except dissertation by the term following the date of the award; minimum one-year membership in AAG required; funding for direct research expenses only.
$ **Given:**   An unspecified number of grants of up to $500 each are awarded annually.
Application Information: Write for application forms.
Deadline: December 31.
Contact: Ehsan Khater.

Association of College and Research Libraries
Doctoral Dissertation Fellowship
50 East Huron Street
Chicago, IL 60611
(312) 280-2510
(800) 545-2433
www.ala.org

Description: Research fellowship for doctoral candidates at dissertation level in library science; recipients chosen on the basis of proposed research.
Restrictions: N/A.
$ **Given:**   One grant of $1,500 is awarded annually; nonrenewable.
Application Information: Write for details.
Deadline: December 1.
Contact: Lisa Grube.

Association of College and Research Libraries Martinus Nijhoff International West European Specialist Study Grant
50 East Huron Street
Chicago, IL 60611
(312) 280-2510
(800) 545-2433

Description: Grant for scholars in library science to travel for up to fourteen days to study West European professional librarianship; recipients chosen on the basis of proposed research.
Restrictions: Personal membership in ALA required.
$ Given: An unspecified number of grants are awarded annually; award covers air travel, surface travel, expenses, room, and board.
Application Information: Write for details.
Deadline: December 1.
Contact: Heleni Marques Pedersoli.

Charles Babbage Institute, University of Minnesota Adelle and Erwin Tomash Fellowship in the History of Information Processing
103 Walter Library
117 Pleasant Street, S.E.
Minneapolis, MN 55455
(612) 624-5050
www.cbi.umn.edu

Description: Research fellowship for doctoral candidates at dissertation level studying the history of information processing; recipients chosen on the basis of academic achievement and quality of proposed research; tenable at any appropriate research institution.
Restrictions: All nationalities eligible.
$ Given: One fellowship awarded annually for $10,000 plus up to $2,000 toward tuition, fees, travel, and research expenses; renewable.
Application Information: Write for details.
Deadline: January 15.
Contact: Jeffrey Yost.

Leo Baeck Institute David Baumgardt Memorial Fellowships
129 East 73rd Street
New York, NY 10021
(212) 744-6400
www.lbi.com

Description: Research fellowships for doctoral candidates studying the writings of Professor Baumgardt or the intellectual history of German-speaking Jewry; recipients chosen on the basis of proposed research.
Restrictions: N/A.
$ Given: One fellowship awarded annually; amount based on project requirements; usually not more than $3,000.
Application Information: Write for details.
Deadline: November 1.
Contact: Carol Kahn Strauss.

Leo Baeck Institute/DAAD German-Jewish History and Culture Fellowships
129 East 73rd Street
New York, NY 10021
(212) 744-6400
www.lbi.com

Description: Research fellowships for doctoral candidates and recent Ph.D.s studying the social, communal, and intellectual history of German-speaking Jewry; recipients chosen on the basis of academic achievement and quality of proposed research; use of the Leo Baeck Institute resources in New York City offered.
Restrictions: United States citizenship required; maximum age range of 32–35.
$ Given: One fellowship of $2,000 is awarded annually; paid in two installments.
Application Information: Write for details.

Deadline: November 1.
Contact: Carol Kahn Strauss.

Leo Baeck Institute
Fritz Halbers Fellowships
129 East 73rd Street
New York, NY 10021
(212) 744-6400
www.lbi.com

Description: Research fellowships for doctoral candidates studying the history and culture of German-speaking Jewry; recipients chosen on the basis of proposed research.
Restrictions: N/A.
$ Given: One fellowship awarded annually; amount based on project requirements; $3,000 maximum.
Application Information: Write for details.
Deadline: November 1.
Contact: Carol Kahn Strauss.

Beta Phi Mu International
Library and Information
Science Honor Society
Frank B. Sessa Scholarship
for Continuing Education
School of Library and
Information Science
University of Pittsburgh
Pittsburgh, PA 15260
(412) 624-9435
www.sis.pitt.edu

Description: Scholarship for scholars of library science, recipients chosen on the basis of proposed study/research plan.
Restrictions: Membership in Beta Phi Mu required.
$ Given: One scholarship of $1,000 is awarded annually.
Application Information: Applicants must submit specific plans for course of continuing education (graduate study or professional development).
Deadline: January 15.
Contact: Executive Secretary.

Bibliographic Society of
America Fellowship Program
P.O. Box 397
Grand Central Station
New York, NY 10163
(212) 647-9171

Description: Fellowship to support research in bibliographic inquiry, the history of the book trades, and publishing history. Eligible topics may concentrate on books and documents in any field, but should focus on the book or manuscript as historical evidence.
Restrictions: None.
$ Given: An unspecified number of fellowships awarded annually, each with a stipend of $1,000.
Application Information: Write for details.
Deadline: December 1.

Brookings Institution
Predoctoral Research
Fellowships in Economic
Studies
1775 Massachusetts Avenue,
N.W.
Washington, DC 20036
(202) 797-6000
www.brook.edu

Description: One-year residential fellowships for doctoral candidates conducting policy-oriented dissertation research in economics as related to public policy; emphasis on economic growth, international economics, industrial organization, regulation, human resources, public finance, and economic stabilization; recipients chosen on the basis of academic achievement, quality of proposed research, and relevance of research topic to Brookings Institution interests; fellowship includes access to Brookings Institution data and staff; women and minorities encouraged to apply.

Restrictions: Applicants must have completed all preliminary doctoral exams.
$ Given: A few fellowships (three to five) awarded annually; each with $17,500 stipend, up to $600 for expenses, and up to $500 for research related travel.
Application Information: Applicants must be nominated by their university graduate departments.
Deadline: December 15 for departmental nomination; February 15 for individual application.

Brookings Institution Predoctoral Research Fellowships in Foreign Policy Studies
1775 Massachusetts Avenue, N.W.
Washington, DC 20036
(202) 797-6000
www.brook.edu

Description: One-year residential fellowships for doctoral candidates conducting policy-oriented dissertation research in United States foreign policy and international relations; emphasis on security policy and economic issues; recipients chosen on the basis of academic achievement, quality of proposed research, and relevance of research topic to United States foreign policy; fellowship includes access to Brookings Institution data and staff; women and minorities encouraged to apply.
Restrictions: N/A.
$ Given: A few fellowships awarded annually; each with $17,500 stipend, up to $600 for research expenses, and up to $500 for research related travel.
Application Information: Applicants must be nominated by their university graduate departments.
Deadline: December 15 for departmental nomination; February 15 for individual application.

Brookings Institution Predoctoral Research Fellowships in Governmental Studies
1775 Massachusetts Avenue, N.W.
Washington, DC 20036
(202) 797-6000
www.brook.edu

Description: One-year residential fellowships for doctoral candidates conducting policy-oriented dissertation research in governmental studies; emphasis on American political institutions, politics, economic and social policy, and government regulation; recipients chosen on the basis of academic achievement, quality of proposed research, and relevance of research topic to Brookings Institution interests; fellowship includes access to Brookings Institution data and staff; women and minorities encouraged to apply.
Restrictions: N/A.
$ Given: A few fellowships awarded annually; each with $17,500 stipend, up to $600 for expenses, and up to $500 for research related travel.
Application Information: Applicants must be nominated by their university graduate departments.
Deadline: December 15 for departmental nomination; February 15 for individual application.

Bunting Institute Fellowship Program
34 Concord Avenue
Cambridge, MA 02138
(617) 495-8136
www.radcliffe.edu/bunting

Description: Postdoctoral fellowships for women to pursue research in all fields of scholarship, professions, creative writing, poetry, visual and performing arts, music, and sciences not included in the Science Scholars Fellowship.
Restrictions: U.S. citizenship required. Limited to women applicants only who have received their doctorate at least two years prior to application.
$ Given: Five to eight fellowships awarded annually, each in the amount $28,500.
Application Information: Write for details.
Deadline: Early October.

Bunting Institute Fellowship Program
34 Concord Avenue
Cambridge, MA 02138
(617) 495-8136
www.radcliffe.edu/bunting

Description: Fellowships to support women actively involved in finding peaceful solutions to conflict or potential conflict among groups of nations.
Restrictions: Limited to women applicants only.
$ Given: One fellowship awarded annually in the amount of $25,000.
Application Information: Write for details.
Deadline: January.

Business and Professional Women's Foundation BPW Career Advancement Scholarships
2012 Massachusetts Avenue, N.W.
Washington, DC 20036
(202) 293-1100
www.bpwusa.org

Description: One-year scholarships for undergraduate and graduate study in all disciplines, with emphasis on computer science, education, science, mathematics, business, humanities, and paralegal training; scholarships are awarded within 24 months of the applicant's completing an undergraduate or graduate program in the United States; recipients chosen on the basis of financial need; funding designed to improve recipients' chances for career advancement/success.
Restrictions: Limited to women only; applicants must be at least 25 years old; no funding for Ph.D. studies, study abroad, or correspondence courses; United States citizenship and affiliation with United States institution required.
$ Given: Approximately 150 scholarships of up to $1,000 each are awarded annually.
Application Information: Request application materials between October 1 and April 1.
Deadline: April 15.
Contact: Assistant Director, Education and Training.

Canada Council Killam Research Fellowships
99 Metcalfe Street
P.O. Box 1047
Ottawa, Ontario
Canada KIP 5V8

Description: Fellowships for senior scholars (eight to twelve years beyond the Ph.D.) to support research in any of the following fields: Humanities, social sciences, natural sciences, health sciences, engineering, and studies linking disciplines within those fields.
Restrictions: Canadian citizenship or landed immigrant resident status required.

$ Given: Fifteen to eighteen fellowships awarded annually, each in the amount $53,000.
Application Information: Write for details.
Deadline: June 30.

Canadian Embassy
Canadian Studies Graduate
Student Fellowships
501 Pennsylvania Avenue,
N.W.
Washington, DC 20001
(202) 682-1740
www.cdnemb.washdc.org

Description: Fellowships for doctoral candidates in the humanities, social sciences, fine arts, business, law, or environmental studies who are working on dissertation topics related in substantial part to Canada; funding for dissertation research in Canada over a three- to nine-month fellowship period.
Restrictions: Applicants must be doctoral students at accredited institutions in Canada or the United States; applicants must have completed all degree requirements other than the dissertation; United States citizenship or permanent resident status required.
$ Given: An unspecified number of fellowships with a maximum of $850/month stipends are awarded annually for a period of up to 9 months; nonrenewable.
Application Information: Write for details.
Deadline: October 30.
Contact: Daniel Abele, Academic Relations Officer.

Canadian Federation of
University Women
Georgette LeMoyne Award
251 Bank Street
Suite 600
Ottawa, Ontario K2P 1X3
Canada
(613) 234-2732
www.cfuw.ca

Description: Award for graduate studies in any field; intended for women taking refresher studies at universities where instruction is in French.
Restrictions: Limited to women only; applicant must hold B.S./B.A. degree and have been accepted to proposed program of graduate study; Canadian citizenship or minimum landed immigrant status required.
$ Given: One award for $1,000 Canadian made annually.
Application Information: Write for details.
Deadline: November 15.
Contact: Chair, Fellowships Committee.

Canadian Federation of
University Women
CFUW Polytechnique
Commemorative Awards
251 Bank Street
Suite 600
Ottawa, Ontario K2P 1X3
Canada
(613) 234-2732
www.cfuw.ca

Description: Award for graduate studies in any field, with preference for studies related to women's issues.
Restrictions: Applicant must hold B.S./B.A. degree and have been accepted to proposed program of graduate study; Canadian citizenship or minimum one-year landed immigrant status required.
$ Given: One grant of $1,400 Canadian awarded annually.
Application Information: Write for details.
Deadline: November 15.
Contact: Fellowships Committee.

Canadian Federation of University Women Margaret Dale Philip Award
251 Bank Street
Suite 600
Ottawa, Ontario K2P 1X3
Canada
(613) 234-2732
www.cfuw.ca

Description: Award to graduate students in the humanities and social sciences, with preference to applicants studying Canadian history; recipients chosen on the basis of academic achievement in college, personal qualities, and potential.
Restrictions: Limited to women only; applicants must hold B.S./B.A. degree and have been accepted to proposed program of graduate study; Canadian citizenship or minimum one-year landed immigrant status required.
$ Given: One grant of $1,000 Canadian is awarded annually.
Application Information: Write for details.
Deadline: November 15.
Contact: Fellowships Committee.

Canadian Institute of Ukrainian Studies Doctoral Thesis Fellowships
352 Athabasca Hall
University of Alberta
Edmonton, Alberta T6G 2E8
Canada

Description: Fellowships for doctoral candidates at dissertation level studying education, law, history, humanities, social sciences, or library sciences as related to Ukrainian or Ukrainian-Canadian topics; recipients chosen on the basis of academic achievement and dissertation topic; tenable in Canada or elsewhere.
Restrictions: Canadian citizenship or landed immigrant status required.
$ Given: An unspecified number of grants, each for $8,000 Canadian, are awarded annually; renewable.
Application Information: Write for details.
Deadline: March 1.

Canadian Institute of Ukrainian Studies Thesis Fellowships
352 Athabasca Hall
University of Alberta
Edmonton, Alberta T6G 2E8
Canada

Description: Fellowships for master's candidates studying education, law, history, humanities, social sciences, or library sciences as related to Ukrainian or Ukrainian-Canadian topics; recipients chosen on the basis of academic achievement and thesis topic; tenable in Canada or elsewhere.
Restrictions: Canadian citizenship or landed immigrant status required.
$ Given: An unspecified number of one-year grants, each for $4,500 Canadian, are awarded annually.
Application Information: Write for details.
Deadline: March 1.

Canadian Library Association CLA Graduate Scholarship
200 Elgin Street
Suite 602
Ottawa, Ontario K2P 1L5
Canada
(613) 232-9625
www.cla.amlibs.ca

Description: Scholarship for B.L.S. and M.L.S. degree holders in library science, for further study; recipients chosen on the basis of academic achievement and financial need.
Restrictions: Canadian citizenship or one-year landed immigrant status required.
$ Given: One grant of up to $2,500 Canadian is awarded annually.
Application Information: Write for details.

Deadline: March 1.
Contact: Scholarships and Awards Committee.

CDS International
Robert Bosch Foundation
Fellowships
871 United Nations Plaza
15th Floor
New York, NY 10017-1814
(212) 497-3500
www.cdsintl.org

Description: Nine-month internships at German government and business institutions (September–May) for master's degree holders and professionals in communications, journalism, economics, political science, public affairs, business administration, law, and German studies; German internships provided in a framework of government and commerce; recipients chosen on the basis of academic achievement, evidence of leadership, and community participation.
Restrictions: Recipients must be proficient in German by the start of the internship (fees for language courses reimbursed); United States citizenship required, age 23–34.
$ Given: Twenty fellowships awarded annually; each with DM3,500/month stipend plus travel expenses and possible spouse stipend.
Application Information: Write for details.
Deadline: October 15.

Center for the Advanced
Study in Behavioral Sciences
Postdoctoral Fellowships
202 Junipero Serra Blvd.
Sanford, CA 94305-6165
(650) 723-9626
www.stanford.edu/group/
CISAC

Description: Nine-to-twelve-month postdoctoral fellowships to support research in any of the following fields: anthropology, art history, biology, classics, economics, education, history, law, linguistics, literature, mathematical and statistical specialties, medicine, musicology, philosophy, political science, psychiatry, psychology, and sociology. Tenable at the Center for Advanced Study in Behavioral Sciences.
Restrictions: None.
$ Given: Approximately fifty fellowships of varying amounts awarded annually.
Application Information: Write for details.
Deadline: Ongoing.

Center for California Studies
Jesse Marvin Unruh Assembly
Fellowship Program
California State University,
Sacramento
6000 J Street
Sacramento, CA 95819-6081
(916) 278-6906
www.csus.edu/calst

Description: Fellowships for graduate students to directly participate in the legislative process in California. Recipients chosen on the basis of their knowledge of California government and current issues important to the State.
Restrictions: None.
$ Given: An unspecified number of fellowships awarded annually, each with a monthly stipend of $1,792 benefits and tuition.
Application Information: Write for details.
Deadline: February 17.

**Center for Defense
Information Internship**
1779 Massachusetts Avenue,
N.W.
Washington, DC 20036
(202) 332-0600
www.cdi.org

Description: Internships for undergraduate and graduate students interested in political science and public
policy as related to military issues; for a minimum four-
month period of full-time work as research and outreach
assistants at CDI; recipients chosen on the basis of academic achievement and interest in United States military
policy and related public policy.
Restrictions: Writing skills essential and computer proficiency.
$ Given: An unspecified number of internships paying
$700/month are awarded annually.
Application Information: Write for details.
Deadlines: October 15, March 15, July 1.
Contact: Intern Program Coordinator.

**Center for International
Security and Cooperation
Predoctoral Fellowships**
Encina Hall
202 Junipero Serra Blvd.
Sanford, CA 94305-6165
(650) 723-9626
www.stanford.edu/group/
CISAC

Description: Predoctoral fellowships for research at the
Center in any field relating to peace and/or international
security.
Restrictions: None.
$ Given: An unspecified number of fellowships awarded
annually, each with a stipend of $18,000.
Application Information: Write for details.
Deadline: February 1.
Contact: Barbara Platt.

**Committee on Scholarly
Communication with the
People's Republic of China
National Program for
Advanced Study and Research
in China—Graduate Program**
228 East 45th Street
New York, NY 10017-3398
(212) 697-1505
FAX (212) 949-8058
www.acls.org

Description: Funding for one academic year of
advanced study/research in China; for master's and doctoral candidates in the humanities and social sciences;
recipients chosen on the basis of academic achievement
and proposed research; tenable at university or research
institute in China.
Restrictions: Three years of Chinese language training;
United States citizenship required.
$ Given: Monthly stipend plus travel.
Application Information: Write for details.
Deadline: December 1.
Contact: Program Officer.

**Dr. M. Aylwin Cotton
Foundation Fellowship Awards**
c/o Albany Trustee Company,
Limited
P.O. Box 232 Pollet House
The Pollet, St. Peter Port
Guerney, Channel Islands
England
Tel: (44) 1481 724 136
FAX (44) 1481 710 478

Description: One-year fellowships for postdoctoral
studies in archaeology, architecture, history, language, and
art of the Mediterranean.
Restrictions: None.
$ Given: An unspecified number of fellowships awarded
annually; each with a maximum stipend of 10,000 British
pounds.
Application Information: Write for details.
Deadline: February 28.

Council for Advancement and Support of Education
John Grenzebach Outstanding Doctoral Dissertation Award
1307 New York Avenue, N.W.
Suite 1000
Washington, DC 20005-4701
(202) 328-5900
www.case.org

Description: Award for outstanding doctoral dissertation addressing philanthropy for education.
Restrictions: N/A.
$ Given: One award of $2,000 for the author, plus travel and lodging expenses for the author and a faculty member to attend the CASE annual assembly.
Application Information: Write for details.
Deadline: February 28.
Contact: Grenzebach Research Awards.

Council for the Advancement of Science Writing
Nate Haseltine Memorial Fellowships in Science Writing
Taylor/Blakeslee University
P.O. Box 404
Greenlawn, NY 11740
www.nasw.org

Description: Fellowships for the study of science writing, available to B.S./B.A. holders in science of journalism professional journalists, and graduate students, enrolled in science writing programs to help defray the cost of tuition; recipients chosen on the basis of academic achievement, quality of writing, and commitment to writing career.
Restrictions: Preference to journalists with two years professional experience who want to specialize in science writing.
$ Given: An unspecified number of grants of up to $2,000 each are awarded annually.
Application Information: Write for details.
Deadline: June 15.
Contact: Executive Director.

Council for European Studies
Pre-Dissertation Fellowship Program
Columbia University
807.I4B
Mail code 3310
New York, NY 10027
(212) 854-4172
www.columbia.edu

Description: Two- to three-month research fellowships in France, Portugal, and the anthropology of Europe for doctoral candidates in European history, sociology, political science, anthropology, and economics.
Restrictions: Applicants must have completed at least two years of graduate study; language proficiency required; United States citizenship or permanent resident status required.
$ Given: Grants of $4,000 each are awarded annually; four for France, two for Portugal, and one for Anthropology.
Application Information: Write for details.
Deadline: February 1.

Council of American Overseas Research Centers
Fellowships for Advanced Multi-Country Research
1100 Jefferson Drive, S.W.
1C 3123, MRC 705
Washington, DC 20560-0705
www.caorc.org

Description: Fellowships for U.S. citizens who have already earned their Ph.D. in the fields of the humanities, social sciences, or allied natural sciences to conduct research of regional significance in more than one country, at least one of which hosts a participating OARC. Recipients will be chosen on the basis of their intellectual capacity, maturity, and fitness for field work, and proposal's significance, relevance, and potential contribution to regional scholarly research. Scholars may apply individually or in teams.

Restrictions: U.S. citizenship required.
$ Given: Eight fellowships awarded annually, each in the amount of up to $6,000 with up to an addition $3,000 for travel.
Application Information: Write for details.
Deadline: December 31.

Council on Social Work Education
CSWE Doctoral Fellowships in Social Work Minority Fellowship Program
1725 Duke Street
Suite 500
Alexandria, VA 22314-3421
(703) 683-8080

Description: One-year fellowships for doctoral candidates to conduct mental health research relevant to ethnic minorities; recipients chosen on the basis of academic achievement, financial need, and quality of proposed research; preference for applicants planning careers in social work specializing in ethnic minority issues of mental health.
Restrictions: Preference for African-American, Hispanic, Native American, and Asian-American applicants, as well as applicants of other ethnic minority groups; M.S.W. degree required; applicants must be full-time doctoral students; United States citizenship or permanent resident status required.
$ Given: An unspecified number of one-year fellowships are awarded annually; each carries a $708/month stipend plus tuition support, as negotiated with recipient's university; renewable.
Application Information: Write for details.
Deadline: June 1.
Contact: Dr. E. Aracelis Francis, Director.

Dibner Institute for the History of Science and Technology
Senior Fellows And Postdoctoral Fellows Program
Dibner Building, MIT E56-100
38 Memorial Drive
Cambridge, MA 02139
(617) 253-6989

Description: Six-month-to-one-year fellowships for senior-level and postdoctoral research at the Bundy Library and the libraries of the consortium universities.
Restrictions: Senior Fellows applicants should have advanced degrees in disciplines relevant to their research and show evidence of substantial scholarly achievement and professional experience. Postdoctoral applicants should have been awarded their Ph.D. within the previous five years. Must reside in Cambridge/Boston area during the term of the grant.
$ Given: Approximately twenty fellowships awarded annually; fellowships provide office space, support facilities, and full privileges of the Bundy Library and consortium libraries. Funds are available for housing, living expenses, and round-trip airfare for international fellows. Average stipend varies.

Application Information: Write for details.
Deadline: December 31.
Contact: Trudy Kontoff, Program Coordinator.

Dirksen Center Congressional Research Awards Program
301 South 4th Street, Suite A
Pekin, IL 61554-4219
(309) 347-7113
www.pekin.net/dirksen/grants

Description: Research grants for individuals studying Congress, especially its historical and contemporary leadership; recipients chosen on the basis of proposed research.
Restrictions: N/A.
$ Given: An unspecified number of grants of up to $3,500 each are awarded annually.
Application Information: Write for details.
Deadline: April 30.
Contact: Frank Mackaman.

Dumbarton Oaks Bliss Prize Fellowships in Byzantine Studies
1703 32nd Street, N.W.
Washington, DC 20007
(202) 339-6400
(202) 339-6410
www.doaks.org

Description: Two-year fellowships for college seniors and B.A. holders entering graduate school in Byzantine studies; participation includes summer travel for improved understanding of Byzantine civilization and culture.
Restrictions: Enrollment in United States or Canadian university required; minimum one-year of Greek required.
$ Given: An unspecified number of fellowships awarded annually; each for graduate school tuition and living expenses (up to $25,000 per year) for two years, plus summer travel (up to $5,000).
Application Information: By advisor nomination only; application must include transcripts, recommendations, study plans, and writing sample.
Deadline: November 1.
Contact: Assistant Director.

Dumbarton Oaks
Dumbarton Oaks Junior Fellowships
1703 32nd Street, N.W.
Washington, DC 20007
(202) 339-6400
(202) 339-6410
www.doaks.org

Description: Travel fellowships for doctoral candidates at dissertation level in Byzantine studies; for independent research; recipients chosen on the basis of academic achievement and quality of proposed research.
Restrictions: Open to all nationalities; working knowledge of relevant languages required; applicants must have completed all coursework and passed preliminary exams.
$ Given: An unspecified number of fellowships are awarded annually; each for $11,000 plus $800 research allowance, $1,300 maximum travel expense allowance, and $1,500 dependents' allowance (if needed).
Application Information: Write for details.
Deadline: November 1.
Contact: Assistant Director.

Dumbarton Oaks
Dumbarton Oaks Summer
Fellowship
1703 32nd Street, N.W.
Washington, DC 20007
(202) 339-6400
(202) 339-6410
www.doaks.org

Description: Six- to nine-week summer fellowships for students of Byzantine studies; for June–August fellowship period; recipients chosen on the basis of academic achievement and quality of proposed research.
Restrictions: N/A.
$ Given: Ten fellowships awarded annually; each for $185/week plus housing, weekday lunches, and up to $1,300 travel allowance.
Application Information: Write for details.
Deadline: November 1.
Contact: Assistant Director.

Friedrich Ebert Foundation
Doctoral Research Fellowships
342 Madison Avenue
New York, NY 10173
(212) 687-0208
FAX (212) 687-0261

Description: Five- to twelve-month residential study/research fellowships in Germany for doctoral candidates at dissertation level in political science, sociology, history, or economics as related to German/European affairs or German-American relations.
Restrictions: Applicants must have completed all degree requirements except dissertation; affiliation with American university required; knowledge of German adequate for research required; United States citizenship required.
$ Given: An unspecified number of fellowships awarded annually; each with DM1,390/month stipend plus airfare, domestic travel allowance, tuition and fees, luggage/books allowance, and dependents' allowance (if needed).
Application Information: Write for details.
Deadline: February 28.
Additional Addresses: 1155 Fifteenth Street, N.W., Suite 1100, Washington, DC 20005, (202) 331-1819; and Godesberger Allee 149, Bonn 2, D-53170, Germany.

Friedrich Ebert Foundation
Pre-Dissertation/Advanced
Graduate Fellowships
342 Madison Avenue
New York, NY 10173
(212) 687-0208
FAX (212) 687-0261

Description: Five- to twelve-month independent study/research fellowships in Germany for doctoral candidates in political science, sociology, history, or economics as related to German/European affairs or German-American relations.
Restrictions: Applicants must have completed at least two years of graduate study at an American university; knowledge of German adequate for research required; United States citizenship required.
$ Given: An unspecified number of fellowships awarded annually; each with DM1,250/month stipend plus airfare, domestic travel allowance, tuition and fees, luggage/books allowance, and dependents' allowance (if needed).
Application Information: Write for details.
Deadline: February 28.
Additional Addresses: 806 Fifteenth Street, N.W., Suite 230, Washington, DC 20005, (202) 331-1819; and Godesberger Allee 149, Bonn 2, D-53170, Germany.

**Educational Testing Service
Second/Foreign Language
Dissertation Research Grants**
P.O. Box 6155
Princeton, NJ 08541
(609) 921-9000

Description: Annual awards for research on second/foreign language testing conducted as part of dissertation work for doctoral degree.
Restrictions: Dissertation level students only.
$ Given: One grant of $2,500 is awarded annually.
Application Information: Write for details.
Deadline: May 15.
Contact: Dr. Carol Taylor, Director, TOEFL Research Program.

**Eisenhower World Affairs
Institute Graduate
Fellowships Program**
Graduate Fellowship Office
Cornell University
155 Caldwell Hall
Ithaca, NY 14853
(607) 255-9110

Description: Fellowships for advanced doctoral candidates in the fields of history, government, economics, business administration, and international affairs to pursue research. Preference will be given to those applicants whose research relates directly to President Eisenhower, the Eisenhower administration, and issues of major concern to him.
Restrictions: None.
$ Given: An unspecified number of fellowships awarded annually, each ranging from $7,000 to $10,000.
Application Information: Write for details.
Deadline: February 6.

**Environmental Protection
Agency STAR Graduate
Fellowship**
Office of Exploratory Research
Room 3102, NEM
401 M Street
Washington, DC 20460
(202) 564-6923
www.epa.gov

Description: One- to three-year fellowships for graduate students in the fields of engineering, sciences, social sciences, or mathematics doing environmentally-oriented research.
Restrictions: U.S. citizenship required or permanent resident status required.
$ Given: One fellowship awarded annually; with a $17,000 stipend, up to $12,000 tuition support, and up to $5,000 expense allowance. Renewable.
Application Information: Write for details.
Deadline: Early November.
Contact: Virginia Broadway, Graduate Fellowship Office.

**Epilepsy Foundation of
America
EFA Behavioral Sciences
Student Research Fellowships**
4351 Garden City Drive
Suite 406
Landover, MD 20785
(301) 459-3700
www.epilepsyfoundation.org

Description: One-year research fellowships for graduate students interested in basic and clinical research in the biological, behavioral, and social sciences designed to advance the understanding, treatment, and prevention of epilepsy; tenable at United States institutions; recipients chosen on the basis of demonstrated competence in epilepsy research.
Restrictions: Funding must be used in the United States no funding for capital equipment.
$ Given: A variable number of fellowships are awarded annually; support limited to $30,000.

Application Information: Write for details.
Deadline: September 1.
Contact: Administrative Assistant, Research and Professional Education.

Eta Sigma Phi National Classics Honor Society Eta Sigma Phi Summer Scholarships
University of South Dakota
Box 171
Vermillion, SD 57069
www.monm.edu

Description: Summer scholarships for study at the American Academy in Rome or the American School of Classical Studies in Athens; for recent college graduates who majored in Latin, Greek, or the classics; recipients can earn six semester hours of graduate-level credit during summer session.
Restrictions: Preference for students planning to teach classics; membership in Eta Sigma Phi required; Ph.D. candidates ineligible; applicants must have graduated from college within the past five years.
$ Given: Two scholarships awarded annually; $2,400 to attend the American Academy in Rome, $2,600 to attend the American School of Classical Studies in Athens.
Application Information: Request application forms from Professor Thomas Sienkewicz, Department of Classics, Monmouth College, Monmouth, IL 61462, (309) 457-2371.
Deadline: December 5.
Contact: Brent M. Froberg, Executive Secretary, Department of Classics.

Florida Education Fund McKnight Doctoral Fellowships
201 East Kennedy Boulevard
Suite 1525
Tampa, FL 33602
www.fl-edu-fd.org/mdf.html

Description: Fellowships for graduate study at one of ten participating doctoral-degree-granting universities in Florida in the fields of business, engineering, agriculture, biology, computer science, mathematics, physical science, and psychology; recipients chosen on the basis of academic achievement.
Restrictions: Limited to African-American applicants only; B.A./B.S. degree required; United States citizenship required.
$ Given: Up to twenty-five fellowships awarded annually; each for a maximum of five years of study, with an annual $11,000 stipend plus up to $5,000 in tuition and fees.
Application Information: Write for details.
Deadline: January 15.
Contact: Dr. Israel Tribble, Jr.

Folger Shakespeare Library Long-Term and Short-Term Research Fellowships
Folger Shakespeare Library
201 East Capitol Street, S.E.
Washington, DC 20003
(202) 675-0333

Description: Six-to-nine-month long-term and one- to three-month short-term residential fellowships for advanced scholars whose research projects are appropriate to the collections of the Folger Library.
Restrictions: Three long-term fellowships restricted to U.S. citizens. Others are open to scholars from any country.
$ Given: Five long-term fellowships awarded annually, four with a stipend of up to $30,000 and one of $45,000. An unspecified number of short-term fellowships awarded annually, each with a monthly stipend of $1,800 per month.
Application Information: Write for details.
Deadline: November 1 for long-term fellowship; March 1 for short-term fellowship.

Foundation for European Language and Educational Centers
Intensive European Language Courses Scholarships
Scholarship Department
Eurocentres
Seestrasse 247
Zurich CH-8038
Switzerland
(01) 485-5251

Description: Partial scholarships for three-month foreign language courses in English, French, German, Italian, and Spanish; each course held in country where language is spoken; recipients chosen on the basis of financial need and prior knowledge of language to be studied.
Restrictions: Applicants must be ages 18–30 and must have at least two years of professional experience in any field.
$ Given: An unspecified number of scholarships are awarded annually; each for between $250 and $750, which covers only part of the course tuition.
Application Information: Write for details.
Deadlines: January 15, March 31, June 15, and October 15.
Contact: Eric Steenbergen, Students' Assistance Department.

French Association of University Women
Dorothy Leet Fellowships
4, rue de Chevreuse
75006 Paris
France

Description: Fellowships for American women who are doctoral candidates or postdoctoral scholars who wish to pursue research in France.
Restrictions: Limited to women applicants. U.S. citizenship required.
$ Given: An unspecified number of fellowships awarded annually, each for $500 to $2,000.
Application Information: Write for details.
Deadline: March 31.
Contact: Danielle Gondard-Cozette, President, Fellowship Committee.

**General Semantics
Foundation
Project Grants**
14 Charcoal Hill
Westport, CT 06880
(203) 226-1394

Description: Grants for master's and doctoral candidates to conduct research in general semantics; recipients chosen on the basis of documentation of ongoing work.
Restrictions: N/A.
$ Given: An unspecified number of grants of $300–$4,500 are awarded annually.
Application Information: Write for details.
Deadline: Applications accepted continuously.
Contact: Harry E. Maynard, President.

**German Academic Exchange
Service
DAAD—American Institute
for Contemporary German
Studies Research Grants**
950 Third Avenue
19th Floor
New York, NY 10022
(212) 758-3223
FAX (212) 755-5780
www.daad.org

Description: Research grant for doctoral candidates and recent Ph.D.s studying postwar Germany; tenable a AICGS.
Restrictions: U.S. or Canadian citizens.
$ Given: One to two grants of $2,500.
Application Information: Write for details.
Deadline: April 15.

**German Academic Exchange
Service
German Studies Summer
Seminar Grants for Graduate
Students and Ph.D.
Candidates**
950 Third Avenue
19th Floor
New York, NY 10022
(212) 758-3223
FAX (212) 755-5780
www.daad.org

Description: Six-week interdisciplinary seminars at the University of Chicago, for advanced graduate students and doctoral candidates in the humanities and social sciences, including students of German intellectual and social history; for the study of Germany after World War II; recipients chosen on the basis of academic achievement; participants eligible for academic credit.
Restrictions: Working knowledge of German required; U.S. or Canadian citizens.
$ Given: An unspecified number of grants are awarded annually; each with a $3,000 stipend.
Application Information: Write for details.
Deadline: March 1.

**German Academic Exchange
Service
German Sur Place Grants**
950 Third Avenue
19th Floor
New York, NY 10022
(212) 758-3223
FAX (212) 755-5780
www.daad.org

Description: Grants for undergraduate upperclassmen and graduate students in German studies; for the study of German affairs from a multidisciplinary perspective.
Restrictions: Applicants must have completed at least two years college-level German and at least three courses in German studies. Must be U.S. or Canadian citizens.
$ Given: An unspecified number of grants of $1,500–$3,000 are awarded annually; each offsets tuition and research costs or summer earnings requirements.
Application Information: Write for details.
Deadlines: May 1, November 1.

**German Academic Exchange
Service
Short-Term Visits to Germany
Research Grants for Ph.D.
Candidates and Recent Ph.D.s**
950 Third Avenue
19th Floor
New York, NY 10022
(212) 758-3223
FAX (212) 755-5780
www.daad.org

Description: One to six months of grant funding for
doctoral candidates and recent Ph.D.s to conduct
research/study in Germany; for work in all fields; recipients chosen on the basis of academic achievement.
Restrictions: Maximum eligible age range of 32–35;
working knowledge of German required; United States or
Canadian citizenship required; affiliation with United
States university required.
$ Given: An unspecified number of grants are awarded
annually; each with monthly stipend, travel allowance, and
health insurance.
Application Information: Write for details.
Deadlines: February 1, August 1.

**German Academic Exchange
Service
Summer Language Study
Grants at Goethe Institutes
for Undergraduate and
Graduate Students**
950 Third Avenue
19th Floor
New York, NY 10022
(212) 758-3223
FAX (212) 755-5780
www.daad.org

Description: Grants for two-month intensive German
language course at the Goethe Institutes in Germany for
undergraduate upperclassmen and graduate students;
recipients chosen on the basis of academic achievement.
Restrictions: Basic knowledge of German required,
three semesters of college-level German preferred; applicants must be between the ages of 18 and 32; United
States or Canadian citizenship required; full-time enrollment in United States university required; individuals
with previous study experience in Germany ineligible;
previous language scholarship recipients ineligible;
majors in modern languages and literatures ineligible.
$ Given: An unspecified number of grants are awarded
annually; each for tuition and fees, plus room and partial
board; no travel allowance.
Application Information: Write for details.
Deadline: January 31.

**Getty Center for the History
of Art and the Humanities
Getty Center Fellowships**
1200 Getty Center Drive
Suite 1100
Los Angeles, CA 90049-1688
(310) 440-7392
www.getty.edu

Description: Twenty-two-month resident fellowships
(October 1–June 30) at the Getty Center for doctoral
candidates at dissertation level and recent Ph.D.s rewriting
dissertations for publication; for work in art, art history,
and interdisciplinary programs in the humanities and
social sciences; recipients chosen on the basis of academic achievement, proposed research, and relevance of
research topic to the interests and resources of the Getty
Center.
Restrictions: N/A.
$ Given: One to two fellowship grants awarded annu-
ally; $36,000/year for predoctoral fellowship,
$44,000/year for postdoctoral fellowship.
Application Information: Write for details.
Deadline: November 1.
Contact: Dr. Herbert H. Hymans, Department of
Visiting Scholars and Conferences.

Florence Gould Foundation Pre-Dissertation Fellowships for Research in France
Council for European Studies
Columbia University
807-807a IAB
New York, NY 10027
(212) 854-4172

Description: Three-month pre-dissertation fellowships for research in France to determine the viability of a projected doctoral dissertation in modern history and the social sciences. Recipients will test the research design of their dissertation, determine availability of archival materials, and contact French scholars in the relevant field. Does not support language training or tuition for courses at a French university.
Restrictions: U.S. Citizenship or Permanent Resident status required. Completion of at least two, but no more than three, years of full-time graduate study required.
$ Given: Six fellowships awarded annually; each with a maximum stipend of $4,000.
Application Information: Write for details.
Deadline: February 1.
Contact: Ionnis Sinanoglou, is8@columbia.edu.

Harry Frank Guggenheim Foundation Dissertation Fellowships
527 Madison Avenue
New York, NY 10022-5304
(212) 644-4907
www.hfg.org

Description: Fellowships for doctoral candidates at dissertation level to write dissertation on dominance, violence, and aggression; relevant disciplines include psychology, sociology, biology, history, anthropology, and political science; recipients chosen on the basis of academic achievement and quality of research.
Restrictions: Open to all nationalities.
$ Given: Ten grants of $10,000 each are awarded annually.
Application Information: Write for details.
Deadline: February 1.
Contact: Program Officer.

Hagley Museum and Library Grants-in-Aid
P.O. Box 3630
Wilmington, DE 19807
(302) 658-2400
www.hagley.w

Description: Grants for two- to eight-week short-term research work conducted at the Hagley Museum and Library, using the imprint, manuscript, pictorial, and artifact collections; grants made available to degree candidates, advanced scholars, independent scholars, and professionals for study of American economic and technological history and French 18th-century history; recipients chosen on the basis of proposed research.
Restrictions: N/A.
$ Given: Several grants of up to $1,200/month each are awarded quarterly.
Application Information: Write for details.
Deadline: Applications accepted continuously.
Contact: Dr. Philip B. Scranton.

Hagley Museum and Library
Hagley-Winterthur Research
Fellowships in Arts and
Industries
Center for the History of
Business, Technology, and
Society
P.O. Box 3630
Wilmington, DE 19807
(302) 658-2400
www.hagley.w

Description: One- to six-month short-term research fellowships for work using both the Hagley and the Winterthur collections and resources; fellowships made available to master's and doctoral candidates, as well as to independent scholars studying historical and cultural relationships of economic life and the arts, including design, architecture, crafts, and the fine arts; recipients chosen on the basis of research abilities and project relevance to both libraries' holdings.
Restrictions: N/A.
$ Given: Six fellowships awarded annually; each with $1,200/month stipend, plus seminar participation and use of both research collections.
Application Information: Write for details.
Deadline: December 1.

Harvard University
Center for International and
Area Studies Fellowships
Program
Center for International Affairs
420 Coolidge Hall
1737 Cambridge Street
Cambridge, MA 02138
(617) 495-2137
www.cfia.harvard.edu

Description: Grants for doctoral candidates at dissertation level and recent Ph.D.s to conduct research in several fields, including area and cultural studies, demography and population studies, economics, geography, history, languages, literatures and linguistics, political science and public policy, psychology, sociology, anthropology, archaeology, law, international affairs, and interdisciplinary programs in the humanities and social sciences; recipients chosen on the basis of academic achievement and proposed research.
Restrictions: Young applicants preferred; preference to individuals pursuing careers involving social science disciplines as relevant to specific geographic areas.
$ Given: A few grants are awarded annually; $22,000–$25,000 stipend for two years of predoctoral research, $32,000–$35,000 stipend for two years of postdoctoral research, plus travel and research allowance.
Application Information: Write for details.
Deadline: October 15.
Contact: Beth Hastie, Fellowship Coordinator.

Herb Society of America
Research and Education
Grants
9019 Kirtland Chardon Road
Kirtland, OH 44094
(440) 256-0514
www.herbsociety.org

Description: Grants to graduate students for study/research in horticulture, science, literature, art, and economics—as related to herbs; recipients chosen on the basis of proposed research, which may be scientific or academic; research period may be up to one year.
Restrictions: N/A.
$ Given: One to two grants totaling $5,000 are awarded annually.
Application Information: Write for details.
Deadline: January 31.
Contact: Grants Administrator.

Herbert Hoover Presidential Library Association
Herbert Hoover Travel Grant Competition
P.O. Box 696
West Branch, IA 52358
(319) 643-5327
www.hoover.rate.gov

Description: Travel grants to support scholarly use of the Herbert Hoover Presidential Library in West Branch, Iowa.
Restrictions: N/A.
$ Given: Several grants of $500–$1,500 each are awarded annually.
Application Information: Write for details.
Deadline: March 1.
Contact: Patricia Hand, Office Manager.

Ed A. Hewett Policy Fellowship Program
National Council for Eurasian and East European Research
910 17th Street, N.W., Suite 300
Washington, DC 20006
(202) 822-6950

Description: Fellowship for U.S. based scholars or researchers to study the countries of the Newly Independent States of the Former Soviet Union (NIS) and/or Central and Eastern Europe (CEE), conducted under the auspices of and placement in a U.S. government agency with responsibility for the administration of some aspect of U.S. foreign policy toward the NIS and CEE.
Restrictions: N/A.
$ Given: One fellowship awarded annually with a maximum stipend of $60,000.
Application Information: Write for details.
Deadline: March 15.
Contact: Robert T. Huber, President, NCEEER.

Hudson Institute
Herman Kahn Fellowship
5395 Emerson Way
P.O. Box 26919
Indianapolis, IN 46226-0919
(317) 545-1000

Description: Fellowships for one year of research/study in Indianapolis or Washington, DC, for doctoral candidates at dissertation level; relevant topics include education, economics, political economy, national security, policy issues, and political theory; recipients chosen on the basis of academic achievement, proposed research, and faculty recommendation.
Restrictions: United States citizenship required.
$ Given: Up to three fellowships awarded annually; each for $18,000 plus travel expenses.
Application Information: Write for details.
Deadline: April 15.
Contact: Director of Programs.

Huntington Library and Art Gallery
W.M. Keck Foundation Fellowship for Young Scholars
1151 Oxford Road
San Marino, CA 91108
(626) 405-2194
www.huntington.org

Description: Approximately one- to five-month residential research fellowships for predoctoral in British and American history, literature, and art; tenable at the Huntington Library.
Restrictions: N/A.
$ Given: A few fellowships awarded annually; each with $2,300/month stipend.
Application Information: Write for application form after October 1.
Deadline: December 15.
Contact: Robert C. Ritchie, Chairman, Committee on Awards.

Institute for European History Research Fellowships
Alte Universitaetsstrasse 19
Mainz 1
D–6500
Germany
(061) 31 39 93 60

Description: Residential fellowships at the Institute for doctoral candidates and postdoctoral scholars studying the history of Europe and European religion from the 16th to the 20th century; recipients chosen on the basis of academic achievement and proposed research.
Restrictions: Open to all nationalities; applicants must have thorough command of German.
$ Given: Twenty fellowships of DM13,080–DM17,280 each are awarded annually.
Application Information: Write for details.
Deadlines: February, June, October.
Contact: For European History program, contact Professor Dr. Karl Otmar Freiherr von Aretin, (06131) 226143; for History of European Religion program, contact Professor Dr. Peter Manns, (06131) 224870.

Institute of Food Technologists Graduate Fellowships
Scholarship Department
221 North LaSalle Street
Suite 300
Chicago, IL 60601
(312) 782-8424
www.ft.org

Description: Fellowships for graduate students doing research in food science and technology; tenable at accredited institutions in the United States and Canada; recipients chosen on the basis of academic achievement.
Restrictions: Applicants must show interest/ability in research; students in such disciplines as genetics, nutrition, microbiology, and biochemistry are ineligible.
$ Given: 33 fellowships for $1,000–$10,000 each are awarded annually; renewable.
Application Information: Application forms are available from school department heads or IFT or can be downloaded from the IFT website; individual application must be submitted to school department head.
Deadline: February 1.
Contact: Fellowship Administrator.

Institute of International Education Colombian Government Study and Research Grants
U.S. Student Programs Division
809 United Nations Plaza
New York, NY 10017-3580
(212) 984-5330
www.iie.org

Description: Grants for B.S./B.A. holders to pursue up to two years of study/research at Colombian Universities; relevant disciplines include agriculture, biology, business administration, economics, chemistry, engineering, education, health services administration, economics, geography, history, Latin American literature, law, linguistics, political science, physics, regulatory development, public health, and remote sensing interpretation.
Restrictions: United States citizenship required.
$ Given: An unspecified number of grants awarded annually; each for modest monthly stipend, plus tuition and fees, health insurance, book/materials allowance, and one-way return airfare upon completion of study.
Application Information: Write for details.
Deadline: October 25.

Institute of International Education Fulbright Fixed Sum–Bulgarian Government Grants
U.S. Student Programs Division
809 United Nations Plaza
New York, NY 10017-3580
(212) 984-5330
www.iie.org

Description: Grants for B.A./B.S. holders in the humanities, physical sciences, and social sciences; for a six- to nine-month residency/exchange in Bulgaria (October–June).
Restrictions: Proficiency in Bulgarian language is desirable; United States citizenship required; applicants must meet all Fulbright eligibility requirements.
$ Given: Five grants awarded annually; Bulgarian government funds stipend, housing, and health/accident insurance; Fulbright provides fixed sum for round-trip transportation plus additional monthly stipend.
Application Information: Write for details.
Deadline: October 25.
Contact: United States Student Program Division.

Institute of International Education Fulbright Fixed Sum–Syrian Government Grants
U.S. Student Programs Division
809 United Nations Plaza
New York, NY 10017-3580
(212) 984-5330
www.iie.org

Description: Grants for degree holders in Arabic language and culture, history, and geography preference for Ph.D candidates, for study at the University of Damascus.
Restrictions: Applicants studying modern social sciences not eligible; minimum two years of Arabic language study or demonstrated proficiency required; United States citizenship required; applicants must meet all Fulbright funding.
$ Given: An unspecified number of grants awarded annually; monthly stipend, tuition, and health insurance, supplemented by Fulbright funding.
Application Information: Write for details.
Deadline: October 25.
Contact: Campus Fulbright program advisor.

Institute of International Education Fulbright–Spanish Government Grants
U.S. Student Programs Division
809 United Nations Plaza
New York, NY 10017-3580
(212) 984-5330
www.iie.org

Description: Grants for B.A./B.S. holders in all fields for study at a Spanish university. Of particular interest are projects dealing with contemporary issues.
Restrictions: Proficiency in Spanish (written and spoken) required; United States citizenship required; applicants must meet all Fulbright eligibility requirements.
$ Given: Thirty-four grants awarded annually; Spanish government funds tuition and stipend; Fulbright funds round-trip transportation, and expense allowance.
Application Information: Write for details.
Deadline: October 25.

Institute of International Education
Fulbright Travel–Iceland Government Grants
U.S. Student Programs Division
809 United Nations Plaza
New York, NY 10017-3580
(212) 984-5330
www.iie.org

Description: Grants for B.A./B.S. holders studying Icelandic language, literature, and history; for eight months of advanced study at the University of Iceland in Reykjavik.
Restrictions: Knowledge of Icelandic, Old Norse, or other Scandinavian language required for language/literature study; United States citizenship required; applicants must meet all Fulbright eligibility requirements.
$ Given: Five grants awarded annually; cash stipend plus tuition.
Application Information: Write for details.
Deadline: October 25.

Institute of International Education
Germanistic Society of America Fellowships
U.S. Student Programs Division
809 United Nations Plaza
New York, NY 10017-3580
(212) 984-5330
www.iie.org

Description: Fellowships for master's degree holders and some B.A./B.S. holders studying German language and literature, art history, history, economics, philosophy, international law, political science, and public affairs; for one academic year of study in Germany.
Restrictions: United States citizenship required; applicants must meet all Fulbright eligibility requirements.
$ Given: Four fellowships awarded annually; each for $11,000 plus consideration for a Fulbright Travel Grant.
Application Information: Write for details.
Deadline: October 25.

Institute of International Education
Lusk Memorial Fellowships
U.S. Student Programs Division
809 United Nations Plaza
New York, NY 10017-3580
(212) 984-5330
www.iie.org

Description: Grants for individuals in the creative and performing arts; for one academic year of study in the United Kingdom and Italy.
Restrictions: Written and spoken proficiency in Italian required for study in Italy; applicants must have completed at least four years of professional study; United States citizenship required.
$ Given: An unspecified number of grants awarded annually; maintenance allowance, health/accident insurance, and round-trip travel allowance.
Application Information: Write for details.
Deadline: October 25.

Institute of International Education
Study and Research Grants for United States Citizens
U.S. Student Programs Division
809 United Nations Plaza
New York, NY 10017-3580
(212) 984-5330
www.iie.org

Description: Grants to support study and research in all fields, as well as professional training in the creative and performing arts; tenable at institutions of higher learning outside of the United States for one year; list of participating countries in any given year may be obtained from IIE.
Restrictions: Open to United States citizens with B.A. or equivalent; acceptable plan of study and proficiency in host country's language required.
$ Given: A variable number of grants awarded annually; covers international transportation, language or orienta-

tion course (where appropriate), tuition, book and maintenance allowances, and health and accident insurance.
Application Information: If currently enrolled in a college or university, apply to the campus Fulbright Program Advisor; applications also available from IIE.
Deadline: October 25.

International Foundation of Employee Benefit Systems Graduate Research Grants
18700 West Bluemound Road
P.O. Box 69
Brookfield, WI 53008-0069
(262) 786-6710

Description: Grants to support doctoral candidates conducting research on labor studies and employee benefit topics, such as health-care benefits, retirement, and income security; recipients chosen on the basis of proposed original research.
Restrictions: United States or Canadian citizenship required.
$ Given: Five to seven grants of up to $5,000 each are awarded annually.
Application Information: Include 20-page proposal (or shorter), curriculum vitae, and two letters of recommendation (one from thesis/dissertation advisor).
Deadline: Applications accepted continuously.
Contact: Director of Research.

International Reading Association Reading/Literacy Research Fellowship
Research and Policy Division
800 Barksdale Road
P.O. Box 8139
Newark, DE 19714-8139
(302) 731-1600

Description: Fellowship for a postdoctoral researcher with exceptional promise in reading research.
Restrictions: Non-U.S. and Canadian citizens only. Limited to Association members. Candidates must have completed their doctorate within the last five years.
$ Given: One fellowship awarded annually for $1,000.
Application Information: Write for details.
Deadline: October 15.

International Research and Exchanges Board
IREX Research Exchange Program with Mongolia
1616 H Street, N.W.
Washington, DC 20006
(202) 628-8188
www.irex.org

Description: One- to four-month exchange program for doctoral candidates to study in Mongolia; relevant disciplines include the humanities, social sciences, and natural sciences; recipients chosen on the basis of proposed research.
Restrictions: Command of host country's language required; United States citizenship required.
$ Given: Three fellowships awarded annually; varying amounts.
Application Information: Write for details.
Deadline: December 15.
Contact: Emili Dickson, Program Officer.

Japan Foundation
Dissertation Fellowships
152 West 57th Street
39th Floor
New York, NY 10019
(212) 489-0299
www.ipf.go.jp

Description: Fellowships for two to 14 months of dissertation research in Japan; funding made available to doctoral candidates at dissertation level in the humanities and social sciences, with emphasis on political science, law, economics, business, and journalism—as related to Japan; recipients chosen on the basis of academic achievement and quality of proposed research.
Restrictions: Applicants must be proficient in Japanese; no funding for Japanese language study; recipients may not hold other fellowships concurrently.
$ Given: Thirteen fellowships awarded annually; each for ¥310,000 plus further allowances including one round trip air ticket.
Application Information: Write for details.
Deadline: December 1.

Japan Ministry of Education,
Science, and Culture
Japanese Government
(Monbusho) Scholarship
Program
2-2 Kasumigaseki, 3-chome
Chiyoda-ku
Tokyo 100
Japan
03-581-4211
www.embjapan.org

Description: Eighteen-month to two-year scholarships for non-Japanese graduate students to study at Japanese universities and research institutes; Research Students Program is specifically designed for graduate students (undergraduate program also available) in the humanities, social sciences, music, fine arts, and natural sciences; open to citizens of countries with educational exchange agreements with Japan.
Restrictions: Language proficiency required (12- to 18-month language training program required if language skills deemed insufficient); applicants must be under age 35.
$ Given: An unspecified number of scholarships awarded annually; each to cover monthly stipend, airfare, tuition, and expense allowance.
Application Information: For further information, contact Japanese Embassy or Consulate.
Deadline: August 14.
Contact: Student Exchange Division, Leslie Fedsta, Japan Information Center, Consulate General of Japan, 100 Colony Square, Suite 2000, Atlanta, GA 30361, (404) 892-2700.

Japanese American Citizens
League
National Scholarship and
Student Aid Program
1765 Sutter Street
San Francisco, CA 94115
(415) 921-5225
www.jacl.org

Description: Scholarships for undergraduate and graduate students, as well as for individuals involved in performing and creative arts projects reflecting the Japanese American experience and culture.
Restrictions: Membership in Japanese American Citizens League (or having parent who is member) preferred; United States citizenship required.
$ Given: An unspecified number of scholarships awarded annually; varying amounts.

Application Information: Application forms are available from local JACL chapters in September; write national office for list of local and regional chapters.
Deadline: March 1 for undergraduates, April for all others.

Lyndon Baines Johnson Foundation
Grants-in-Aid of Research
2313 Red River Street
Austin, TX 78705
(512) 478-7829
www.lbjib.utexas.adu

Description: Grants for individuals to conduct research at the LBJ Library; relevant fields include communications, economics, environmental policy and resource management, history, political science, and public policy; recipients chosen on the proposed research.
Restrictions: N/A.
$ Given: A few grants awarded annually to help defray the costs of living, travel, and related expenses; grants normally range from $300–$1,400.
Application Information: Contact the Chief Archivist regarding the availability of proposed material before applying.
Deadlines: January 31, July 31.
Contact: Assistant Executive Director.

Kaiser Media Fellowships in Health
Henry J. Kaiser Family Foundation
2400 Sand Hill Road
Menlo Park, CA 94025
(650) 854-9400

Description: One-year fellowships for journalists, editors, and producers who cover health issues to research specific topics in the field of health policy, health financing, or public health issues.
Restrictions: U.S. citizenship or employment by an accredited U.S. media organization required.
$ Given: Up to six fellowships awarded annually, each with a basic annual stipend of $45,000.
Application Information: Write for details.
Deadline: March 12.
Contact: Penny Duckham, Executive Director, Fellowships Program.

Kaiser Media Mini-Fellowships in Health
Henry J. Kaiser Family Foundation
2400 Sand Hill Road
Menlo Park, CA 94025
(650) 854-9400

Description: Limited grants for journalists, editors, and producers who cover health issues to undertake a specific research project in the field of health policy, health financing, or public health issues.
Restrictions: U.S. citizenship or employment by an accredited U.S. media organization required.
$ Given: An unspecified number of fellowships awarded annually, each for an average of $5,000 for project-related travel and expenses.
Application Information: Write for details.
Deadline: March 12.
Contact: Penny Duckham, Executive Director, Fellowships Program.

Kennan Institute Short-Term Grants
One Woodrow Wilson Plaza
1300 Pennsylvania Avenue, N.W.
Washington, DC 20004-3027
(202) 691-4246

Description: Grants for scholars whose research in the social sciences or humanities focuses on the former Soviet Union and who demonstrate a particular need to use the library, archival and other specialized resources of the Washington, DC area.
Restrictions: Academic participants must either possess a doctoral degree or be doctoral candidates who have nearly completed their dissertations. Recipients required to be in residence in Washington, DC for the duration of their grant.
$ Given: An unspecified number of grants awarded annually, each with a stipend of $100 per day.
Application Information: Write for details.
Deadlines: December 1, March 1, June 1, September 1.
Contact: Jennifer Giglio.

Kosciuszko Foundation
15 East 65th Street
New York, NY 10021-6595
(212) 734-2130
FAX (212) 628-4552
www.kosciuszkofoundation.org

Description: One-year scholarships to U.S. citizens of Polish descent for graduate studies in any field at colleges and universities in the United States and to Americans of non-Polish descent whose studies at American universities are primarily focused on Polish subjects. Recipients chosen on the basis of academic achievement and financial need.
Restrictions: Must be enrolled in a graduate program at a U.S. university. Applicants must be U.S. citizens or of Polish descent.
$ Given: An unspecified number of scholarships of $1,000–$5,000 each are awarded annually.
Deadline: January 16.
Contact: Grants office.

Kosciuszko Foundation Graduate Studies and Research in Poland Program
15 East 65th Street
New York, NY 10021-6595
(212) 734-2130
FAX (212) 628-4552

Description: Grants to allow Americans to pursue graduate and postgraduate studies in Poland in any subject.
Restrictions: Applicants must have strong command of Polish language; United States citizenship or permanent resident of Polish descent; Polish studies background required.
$ Given: An unspecified number of grants of $1,000–$5,000 awarded annually; each for tuition, room, board, and monthly stipend for living expenses.
Application Information: Write for details.
Deadline: January 16.
Contact: Grants Office.

Kosciuszko Foundation
Year Abroad at the University
of Cracow Program
15 East 65th Street
New York, NY 10021-6595
(212) 734-2130
FAX (212) 628-4552

Description: Grants to support participation in one-year program of academic study at the University of Cracow (Jagiellonian University) in Poland; funding made available to undergraduate upperclassmen and graduate students in the fields of Polish language, literature, history, and culture.
Restrictions: Applicants must have Polish background; United States citizenship or permanent resident.
$ Given: An unspecified number of grants awarded annually; each for tuition, housing, and monthly food/expense allowance; round-trip travel not covered.
Application Information: Write for details.
Deadline: November 15.
Contact: Grants Office.

Samuel H. Kress Foundation
Art Conservation Advanced
Training Fellowships
174 East 80th Street
New York, NY 10021
(212) 861-4993
www.shkf.org

Description: One-year fellowships in special areas of fine arts conservation; tenable at appropriate institutions.
Restrictions: Applicants must have completed initial conservation training; United States citizenship or enrollment in United States university required.
$ Given: Ten fellowships of $2,500 each are awarded annually.
Application Information: Write for details.
Deadline: March 1.
Contact: Lisa Ackerman, Chief Administrative Officer.

Samuel H. Kress Foundation
Art History Travel Fellowships
174 East 80th Street
New York, NY 10021
(212) 861-4993
www.shkf.org

Description: Fellowships for doctoral candidates at dissertation level in art history to travel for the purpose of viewing original materials/works; recipients chosen on the basis of academic achievement, financial need, and necessity of travel.
Restrictions: United States citizenship or enrollment in United States university required.
$ Given: Fifteen to twenty fellowships of $1,000–$5,000 awarded annually.
Application Information: Applicants must be nominated by their art history departments.
Deadline: November 30.
Contact: Lisa Ackerman, Chief Administrative Officer.

Samuel H. Kress Foundation
Predoctoral Fellowships for
Research in Art History
174 East 80th Street
New York, NY 10021
(212) 861-4993
www.shkf.org

Description: Two-year fellowships for dissertation research in art history at Institutes in Florence, Jerusalem, Leiden, London, Munich, Nicosea, Paris, Rome, or Zurich; recipients chosen on the basis of academic achievement, financial need, and proposed research.
Restrictions: Affiliation with United States university required.
$ Given: Four fellowships of $18,000 are awarded annually.

Application Information: Write for details; applicants must be nominated by their department, one nomination per department.
Deadline: November 30.
Contact: Lisa Ackerman, Chief Administrative Officer.

L.S.B. Leakey Foundation
Franklin Mosher Baldwin
Memorial Fellowships
P.O. Box 29346
Presidio Building 10024
O'Reilly Avenue
San Francisco, CA 94129-0346
www.leakeyfoundation.org

Description: Fellowship for master's candidates in anthropology; tenable at any qualified institution in the world.
Restrictions: Limited to citizens of African nations.
$ Given: One fellowship of up to $12,000 awarded annually for expenses.
Application Information: Write for details.
Deadline: February 15.
Contact: D. Karla Savage, Ph.D., Program and Grants Officer.

L.S.B. Leakey Foundation
Foraging Peoples Study
Fellowships
P.O. Box 29346
Presidio Building 10024
O'Reilly Avenue
San Francisco, CA 94129-0346
www.leakeyfoundation.org

Description: Fellowship for doctoral candidates studying contemporary foraging peoples; recipients chosen on the basis of proposed research; preference for urgent research projects that might not ordinarily be funded by other agencies.
Restrictions: N/A.
$ Given: One occasional fellowship of up to $40,000 awarded for one to two years of field expenses.
Application Information: Write for details.
Deadlines: Preapplication and curriculum vitae due October 15; formal application due January 2.
Contact: D. Karla Savage, Ph.D., Program and Grants Officer.

L.S.B. Leakey Foundation
General Grants
P.O. Box 29346
Presidio Building 10024
O'Reilly Avenue
San Francisco, CA 94129-0346
www.leakeyfoundation.org

Description: Fellowship for professional and doctoral candidates, if supported by faculty advisors, for the study of human evolution; priority to new projects in exploratory phases and novel opportunities to establish projects.
Restrictions: N/A.
$ Given: An unspecified number of grants for $3,000–$12,000 each are awarded twice annually.
Application Information: Write for details.
Deadlines: January 5, August 15.
Contact: D. Karla Savage, Ph.D., Program and Grants Officer.

Library and Information Technology Association
Scholarship in Library and Information Technology
50 East Huron Street
Chicago, IL 60611
(312) 944-6780
www.lila.org

Description: Scholarship for master's candidates in library science; recipients chosen on the basis of academic achievement, leadership qualities, commitment to career in library automation, and prior experience with library automation; financial need considered.
Restrictions: N/A.
$ Given: One scholarship of $2,500 is awarded annually.
Application Information: Write for details.
Deadline: April 1.
Contact: Rebecca Falkner, Program Officer.

The Library Company of Philadelphia
American History and Culture Research Fellowships
1314 Locust Street
Philadelphia, PA 19107
(215) 546-3181
www.librarycompany.org

Description: Research fellowships at the Library Company of Philadelphia for doctoral candidates and postdoctoral scholars in most disciplines as related to the history and culture of 18th- to 19th-century America; tenable for one or more months; recipients chosen on the basis of proposed research.
Restrictions: N/A.
$ Given: An unspecified number of fellowships awarded annually; each with $1,500/month stipend.
Application Information: Write for details.
Deadline: March 1.
Contact: James Green, Curator.

Charles A. Lindbergh Foundation
Lindbergh Grants Program
2150 Third Avenue North
Suite 310
Anoka, MN 55303
(612) 576-1596
www.isd.net/lindbergh

Description: Grants for individuals to conduct research into the balance of technology and the human/natural environment; relevant fields include humanities, biomedical research, conservation of natural resources, waste disposal management, wildlife preservation, intercultural communications, aviation, aeronautics, agriculture, astronautics, adaptive technology, the arts, health and population studies, and oceanography.
Restrictions: Open to all nationalities.
$ Given: Ten grants of up to $10,580 each are awarded annually.
Application Information: Write for details.
Deadline: June 14.
Contact: Shelley Nehl, Grants Coordinator.

Henry Luce Foundation
Luce Scholars Program
111 West 50th Street
Rm. 4601
New York, NY 10020
(212) 489-7700
www.hluce.org

Description: Internship programs for graduate students in all disciplines relevant to Asian area and cultural studies to work in chosen disciplines in East and Southeast Asia; recipients chosen on the basis of academic achievement and leadership potential. Must be nominated by academic institution. No individual applications accepted.
Restrictions: Maximum age 29; not intended for specialists in Asian affairs; United States citizenship required.

$ Given: Fifteen grants of $1,400–$1,700 each awarded annually.
Application Information: Applicants must be nominated by one of 67 participating colleges or universities.
Deadline: Nominations by schools by first Monday in December.
Contact: Helene Redall, Grants Coordinator.

MacArthur Foundation Grants for Research and Writing
MacArthur Foundation
140 South Dearborn Street
Chicago, IL 60603
(312) 726-8000
www.macfdn.org

Description: Grants for research and writing in any academic discipline or profession to support innovation and excellence in the analysis of the causes, nature, and consequence of international conflict and cooperation; and in the development of improved understandings of human security; and to broaden and strengthen the community of writers and peace, security and sustainability.
Restrictions: Not for dissertation research.
$ Given: Applicants may request up to $75,000 for individual projects, or $100,000 for two-person collaborations.
Application Information: Write for details.
Deadline: February 2.

Marshall Scholarships
Marshall Aid Commemorating Commission
Association of Commonwealth Universities
36 Gordon Square
London WC1H0PF
(44) 1713878572
www.aca.ac.uk/marshall

Description: Two- to three-year scholarships for undergraduate or graduate level study at any university in the United Kingdom, in any discipline leading to the award of a British university degree.
Restrictions: U.S. citizenship required; limited to graduates of accredited four-year colleges and universities in the United States with at least a 3.75 GPA since freshman year.
$ Given: Up to forty scholarships awarded annually; each worth approximately $25,000 per year and comprising a personal allowance for cost of living and residence, tuition fees, books, travel in connection with studies, and to and from the United States.
Application Information: Write for details. Application forms also available from colleges and universities in the United States, British consulates in Atlanta, Boston, Chicago, Houston, and San Francisco, the British Council in Washington, DC, British Information Services in New York.
Deadline: N/A.

James Madison Foundation Fellowships
P.O. Box 4030
Iowa City, IA 52243-4030
(800) 525-6928
www.jamesmadison.com

Description: Fellowships for graduate study leading to a master's degree in American history or political science; a master's of Arts in Teaching or a master's of Education degree concentrating in constitutional history or American government or political theory. Fellowship includes the four-week Summer Institute on the Constitution at Georgetown University.
Restrictions: None.
$ Given: Up to $24,000 annually for tuition, fees, books, room, board.
Application Information: Write for details.
Deadline: March 1.

Massachusetts Historical Society
Andrew W. Mellow Research Fellowships
1154 Boylston Street
Boston, MA 02215
(617) 536-1608

Description: Short-term fellowships for advanced graduate students and holders of a Ph.D. or the equivalent to conduct research at the Massachusetts Historical Society. Any project for which the Society's collections are appropriate is eligible for consideration, including specifically the study of the history of colonial New England; study of the Society's collection of portraits, engravings, silhouettes, and other graphic material; study of African American history, study of Paul Revere; women's history; the American Revolution.
Restrictions: Preference will be given to candidates who live fifty or more miles from Boston.
$ Given: Approximately eighteen fellowships are awarded annually; each with a four-week stipend of $1,500.
Application Information: Write for details.
Deadline: March 1.
Contact: Len Travers, Assistant Director, Center for the Study of New England History.

Medical Library Association
MLA Doctoral Fellowships
65 East Wacker Place
Suite 1900
Chicago, IL 60601
(312) 419-9094
www2.mc.duke.edu/misc.
MLA/HHSS/hhss.htm

Description: One-year fellowships for doctoral candidates in health sciences librarianship, with emphasis on biomedical and health-related information science; funding intended to support research or travel, not tuition; recipients chosen on the basis of academic achievement.
Restrictions: Applicants must hold master's degrees from ALA-accredited schools; United States or Canadian citizenship required.
$ Given: One fellowship of $2,000 is awarded biannually; non-renewable.
Application Information: Write for details.
Deadline: December 1.
Contact: Coordinator of Research and Professional Recognition.

Medical Library Association
MLA Graduate Scholarships
65 East Wacker Place
Suite 1900
Chicago, IL 60601
(312) 419-9094
www2.mc.duke.edu/misc
MLA/HHSS/hhss.htm

Description: Scholarships for master's candidates in medical librarianship; recipients chosen on the basis of academic achievement and professional potential.
Restrictions: Applicants must be entering an ALA-accredited school or have at least one-half the academic requirements yet to complete during the scholarship year; United States or Canadian citizenship required.
$ Given: One scholarship for $2,000 is awarded annually.
Application Information: Write for details.
Deadline: December 1.
Contact: Coordinator of Research and Professional Recognition.

Medical Library Association
MLA Graduate Scholarships
for Minority Students
65 East Wacker Place
Suite 1900
Chicago, IL 60601
(312) 419-9094
www2.mc.duke.edu/misc
MLA/HHSS/hhss.htm

Description: Scholarships for master's candidates in health sciences librarianship; recipients chosen on the basis of academic achievement and professional potential.
Restrictions: Limited to minority group applicants only; applicants must be entering an ALA-accredited school or have at least one-half the academic requirements yet to complete during the scholarship year; United States or Canadian citizenship required.
$ Given: One scholarship for $2,000 is awarded annually.
Application Information: Write for details.
Deadline: December 1.
Contact: Coordinator of Research and Professional Recognition.

Memorial Foundation for
Jewish Culture
International Doctoral
Scholarship for Jewish Studies
15 East 26th Street
Room 1901
New York, NY 10010
(212) 679-4074

Description: Scholarships for doctoral candidates in Jewish studies; recipients chosen on the basis of academic achievement, financial need, and proposed research.
Restrictions: N/A.
$ Given: An unspecified number of scholarships awarded annually; each for $2,500–$7,500 per year; renewable for up to 4 years.
Application Information: Submit written request for application form; references required.
Deadline: October 31.
Contact: Executive Vice President.

Metropolitan Museum of Art
Bothmer Fellowship
Office of Academic Programs
Fifth Avenue and 82nd Street
New York, NY 10028
(212) 570-3874
www.metmuseum.org

Description: Fellowship for doctoral students studying Greek and Roman art at United States universities, for thesis-related work using the Metropolitan's Department of Greek and Roman Art resources; recipients chosen on the basis of academic achievement and proposed thesis topic.
Restrictions: Applicant's thesis topic must have been accepted by thesis advisor; fellowship not for exhibition projects.

$ Given: One fellowship awarded annually; $18,000, plus up to $3,000 travel allowance.
Application Information: Write for details.
Deadline: November 5 (or first Friday in November).
Contact: Marcie Karp, Fellowships Coordinator.

**Metropolitan Museum of Art
Chester Dale Fellowships**
Office of Academic Programs
Fifth Avenue and 82nd Street
New York, NY 10028
(212) 570-3874
www.metmuseum.org

Description: Three-month to one-year residential fellowships for doctoral students studying fine art of the Western world, for research using the Metropolitan's resources; recipients chosen on the basis of academic achievement and proposed research.
Restrictions: Preferred maximum age 40; United States citizenship preferred; fellowships not for exhibition projects.
$ Given: An unspecified number of fellowships awarded annually; plus $2,500.
Application Information: Write for details.
Deadline: November 5.
Contact: Marcie Karp, Fellowships Coordinator.

**Metropolitan Museum of Art
Andrew W. Mellon
Fellowships**
Office of Academic Programs
Fifth Avenue and 82nd Street
New York, NY 10028
(212) 570-3874
www.metmuseum.org

Description: Residential fellowships for doctoral students in art history, for research using the Metropolitan's collections; maximum one-year fellowship period; recipients chosen on the basis of academic achievement and proposed research.
Restrictions: Fellowships not for exhibition projects.
$ Given: An unspecified number of fellowships awarded annually.
Application Information: Write for details.
Deadline: November 5.
Contact: Marcie Karp, Fellowships Coordinator.

**Metropolitan Museum of Art
Andrew W. Mellon
Fellowships in Conservation**
Office of Academic Programs
Fifth Avenue and 82nd Street
New York, NY 10028
(212) 570-3874
www.metmuseum.org

Description: One-year residential fellowships for doctoral students in fine arts conservation, for work in specific departments of the Metropolitan, including Paintings Conservation, Objects Conservation, Musical Instruments, Arms and Armor, Paper Conservation, Costume Institute, Textile Conservation, and Asian Art Conservation; recipients chosen on the basis of training and proposed research.
Restrictions: Applicants must be planning employment in conservation.
$ Given: An unspecified number of fellowships awarded annually; stipends commensurate with training and experience; renewable for two more years.
Application Information: Write for details.
Contact: Marcie Karp, Fellowships Coordinator.

**Metropolitan Museum of Art
J. Clawson Mills Scholarships**
Office of Academic Programs
Fifth Avenue and 82nd Street
New York, NY 10028
(212) 570-3874
www.metmuseum.org

Description: One-year residential scholarships for doc-
toral students in fine arts, for study/research using the
Metropolitan's collections; recipients chosen on the basis
of academic achievement and proposed research.
Restrictions: N/A.
$ Given: An unspecified number of scholarships
awarded annually.
Application Information: Write for details.
Deadline: November 5.
Contact: Marcie Karp, Fellowships Coordinator.

**Metropolitan Museum of Art
Theodore Rousseau
Scholarships**
Office of Academic Programs
Fifth Avenue and 82nd Street
New York, NY 10028
(212) 570-3874
www.metmuseum.org

Description: Fellowships for master's and doctoral candidates in art history, for study in Europe; intended to
allow recipients first-hand examination of painting in
major European collections.
Restrictions: Applicants must have completed at least
one year of graduate training; applicants should be planning careers as museum curators of painting.
$ Given: An unspecified number of fellowships awarded
annually.
Application Information: Write for details.
Deadline: November 5.
Contact: Marcie Karp, Fellowships Coordinator.

**Metropolitan Museum of Art
Norbert Schimmel
Fellowships for
Mediterranean Art and
Archaeology**
Office of Academic Programs
Fifth Avenue and 82nd Street
New York, NY 10028
(212) 570-3874
www.metmuseum.org

Description: Residential fellowships for doctoral candidates studying Near Eastern art and archaeology, Greek
art, and/or Roman art at United States universities, for
thesis-related research using the Metropolitan's art collection; recipients chosen on the basis of academic achievement, financial need, and proposed research.
Restrictions: N/A.
$ Given: One fellowship awarded annually.
Application Information: Write for details.
Deadline: November 5.
Contact: Marcie Karp, Fellowships Coordinator.

**Metropolitan Museum of Art
Summer Graduate
Internships**
Office of Academic Programs
Fifth Avenue and 82nd Street
New York, NY 10028
(212) 570-3874
www.metmuseum.org

Description: Nine-week internships to provide master's
and doctoral candidates in museum studies with practical
experience in various museum departments; recipients
chosen on the basis of academic achievement and future
career goals.
Restrictions: Applicants must have completed at least
one year of museum studies and have strong art history
background.
$ Given: An unspecified number of internships awarded
annually.
Application Information: Write for details.
Contact: Coordinator of Internships.

Metropolitan Museum of Art
Polaire Weissman Fund
Fellowships
Office of Academic Programs
Fifth Avenue and 82nd Street
New York, NY 10028
(212) 570-3874
www.metmuseum.org

Description: Fellowships for graduate students in fine arts and costume history, to provide experience with costume history and conservation at the Metropolitan Museum; preference for those interested in museum and teaching careers in these areas; fellowships offered in alternate years only.
Restrictions: N/A.
$ Given: An unspecified number of internships awarded in alternate years.
Application Information: Fellowships offered in academic years 92/93, 94/95, etc.
Deadline: November 5.
Contact: Marcie Karp, Fellowships Coordinator.

Metropolitan Museum of Art
Jane and Morgan Whitney
Fellowships
Office of Academic Programs
Fifth Avenue and 82nd Street
New York, NY 10028
(212) 570-3874
www.metmuseum.org

Description: One-year fellowships for graduate students in fine arts, for study/research in fields related to Metropolitan's collections; preference for decorative arts.
Restrictions: Applicants under age 40 preferred.
$ Given: An unspecified number of internships awarded annually.
Application Information: Write for details.
Deadline: November 5.
Contact: Marcie Karp, Fellowships Coordinator.

Monticello College
Foundation and Washington
University
Spencer T. Olin Fellowships
for Women in Graduate Study
Graduate School of Arts and
Sciences
Washington University
Campus Box 1187
One Brookings Drive
St. Louis, MO 63130-4899
(314) 935-6848

Description: Fellowships for graduate students to prepare for careers in higher education and professions in the fields of biological and biomedical sciences, humanities, physical sciences and mathematics, social and behavioral sciences, architecture, business administration, engineering, fine arts, law, medicine, and social work. Tenable at Washington University.
Restrictions: Limited to women applicants only.
$ Given: An unspecified number of fellowships awarded annually, each ranging from $20,000 to $33,000.
Application Information: Write for details.
Deadline: February 1.

National Air and Space
Museum
Guggenheim Fellowships
6th and Independence Avenue,
S.W.
Washington, DC 20560-0312
(202) 357-2700
www.nasm.edu

Description: Three- to twelve-month residential fellowships for doctoral candidates at dissertation level, as well as recent Ph.D.s (within past seven years), for historical/scientific research on aviation and space; relevant disciplines include history, aerospace, and engineering.
Restrictions: N/A.
$ Given: An unspecified number of fellowships awarded annually; $15,000–$27,000 predoctoral stipend, $25,000 postdoctoral stipend.
Application Information: Write for details.
Deadline: January 15.
Contact: Fellowship Coordinator.

National Air and Space Museum
Verville Fellowships
6th and Independence Avenue, S.W.
Washington, DC 20560 0312
(202) 357-2700
www.nasm.edu

Description: Nine- to twelve-month fellowships for analysis of major developments, trends, and accomplishments in history of aviation/space studies; relevant disciplines include history, aerospace, and engineering.
Restrictions: Applicants must demonstrate skills in research and writing.
$ Given: An unspecified number of fellowships for $35,000 each are awarded annually.
Application Information: Write for details.
Deadline: January 15.
Contact: Fellowship Coordinator.

National Association for Core Curriculum
Bossing-Edwards Research Scholarships
404 East White Hall
Kent State University
Kent, OH 44242
(216) 672-2792
www.wkans.edu/~graduate/gfog

Description: Scholarships for master's and doctoral candidates studying core curriculum, interdisciplinary studies, and integrated curriculum; intended as support for research promoting development of secondary education programs; recipients chosen on the basis of proposed research project's relevance to core curriculum.
Restrictions: Applicants must have been core teachers for at least one year; funding must be used at institution with adequate resources for core research; summary of research findings must be submitted to NACC.
$ Given: An unspecified number of scholarships for $100–$500 each are awarded annually.
Application Information: Write for details.
Deadline: October 1.
Contact: Dr. Gordon F. Vars, Executive Secretary-Treasurer.

National Association of Broadcasters
Grants for Research in Broadcasting
1771 N. Street, N.W.
Washington, DC 20036
(202) 429-5389
www.nab.org

Description: Grants for graduate students to conduct research on the social, cultural, political, and economic aspects of the United States commercial broadcast industry.
Restrictions: N/A.
$ Given: An unspecified number of grants on average of $5,000 each are awarded annually.
Application Information: Write for details.
Deadline: January 28.
Contact: Vice President.

National Collegiate Athletic Association
NCAA Postgraduate Scholarships
P.O. Box 6222
Indianapolis, IN 46206-6222
(317) 917-6222
www.ncaa.org

Description: Scholarships for varsity college athletes in sports which NCAA conducts national championships; for full-time graduate study in any field; recipients chosen on the basis of academic achievement (minimum 3.0 GPA), athletic achievement, and capability for graduate study.
Restrictions: N/A.
$ Given: One hundred and seventy-four scholarships are awarded annually: 35 in football, 32 in basketball (16 to men, 16 to women), and 107 in other varsity sports (36 to men, 71 to women); of $5,000 each.

Application Information: Applicants must be nominated by college director of athletics during final season of NCAA eligibility; maximum two football, two basketball (one man, one woman), and four other sports (two men, two women) nominations per NCAA member school per year.
Deadlines: February 1 for football; March 1 for basketball; April 24 for other varsity sports.
Contact: John Williams.

National Foundation for Jewish Culture
Doctoral Dissertation Fellowships in Jewish Studies
330 Seventh Avenue
21st Floor
New York, NY 10001
(212) 629-0500
www.jewishculture.org

Description: Fellowships for doctoral candidates at dissertation level in Jewish studies; recipients chosen on the basis of academic achievement and dissertation topic.
Restrictions: Preference for applicants planning careers in Jewish studies; United States citizenship or permanent resident status required.
$ Given: An unspecified number of fellowships of $7,000–$10,000 each are awarded annually.
Application Information: Write for details.
Deadline: January 3.
Contact: Kim Bistrong.

National Gallery of Art
Chester Dale Predoctoral Fellowships
Center for Advanced Study in the Visual Arts
4th and Constitution Avenue, N.W.
Washington, DC 20565
(202) 842-6482
FAX (202) 842-6733
www.nga.gov

Description: One-year fellowships for doctoral candidates in Western art to advance their dissertation through research and/or travel; recipients chosen on the basis of academic achievement.
Restrictions: Applicants must be proficient in two foreign languages related to dissertation topic; recipients may not hold outside job during fellowship tenure; United States citizenship or enrollment in United States university required.
$ Given: Two fellowships for $16,000 each are awarded annually; non-renewable.
Application Information: Applicants must be sponsored by the chairperson of the art history graduate department.
Deadline: November 15.
Contact: Henry A. Millon, Dean.

National Gallery of Art
Mary Davis Predoctoral Fellowship
Center for Advanced Study in the Visual Arts
4th and Constitution Avenue, N.W.
Washington, DC 20565
(202) 842-6402
FAX (202) 842-6733
www.nga.gov

Description: Two-year fellowships for doctoral candidates at dissertation level in Western art; to support one year of dissertation research within the United States or abroad, and one year in residence at the Center, working on research projects and gaining curatorial experience.
Restrictions: Applicants must have completed all preliminary coursework and exams for doctorate; applicants must be proficient in two foreign languages related to dissertation topic; United States citizenship or enrollment in United States university required.
$ Given: One fellowship for $16,000 per year (for two years) is awarded annually.

Application Information: Applicants must be sponsored by the chairperson of the art history graduate department.
Deadline: November 15.
Contact: Henry A. Millon, Dean.

National Gallery of Art
David E. Finley Predoctoral
Fellowship
Center for Advanced Study in
the Visual Arts
4th and Constitution Avenue,
N.W.
Washington, DC 20565
(202) 842-6402
FAX (202) 842-6733
www.nga.gov

Description: Three-year fellowships for doctoral candidates at dissertation level in history of art/architecture/urban design; for two years of dissertation-related research and travel, plus one year of residency at Center for Advanced Study in the Visual Arts; recipients chosen on the basis of academic achievement and proposed research.
Restrictions: Applicants must be proficient in two foreign languages related to dissertation topic; applicants must have significant interest in museum work; recipients may not hold outside job during fellowship tenure; United States citizenship or enrollment in United States university required.
$ Given: One fellowship for $16,000 per year (for three years) is awarded annually; non-renewable.
Application Information: Applicants must be sponsored by the chairperson of the art history graduate department.
Deadline: November 15.
Contact: Henry A. Millon, Dean.

National Gallery of Art
Ittleson Predoctoral
Fellowship
Center for Advanced Study in
the Visual Arts
4th and Constitution Avenue,
N.W.
Washington, DC 20565
(202) 842-6482
FAX (202) 842-6733
www.nga.gov

Description: Two-year fellowships for doctoral candidates at dissertation level in art and art history exclusive of Western art; for one year of dissertation-related research and travel, plus one year of residency at Center for Advanced Study in the Visual Arts; recipients chosen on the basis of academic achievement and proposed research.
Restrictions: United States citizenship or enrollment in United States university required.
$ Given: One fellowship for $16,000 per year (for two years) is awarded annually; non-renewable.
Application Information: Applicants must be sponsored by the chairperson of the art history graduate department.
Deadline: November 15.
Contact: Henry A. Millon, Dean.

**National Gallery of Art
Samuel H. Kress Predoctoral
Fellowship**
Center for Advanced Study in
the Visual Arts
4th and Constitution Avenue,
N.W.
Washington, DC 20565
(202) 842-6482
FAX (202) 842-6733
www.nga.gov

Description: Two-year fellowships for doctoral candidates at dissertation level in history of western art; for one year of dissertation-related research and travel, plus one year of residency at Center for Advanced Study in the Visual Arts (half-time devoted to dissertation completion, half-time devoted to Gallery research projects); recipients chosen on the basis of academic achievement and proposed research.
Restrictions: Applicants must be proficient in two foreign languages related to dissertation topic; recipients may not hold outside job during fellowship tenure; United States citizenship or enrollment in United States university required.
$ Given: One fellowship for $16,000 per year (for two years) is awarded annually; non-renewable.
Application Information: Applicants must be sponsored by the chairperson of the art history graduate department.
Deadline: November 15.
Contact: Henry A. Millon, Dean.

**National Gallery of Art
Andrew W. Mellon
Predoctoral Fellowship**
Center for Advanced Study in
the Visual Arts
4th and Constitution Avenue,
N.W.
Washington, DC 20565
(202) 842-6482
FAX (202) 842-6733
www.nga.gov

Description: Two-year fellowships for doctoral candidates at dissertation level in art and art history, excluding Western art; to support one year of dissertation research within the United States or abroad, and one year in residence at the Center, completing dissertation.
Restrictions: Applicants must have completed all preliminary coursework and exams for doctorate; applicants must be proficient in two foreign languages related to dissertation topic; United States citizenship or enrollment in United States university required.
$ Given: One fellowship for $16,000 per year (for two years) is awarded annually; non-renewable.
Application Information: Applicants must be sponsored by the chairperson of the art history graduate department.
Deadline: November 15.
Contact: Henry A. Millon, Dean.

**National Gallery of Art
Paul Mellon Fellowship**
Center for Advanced Study in
the Visual Arts
4th and Constitution Avenue,
N.W.
Washington, DC 20565
(202) 842-6482
FAX (202) 842-6733
www.nga.gov

Description: Three-year fellowships for doctoral candidates at dissertation level in history of Western art; for two years of dissertation-related research and travel, plus one year of residency at Center for Advanced Study in the Visual Arts; recipients chosen on the basis of proposed research.
Restrictions: Applicants must be proficient in two foreign languages related to dissertation topic; recipients must have devoted at least six months full-time research to proposed dissertation topic before beginning fellow-

ship; recipients may not hold outside job during fellow-ship tenure; United States citizenship or enrollment in United States university required.
$ Given: One fellowship for $16,000 per year (for three years) is awarded annually; non-renewable.
Application Information: Applicants must be sponsored by the chairperson of the art history graduate department.
Deadline: November 15.
Contact: Henry A. Millon, Dean.

National Gallery of Art
Predoctoral Fellowship
Center for Advanced Study in the Visual Arts
4th and Constitution Avenue, N.W.
Washington, DC 20565
(202) 842-6482
FAX (202) 842-6733
www.nga.gov

Description: One- to three-year fellowships for doctoral candidates at dissertation level in history of art/architecture/urban design; to support dissertation research.
Restrictions: Applicants must have completed all preliminary coursework and exams for doctorate; United States citizenship or enrollment in United States university required.
$ Given: Ten fellowships for $11,000 per year (for one to three years) are awarded annually; non-renewable.
Application Information: Applicants must be sponsored by the chairperson of the art history graduate department.
Deadline: November 15.
Contact: Henry A. Millon, Dean.

National Gallery of Art
Robert H. and Clarice Smith
Predoctoral Fellowship
Center for Advanced Study in the Visual Arts
4th and Constitution Avenue, N.W.
Washington, DC 20565
(202) 842-6482
FAX (202) 842-6733
www.nga.gov

Description: One-year fellowship for doctoral candidates at dissertation level in Dutch or Flemish art history; for use within the United States or abroad; tenure at the Center not required; recipients chosen on the basis of academic achievement and proposed research.
Restrictions: Applicants must be proficient in two foreign languages related to dissertation topic; recipients may not hold outside job during fellowship tenure; United States citizenship or enrollment in United States university required.
$ Given: One fellowship for $16,000 is awarded annually; non-renewable.
Application Information: Applicants must be sponsored by the chairperson of the art history graduate department.
Deadline: November 15.
Contact: Henry A. Millon, Dean.

National Gallery of Art
Wyeth Predoctoral Fellowship
Center for Advanced Study in
the Visual Arts
4th and Constitution Avenue,
N.W.
Washington, DC 20565
(202) 842-6482
FAX (202) 842-6733
www.nga.gov

Description: Two-year fellowship for doctoral candidates at dissertation level in American art; for one year of dissertation-related research and travel, plus one year of residency at Center for Advanced Study in the Visual Arts; recipients chosen on the basis of academic achievement and proposed research.
Restrictions: Applicants must be proficient in two foreign languages related to dissertation topic; recipients may not hold outside job during fellowship tenure; United States citizenship or enrollment in United States university required.
$ Given: One fellowship for $16,000 per year (for two years) is awarded annually; non-renewable.
Application Information: Applicants must be sponsored by the chairperson of the art history graduate department.
Deadline: November 15.
Contact: Henry A. Millon, Dean.

National Historical
Publications and Records
Commission
NHPRC Historical Editing
Fellowships
National Archives Building
Washington, DC 20408
(202) 501-5610
www.nara.gov/nhprc

Description: Fellowships for doctoral candidates at dissertation level and postdoctoral scholars in United States history and editing, to participate in advanced editing of documentary sources for United States history; fellowship involves ten months of training, with concentration on one project; instruction in transcription, annotation, copyediting, and proofreading included.
Restrictions: United States citizenship or legal resident status required.
$ Given: A few fellowships awarded annually; varying amounts, average grant $39,000.
Application Information: Write for details.
Deadline: N/A.
Contact: Program Director.

National Historical
Publications and Records
Commission
NHPRC/The Andrew M.
Mellon Foundation Fellowship
in Archival Administration
National Archives Building
Washington, DC 20408
(202) 501-5610
www.nara.gov/nhprc

Description: Nine- to twelve-month fellowships for master's degree holders in archival administration, to work at host archival institutions/organizations.
Restrictions: Applicants must have two to five years experience in an archival setting, performing archival work; United States citizenship or legal resident status required.
$ Given: Two fellowships awarded annually; average $39,000.
Application Information: Write for details.
Deadline: March 1.
Contact: Program Director.

National Italian American Foundation Scholarship Program
Doctoral Research in Italy Fellowship
1860 19th Street, N.W.
Washington, DC 20009
(202) 638-2137
FAX (202) 638-0002

Description: Scholarship for Ph.D. candidates for doctoral research in Italy in modern history, politics, or economics.
Restrictions: Applicants must be of Italian descent. Must provide letter of support from advisor.
$ Given: One scholarship awarded annually for $5,000
Application Information: Send SASE for details.
Deadline: May 31.
Contact: Dr. Maria Lombardo, Education Director.

National Italian American Foundation Scholarship Program
Vincent Visceglia General Graduate Scholarships
1860 19th Street, N.W.
Washington, DC 20009
(202) 387-0600
www.niaf.org

Description: Scholarships for master's and doctoral candidates in Italian studies; recipients chosen on the basis of academic achievement and financial need and community service.
Restrictions: Applicants must be of Italian descent or be working on M.A. or Ph.D. in Italian studies.
$ Given: One fellowship for $2,000 is awarded annually.
Application Information: Application must be filled in triplicate; write for details.
Deadline: May 31.
Contact: Dr. Maria Lombardo, Education Director.

National Italian American Foundation Scholarship Program
Silvio Conte Internship
1860 19th Street, N.W.
Washington, DC 20009
(202) 387-0600
www.niaf.org

Description: Internship for undergraduate and graduate students to work for one semester in Congressman Conte's Washington, DC office.
Restrictions: Applicants must be of Italian descent; recipient must write paper about the internship experience and its expected benefit to recipient's future career.
$ Given: One internship paying $2,000 is awarded annually.
Application Information: Send SASE for details.
Deadline: May 31.
Contact: Dr. Maria Lombardo, Education Director.

National Italian American Foundation Scholarship Program
Italian American Regional Scholarships
1860 19th Street, N.W.
Washington, DC 20009
(202) 387-0600
www.niaf.org

Description: Scholarships for high school, undergraduate, and graduate students in all fields; regions are East Coast, Midwest, Southwest, and Mid-Atlantic; recipients chosen on the basis of academic achievement and financial need and community service.
Restrictions: Applicants must be of Italian descent.
$ Given: Twenty-four scholarships awarded annually; each $5,000.
Application Information: Send SASE for details.
Deadline: May 31.
Contact: Dr. Maria Lombardo, Education Director.

National Research Council Ford Foundation Predoctoral and Dissertation Fellowships FF/TJ2041
2101 Constitution Avenue
Washington, DC 20418
(202) 334-2872
FAX (202) 334-3419

Description: Three-year predoctoral fellowships and nine- to twelve-month dissertation fellowships for study in selected disciplines (humanities, social sciences, sciences, mathematics, and engineering). Recipients chosen on the basis of academic achievement and commitment to scholarship, research and careers in teaching.
Restrictions: Limited to U.S. citizens or nationals only. Limited to members of the following groups: Alaskan Natives, African Americans, Mexican Americans, Native American Indians, Native Pacific Islanders, Puerto Ricans. Applicants must be enrolled in or planning to enroll in a research-based Ph.D. or Sc.D program.
$ Given: Fifty predoctoral fellowships and twenty-nine dissertation fellowships awarded annually; predoctoral fellowships have annual stipend of $14,000 and institutional award of $7,500. Dissertation fellowships offer stipend of $21,500.
Application Information: Write for details.
Deadline: November 12.

National Research Council NRC/Ford Predoctoral and Dissertation Fellowships for Minorities
Fellowships Office
2101 Constitution Avenue, N.W.
Washington, DC 20418
(202) 334-2872
www.nas.edu/nre

Description: Fellowships for graduate students in the humanities, social sciences, biological and agricultural sciences, physical sciences and mathematics, and engineering and applied sciences; recipients chosen on the basis of academic achievement and proposed research.
Restrictions: Limited to members of minority groups; United States citizenship required.
$ Given: Fifty-three predoctoral fellowships awarded; $14,000 for fellow, $7,500 to institution in fellow's name; 25 dissertation fellowships of $21,500 for a one-year period.
Application Information: Write for details.
Deadline: November 5.

National Right to Work Committee William B. Ruggles Journalism Scholarship
8001 Braddock Road
Suite 500
Springfield, VA 22160
(703) 321-9820
www.nilrr.org

Description: Scholarship for undergraduate and graduate students in journalism, mass media, and mass communications; award for best 500-word essay on the right to work principle.
Restrictions: Applicant must be enrolled in accredited United States journalism schools; scholarship must be used within the United States.
$ Given: One scholarship for $2,000 awarded annually.
Application Information: Submit application between January 1 and March 31.
Deadline: March 31.
Contact: Mary Kay Grover.

National Science Foundation Behavioral and Neural Sciences Research Grants
4201 Wilson Boulevard
Arlington, VA 22230
(703) 306-1234
www.nsf.gov

Description: Grants to support research on nervous systems and human/animal behavior; awarded in the following subprogram categories: cultural/physical anthropology, archaeology, animal behavior, behavioral neuroendocrinology, cellular neuroscience, developmental neuroscience, human cognition/perception, linguistics, neural mechanisms of behavior, neurobiology of learning/memory, sensory system, and social psychology; recipients chosen on the basis of proposed research.
Restrictions: N/A.
$ Given: An unspecified number of grants awarded annually; varying amounts.
Application Information: Write for subprogram details.
Deadlines: Accepted continuously; January 10, July 10.
Contact: Specific contacts for different areas.

National Science Foundation Graduate Research Fellowship Program
Oak Ridge Associated Universities
P.O. Box 3010
Oak Ridge, TN 37831-3010
(865) 241-4300

Description: Three-year fellowships for graduate study leading to research-based master's or doctoral degrees in the mathematical, physical, biological, engineering, and behavioral and social sciences.
Restrictions: U.S. citizenship or permanent resident status required.
$ Given: An unspecified number of fellowships awarded annually; each with an annual stipend of $15,000, and a cost-of-education allowance of $10,500 per tenure year.
Application Information: Write for details.
Deadline: November 4.

National Security Education Program Graduate International Fellowships
Academy for Educational Development
1825 Connecticut Avenue
Washington, DC 20009-5721
(800) 498-9360
www.aed.org/nsep

Description: One- to six-semester (twenty-four-month) fellowships for graduate students to pursue specialization in area and language study in a diverse list of fields of study, specifically business, economics, history, international affairs, law, applied sciences and engineering, health and biomedical sciences, political science, and other social sciences, which are connected to U.S. national security.
Restrictions: U.S. citizenship required. Application to or enrollment in a graduate program in an accredited U.S. college or university located within the United States. Must be willing to enter into service agreement to seek employment with an agency or office of the federal government involved in national security affairs. Recipients chosen on the basis of the relationship of the applicant's proposed study to U.S. national security and how the applicant proposes to use knowledge and experience gained from NSEP support to contribute to U.S. national security.

$ Given: An unspecified number of fellowships awarded annually; each for $2,000 per semester for language or area studies coursework at your home university and $10,000 per semester for two semesters of overseas study program expenses.
Application Information: Write for details.
Deadline: January 15.

National Women's Studies Association
NAIAD-NWSA Graduate Scholarships in Lesbian Studies
7100 Baltimore Avenue
Suite 500
College Park, MD 20742
(301) 403-0525
www.nwsa.org

Description: Scholarships for master's and doctoral candidates in lesbian studies; recipients chosen on the basis of financial need and thesis/dissertation topic.
Restrictions: Membership in NWSA preferred.
$ Given: One scholarship of $500 awarded annually.
Application Information: Write for details.
Deadline: February 15.
Contact: Loretta Younger, Office Manager.

National Women's Studies Association
NWSA Scholarship in Jewish Women's Studies
7100 Baltimore Avenue
Suite 500
College Park, MD 20742
(301) 403-0525
www.nwsa.org

Description: Scholarship for graduate students in Jewish women's studies; recipients chosen on the basis of financial need and academic achievement.
Restrictions: N/A.
$ Given: One scholarship of $500 is awarded annually.
Application Information: Write for details.
Deadline: March 15.
Contact: Loretta Younger, Office Manager.

National Women's Studies Association
Pergamon–NWSA Graduate Scholarships in Women's Studies
7100 Baltimore Avenue
Suite 500
College Park, MD 20742
(301) 403-0525
www.nwsa.org

Description: Scholarship for master's and doctoral candidates in women's studies; recipients chosen on the basis of financial need and proposed research.
Restrictions: Membership in NWSA preferred.
$ Given: One scholarship of $1,000 is awarded annually.
Application Information: Write for details.
Deadline: February 15.
Contact: Loretta Younger, Office Manager.

Natural Sciences and Engineering Research Council of Canada
NSERC Postgraduate Scholarships in Science Librarianship and Documentation
350 Albert Street
Ottawa, Ontario K1A 1H5
Canada
(613) 995-5992
www.nscrc.ca

Description: One-year scholarships for first- and second-year study toward M.L.S. degree in library science; recipients chosen on the basis of academic achievement, commitment to field, and relevant experience.
Restrictions: Applicants must have B.S. degree in science or engineering, Canadian citizenship or permanent resident status required.
$ Given: A few scholarships awarded annually; each for $13,500 Canadian plus travel allowance.
Application Information: Write for details.
Deadline: December 1.
Contact: Information Officer.

New York State Senate Graduate/Post-Graduate Fellowship Program
Richard J. Roth Journalism Fellowship
Room 416
90 South Swan Street
Albany, NY 12247
(518) 455-2611

Description: Graduate fellowships to support one year of working as a full-time staff member in the Senate Press Office. Preference will be given to those candidates pursuing careers in journalism or public relations.
Restrictions: U.S. Citizenship required. Applicants must be residents of New York or enrolled in a New York state graduate school who have completed at least two semesters of graduate study.
$ Given: One fellowship in the amount of $25,000 awarded annually.
Application Information: Write for details.
Deadline: May 1.
Contact: Dr. Russell J. Williams, Director

New York University
AEJMC Summer Internship for Minorities in Journalism
269 Mercer Street
Suite 601
New York, NY 10003
(212) 998-2130
www.nyu.edu

Description: Summer internships for college upperclassmen and graduate students; participation includes actual work, journalism courses, workshops, and onsite visits; media worksites include *TV Guide*, *New York Times*, radio stations, public relations companies, advertising firms, and broadcasting companies.
Restrictions: Limited to minority group members only, especially African-American, Hispanic, Native American, Eskimo, and Asian-American applicants.
$ Given: An unspecified number of internships awarded annually; each pays at least $200/week.
Application Information: Request form by December 3.
Deadline: December 11.
Contact: Glenda Noel-Doyle, AEJMC Internship Coordinator, Institute of Afro-American Affairs.

**New York University
Publishing Studies Fellowships**
11 West 42nd Street
Room 400
New York, NY 10036
(212) 790-3232

Description: Fellowships sponsored by North American publishing houses to train graduate students in book/magazine publishing; participation requires enrollment in two-year M.A. program (first year, full-time coursework; second year, paid internship in New York City). Must be accepted and attend one semester at NYU Center for Publishing before applying for fellowships.
Restrictions: Applicants must be college graduates with minimum 3.0 GPA.
$ Given: Nine fellowships for $5,500 each are awarded annually.
Application Information: Application requires college transcripts, two letters of recommendation, and interview.
Deadline: March 1.
Contact: Mary Witty, Publishing Studies Program Coordinator, Gallatin Division.

**Newberry Library
Frances C. Allen Fellowships**
Committee on Awards
60 West Walton Street
Chicago, IL 60610-3380
(312) 943-9090
www.newberry.org

Description: One-month to one-year research fellowships for master's and doctoral candidates in the humanities and social sciences; tenable primarily at the D'Arcy McNickle Center for the History of the American Indian.
Restrictions: Limited to female Native American applicants.
$ Given: An unspecified number of fellowships awarded annually; each with stipend for living and travel expenses.
Application Information: Write for details.
Deadline: March 1.

**Newberry Library Monticello
College Foundation Fellowship
for Women**
60 West Walton Street
Chicago, IL 60610-3380
(312) 255-3595
www.newberry.org

Description: Six-month fellowships for women at the early stages of their professional careers to pursue six months of research and writing in any field appropriate to the Newberry's Collections, specifically American and European history and literature or women's studies.
Restrictions: U.S. citizenship or permanent resident status required. Limited to women applicants possessing a Ph.D.
$ Given: One fellowship awarded annually, with a $12,000 stipend.
Application Information: Write for details.
Deadline: January 20.

**Newberry Library
Short-Term Resident
Fellowships for Individual
Research**
Committee on Awards
60 West Walton Street
Chicago, IL 60610-3380
(312) 943-9090 ext. 267
www.newberry.org

Description: Two- to three-month research fellowships for Ph.D.s and doctoral candidates at dissertation level in any field appropriate to the Newberry Library collections, including history and the humanities in Western civilization, from the Middle Ages through the early 20th century; recipients chosen on the basis of proposed research.
Restrictions: Preference to applicants needing to use Newberry facilities; preference to individuals living outside the Chicago area; open to all nationalities.

$ Given: An unspecified number of fellowships awarded annually; on average of $1,200 each.
Application Information: Write for details.
Deadlines: March 1, October 15.

Newberry Library
Herman Dunlap Smith Center
for the History of
Cartography Research
Fellowships
Committee on Awards
60 West Walton Street
Chicago, IL 60610-3380
(312) 943-9090
www.newberry.org

Description: Short-term (up to three months) and long-term (6–12 months) residential research fellowships for doctoral candidates and postdoctoral scholars in the history of cartography; tenable at the Newberry Library; recipients chosen on the basis of proposed research and its applicability to Library's holdings.
Restrictions: N/A.
$ Given: An unspecified number of fellowships awarded annually; each with $1,200 monthly stipend for living and travel expenses, reaching a maximum $30,000 stipend for long-term projects.
Application Information: Write for details.
Deadlines: March 1 for long- and short-term projects; October 15 for short-term projects only.

Norwegian Information
Service in the United States
Norwegian Emigration Fund
of 1975 Scholarships and
Grants for Americans
825 Third Avenue
17th Floor
New York, NY 10022
(212) 421-7333
www.norway.org

Description: Grants for American master's and doctoral candidates to visit Norway to study emigration history and relations between the United States and Norway.
Restrictions: United States citizenship or permanent resident status required.
$ Given: An unspecified number of grants of NKr5,000–NKr40,000 each are awarded annually.
Application Information: Write for details.
Deadline: July 1.
Contact: Grants and Scholarships Section.

Norwegian Information
Service in the United States
Norwegian Marshall Fund
Grants
825 Third Avenue
17th Floor
New York, NY 10022
(212) 421-7333
www.norway.org

Description: Grants for American master's and doctoral candidates in science and the humanities to conduct research abroad.
Restrictions: United States citizenship required.
$ Given: An unspecified number of grants of up to $5,000 each are awarded annually.
Application Information: Request application forms from Norway-American Association, Drammensveien 20 C, Oslo 2, 0255, Norway, (02) 44.76.83.
Deadline: March 15.
Contact: Grants and Scholarships Section.

Norwegian Information Service in the United States SASS Travel Grants
825 Third Avenue
17th Floor
New York, NY 10022
(212) 421-7333
www.norway.org

Description: Grants for master's and doctoral candidates who have passed preliminary exams, as well as for Norwegian language/culture teachers, for study/research in Norway.
Restrictions: United States citizenship or permanent resident status required; membership in SASS (Society for the Advancement of Scandinavian Study) required.
$ Given: An unspecified number of grants of $750–$1,500 each are awarded annually.
Application Information: Write for details.
Deadline: April 15.
Contact: Grants and Scholarships Section.

Oak Ridge Institute for Science and Education Department of Energy Research Participation Program
P.O. Box 117
Oak Ridge, TN 37831
(865) 576-3146
www.orau.gov/orise.htm

Description: Program for undergraduate and graduate students, as well as faculty members, to conduct/participate in research programs at seven Department of Energy facilities; summer and academic-year programs available; research programs are related to energy production, utilization, and conservation.
Restrictions: Applicants must have done degree work in life/physical/social sciences, mathematics, toxicology, or engineering; United States citizenship or permanent resident status required.
$ Given: An unspecified number of fellowships awarded annually; each with $20,000–$48,000 stipend, based on degree, program, and area of research.
Application Information: Write for application forms.
Deadline: February 29.
Contact: Al Wohlpart, Science and Engineering Education Division.

Omega Psi Phi Fraternity George E. Meares Memorial Scholarships
1004 Spencer Avenue
Gastonia, NC 28052

Description: Scholarships for graduate students in social work, social sciences, and criminal justice; recipients chosen on the basis of academic achievement (transcripts).
Restrictions: United States citizenship required.
$ Given: An unspecified number of $1,000 scholarships are awarded annually.
Application Information: Write for details.
Deadline: April 1.
Contact: Minnie Meares Draughn.

Onohundro Institute of Early American History and Culture
Andrew W. Mellon Postdoctoral Research Fellowship
P.O. Box 8781
Williamsburg, VA 23187-8781
(757) 221-1116
www.oieahc.h-net.msu.edu

Description: One-year postdoctoral fellowships for research in any area of American studies at the Institute. Recipients chosen on the basis of their manuscript's potential for publication as a distinguished, book-length contribution to scholarship.
Restrictions: Limited to applicants who have received their Ph.D. at least twelve months prior to application.
$ Given: One fellowship awarded annually for an unspecified amount.
Application Information: Write for details.
Deadline: November 1.

Pacific Cultural Foundation Grants for Chinese Studies
Palace Office Building
Suite 807
346 Nanking East Road
Section 3
Taipei, Taiwan 10567
Republic of China
(02) 752-7424 through -7429
(six phone lines)

Description: Grants for master's degree holders for research in Chinese studies; four types of studies grants: research, writing, publication, and seminar; recipients chosen on the basis of proposed work/research.
Restrictions: Applicants must be residents of the free world.
$ Given: Approximately 80 grants of $2,000–$5,000 each are awarded annually.
Application Information: Separate application for travel grant available.
Deadlines: March 1, September 1.

Parapsychology Foundation Eileen J. Garrett Scholarship
228 East 71st Street
New York, NY 10021
(212) 628-1550

Description: Scholarship for research and study in parapsychology; funding made available to students at accredited universities; recipients chosen on the basis of academic achievement, quality of proposed research, and plans to pursue career in parapsychology.
Restrictions: N/A.
$ Given: One scholarship for $3,000 is awarded annually.
Application Information: Write for details.
Deadline: July 15.

Phi Alpha Theta International Honor Society in History Journalism Prizes for Graduate Students in History
2333 Liberty Street
Allentown, PA 18104
(610) 336-4925

Description: Prizes for best undergraduate and graduate history essays; judged on combination of original research and good composition.
Restrictions: Membership in PAT required.
$ Given: Six prizes awarded annually—one Hammond Prize of $200 for best graduate essay; one Turner Prize of $150 for best undergraduate essay; four additional unnamed prizes of $100 each, open to both undergraduate and graduate students.
Application Information: Submit manuscript and letter of faculty recommendation to Dr. Marsha L. Frey, Kansas State University, Manhattan, KS 66506.
Deadline: July 1.
Contact: Dr. Marsha L. Frey, Secretary.

Phi Alpha Theta International Honor Society in History Scholarships
2333 Liberty Street
Allentown, PA 18104
(610) 336-4925

Description: Scholarships for graduate study in history; Zimmerman Scholarship for individuals entering graduate school for M.A. degree in history; Pine Memorial Scholarship for advanced graduate study; and a number of other smaller graduate scholarships.
Restrictions: Membership in PAT required.
$ Given: Zimmerman Scholarship, $1,250; Pine Memorial Scholarship, $1,000; other scholarships, $750 each—all awarded annually.
Application Information: Write for details.
Deadline: March 15.
Contact: Donald B. Hoffman, Ph.D., Secretary-Treasurer.

Phi Beta Kappa Society Mary Isabel Sibley Fellowship
1785 Massachusetts, N.W.
4th Floor
Washington, DC 20036
(202) 265-3808
www.pbk.org

Description: One-year fellowship for postdoctoral scholars and doctoral candidates at dissertation level for research on French language and literature or Greek language, literature, history and archaeology; recipients chosen on the basis of academic achievement and quality of proposed research during fellowship year.
Restrictions: Limited to unmarried women ages 25–35 only; recipients must devote full-time efforts to research.
$ Given: One fellowship of $20,000 is awarded annually; non-renewable.
Application Information: French fellowship awarded in even-numbered years; Greek fellowship awarded in odd-numbered years.
Deadline: January 15.
Contact: Linda D. Surles, Program Officer.

Pitt Rivers Museum James A. Swan Fund
Oxford University
South Parks Road
Oxford, England OX1 3PP
0865-270927
www.prm.ox.ac.uk

Description: Grants for individuals to travel to Africa to pursue study/research on the hunter-gatherer peoples of Africa; recipients chosen on the basis of proposed research.
Restrictions: N/A.
$ Given: Ten grants of 1,000 pounds–2,000 pounds each are awarded annually; renewable.
Application Information: No form; submit research proposal and proposed budget.
Deadline: Accepted continuously.
Contact: Dr. Schuyler Jones, Curator.

Population Council
Population Council
Fellowships in the Social
Sciences
1 Dag Hammarskjold Plaza
New York, NY 10017
(212) 339-0500
www.popcouncil.org

Description: Fellowships for doctoral candidates at dissertation level and mid-career professionals seeking Ph.D degrees; for study/research combining population studies and such other social science disciplines as anthropology, sociology, economics, geography, public health; recipients chosen on the basis of academic achievement and proposed research.
Restrictions: Research/study must be carried out at institution with strong program in population studies; preference to applicants with employment experience in population studies or family planning; strong preference for nationals of developing countries who are committed to returning to their home countries in population-related careers.
$ Given: An unspecified number of fellowships awarded annually; monthly stipend based on place of study and other factors.
Application Information: Women encouraged to apply.
Deadline: December 15.
Contact: Manager, Fellowships Program.

President's Commission on
White House Fellowships
White House Fellowships
712 Jackson Place, N.W.
Washington, DC 20503
(202) 395-4522
www2.whitehouse.gov WH-fellows/index.html

Description: Twelve-month appointments as special assistants to the Vice President, Cabinet members, and the Presidential staff; fellowships include participation in educational program; positions available for students in public affairs, education, the sciences, business, and the professions; recipients chosen on the basis of leadership qualities, commitment to community service, and career/academic achievement.
Restrictions: Limited to young adults, ages 30–39; civilian federal employees are ineligible; recipients may not hold official state or local office while serving as White House fellows; United States citizenship required.
$ Given: Eleven to nineteen wage-earning fellowships for up to a maximum of $70,500 are awarded annually.
Application Information: Write for details.
Deadline: February 1.

The Radcliffe Research
Support Program
Henry A. Murray Research
Center
10 Garden Street
Cambridge, MA 02138
(617) 495-8140
FAX (617) 495-8422
www.radcliffe.edu/murray/grants/rrsprog.htm

Description: Grants for postdoctoral scholars for research drawing on the Henry A. Murray Research Center's data resources. The Research Center is a repository for social science data on human development and social change, particularly the changing life experiences of American women. Recipients chosen on the basis of scientific merit of proposed research, potential contribution to the relevant field of study, the extent to which the project takes advantage of data in the Murray Center archive, and the adequacy of the budget for proposed work.

Restrictions: None.
$ Given: An unspecified number of grants awarded annually, each for up to $5,000.
Application Information: Write for details.
Deadline: January 15.
Contact: Grants Administrator.

REFORMA, The National Association to Promote Library Services to the Spanish Speaking REFORMA Scholarships in Library and Information Science
Auroria Library
Lawrence at 11th Street
Denver, CO 80204-2096
(303) 556-3526
www.clnet.ucr.edu/library/reforma

Description: Scholarships for individuals studying library and information science; recipients chosen on the basis of academic achievement and financial need.
Restrictions: Applicants must speak Spanish and must demonstrate a desire to serve the Spanish-speaking community. Must be U.S. citizen or resident.
$ Given: An unspecified number of $1,000 minimum scholarships are awarded annually.
Application Information: Write for details.
Deadline: May 15.
Contact: Ninfa Trejo, Chair, REFORMA scholarship, University of Arizona Library, P.O. Box 210005, Tucson, AZ 85721-0055, (520) 621-4868.

Rockefeller University Rockefeller Archive Center Research Grants
15 Dayton Avenue
Pocantico Hills
North Tarrytown, NY
10591-1598
(914) 631-4505
www.rockefeller.edu/archives.ctr

Description: Residential research fellowships for graduate students and postdoctoral scholars pursuing research using Archive Center resources; relevant disciplines including philanthropy, education, science, medicine, black history, agriculture, labor, social welfare, social sciences, politics, religion, population, economic development, and the arts; recipients chosen on the basis of proposed research and necessity of using Archive Center resources.
Restrictions: N/A.
$ Given: An unspecified number of grants awarded annually; each for up to $2,500 for travel, lodging, and research expenses.
Application Information: Write for details.
Deadline: November 30.
Contact: Pamela Harris, Director.

School of American Research Katrin H. Lamon Resident Scholar Program for Native Americans
P.O. Box 2188
Santa Fe, NM 87504
www.sarweb.org

Description: Nine-month residential fellowship for postdoctoral scholars and doctoral candidates at dissertation level in anthropology and related social sciences; intended to provide recipients with intellectual stimulation of campus life plus time to write up results of compiled field work/research.
Restrictions: Limited to Native American applicants.
$ Given: One fellowship awarded annually; maximum $29,000 stipend plus housing and office; non-renewable.
Application Information: Write for details.
Deadline: November 15.
Contact: Resident Scholar Coordinator.

**School of American Research
Resident Scholar Fellowships**
P.O. Box 2188
Santa Fe, NM 87504
www.sarweb.org

Description: Nine-month residential fellowship for postdoctoral scholars and doctoral candidates at dissertation level in anthropology and related humanities and social sciences; National Endowment for the Humanities funds three fellowships for Ph.D.s; Weatherhead Foundation funds two fellowships for doctoral candidates working on their dissertations.
Restrictions: Preference to applicants who have completed research and need time to write up results; United States citizenship required.
$ Given: An unspecified number of fellowships awarded annually; each with stipend plus housing, office and medical insurance.
Application Information: Send registered mail.
Deadline: November 15.
Contact: Resident Scholar Coordinator.

**Sinfonia Foundation Research
Assistance Grants**
10600 Old State Road
Evansville, IN 47711
(812) 867-2433
(800) 473-2649
www.sinfonia.org/foundation

Description: Grants for musicians and music teachers to pursue post-graduate research in American music and music education; recipients chosen on the basis of financial need.
Restrictions: Applicants must demonstrate competence in writing and research; open to all nationalities.
$ Given: An unspecified number of grants averaging $1,000 each are awarded annually.
Application Information: Write for details.
Deadline: April 1.
Contact: Dr. Gary Ingle.

**Smithsonian Institution
Graduate Student Research
Fellowships**
Office of Fellowships and
Grants
955 L'Enfant Plaza
Suite 7000
Washington, DC 20560
(202) 287-3271

Description: Ten-week residential fellowships for graduate students to pursue research at the Smithsonian; relevant disciplines include art history, anthropology, ecology, biology, environmental science, astrophysics, history of science, Oriental art, natural history, African art and culture, and American cultural/sociological history; recipients chosen on the basis of proposed research.
Restrictions: N/A.
$ Given: Approximately 38 fellowships are awarded annually; each with maximum $3,500 stipend.
Application Information: Write for details.
Deadline: January 15.
Contact: Program Assistant.

Smithsonian Institution Minority Students Internships
Office of Fellowships and Grants
955 L'Enfant Plaza
Suite 7000
Washington, DC 20560
(202) 287-3271

Description: Ten-week internships for undergraduate upperclassmen and graduate students in the humanities, social sciences, natural sciences, and physical sciences; internship program includes participation in ongoing research or activities at the Museum plus supervised independent research in any bureau; recipients chosen on the basis of academic achievement and proposed research.
Restrictions: Limited to minority group applicants.
$ Given: An unspecified number of internship positions are awarded annually; $300/week undergraduate stipend, $300/week graduate stipend.
Application Information: Write for details.
Deadlines: January 15 and October 15.

Smithsonian Institution Predoctoral Research Fellowships in Anthropology
Office of Fellowships and Grants
955 L'Enfant Plaza
Suite 7000
Washington, DC 20560
(202) 287-3271

Description: One-year residential fellowships for doctoral candidates at dissertation level in anthropology to pursue independent research using the Smithsonian's collections, resources, and staff expertise; relevant disciplines include anthropology, ethnology, ethnohistory, archaeology, and carbon-14 dating; recipients chosen on the basis of proposed research.
Restrictions: Applicants must have completed all preliminary coursework and exams for degree.
$ Given: An unspecified number of fellowships are awarded annually; each with $15,000 stipend.
Application Information: Write for details.
Deadline: January 15.
Contact: Program Assistant.

Smithsonian Institution Predoctoral Research Fellowships in Cultural History
Office of Fellowships and Grants
955 L'Enfant Plaza
Suite 7000
Washington, DC 20560
(202) 287-3271

Description: One-year residential fellowships for doctoral candidates at dissertation level in cultural history to pursue independent research using the Smithsonian's collections, resources, and staff expertise; recipients chosen on the basis of proposed research.
Restrictions: Applicants must have completed all preliminary coursework and exams for degree.
$ Given: An unspecified number of fellowships are awarded annually; each with $15,000 stipend.
Application Information: Write for details.
Deadline: January 15.
Contact: Program Assistant.

Smithsonian Institution Predoctoral Research Fellowships in the History of Art
Office of Fellowships and Grants
955 L'Enfant Plaza
Suite 7000
Washington, DC 20560
(202) 287-3271

Description: One-year residential fellowships for doctoral candidates at dissertation level in art history to pursue independent research using the Smithsonian's collections, resources, and staff expertise; recipients chosen on the basis of proposed research.
Restrictions: Applicants must have completed all preliminary coursework and exams for degree.
$ Given: An unspecified number of fellowships are awarded annually; each with $15,000 stipend.
Application Information: Write for details.
Deadline: January 15.
Contact: Program Assistant.

Smithsonian Institution Predoctoral Research Fellowships in the History of Science and Technology
Office of Fellowships and Grants
955 L'Enfant Plaza
Suite 7000
Washington, DC 20560
(202) 287-3271

Description: One-year residential fellowships for doctoral candidates at dissertation level in the history of science and technology, to pursue independent research using the Smithsonian's collections, resources, and staff expertise; relevant disciplines include history of mathematics, physical sciences, pharmacy, medicine, civil and mechanical engineering, electrical technology, and history of American science; recipients chosen on the basis of proposed research.
Restrictions: Applicants must have completed all preliminary coursework and exams for degree.
$ Given: An unspecified number of fellowships are awarded annually; each with $15,000 stipend.
Application Information: Write for details.
Deadline: January 15.
Contact: Program Assistant.

Smithsonian Institution James Renwick Fellowships
Office of Fellowships and Grants
955 L'Enfant Plaza
Suite 7000
Washington, DC 20560
(202) 357-2531

Description: Three- to twelve-month fellowships for doctoral candidates and postdoctoral scholars to pursue study/research on modern American crafts, including 20th century art, craft and design; preference for work with post-1930 crafts.
Restrictions: N/A.
$ Given: An unspecified number of fellowships are awarded annually; $15,000 for predoctoral fellow; $27,000 for postdoctoral fellow, plus travel allowance.
Application Information: Write for details.
Deadline: January 15.
Contact: Renwick Gallery.

Smithsonian Institution Libraries
Dibner Library
Resident Scholar Program Grants
NHB 24 Mail Stop 154
Washington, DC 20560
202-357-2240

Description: Grants for doctoral candidates, postdoctoral scholars, and professionals studying the history of science and technology, to support one to three months of research/study at Dibner Library of the History of Science and Technology and other libraries of the Smithsonian.
Restrictions: N/A.
$ Given: An unspecified number of grants awarded annually; each with $1,500/month stipend to cover expenses.

Application Information: Write for details.
Deadline: December 1.

Social Science Research Council Advanced German and European Studies Doctoral Dissertation Fellowships
810 Seventh Avenue
New York, NY 10019
212 377-2700
www.ssrc.org

Description: Nine- to twelve-month residential fellowships for doctoral candidates at dissertation level to study at Free University of Berlin; for dissertation work addressing the economic, political, and social aspects of modern and contemporary German and European affairs; recipients chosen on the basis of academic achievement and proposed research.
Restrictions: Good command of German required; United States citizenship or permanent resident status required.
$ Given: An unspecified number of fellowships awarded annually; each covers monthly stipend and travel expenses.
Application Information: Write for details.
Deadline: February 1.

Social Science Research Council International Migration Program Dissertation and Postdoctoral Fellowships
810 Seventh Avenue
New York, NY 10019
(212) 377-2700
www.ssrc.org

Description: One-year fellowships for the study of international migration to the United States, specifically the process of settlement, and outcomes for immigrants, refugees, and native-born Americans. Recipients chosen on the basis of the theoretical contributions that their research can make in interpreting U.S. immigration.
Restrictions: United States citizenship, permanent resident status, or enrollment at U.S. institution required.
$ Given: Approximately seven dissertation fellowships and five postdoctoral fellowships awarded annually; maximum dissertation award is $12,000 and up to $3,000 in research expenses, maximum postdoctoral award is $20,000.
Application Information: Write for details.
Deadline: January 12.

Social Science Research Council International Predissertation Research Fellowships
Contact individual universities for details and deadline information

Description: Fellowships for doctoral candidates in the early stages of Ph.D. programs in the social sciences, to promote internationalization of graduate training and to focus research on the developing world; relevant disciplines include political science, economics, and sociology; tenable for twelve months of support over two-year period, for domestic and overseas study.
Restrictions: Applicants must be full-time students in Ph.D. degree-granting programs at the following schools: University of California at Berkeley, UCLA, University of California at San Diego, University of Chicago, Columbia, Cornell, Duke, Harvard, University of Illinois, Indiana University at Bloomington, Massachusetts

Institute of Technology, Michigan State University, University of Michigan, University of Minnesota at Twin Cities, University of North Carolina, Northwestern, University of Pennsylvania, Princeton, Stanford, University of Texas at Austin, University of Washington, University of Wisconsin at Madison, and Yale; no funding for dissertation research.
$ Given: An unspecified number of fellowships awarded annually; each $1,500 for domestic study plus allowance for overseas expenses.
Application Information: Write for details.
Deadline: N/A.
Contact: Dr. Ellen Perecman, Program Director.

Social Sciences and Humanities Research Council of Canada
Jules and Gabrielle Leger Fellowships
Fellowships Division
350 Albert Street
Box 1610
Ottawa, Ontario K1P 6G4
Canada
(613) 943-7777
www.sshrc.ca

Description: One-year fellowships for university-affiliated and private scholars at graduate level in the humanities and social sciences, to support research and writing on the historical/contemporary contribution of the Crown and its representatives; tenable at recognized university/institution for at least eight months of full-time work; recipients chosen on the basis of academic achievement.
Restrictions: Canadian citizenship required.
$ Given: An unspecified number of fellowships awarded in alternate years; each for $40,000 Canadian plus $10,000 Canadian for research/travel expenses.
Application Information: Fellowships offered in odd-numbered years.
Deadline: October 1.

Social Sciences and Humanities Research Council of Canada
SSHRC Doctoral Fellowships
Fellowships Division
350 Albert Street
Box 1610
Ottawa, Ontario K1P 6G4
Canada
(613) 943-7777
www.sshrc.ca

Description: Six- to forty-eight-month renewable fellowships for doctoral candidates in the humanities, and social sciences; tenable in Canada or abroad; recipients chosen on the basis of academic achievement and proposed research.
Restrictions: Applicants must have completed one year of doctoral study; Canadian citizenship or permanent resident status required.
$ Given: Six hundred fellowships awarded annually, plus 600 annual renewables; each for up to $16,620 Canadian per year plus relocation costs.
Application Information: Write for details.
Deadline: November 15.

Social Sciences and Humanities Research Council of Canada
SSHRC Queen's Fellowships
Fellowships Division
350 Albert Street
Box 1610
Ottawa, Ontario K1P 6G4
Canada
(613) 943-7777
www.sshrc.ca

Description: One-year fellowships for graduate students in social sciences and humanities, to support study toward Ph.D. in Canadian studies at Canadian institutions.
Restrictions: Canadian citizenship required; must have completed one year of graduate study.
$ Given: One to two fellowships awarded annually; each for up to $16,620 Canadian plus tuition and travel allowance; non-renewable.
Application Information: Applicants automatically eligible if currently studying Canadian studies at Canadian University; no application.
Deadline: October 15.

W. Stull Holt Dissertation Fellowship
Wright State University
Department of History
Dayton, OH 45435
(937) 775-3333

Description: Fellowship for doctoral candidate to conduct dissertation research on topic relevant to the history of American foreign relations; recipients chosen on the basis of proposed research.
Restrictions: N/A.
$ Given: One fellowship of $1,500 is awarded annually.
Application Information: Application information and materials from Katherine Siegel, Department of History, St. Josephs University, 5600 City Avenue, Philadelphia, PA 19131, (610) 660-1000.
Deadline: April 1.

Society of Architectural Historians
Rosann Berry Fellowship
Charnley Parsky House
1365 North Astor Street
Chicago, IL 60610-1365
(312) 573-1365
FAX (312) 573-1141
www.sah.org

Description: Fellowship to allow one doctoral student to attend the Society's annual meeting; relevant disciplines includes history of architecture, city planning, decorative arts, and historic preservation; recipients chosen on the basis of academic achievement and quality to work.
Restrictions: N/A.
$ Given: One fellowship awarded annually; Society fee waived, plus $500 to cover travel/lodging; meals reimbursed.
Application Information: Write for details.
Deadline: November 15.
Contact: Assistant to the Executive Director.

Paul and Daisy Soros Fellowships for New Americans
400 West 59th Street
New York, NY 10019
(212) 547-6926
FAX (212) 548-4623
www.pdsoros.org

Description: Fellowships for up to two years of graduate study in the United States in any professional field or scholarly discipline in the Arts, Humanities, Social Sciences, and Sciences. Recipients chosen on the basis of the relevance of graduate school to their long-term career goals, their potential for enhancing their contributions to society, academic achievement, creativity, originality, and initiative.
Restrictions: Limited to applicants under 30 years of age. Applicants must either be a resident alien (holding a

Green Card), naturalized as a U.S. citizen, or the child of two parents who are both naturalized citizens.
$ Given: Thirty fellowships awarded annually, each with a maintenance grant of $20,000 and a tuition grant of one-half the tuition costs of the graduate program.
Application Information: Write for details.
Deadline: November 30.

Sourisseau Academy for California State and Local History
Sourisseau Academy Research Grants
History Department
San Jose State University
San Jose, CA 95192
(408) 924-6510 or
(408) 227-2657

Description: Grants to support research related to any aspect of California and Santa Clara County history.
Restrictions: N/A.
$ Given: Up to ten grants for $500 each are awarded annually.
Application Information: Write for details.
Deadlines: April 1, November 1.
Contact: Executive Secretary.

Special Libraries Association Affirmative Action Scholarship
1700 Eighteenth Street, N.W.
Washington, DC 20009
(202) 234-4700
www.sla.org

Description: Scholarship for master's candidates and graduating college seniors; tenable at United States or Canadian institution of library and information science; preference to students with interest in special librarianship; recipients chosen on the basis of academic achievement and financial need.
Restrictions: Limited to minority group applicants only; United States or Canadian citizenship required.
$ Given: One scholarship for $6,000 is awarded annually.
Application Information: Write for details.
Deadline: October 31.

Special Libraries Association Plenum Scholarships
1700 Eighteenth Street, N.W.
Washington, DC 20009
(202) 234-4700

Description: Research scholarships for doctoral candidates with approved dissertation topics; tenable at United States or Canadian institution of library and information science; preference to students with interest in special librarianship; recipients chosen on the basis of academic achievement, financial need, and proposed research.
Restrictions: United States or Canadian citizenship required. Membership in SLA required.
$ Given: One scholarship for $1,000 is awarded annually.
Application Information: Write for details.
Deadline: October 31.

State Historical Society of Wisconsin
Alice E. Smith Fellowship
816 State Street
Madison, WI 53706
(608) 264-6400
www.shsw.wisc.edu

Description: Research fellowship for master's and doctoral candidates studying American history, especially that of Wisconsin or the Midwest; recipients chosen on the basis of proposed research.
Restrictions: Limited to women only.
$ Given: One fellowship for $2,000 is awarded annually.
Application Information: Write for details.
Deadline: July 15.
Contact: Michael E. Stevens, State Historian.

Donald E. Stokes Dissertation Research Fellowship of the British Politics Group
West Virginia University, Eberly College of Arts and Sciences
P.O. Box 6317
Morgantown, WV 26506-6317
(304) 293-3811, ext: 5269
FAX (304) 293-8644

Description: Fellowship for a North American graduate student doing Ph.D. dissertation research on British politics to conduct research in the United Kingdom, including comparative and historical work as well as contemporary British politics.
Restrictions: None.
$ Given: One fellowship awarded annually for $500 U.S. or 300 pounds sterling (choice of recipient).
Application Information: Write for details.
Deadline: March 15.
Contact: Donly T. Studlar, Ph.D.

Swann Foundation for Caricature and Cartoon Fellowships for the Study of Caricature and Cartoon
Swann Foundation Fund
Prints and Photographics Division
Library of Congress
101 Independence Avenue, S.E.
Washington, DC 20540-4730
www.lcweb.loc.gov

Description: Fellowships for doctoral candidates at dissertation level in any university discipline as related to caricature and cartoon; recipients chosen on the basis of academic achievement, financial need, and quality of proposed research.
Restrictions: Enrollment at United States or Canadian university required.
$ Given: One fellowship for $15,000 is awarded annually.
Application Information: Write for details.
Deadline: February 15.
Contact: Harry Katz, President.

Truman Foundation
Truman Scholarships
712 Jackson Place, N.W.
Washington, DC 20006
(202) 395-4831
www.truman.gov

Description: Scholarships for undergraduate and graduate studies in any discipline; preference given to candidates proposing to enroll in professional programs oriented to careers in public service, including public administration, public policy analysis, public health, international relations, government, economics, social services, education and human resource development, and conservation and environmental protection. Recipients chosen on the basis of public and community service, commitment to careers in government and public service, leadership potential and communications skills.
Restrictions: U.S. citizenship required.

$ Given: Seventy-five to eighty scholarships awarded annually for varying amounts; up to $27,000 for graduate studies.
Application Information: Write for details.
Deadline: February 1.

Harry S. Truman Library Institute
Dissertation Year Fellowships
500 West U.S. Highway 24
Independence, MO 64050
(816) 833-1400
www.trumanlibrary.org

Description: One-year fellowships for doctoral candidates who have completed their dissertation research; to support the writing of dissertations on Truman's public career and administration; Library residency not required.
Restrictions: Recipients must provide the Library with copies of finished dissertations.
$ Given: Two fellowships for $16,000 each are awarded annually.
Application Information: Write for details.
Deadline: February 1.
Contact: Secretary.

Harry S. Truman Library Institute
Research Grants
500 West U.S. Highway 24
Independence, MO 64050
(816) 833-1400
www.trumanlibrary.org

Description: Grants to support one to three weeks of research at the Library on projects concerning Truman's public career or administration; for master's and doctoral candidates, as well as postdoctoral scholars; recipients chosen on the basis of proposed research.
Restrictions: N/A.
$ Given: An unspecified number of grants for up to $2,500 each are awarded annually; intended to cover round-trip airfare and living expenses.
Application Information: Submit written proposal.
Deadline: April 1 and October 1.
Contact: Secretary.

Morris K. Udall Scholarship and Excellence in Environmental Policy Foundation
2301 North Dodge Street
Iowa City, IA 52243-4030
(319) 336-1650

Description: One-year fellowship for doctoral candidates in the area of environmental public policy and conflict resolution. Recipients chosen on the basis of their commitment to this field and their potential to make a significant contribution.
$ Given: Up to two fellowships are awarded annually, each for up to $24,000.
Application Information: Write for details.
Deadline: January 15.

United Daughters of the Confederacy
Mrs. Simon Baruch University Award
328 North Boulevard
Richmond, VA 23220
(804) 355-1636
www.ngudc.org

Description: Award for best submitted scholarly book or monograph on Southern history and the Confederacy; open to master's degree holders, doctoral candidates, and postdoctoral scholars.
Restrictions: Submitted work must be unpublished.
$ Given: One author's award of $500, plus $2,000 to aid publication of the manuscript.

Application Information: Offered only in even-numbered years.
Deadline: May 1 of even-numbered years.

U.S. Arms Control and Disarmament Agency Hubert H. Humphrey Doctoral Fellowships in Arms Control and Disarmament
U.S. Department of State
Bureau of Arms Control
2201 C Street
Room 3643
Washington, DC 20520
(202) 736-9022

Description: Fellowships for doctoral candidates at dissertation level, as well as third-year law students; to support up to twelve months of research on arms control and disarmament; recipients chosen on the basis of academic achievement and proposed research.
Restrictions: United States citizenship or legal residency required.
$ Given: Two fellowships awarded annually; each with $8,000 stipend, plus up to $6,000 paid to institution to cover tuition and fees.
Application Information: Write for details.
Deadline: March 31.
Contact: Robert Waters.

U.S. Army Center of Military History Dissertation Year Fellowships
U.S. Army Center of Military History
Building 35
103 3rd Avenue
Ft. McNair, DC 20319-5058
FAX (202) 685-2077
www.army.mil

Description: One-year fellowships for doctoral candidates at dissertation level studying the history of war on land, especially the history of the United States Army; recipients chosen on the basis of academic achievement and proposed research.
Restrictions: Open to civilians only; United States citizenship or legal residency required.
$ Given: An unspecified number of fellowships for $9,000 each are awarded annually.
Application Information: Write for details.
Deadline: January 15.
Contact: Executive Secretary.

U.S. Army Military History Institute Advanced Research Grant Program
22 Ashburn Drive
Carlisle Barracks, PA
17013-5008
(717) 245-3611

Description: Grants to graduate degree holders and professionals to support on-site Institute research on a topic related to military history, within the Institute's scope of holdings; recipients chosen on the basis of proposed research, use of Institute's holdings, and potential benefit to United States Army.
Restrictions: N/A.
$ Given: An unspecified number of grants up to $1,500 each are awarded annually; renewable.
Application Information: Write for details.
Deadline: January 1.
Contact: Tom Hendricks, Director for Educational Services.

U.S. Department of Education
FLAS Fellowships
Center for International
Education
400 Maryland Avenue, S.W.
Washington, DC 20024-5329
(202) 401-9785
www.ed.gov

Description: Fellowships for graduate students at
accredited United States institutions studying foreign languages and area studies; recipients chosen on the basis of
academic achievement and proposed research.
Restrictions: Applicants must be preparing for careers
as specialists in uncommon languages and area studies;
United States citizenship or permanent resident status
required.
$ Given: Six hundred fellowships awarded annually;
each covers tuition and fees ($17,863 academic year;
$3,726 summer), plus $5,000 stipend; renewable.
Application Information: Write for details.
Deadline: Varies.

U.S. Department of Education
Jacob K. Javits Fellows
Program
400 Maryland Avenue, S.W.
Portals, Suite 600
Washington, DC 20024-5329
www.ed.gov

Description: Fellowships for doctoral candidates with
fewer than 20 semester hours; relevant disciplines include
most humanities, arts, and social sciences; recipients chosen on the basis of academic achievement and proposed
research.
Restrictions: United States citizenship or permanent
resident status required.
$ Given: Approximately 80 fellowships awarded annu-
ally; average award of $25,000 per year; renewable for up
to 48 months.
Application Information: Write for details.
Deadline: March.
Contact: Melissa Burton, Director.

University of Illinois at
Urbana-Champaign
Kate Neal Kinley Memorial
Fellowship
College of Fine and Applied
Arts
110 Architecture Building
608 East Lorado Taft Drive
Champaign, IL 61820
(217) 333-1661
www.grad.uiuc.edu

Description: One-year fellowships for B.S./B.A. holders
in the fields of applied arts and design, architecture, art,
and music; recipients chosen on the basis of artistic talent
and academic achievement.
Restrictions: Limited to graduates of the College of
Fine and Applied Arts of the University of Illinois at
Urbana-Champaign or similar institutions; preference for
applicants under age 25.
$ Given: Three fellowships for $7,000 awarded annu-
ally.
Application Information: Write for details.
Deadline: February 1.
Contact: Dean Kathleen Conlin.

University of North Carolina at Chapel Hill
Gilbert Chinard French History and Literature Research Grants
Romance Languages Department
CB3170
Chapel Hill, NC 27599
(919) 962-2062
www.unc.edu

Description: Grants for doctoral candidates at dissertation level and recent Ph.D.s (within past six years) for two months' study of French history and literature in France; recipients chosen on the basis of academic achievement and proposed work.
Restrictions: Applicants must be affiliated with United States universities; United States citizenship or permanent resident status required.
$ Given: Two to three grants for $1,000 each are awarded annually.
Application Information: Write for details.
Deadline: January 15.
Contact: Catherine Maley, President, Institut Français de Washington.

Virginia State Council of Higher Education
Virginia Tuition Assistance Grant Program
101 North 14th Street
James Monroe Building
9th Floor
Richmond, VA 23219
(804) 225-2137
www.schev.edu

Description: Grants for full-time undergraduates and graduate students, including medical and law school students; tenable at eligible private universities in Virginia; some recipients chosen without regard to financial need.
Restrictions: Limited to Virginia residents.
$ Given: An unspecified number of grants awarded annually; each for up to $1,440 per academic year.
Application Information: Write for details.
Deadline: January 31.
Contact: Elizabeth J. Waddy, Student Aid Program Specialist.

Wellesley College
Anne Louise Barett Fellowship
Office of Financial Aid
106 Central Street
Wellesley, MA 02481
(617) 235-0320
www.wellesley.edu

Description: Fellowship for B.S./B.A. holders and graduating college seniors in the fields of music theory, composition and history; tenable for full-time graduate study in the United States or abroad at institutions other than Wellesley; recipients chosen on the basis of merit and financial need.
Restrictions: Limited to Wellesley graduates.
$ Given: One fellowship of up to $4,000 is awarded annually.
Application Information: Request application form before November 25.
Deadline: December 11.
Contact: Secretary to the Committee on Graduate Fellowships.

Wellesley College
Ruth Ingersoll Goldmark Fellowship
Office of Financial Aid
106 Central Street
Wellesley, MA 02181
(617) 235-02481
www.wellesley.edu

Description: Fellowship for B.S./B.A. holders and graduating college seniors in the fields of English literature, composition, and the classics; tenable for full-time graduate study in the United States or abroad at institutions other than Wellesley; recipients chosen on the basis of merit and financial need.
Restrictions: Limited to women graduates of Wellesley.
$ Given: One fellowship of up to $1,500 is awarded annually.

Application Information: Request application form before November 25.
Deadline: December 11.
Contact: Secretary to the Committee on Graduate Fellowships.

Wellesley College
Edna V. Moffett Fellowship
Office of Financial Aid
106 Central Street
Wellesley, MA 02481
(617) 235-0320
www.wellesley.edu

Description: Fellowship for B.S./B.A. holders and graduating college seniors in the field of history; tenable for full-time graduate study in the United States or abroad at institutions other than Wellesley; preference for individuals entering their first year of graduate study recipients chosen on the basis of merit and financial need.
Restrictions: Limited to women graduates of Wellesley.
$ Given: One fellowship of up to $4,000 is awarded annually.
Application Information: Request application form before November 25.
Deadline: December 11.
Contact: Secretary to the Committee on Graduate Fellowships.

Wellesley College
Mary McEwin Schimke
Scholarships
Office of Financial Aid
Box GR
106 Central Street
Wellesley, MA 02481
(617) 235-0320
www.wellesley.edu

Description: Scholarships for B.S./B.A. in the fields of literature, history, and American studies; recipients chosen on the basis of merit and financial need; tenable for graduate study at institutions other than Wellesley; intended to afford relief from costs of household and child care during graduate study.
Restrictions: Limited to women applicants; minimum age 30; applicants must have received their bachelor's degrees from United States institutions.
$ Given: An unspecified number of scholarships of up to $1,000 each are awarded annually.
Application Information: Request application form before November 25.
Deadline: December 11.
Contact: Secretary to the Committee on Graduate Fellowships.

Wellesley College
Vida Dutton Scudder
Fellowship
Office of Financial Aid
106 Central Street
Wellesley, MA 02481
(617) 235-0320
www.wellesley.edu

Description: Fellowship for B.S./B.A. holders and graduating college seniors in the fields of literature, political science, and the social sciences; tenable for full-time graduate study in the United States or abroad at institutions other than Wellesley; recipients chosen or the basis of merit and financial need.
Restrictions: Limited to Wellesley graduates.
$ Given: One fellowship of up to $4,000 is awarded annually.

Application Information: Request application form before November 25.
Deadline: December 11.
Contact: Secretary to the Committee on Graduate Fellowships.

Wellesley College
Harriet A. Shaw Fellowship
Office of Financial Aid
106 Central Street
Wellesley, MA 02481
(617) 235-0320
www.wellesley.edu

Description: Fellowship for B.S./B.A. in the fields of music and allied arts; tenable for full-time graduate study in the United States or abroad; recipients chosen on the basis of academic achievement and financial need.
Restrictions: Limited to Wellesley graduates.
$ Given: One fellowship of up to $4,000 is awarded annually.
Application Information: Request application form before November 25.
Deadline: December 11.
Contact: Secretary to the Committee on Graduate Fellowships.

Whatcom Museum of History and Art
Jacobs Research Fund Small Grants Program
121 Prospect Street
Bellingham, WA 98225
(360) 676-6981
www.cob.org

Description: Grants to support field research on living Native Americans; relevant disciplines include folklore, languages, literatures and linguistics, music, dance, drama, sociocultural anthropology, and ethnoscience; preference for Pacific Northwest focus; recipients chosen on the basis of proposed research.
Restrictions: Native American applicants encouraged.
$ Given: Ten grants of up to $1,200 each are awarded annually.
Application Information: Write for details.
Deadline: February 15.
Contact: Rebecca Schlotterback, Administrator.

Williams College
Committee on Institutional Cooperation
Hopkins Hall
Williamstown, MA 01267
(413) 597-4352
www.williams.edu

Description: One-year residential fellowships at Williams College for doctoral candidates at dissertation level in engineering, the humanities, mathematics, or social sciences.
Restrictions: Limited to minority group applicants. U.S. citizenship required. Tenable at any Big Ten University or the University of Chicago.
$ Given: Full tuition plus $8,000 stipend.
Application Information: Write for details.
Deadline: January 15.
Contact: Peter Grudin, Dean of the Faculty.

Woodrow Wilson Johnson & Johnson Dissertation Grants in Children's Health
CN 5281
Princeton, NJ 08543-5281
(609) 452-7007
www.woodrow.org/womens-studies/health

Description: Grants for dissertation research on issues related to children's health, specifically its significance for public policy or treatment. Recipients chosen on the basis of originality and significance, scholarly validity, commitment to children's health, academic achievement.
Restrictions: Applicants must have completed all pre-dissertation requirements at graduate schools in the United States.
$ Given: Five grants awarded annually, each for $2,000 to be used for expenses connected with dissertation.
Application Information: Write for details.
Deadline: November 8.

Woodrow Wilson Johnson & Johnson Dissertation Grants in Women's Health
CN 5281
Princeton, NJ 08543-5281
(609) 452-7007
www.woodrow.org/womens-studies/health

Description: Grants for dissertation research on issues related to women's health, specifically its significance for public policy or treatment. Recipients chosen on the basis of originality and significance, scholarly validity, commitment to women's health, academic achievement.
Restrictions: Applicants must have completed all pre-dissertation requirements at graduate schools in the United States.
$ Given: Ten grants awarded annually, each for $2,000 to be used for expenses connected with dissertation.
Application Information: Write for details.
Deadline: November 8.

Woodrow Wilson National Fellowship Foundation Mellon Fellowships in the Humanities
CN 5329
Princeton, NJ 08543
(609) 452-7007
www.woodrow.org

Description: Two-year fellowships for graduating college seniors and recent college graduates planning to pursue Ph.D. degrees in the humanities; to both teach and do research tenable at any United States or Canadian institution, subject to cost ceiling; recipients chosen on the basis of outstanding academic achievement.
Restrictions: United States or Canadian citizenship or permanent resident status required.
$ Given: Eighty fellowships awarded annually; each for $14,750 plus tuition and fees for the first year.
Application Information: Application by faculty nomination only.
Deadline: November 4 for nomination; December 2 for application.
Contact: Dr. Robert Weisbuch, Director.

**Woodrow Wilson National
Fellowship Foundation
Charlotte W. Newcombe
Doctoral Dissertation
Fellowships**
CN 5281
Princeton, NJ 08543
(609) 452-7007
www.woodrow.org

Description: Twelve-month research fellowships for doctoral candidates at dissertation level, for dissertation research on ethical or religious values in all fields of social sciences, humanities, and education.
Restrictions: Applicants must be enrolled in United States graduate schools.
$ Given: Thirty-five fellowships for $15,000 each are awarded annually.
Application Information: Write for details.
Deadline: Early December.
Contact: Program Officer.

**Woodrow Wilson National
Fellowship Foundation
˙Women's Studies Doctoral
Research Grants**
CN 5281
Princeton, NJ 08543
(609) 452-7007
www.woodrow.org

Description: Research grants for doctoral candidates at dissertation level in women's studies specifically to encourage research on issues related to women's health; recipients chosen on the basis of proposed dissertation research.
Restrictions: Applicants should have completed all Ph.D. requirements except dissertation at United States graduate schools.
$ Given: Fifteen research grants for $2,000 each are awarded annually.
Application Information: Write for details.
Deadline: November 8.
Contact: Director, Women's Studies Program.

**Woodrow Wilson Postdoctoral
Fellowships in the Humanities**
5 Vaugh Drive, Suite 300
Princeton, NJ 08540-6313
(609) 452-7007
www.woodrow.org

Description: Two-year fellowships to enable young teachers and scholars to remain in academia, providing fellows the time and resources necessary to continue their research, turn a dissertation into a publication, and broaden their teaching experience. Recipients chosen on the basis of teaching experience.
Restrictions: U.S. citizenship or permanent resident status required. Applicants must have completed their Ph.D. requirements.
$ Given: Host institutions are to provide a minimum salary of $30,000 and benefits (with partial support from WWNFF), office space, and research and library support.
Application Information: Write for details.
Deadline: November 19.

**Winterthur Museum, Garden
and Library
Winterthur Museum Visiting
Research Scholars**
Office of Advanced Studies
Winterthur, DE 19735
(302) 888-4649

Description: One-month to one-year residential fellowships for doctoral candidates in all disciplines related to the Winterthur collections; intended for scholars who have been granted awards from other institutions but need a place to work/research; fellowship tenure features full access to museum resources and rental housing on Winterthur grounds; recipients chosen on the basis of proposed research.

Restrictions: N/A.
$ Given: Short term grants of $1,500/month.
Application Information: Write for details.
Deadline: January 15.
Contact: Research Fellowship Program.

Women's Research and Education Institute Congressional Fellowships on Women and Public Policy
1750 New York Avenue, N.W.
Suite 350
Washington, DC 20006
(202) 328-7070
www.wrei.org

Description: Congressional fellowship program designed to train women as potential public policy leaders; fellowship runs January through September and involves 30 hrs/wk work in a United States Congress office as a legislative aide on policy issues affecting women; open to master's and doctoral candidates at United States institutions; relevant disciplines include humanities, social sciences, biology and biomedical sciences, engineering and applied sciences, biomedical engineering, technology management and policy, business administration and management, health services management and hospital administration, education, allied health professionals, medicine, nursing, public and community health, and law; recipients chosen on the basis of political/civic activity and interest in women's issues.
Restrictions: Limited to women applicants; nine hours previous graduate coursework preferred; United States citizenship preferred.
$ Given: Eight to fifteen fellowships awarded annually; each with $9,500 stipend plus $500 for health insurance and up to $1,500 toward six hours tuition at home institution.
Application Information: Request application after November 1.
Deadline: February 14.
Contact: Alison Dineen, Fellowship Director.

Yale University Summer Fellowships
Walpole Library
154 Main Street
Farmington, CT 06032
(860) 677-2140

Description: Summer fellowships for students enrolled in doctoral programs at Yale University to pursue research in the Lewis Walpole collections.
Restrictions: Limited to graduate students enrolled at Yale University.
$ Given: An unspecified number of fellowships awarded annually, each with an eight-week stipend of $3,900 or a four-week stipend of $1,950.
Application Information: Write for details.
Deadline: March 15.
Contact: The Librarian.

Biological and Agricultural Sciences

Alcohol, Drug Abuse, and Mental Health Administration Predoctoral National Research Service Awards
5600 Fishers Lane
Rockville, MD 20857

Description: Predoctoral awards for students who are enrolled in an academic program which leads to a combined MD/Ph.D Degree to pursue research as they relate to alcohol-derived, drug abuse, or mental health/mental illness and their basic processes, incidence and prevalence, etiology, description, diagnosis, and pathogenesis, treatment, development, assessment and evaluation, prevention.
Restrictions: U.S. citizenship or permanent resident status required.
$ Given: An unspecified number of fellowships awarded annually, each with a stipend of $12,000.
Application Information: Write for details.
Deadline: September 10.

American Association for the Advancement of Science Mass Media Science and Engineering Fellows Program
1333 H Street, N.W.
Washington, DC 20005
(202) 326-6760
www.asg.org

Description: Ten-week summer fellowships for science graduate students to work as journalists (print, radio, or television and internet sites) to increase their understanding of the news media; available to students at any graduate and postgraduate level of study in family policy, child and family development, physical sciences, the natural and social sciences, as well as engineering; recipients chosen on the basis of academic achievement and demonstrated commitment of conveying to the public a better understanding and appreciation of science and technology.
Restrictions: No funding to non-technical applicants; United States citizenship required; no concurrent funding allowed.
$ Given: Twenty-five to thirty fellowships awarded annually; weekly living stipend for ten weeks plus travel costs.
Application Information: Write for details and application form; minorities and individuals with disabilities encouraged to apply.
Deadline: January 15.
Contact: Katrina Malby, Program Manager.

American Association of
University Women
Educational Foundation
AAUW Selected Professions
Fellowships
111 Sixteenth Street
Washington, DC 20036
(319) 337-1716
www.aauw.org

Description: Fellowships for graduate students entering their final year of study in fields with traditionally low female representation, including architecture, business administration, computer science, dentistry, engineering, law, mathematics/statistics, medicine; recipients chosen on the basis of academic achievement; tenable for full-time study at accredited United States institutions.
Restrictions: Limited to women who are members of minority groups in final year of study in law, medicine, or business; United States citizenship or permanent resident status required.
$ Given: Twenty-five fellowships of $5,000–$12,000 each are awarded annually.
Application Information: Application forms available August 1 through December 20.
Deadline: January 10 postmark deadline–November 15 for engineering.

American Cancer Society
Postdoctoral Fellowships
Research Department
1599 Clifton Road
Atlanta, GA 30329
(800) ACS-2345
www.cancer.org

Description: One- to three-year postdoctoral fellow-ships in the biomedical fields, as related to neoplasia.
Restrictions: U.S. citizenship or permanent resident sta-tus required.
$ Given: An unspecified number of fellowships awarded annually, each with an annual stipend ranging from $24,000 to $26,000.
Application Information: Write for details.
Deadline: March 1 and October 1.

American Foundation for
Pharmaceutical Education
Graduate Fellowships
618 Somerset Street
P.O. Box 7126
North Plainfield, NJ 07060

Description: One-year graduate and postdoctoral fel-lowships to support research in the pharmaceutical sci-ences.
Restrictions: U.S. citizenship required.
$ Given: An unspecified number of fellowships awarded annually, each with a stipend ranging from $6,000 to $16,000.
Application Information: Write for details.
Deadline: March 1.

American Geological Institute
AGI Minority Geoscience
Scholarships
4220 King Street
Alexandria, VA 22302-1507
(703) 379-2480
www.agiweb.org

Description: Scholarships for undergraduate and gradu-ate students who are geoscience and geoscience education majors at accredited institutions; relevant disciplines included geology, geophysics, geochemistry, hydrology, oceanography, planetary geology, and geoscience educa-tion; tenable in the United States; recipients chosen on the basis of academic achievement and financial need.
Restrictions: Limited to unrepresented minority group applicants in the geosciences; United States citizenship required.

$ Given: An unspecified number of scholarships awarded annually.
Application Information: Application form required.
Deadline: February 1.
Contact: Marilyn J. Suiter, Administrator, Special Programs.

American Geophysical Union Horton Research Grant in Hydrology and Water Resources
2000 Florida Avenue, N.W.
Washington, DC 20009
(202) 462-6900
www.agu.org

Description: Grants for doctoral candidates, to support research projects in hydrology and water resources; relevant disciplines include physical/chemical/biological aspects of hydrology, as well as water resources policy sciences (economics, sociology, and law).
Restrictions: Membership in American Geophysical Union required.
$ Given: One or more grants awarded annually; approximately $9,000 plus travel allowance to ensure attendance at awards luncheon.
Application Information: Proposal must be signed by faculty advisor; application forms required.
Deadline: March 1.
Contact: Winetta Singhateh.

American Heart Association Postdoctoral Fellowships
Division of Research
Administration
7272 Greenville Avenue
Dallas, TX 75231-4596
(717) 393-0725

Description: Five-year postdoctoral fellowships to support research in the field of cardiovascular functions and disease, and stroke.
Restrictions: U.S. citizenship or permanent resident status required.
$ Given: A variable number of fellowships awarded annually, each in the amount of $45,000.
Application Information: Write for details.
Deadline: June 1.

**American Museum of Natural History
Frank M. Chapman Memorial Grants for Ornithological Research**
Ornithology Department
Central Park West
at 79th Street
New York, NY 10024
(212) 769-5775
www.amnh.org

Description: Grants to support advanced graduate and postdoctoral scholars in research in both neontological and paleontological ornithology from a broad, international perspective; tenable at the American Museum of Natural History or elsewhere.
Restrictions: N/A.
$ Given: An unspecified number of grants awarded annually; each for $200–$1,000.
Application Information: Write for details.
Deadline: January 15.

American Museum of Natural History Collection Study Grants
Office of Grants and Fellowships
Central Park West
at 79th Street
New York, NY 10024
(212) 769-5040
www.amnh.org

Description: Grants to supoprt four or more days of residential study at the American Museum of Natural History; for doctoral candidates and recent postdoctoral scholars studying vertebrate and invertebrate zoology, paleozoology, anthropology, mineral sciences, and astrophysics.
Restrictions: Limited to investigators living more than daily commute distance from the American Museum of Natural History.
$ Given: An unspecified number of grants awarded annually; each for up to $1,500 toward travel and subsistence; no funding for tuition; non-renewable.
Application Information: Write for details.
Deadline: Applications accepted continuously.
Contact: Grants Administrator.

American Museum of Natural History Fellowship Program
Central Park West
at 79th Street
New York, NY 10024
(212) 769-5040
www.amnh.org

Description: Postdoctoral fellowship to support research in any of the following fields: anthropology, mineral sciences, vertebrate and invertebrate zoology, and paleontology.
Restrictions: None.
$ Given: Twelve fellowships awarded annually, each in the amount of $21,000.
Application Information: Write for details.
Deadline: January 15.

American Museum of Natural History
Lerner-Gray Grants for Marine Research
Office of Grants and Fellowships
Central Park West
at 79th Street
New York, NY 10024
(212) 769-5040
www.amnh.org

Description: Grants to support advanced graduate students and postdoctoral scholars in marine zoology in early career research projects involving systematics, evolution, ecology, and field studies of behavior of marine animals; tenable at the American Museum of Natural History or elsewhere.
Restrictions: N/A.
$ Given: An unspecified number of grants awarded annually; each for $200–$1,000.
Application Information: Write for details.
Deadline: March 15.
Contact: Grants Administrator.

American Museum of Natural History
Theodore Roosevelt Memorial Grants
Office of Grants and Fellowships
Central Park West
at 79th Street
New York, NY 10024
(212) 769-5040
www.amnh.org

Description: Short-term grants to support advanced graduate students and postdoctoral scholars in paleontology research of the fauna of North America related to wildlife conservation or natural history; recipients chosen on the basis of academic achievement and proposed research.
Restrictions: N/A.
$ Given: An unspecified number of grants awarded annually; each for $200–$1,000 toward continuing research; no funding for tuition.
Application Information: Write for details.

Deadline: February 15.
Contact: Grants Administrator.

**American Philosophical
Society Library
Mellon Resident Research
Fellowships**
104 South Fifth Street
Philadelphia, PA 19106
(215) 440-3400
www.amphilsoc.org

Description: One- to three-month residential fellowships for doctoral candidates at dissertation level and postdoctoral scholars pursuing study relevant to APS collections; tenable at the Society Library, for short-term research using the library's collections.
Restrictions: N/A.
$ Given: An unspecified number of fellowships awarded annually; each for $1,900/month.
Application Information: Write for details.
Deadline: March 1.
Contact: Associate Librarian for Research Programs.

**American Psychological
Association
APA Minority Fellowship
Program in Neuroscience**
750 First Street, N.E.
Washington, DC 20002-4242
(202) 336-6027 or
(202) 336-6012
www.apa.org

Description: Ten-month fellowships for doctoral candidates in neuroscience; recipients chosen on the basis of academic achievement, financial need, and commitment to future career in neuroscience research as well as researchers and teachers whose work focuses on minority people and relevant issues.
Restrictions: African-American, Hispanic, Native American, Alaskan Native, Asian-American, and Pacific Islander applicants preferred; applicants must be planning careers in neuroscience; United States or Canadian citizenship or permanent resident status required.
$ Given: An unspecified number of fellowships awarded annually; $12,240 for ten months, $14,688 for twelve months, funding for postdoctorates varies, plus cost-sharing arrangement for full tuition scholarship and travel funds depending on experience; renewable for up to three years if recipient maintains good academic standing.
Application Information: Write for details.
Deadline: January 15.
Contact: Dr. James M. Jones, Director; Guerra, Minority Fellowship Program.

**American Society for
Engineering Education
Natural Defense Science and
Engineering Fellowship
Office of Naval Research
Graduate Fellowships**
1818 N Street, N.W.
Suite 600
Washington, DC 20036
(202) 331-3525
www.asee.org/ndseg

Description: Thirty-six-month fellowships (tenable over four years) for college seniors in engineering, mathematics, and science to support graduate work toward Ph.D. beginning the following September; fellowship includes summer work at Department of Defense Laboratories in freshman or sophomore year; relevant disciplines include biology/biomedical sciences, oceanography, mathematics, computer science, electrical engineering, material science, cognitive and neural sciences, naval architecture and ocean engineering, physics, chemistry, and aerospace/mechanical engineering; recipients chosen on the basis of academic achievement.

Restrictions: United States citizenship required; applicants already in graduate school ineligible.
$ Given: Up to 150 fellowships awarded annually; each for $18,500 for the first twelve months, $19,500 for the second twelve months, and $20,500 for the third twelve months, plus full tuition paid directly to the United States university.
Application Information: Write for details.
Deadline: January 14.
Contact: Projects Officer.

American Statistical Association ASA and USDA/NASS Research Fellow and Associate Program
1429 Duke Street
Alexandria, VA 22314-3402
(703) 684-1221
www.amstat.org

Description: Nine- to twelve-month fellowships and associateships for doctoral candidates and postdoctoral researchers in agricultural statistics, for residential research/work at the National Agricultural Statistics Service; recipients chosen on the basis of academic achievement and proposed research.
Restrictions: N/A.
$ Given: An unspecified number of fellowship/associateship positions awarded annually; each with stipend.
Application Information: Write for details.
Deadline: March 1.
Contact: Judy Dill, Director.

American Water Works Association LARS Scholarships
6666 West Quincy Avenue
Denver, CO 80235
(303) 794-7711
FAX (303) 794-6303
www.awwa.org

Description: Scholarships for outstanding graduate students in fields of water treatment, corrosion control, and aquatic/analytic/environmental chemistry.
Restrictions: Applicants must be graduate students at institutions in the United States, Canada, Guam, Puerto Rico, or Mexico who will complete their degree requirements after August 31 of the deadline year.
$ Given: Two scholarships awarded annually; $5,000 for M.S. candidate; $7,000 for Ph.D. candidate.
Application Information: Write for details.
Deadline: January 15.
Contact: Scholarship Coordinator, Volunteer and Technical Support Group.

American Water Works Association Abel Wolman Doctoral Fellowships
6666 West Quincy Avenue
Denver, CO 80235
(303) 794-7711
FAX (303) 794-6303
www.awwa.org

Description: Twelve-month fellowships for outstanding doctoral candidates, to support research and training in water supply and treatment.
Restrictions: Applicants must be within two years of completing Ph.D. requirements; United States, Canadian, or Mexican citizenship required.
$ Given: One fellowship awarded annually; $15,000 stipend plus $1,000 research supplies/equipment allowance and $4,000 for tuition and fees.
Application Information: Write for details.
Deadline: January 15.

Arctic Institute of North America
Grant-in-Aid Program
University of Calgary
2500 University Drive, N.W.
Calgary, Alberta T2N 1N4
Canada
(403) 220-7515

Description: Grants for graduate students for natural/social sciences field work in the northern regions; recipients chosen on the basis of academic achievement and quality of proposed research.
Restrictions: N/A.
$ Given: An unspecified number of grants of up to $5,000 Canadian are awarded annually.
Application Information: Write for details.
Deadline: January 15.
Contact: Executive Director.

Arthritis Foundation
Doctoral Dissertation Awards for Nonphysical Health Professionals
1314 Spring Street, N.W.
Atlanta, GA 30309
(404) 872-7100
www.arthritis.org

Description: One to two years of grant support for doctoral candidates conducting dissertation-level research related to arthritis; recipients chosen on the basis of proposed research.
Restrictions: Applicants must be planning careers in arthritis research; membership in or eligibility for professional organization required.
$ Given: An unspecified number of grants awarded annually; each for up to $10,000/year.
Application Information: Applicant's doctoral chairperson must approve the project.
Deadline: September 1.
Contact: Administrative Assistant, Research Administrator.

Arthritis Foundation
Doctoral Dissertation Physical Scientist Development Award
1314 Spring Street, N.W.
Atlanta, GA 30309
(404) 872-7100
www.arthritis.org

Description: Two years of grant support for medical students in M.D. or M.D./Ph.D. programs at accredited United States medical schools pursuing arthritis-related research; recipients chosen on the basis of proposed research and potential as biomedical investigators.
Restrictions: Applicants must be planning careers in medicine; applicants must have research advisors who agree to provide the necessary space, facilities, and guidance for the proposed research.
$ Given: An unspecified number of grants awarded annually; each for $27,000–$32,000/year.
Application Information: Write for details.
Deadline: September 1.

Association for Women in Science Educational Foundation
AWIS Predoctoral Award
1522 K Street, N.W. Suite 820
Washington, DC 20005
(202) 326-8490 or
1-800-886-Awis
FAX (202) 408-0742
www.awis.org

Description: Awards for doctoral candidates in life sciences, physical sciences, social sciences, engineering, mathematics, and behavioral sciences; recipients chosen on the basis of academic achievement and quality of proposed research.
Restrictions: Limited to women only; United States citizenship and enrollment in United States institution required.
$ Given: An unspecified number of grants of $1,000 each are awarded annually.

Application Information: Write for details.
Deadline: January 15.

Atlantic Salmon Federation
Olin Fellowships
P.O. Box 429
Saint Andrews,
New Brunswick
E0G 2X0
Canada
(506) 529-4581

Description: Fellowship to support research on Atlantic salmon conservation and management; tenable at any accredited university or research laboratory; recipients chosen on the basis of academic achievement and benefit of proposed research.
Restrictions: United States or Canadian citizenship required.
$ Given: Two to six fellowships awarded annually; each for $1,000–$3,000 Canadian.
Application Information: For application form, contact the United States office, Atlantic Salmon Federation, P.O. Box 807, Calais, ME 04619.
Deadline: March 15.
Contact: Ellen Merrill.

Bunting Institute
Science Scholars Fellowship
Program
34 Concord Avenue
Cambridge, MA 02138
(617) 495-8136
www.radcliffe.edu/bunting

Description: Postdoctoral fellowships to support women scientists in any level in any of the following fields: astronomy, molecular and cellular biology, biochemistry, chemistry, cognitive and neural sciences, mathematics, computer science, electrical, aerospace, and mechanical engineering, materials science, naval architecture, ocean engineering, oceanography, physics, and geology.
Restrictions: U.S. citizenship required. Limited to women applicants only who have received their doctorate at least two years prior to application.
$ Given: Eight fellowships awarded annually, each in the amount of $31,300.
Application Information: Write for details.
Deadline: Early October.

Business and Professional
Women's Foundation
Education Program
Wyeth-Ayerst Laboratories
Scholarship for Women in
Graduate Medical and Health
Business Programs
2012 Massachusetts Avenue,
N.W.
Washington, DC 20036
(202) 296-9118

Description: Fellowships to support women seeking entry into underrepresented and underutilized health-related occupations in the fields of biomedical engineering, biomedical research, medical technology, pharmaceutical marketing, public health, and public health policy. Recipients chosen on the basis of financial need.
Restrictions: U.S. citizenship required. Limited to women 25 years of age or older.
$ Given: An unspecified number of fellowships awarded annually, each for $2,000.
Application Information: Send SASE.
Deadline: April 15.

Canada Council Killam Research Fellowships
99 Metcalfe Street
P.O. Box 1047
Ottawa, Ontario
Canada K1P 5V8

Description: Fellowships for senior scholars (eight to twelve years beyond the Ph.D.) to support research in any of the following fields: humanities, social sciences, natural sciences, health sciences, engineering, and studies linking disciplines within those fields.
Restrictions: Canadian citizenship or landed immigrant resident status required.
$ Given: Fifteen to eighteen fellowships awarded annually, each in the amount $53,000.
Application Information: Write for details.
Deadline: June 30.

Carnegie Institution of Washington
Carnegie Developmental Biology Research Fellowships
1530 P Street, N.W.
Washington, DC 20005
(202) 387-6400
FAX (202) 387-6411
www.ciw.edu

Description: One-year residential research fellowships at the Department of Embryology in Baltimore, Maryland, for doctoral candidates at dissertation level and postdoctoral scholars studying developmental biology and embryology; recipients chosen on the basis of academic achievement and proposed research.
Restrictions: N/A.
$ Given: An unspecified number of fellowships awarded annually; varying amounts; renewable for two additional years.
Application Information: Applicants should establish contact with staff member with whom they plan to study; application materials include educational record, record of work experience, list of publications, essay, and three letters of recommendation; completed applications should be sent to Director, Carnegie Institution, Department of Embryology, 115 West University Parkway, Baltimore, MD 21210-3301.
Deadline: One year in advance of fellowship.
Contact: Publications Officer.

Carnegie Institution of Washington
Carnegie Plant Biology Fellowships
1530 P Street, N.W.
Washington, DC 20005
(202) 387-6400
FAX (202) 387-6411
www.ciw.edu

Description: One-year residential research fellowship at the Department of Plant Biology in Stanford, California, for doctoral candidates at dissertation level and postdoctoral scholars studying plant biology; recipients chosen on the basis of academic achievement and proposed research.
Restrictions: N/A.
$ Given: Ten to twelve fellowships awarded annually; varying amounts; renewable for two additional years.
Application Information: Applicants should establish contact with staff member with whom they plan to study; application materials include educational record, record of work experience, list of publications, essay, and three letters of recommendation; completed applications should be sent to Director, Carnegie Institution,

Department of Plant Biology, 290 Panama Street, Stanford, CA 94305-4101.
Deadline: January 1.
Contact: Publications Officer.

Carnegie Institute of Washington Fellowship in Embryology
Department of Embryology
115 West University Parkway
Baltimore, MD 21210
(202) 387-6400
www.carnegie-institute.com

Description: One- to two-year predoctoral and postdoctoral fellowships to support research in the field of embryology.
Restrictions: None. Qualified women and minorities encouraged to apply.
$ Given: An unspecified number of fellowships of varying amounts awarded annually.
Application Information: Write for details.
Deadline: Varies.

Carnegie Institute of Washington Fellowship in Plant Biology
Department of Plant Biology
290 Panama Street
Stanford, CA 94305
www.carnegie-institute.com

Description: One- to two-year predoctoral and postdoctoral fellowships to support research in the field of photosynthesis and the physiological and biochemical mechanisms that underlie the financial diversity and adaptations of plants.
Restrictions: None. Qualified women and minorities encouraged to apply.
$ Given: An unspecified number of fellowships of varying amounts awarded annually.
Application Information: Write for details.
Deadline: Varies.

Center for the Advanced Study in Behavioral Sciences Postdoctoral Fellowships
202 Junipero Serra Boulevard
Stanford, CA 94305-6165
(650) 723-9626
www.stanford.edu/group/CISAC

Description: Nine- to twelve-month postdoctoral fellowships to support research in any of the following fields; anthropology, art history, biology, classics, economics, education, history, law, linguistics, literature, mathematical and statistical specialties, medicine, musicology, philosophy, political science, psychiatry, psychology, and sociology. Tenable at the Center for Advanced Study in Behavioral Sciences.
Restrictions: None.
$ Given: Approximately fifty fellowships of varying amounts awarded annually.
Application Information: Write for details.
Deadline: Ongoing.

Council for the Advancement of Science Writing Fellowships in Science Writing
P.O. Box 404
Greenlawn, NY 11740

Descriptions: Fellowships for the study of science writing, available to B.S./B.A. holders in science of journalism, as well as to professional reporters and graduate students; recipients chosen on the basis of academic achievement, quality of writing, and commitment to writing career.

Restrictions: Preference to journalists with two years professional experience who want to specialize in science writing.
$ Given: An unspecified number of grants of up to $2,000 each are awarded annually.
Application Information: Write for details.
Deadline: June 1.
Contact: Diane McGurgan.

Deafness Research Foundation
Research Grants
575 Fifth Avenue
11th Floor
New York, NY 10017
(212) 599-0027
(212) 599-0039
www.drf.org

Description: Grant for doctoral candidates, faculty and staff members, to support research on any aspect of the ear—its function, physiology, biochemistry, genetics, anatomy, pathology, or rehabilitation; recipients chosen on the basis of proposed research.
Restrictions: Funding must be used at United States or Canadian facility; applicants must disclose any other sources of funding for the project.
$ Given: Twenty grants of up to $15,000 are awarded annually; renewable for one to two additional years.
Application Information: Write for details.
Deadline: June 1.
Contact: Medical Director.

Epilepsy Foundation of America
EFA Behavioral Sciences Student Research Fellowships
4351 Garden City Drive
Suite 406
Landover, MD 20785
(301) 459-3700
www.efa.org

Description: One-year research fellowships for graduate students interested in basic and clinical research in the biological, behavioral, and social sciences designed to advance the understanding, treatment, and prevention of epilepsy; tenable at United States institutions; recipients chosen on the basis of demonstrated competence in epilepsy research.
Restrictions: Funding must be used in the United States; no funding for indirect costs.
$ Given: An unspecified number of fellowships awarded annually.
Application Information: Write for details.
Deadline: March 1.
Contact: Kathy Morris.

Epilepsy Foundation of America
Medical Student Fellowships
4351 Garden City Drive
Suite 406
Landover, MD 20785
(301) 459-3700
www.efa.org

Description: Short-term fellowships (three months) for medical students interested in careers in epilepsy research; tenable for research at United States institutions with ongoing epilepsy research/service projects; recipients chosen on the basis of submitted statement addressing relevant experiences and interest.
Restrictions: End-of-project report required.
$ Given: An unspecified number of fellowships for $2,000 each are awarded annually.

Application Information: Submit outline of proposed eight- to twelve-week program of research, plus personal statement addressing interest in epilepsy research.
Deadline: March 1.
Contact: Kathy Morris.

Florida Education Fund McKnight Doctoral Fellowships
201 East Kennedy Boulevard
Suite 1525
Tampa, FL 33602
www.fl-educ-fd.org

Description: Fellowships for graduate study at one of eleven participating doctoral-degree-granting universities in Florida in the fields of business, engineering, agriculture, biology, computer science, mathematics, physical science, and psychology; recipients chosen on the basis of academic achievement.
Restrictions: Limited to African-American applicants only; B.A./B.S. degree required; United States citizenship required.
$ Given: Twenty-five fellowships awarded annually; each for a maximum of five years of study, with an annual $11,000 stipend plus up to $5,000 in tuition and fees.
Application Information: Write for details.
Deadline: January 15.
Contact: President.

French Embassy Scientific Services Chateaubriand Research Scholarships for the Exact Sciences, Engineering, and Medicine
Department of Science and Technology
4101 Reservoir Road, N.W.
Washington, DC 20007
(202) 944-6246
www.info-france-usa.org

Description: Six- to twelve-month research scholarship for doctoral candidates at dissertation level, as well as postdoctoral scholars, to conduct research in France at French universities, engineering schools, and private laboratories; language training sessions provided; relevant disciplines include biological and agricultural sciences, physical sciences and mathematics, engineering and applied sciences, medicine, nutrition, optometry and vision sciences, pharmacy and pharmaceuticals sciences, and veterinary medicine and sciences; recipients chosen on the basis of proposed research.
Restrictions: Each applicant must be registered at United States university and already in contact with French host institution; United States citizenship required.
$ Given: Twenty to thirty scholarships awarded annually; monthly stipend plus airfare and health insurance.
Application Information: Application forms must be submitted with faculty recommendation.
Deadline: December 1.
Contact: Pierre N'guyen.

Garden Club of America
Catherine H. Beattie
Fellowship
Center for Plant Conservation
Missouri Botanical Garden
P.O. Box 299
St. Louis, MO 63166-0299
(314) 577-9503
www.mobot.org/cpc/beattie.
html

Description: Graduate fellowships to promote conservation of rare and endangered flora in the U.S. through
research in any of the following fields: botany, horticulture, conservation, or ecology. Preference given to students whose projects focus on the endangered flora of the
Carolinas and southeastern U.S.
Restrictions: None.
$ Given: One fellowship awarded annually in the
amount of $4,000.
Application Information: Write for details.
Deadline: December 31.

Hertz Foundation
Graduate Fellowship Awards
P.O. Box 5032
Livermore, CA 94551-5032
(925) 373-6329
www.hertzfoundation.org

Description: Fellowships for graduate study in any discipline at one of several tenable schools. Recipients chosen on the basis of merit.
Restrictions: None.
$ Given: One fellowship awarded annually, annual
stipend of $25,000 and tuition covered for a maximum
tenure of five years.
Application Information: Write for details.
Deadline: N/A.

Horticultural Research
Institute
HRI Grants
1250 I Street, N.W.
Suite 500
Washington, DC 20005
(202) 789-2900
www.anla.org

Description: Research grants to support work on
improving the efficiency of the landscape/nursery trade;
recipients chosen on the basis of proposed research.
Restrictions: N/A.
$ Given: Fifteen to twenty grants for $500–$10,000
each are awarded annually.
Application Information: Write for details.
Deadline: May 1.
Contact: Ashby P. Ruden, Administrator.

Howard Hughes Medical
Institute
Predoctoral Fellowships in
Biological Sciences
National Research Council
2101 Constitution Avenue,
N.W.
Washington, DC 20418
(202) 334-3419

Description: Three-year international fellowships to
support full-time study toward Ph.D. degree in biological
sciences; intended for students at or near the beginning of
graduate studies; relevant fields include biochemistry,
biophysics, biostatistics, mathematical biology, cell biology, developmental biology, epidemiology, genetics,
immunology, microbiology, molecular biology, neuroscience, pharmacology, physiology, structural biology, and
virology; tenable at United States institutions; recipients
chosen on the basis of academic achievement and future
promise in biomedical research; women and minorities
encouraged to apply.
Restrictions: Open to all nationalities.
$ Given: Eighty fellowships awarded annually; each
with $16,000/year stipend and $14,000 annual cost-of-
education allowance in lieu of tuition and fees; available
for four years contigent on academic progress.

Application Information: Write for details.
Deadline: November 4.
Contact: Fellowship Office, National Research Council.

Howard Hughes Medical Institute
The NIH Cloister Program
Research Scholars Program
One Cloister Court,
Department G
Bethesda, MD 20814-1460
(301) 951-6770
(800) 424-9924
www.hhmi.org

Description: One-year research scholar positions for medical students to participate in laboratory research at the National Institutes of Health in Bethesda, Maryland; sponsored by HHMI and NIH.
Restrictions: Applicants must be attending medical school (usually in second year) in the United States or Puerto Rico; United States citizenship or permanent resident status required.
$ Given: An unspecified number of positions given annually; each with $17,800 stipend, plus benefits (i.e., moving expenses, travel funds, cost of books). Funding available for second year of study.
Application Information: Kits and brochures available from medical school deans' offices.
Deadline: December 2.
Contact: Program Officer.

Hudson River Foundation for
Science and Environmental
Research Graduate
Fellowships
40 West 20th Street
9th Floor
New York, NY 10011
(212) 924-8290
FAX (212) 924-8325
www.hudsonriver.org

Description: Graduate fellowships for research in the fields of the life sciences, environmental studies, or public policy, as they relate to the Hudson River System.
Restrictions: Applicants must be enrolled in an accredited doctoral or master's program, must have a research plan approved by their department.
$ Given: An unspecified number of fellowships awarded annually; doctoral in the amount of $15,000, with up to $1,000 incidental research; master's in the amount of $11,000 with up to $1,000 incidental research.
Application Information: Write for details.
Deadline: March 6.
Contact: Science Director.

Edmund Niles Huyck
Preserve Graduate and
Postgraduate Research Grants
P.O. Box 189
Rensselaerville, NY 12147
(518) 797-3440
http:capital.net/com/huyck

Description: Grants for graduate students, as well as postdoctoral investigators, to support up to one year of research in animal behavior, evolution, and forest biology; research to be conducted using the Biological Station of the Huyck Preserve; recipients chosen on the basis of proposed research.
Restrictions: N/A.
$ Given: Ten grants awarded annually; each for up to $2,500, plus housing and laboratory space.
Application Information: Write for details.
Deadline: February 1.
Contact: Dr. Richard L. Wyman, Executive Director.

Institute of International Education Colombian Government Study and Research Grants
U.S. Student Programs Division
809 United Nations Plaza
New York, NY 10017-3580
(212) 984-5330
www.iie.org/fulbright

Description: Grants for B.S./B.A. holders to pursue up to two years of study/research at Colombian universities; relevant disciplines include agriculture, biology, business administration, economics, chemistry, engineering, education, health services administration, economics, chemistry, engineering, education, geography, history, Latin American literature, law, linguistics, political science, physics, regulatory development, public health, and remote sensing interpretation.
Restrictions: United States citizenship required.
$ Given: An unspecified number of grants awarded annually; each for modest monthly stipend, plus tuition and fees, health insurance, book/materials allowance, and one-way return airfare upon completion of study.
Application Information: Write for details.
Deadline: October 23.

Institute of International Education Study and Research Grants for U.S. Citizens
U.S. Student Programs Division
809 United Nations Plaza
New York, NY 10017-3580
(212) 984-5330
www.iie.org/fulbright

Description: Grants to support study and research in all fields, as well as professional training in the creative and performing arts; tenable at institutions of higher learning outside of the United States for one year; list of participating countries in any given year may be obtained from IIE.
Restrictions: Open to United States citizens with B.A. or equivalent; acceptable plan of study and proficiency in host country's language required.
$ Given: A variable number of grants awarded annually; covers international transportation, language or orientation course (where appropriate), tuition, book and maintenance allowances, and health and accident insurance.
Application Information: If currently enrolled in a college or university, apply to the campus Fulbright Program Advisor; applications also available from IIE.
Deadline: October 23.

International Research and Exchanges Board IREX Research Exchange Program with Mongolia
1616 H. Street, N.W.
Washington, DC 20006
(202) 628-8188
www.irex.org

Description: One- to four-month exchange program for predoctoral and postdoctoral candidates to study in Mongolia; relevant disciplines include the humanities and social sciences; recipients chosen on the basis of proposed research.
Restrictions: Command of host country's language required; United States citizenship required.
$ Given: Two to three fellowships awarded annually.
Application Information: Write for details.
Deadline: December 15.
Contact: Emilie Dickson.

Japan Ministry of Education, Science, and Culture Japanese Government (Monbusho) Scholarship Program
2-2 Kasumigaseki, 3-chome
Chiyoda-ku
Tokyo 100
Japan
03-581-4211

Description: Eighteen-month to two-year scholarships for non-Japanese graduate students to study at Japanese universities and research institutes; Research Students Program is specifically designed for graduate students (undergraduate program also available) in the humanities, social sciences, music, fine arts, and natural sciences; open to citizens of countries with educational exchange agreements with Japan.
Restrictions: Language proficiency required (twelve- to eighteen-month language training program required if language skills deemed insufficient); applicants must be under age thirty-five.
$ Given: An unspecified number of scholarships awarded annually; each to cover monthly stipend, airfare, tuition, and expense allowance.
Application Information: For further information, contact Japanese Embassy or Consulate.
Deadlines: June 15, September 30.
Contact: Student Exchange Division.

Kosciuszko Foundation
15 East 65th Street
New York, NY 10021-6595
(212) 734-2130
FAX (212) 628-4552
www.kosciuszkofoundation.org

Description: One-year scholarships to U.S. citizens of Polish descent for graduate studies in any field at colleges and universities in the United States and to Americans of non-Polish descent whose studies at American universities are primarily focused on Polish subjects. Recipients chosen on the basis of academic achievement and financial need.
Restrictions: Must be enrolled in a graduate program at a U.S. university. Applicants must be U.S. citizens or of Polish descent.
$ Given: An unspecified number of scholarships of $1,000–$5,000 each are awarded annually.
Deadline: January 16.
Contact: Grants office.

The Library Company of Philadelphia American History and Culture Research Fellowships
1314 Locust Street
Philadelphia, PA 19107
(215) 546-5167
www.librarycompany.org

Description: Residential research fellowships at the Library Company of Philadelphia for doctoral candidates and postdoctoral scholars in most disciplines as related to the history and culture of 18th- to 19th-century America; tenable for one or more months; recipients chosen on the basis of proposed research.
Restrictions: N/A.
$ Given: An unspecified number of fellowships awarded annually; each with $1,500/month stipend.
Application Information: Write for details.
Deadline: April 15.
Contact: James Green, Curator.

Marshall Scholarships
Marshall Aid Commemorating
Commission
Association of Commonwealth
Universities
36 Gordon Square
London WC1H0PF
(44) 1713878572
www.aca.ac.uk/marshall

Description: Two- to three-year scholarships for under-graduate or graduate level study at any university in the United Kingdom, in any discipline leading to the award of a British university degree.
Restrictions: U.S. citizenship required; limited to grad-uates of accredited four-year colleges and universities in the United States with at least a 3.75 GPA since freshman year.
$ Given: Up to forty scholarships awarded annually; each worth approximately $25,000 per year and compris-ing a personal allowance for cost of living and residence, tuition fees, books, travel in connection with studies, and to and from the United States.
Application Information: Write for details. Application forms also available from colleges and universities in the United States, British consulates in Atlanta, Boston, Chicago, Houston, and San Francisco, the British Council in Washington, DC, British Information Services in New York.
Deadline: N/A.

**Monticello College
Foundation and Washington
University
Spencer T. Olin Fellowships
for Women in Graduate Study**
Graduate School of Arts and
Sciences
Washington University
Campus Box 1187
One Brookings Drive
St. Louis, MO 63130-4899
(314) 935-6848

Description: Fellowships for graduate students to pre-pare for careers in higher education and professions in the fields of biological and biomedical sciences, humanities, physical sciences and mathematics, social and behavioral sciences, architecture, business administration, engineer-ing, fine arts, law, medicine, and social work. Tenable at Washington University.
Restrictions: Limited to women applicants only.
$ Given: An unspecified number of fellowships awarded annually, each ranging from $20,000 to $33,000.
Application Information: Write for details.
Deadline: February 1.

**National Geographic Society
Research Grants
Committee for Research and
Exploration**
1145 17th Street, N.W.
Washington, DC 20036
(202) 857-7439
www.nationalgeographic.com

Description: Grants for research in anthropology, archaeology, astronomy, biology, glaciology, botany, ecol-ogy, physical and human geography, mineralogy, geology, oceanology, paleontology, zoology, and other sciences pertinent to geography; funding primarily for postdoctoral researchers, but occasionally awarded to exceptional doc-toral candidates; recipients chosen on the basis of pro-posed research.
Restrictions: Open to all nationalities.
$ Given: An unspecified number of grants of $15,000–$20,000 average each are awarded annually.
Application Information: Write for details.
Deadline: Applications accepted continuously.
Contact: Committee for Research and Exploration.

National Medical Fellowships, Inc.
The Commonwealth Fund Medical Fellowships for Minorities
110 West 32nd Street
8th Floor
New York, NY 10001
(212) 714-1007
www.nmf-online.org

Description: Eight- to twelve-week fellowships for second- and third-year medical students to work in major research laboratories under the supervision/tutelage of prominent biomedical scientists; recipients chosen on the basis of academic achievement.
Restrictions: Limited to minority group members only; applicants must attend accredited United States medical schools and must be interested in careers in research/academic medicine.
$ Given: Thirty-five fellowships awarded annually; each for $6,000.
Application Information: Applicants must be nominated by medical school deans.
Deadlines: September for nomination; application deadline follows.
Contact: Programs Department.

National Research Council Postdoctoral and Senior Research Associateship Awards
2101 Constitution Avenue, N.W.
Washington, DC 20418
FAX (202) 334-2759
www.nas.edu/rap/welcome/html

Description: Twelve-month awards for recent Ph.D. or M.D. graduates for independent research in chemistry, earth and atmospheric sciences, engineering, mathematics, and applied sciences, life and medical sciences, space and planetary sciences, and physical sciences. Tenable at over 100 laboratories representing nearly all U.S. government agencies with research facilities.
Restrictions: None.
$ Given: Three hundred and fifty awards for $30,000 to $47,000 depending upon sponsoring laboratory. Renewable for up three years. Support for relocation and professional travel.
Application Information: Write for details.
Deadlines: January 15, April 15, August 15.

National Science Foundation Behavioral and Neural Sciences Research Grants
4201 Wilson Boulevard
Arlington, VA 22230
(703) 306-1416
www.nsf.gov

Description: Grants to support research on nervous systems and human/animal behavior; awarded in the following subprogram categories: cultural/physical anthropology, archaeology, animal behavior, behavioral neuroendocrinology, cellular neuroscience, developmental neuroscience, human cognition/perception, linguistics, neural mechanisms of behavior, neurobiology of learning/memory, sensory system, and social psychology; recipients chosen on the basis of proposed research.
Restrictions: N/A.
$ Given: An unspecified number of grants awarded annually; varying amounts.
Application Information: Write for subprogram details.
Deadlines: Applications accepted continuously; January 15, July 15.
Contact: Program Director, Division of Integrative Biology and Neuroscience.

National Science Foundation Graduate Research Fellowship Program
Oak Ridge Associated Universities
P.O. Box 3010
Oak Ridge, TN 37831-3010
(865) 241-4300

Description: Three-year fellowships for graduate study leading to research-based master's or doctoral degrees in the mathematical, physical, biological, engineering, and behavioral and social sciences.
Restrictions: U.S. citizenship or permanent resident status required.
$ Given: An unspecified number of fellowships awarded annually; each with an annual stipend of $15,000, and a cost-of-education allowance of $10,500 per tenure year.
Application Information: Write for details.
Deadline: November 4.

National Science Foundation Postdoctoral Research Fellowships in Biological Informatics
P.O. Box 218
Jessup, MD 20794-0218
(301) 947-2722
www.nsf.gov

Description: Fellowships for postdoctoral-level research and training at the intersection of biology and the informational, computational, mathematical, and statistical sciences. Research may be conducted at any appropriate U.S. or foreign host institution. Recipients chosen on the basis of their ability, accomplishments, and potential, the research and training plan's scientific merit, feasibility, significance in generating new biological knowledge, and impact on the career development of the applicant.
Restrictions: U.S. citizenship or permanent resident status required. Fellows must affiliate with a host institution during the entire tenure of the fellowship.
$ Given: Approximately twenty fellowships awarded annually, each for $50,000 per year for two or three years.
Application Information: Write for details.
Deadline: First Monday in November.

National Security Education Program Graduate International Fellowships
Academy for Educational Development
1825 Connecticut Avenue
Washington, DC 20009-5721
(800) 498-9360
www.aed.org/nsep

Description: One- to six-semester (twenty-four-month) fellowships for graduate students to pursue specialization in area and language study in a diverse list of fields of study, specifically business, economics, history, international affairs, law, applied sciences and engineering, health and biomedical sciences, political science and other social sciences, which are connected to U.S. national security.
Restrictions: U.S. citizenship required. Application to or enrollment in a graduate program in an accredited U.S. college or university located within the United States. Must be willing to enter into service agreement to seek employment with an agency or office of the federal government involved in national security affairs. Recipients chosen on the basis of the relationship of the applicant's proposed study to U.S. national security and how the applicant proposes to use knowledge and experience gained from NSEP support to contribute to U.S. national security.

$ Given: An unspecified number of fellowships awarded annually; each for $2,000 per semester for language or area studies coursework at your home university and $10,000 per semester for two semesters of overseas study program expenses.
Application Information: Write for details.
Deadline: January 15.

Natural Sciences and Engineering Research Council of Canada
NSERC Postgraduate Scholarships in Science Librarianship and Documentation
200 Kent Street
Ottawa, Ontario K1A 1H5
Canada
(613) 992-8203
(613) 995-5521
www.nserc.ca

Description: One-year scholarships for first- and second-year study toward M.L.S. degree in library science; recipients chosen on the basis of academic achievement, commitment to field, and relevant experience.
Restrictions: Applicants must have B.S. degree in science or engineering; Canadian citizenship or permanent resident status required.
$ Given: A few scholarships awarded annually; each for $13,500 Canadian plus travel allowance.
Application Information: Write for details.
Deadline: December 1.
Contact: Nadine Bohan; Information Officer.

Parenteral Drug Association Foundation for Pharmaceutical Sciences
Foundation Grant in Biotechnology
PDA Headquarters
7500 Old Georgetown Road
Suite 620
Bethesda, MD 20814
(301) 986-0293
FAX (301) 986-0296
www.pda.org

Description: One- to three-year grant for research in developing biotechnology analytical methodology; recipients chosen on the basis of proposed research.
Restrictions: No geographic restrictions.
$ Given: One grant of $15,000 is awarded annually.
Application Information: Application form and eight copies of proposal required.
Deadline: June 15.
Contact: Grants Administrator.

Parenteral Drug Association Foundation for Pharmaceutical Sciences
PDAF Research Grants
PDA Headquarters
7500 Old Georgetown Road
Suite 620
Bethesda, MD 20814
(301) 986-0293
FAX (301) 986-0296
www.pda.org

Description: One-year grants to support research in parenteral technology and related fields; recipients chosen on the basis of proposed research.
Restrictions: United States citizenship required.
$ Given: Two grants of $15,000 each are awarded annually; renewable once.
Application Information: Write for details.
Deadline: June 15.
Contact: Grants Administrator.

Parenteral Drug Association Foundation for Pharmaceutical Sciences Charles P. Schaufus Parenteral Processing Technology Research Grant
PDA Headquarters
7500 Old Georgetown Road
Suite 620
Bethesda, MD 20814
(301) 986-0293
FAX (301) 986-0296
www.pda.org

Description: One- to three-year grants to support research in parenteral technology; recipients chosen on the basis of proposed research.
Restrictions: United States citizenship required.
$ Given: One grant of $10,000 is awarded annually; renewable.
Application Information: Write for details.
Deadline: June 15.
Contact: Grants Administrator.

President's Commission on White House Fellowships White House Fellowships
712 Jackson Place, N.W.
Washington, DC 20503
(202) 395-4522
www.whitehouse.gov/
wh_fellows

Description: Twelve-month appointments as special assistants to the Vice President, Cabinet members, and the Presidential staff; fellowships include participation in educational program; positions available for students in public affairs, education, the sciences, business, and the professions; recipients chosen on the basis of leadership qualities, commitment to community service, and career/academic achievement.
Restrictions: Limited to young adults, ages 30–39; civilian federal employees are ineligible; recipients may not hold official state or local office while serving as White House fellows; United States citizenship required.
$ Given: Eleven to nineteen wage-earning fellowships for up to a maximum of $65,000 are awarded annually.
Application Information: Write for details.
Deadline: February 1.

Population Council Reproductive Biomedicine Fellowships
1230 York Avenue
Box 273
New York, NY 10021
(212) 339-0500

Description: One- to two-year fellowships for doctoral candidates for study of physiology and biochemistry of reproduction. Training in any aspect of reproductive biology may be considered.
Restrictions: None.
$ Given: An unspecified number of fellowships awarded annually; annual stipend of $30,000.
Application Information: Write for details.
Deadline: None.
Contact: The Fellowship Secretary.

Purina Mills Company
Purina Mills Research
Fellowships
Purina Research Awards
Committee
P.O. Box 66812
St. Louis, MO 63166-6812
(800) 227-8941
FAX (314) 768-4894
www.purina-mills.com

Description: Fellowships for graduate students at agri-cultural colleges, for nutrition and physiology research as related to dairy, poultry, and animal sciences; recipients chosen on the basis of academic achievement and pro-posed research.
Restrictions: N/A.
$ Given: Four fellowships awarded annually; each for $12,500/year.
Application Information: Write for guidelines.
Deadline: February 5.
Contact: Mary E. Timpe-2E.

Rockefeller University
Rockefeller Archive Center
Research Grants
15 Dayton Avenue
Pocantico Hills
North Tarrytown, NY
10591-1598
(914) 631-4505
www.rockefeller.edu/archives.
ctr

Description: Residential research fellowships for gradu-ate students and postdoctoral scholars pursuing research using Archive Center resources; relevant disciplines including philanthropy, education, science, medicine, black history, agriculture, labor, social welfare, social sci-ences, politics, religion, population, economic develop-ment, and the arts; recipients chosen on the basis of proposed research and necessity of using Archive Center resources.
Restrictions: N/A.
$ Given: An unspecified number of grants awarded annually; each for up to $2,500 for travel, lodging, and research expenses.
Application Information: Write for details.
Deadline: November 30.
Contact: Pamela Harcia, Director.

Sigma Xi, The Scientific
Research Society
Grants-in-Aid of Research
P.O. Box 13975
Research Triangle Park, NC
27709
(800) 243-6534
(919) 549-4691
www.sigmaxi.org

Description: Research grants to graduate and under-graduate students in science and engineering, to support research projects; recipients chosen on the basis of pro-posed research.
Restrictions: Open to all nationalities.
$ Given: An unspecified number of grants awarded annually; each for up to $1,000 (average $500).
Application Information: Application forms required.
Deadlines: February 1, May 1, and November 1.
Contact: Committee on Grants-in-Aid of Research.

Alfred P. Sloan Foundation
DOE Joint Postdoctoral
Fellowships in Computational
Molecular Biology
630 Fifth Avenue, Suite 2550
New York, NY 10111-0242
(212) 649-1649
www.sloan.org

Description: Two-year postdoctoral fellowships for sci-entists interested in computational molecular biology to work in an appropriate molecular biology department or laboratory in the U.S. or Canada. Recipients chosen on the basis of strong educational backgrounds in such fields as physics, mathematics, computer science, chemistry, engineering, and related fields who wish to bring these backgrounds to bear upon computational molecular research questions.

Restrictions: N/A.
$ Given: Up to ten fellowships awarded annually, each with an annual stipend of $42,000, plus research expenses up to $1,500.
Application Information: Write for details.
Deadline: February 1.

Smithsonian Institution Graduate Student Research Fellowships
Office of Fellowships and Grants
955 L'Enfant Plaza
Suite 7300
Washington, DC 20560
(202) 287-3271
www.si.edu/research+study/

Description: Ten-week residential fellowships for graduate students to pursue research at the Smithsonian; relevant disciplines include art history, anthropology, ecology, biology, environmental science, astrophysics, history of science, Oriental art, natural history, African art and culture, and American cultural/sociological history; recipients chosen on the basis of proposed research.
Restrictions: Applicants must be formally enrolled in a graduate program of study, must have completed at least one semester, and must not yet have advanced to candidacy in a doctoral program.
$ Given: Approximately thirty-eight fellowships are awarded annually; each with maximum $5,000 stipend.
Application Information: Write for details.
Deadline: January 15.
Contact: Program Assistant.

Smithsonian Institution Minority Students Internships
Office of Fellowships and Grants
955 L'Enfant Plaza
Suite 7300
Washington, DC 20560
(202) 287-3271
www.si.edu/research+study/

Description: Nine- to twelve-week internships for undergraduate upperclassmen and graduate students in the humanities, social sciences, natural sciences, and physical sciences; internship program includes participation in ongoing research or activities at the museum plus supervised independent research in any bureau; recipients chosen on the basis of academic achievement and proposed research.
Restrictions: Limited to minority group applicants.
$ Given: An unspecified number of internship positions are awarded annually; $250/week undergraduate stipend, $300/week graduate stipend.
Application Information: Write for details.
Deadlines: January 15, and October 15.

Smithsonian Institution Predoctoral Research Fellowships in the History of Science and Technology
Office of Fellowships and Grants
955 L'Enfant Plaza
Suite 7300
Washington, DC 20560
(202) 287-3271
www.si.edu/research+study/

Description: Three- to twelve-month residential fellowships for doctoral candidates at dissertation level and postdoctoral students in the history of science and technology, to pursue independent research using the Smithsonian's collections, resources, and staff expertise; relevant disciplines include history of mathematics, physical sciences, pharmacy, medicine, civil and mechanical engineering, electrical technology, and history of American science; recipients chosen on the basis of proposed research.
Restrictions: Applicants must have completed all preliminary coursework and exams for degree.

$ Given: An unspecified number of fellowships are awarded annually; each with $15,000 for predoctoral candidates; $27,000 for postdoctoral candidates.
Application Information: Write for details. Applications available in September.
Deadline: January 15.
Contact: Program Assistant.

Soil and Water Conservation Society
Kenneth E. Grant Research Awards
7515 N.E. Ankeny Road
Ankeny, IA 50021
(515) 289-2331
(800) 843-7645
www.swcs.org

Description: Awards for graduate students to conduct research (thesis/dissertation related or other) on good land use; relevant disciplines include agronomy and soil sciences, natural resources, water resources, and economics; recipients chosen on the basis of academic achievement and financial need.
Restrictions: SWCS membership required.
$ Given: An unspecified number of awards of up to $1,400 each are awarded annually.
Application Information: Request application from university department head or SWCS.
Deadline: April 1.
Contact: Max Schnepf, Director of Public Affairs.

Paul and Daisy Soros Fellowships for New Americans
400 West 59th Street
New York, NY 10019
(212) 547-6926
FAX (212) 548-4623
www.pdsoros.org

Description: Fellowships for up to two years of graduate study in the United States in any professional field or scholarly discipline in the Arts, Humanities, Social Sciences, and Sciences. Recipients chosen on the basis of the relevance of graduate school to their long-term career goals, their potential for enhancing their contributions to society, academic achievement, creativity, originality, and initiative.
Restrictions: Limited to applicants under 30 years of age. Applicants must either be a resident alien (holding a Green Card), naturalized as a U.S. citizen, or the child of two parents who are both naturalized citizens.
$ Given: Thirty fellowships awarded annually, each with a maintenance grant of $20,000 and a tuition grant of one-half the tuition costs of the graduate program.
Application Information: Write for details.
Deadline: November 30.

Southern Illinois University at Carbondale
Minority Doctoral Fellowships in Science and Engineering
Graduate School
Woody Hall, B-114
Carbondale, IL 62901
(618) 536-7791
www.sin.edu

Description: Three-year fellowships for doctoral candidates in the life sciences, physical sciences, and engineering; recipients chosen on the basis of GRE or other national standardized test scores.
Restrictions: Limited to minority group applicants; applicants of Mexican or Puerto Rican descent preferred; United States citizenship required.
$ Given: An unspecified number of fellowships awarded annually; each for $15,000/year plus full tuition & fees (for three years).

Application Information: Write for details.
Deadline: February 1.
Contact: Jane Meuth.

Southern Illinois University at Carbondale Minority Graduate Incentive Program
Woody Hall, B-114
Carbondale, IL 62901
(618) 453-4558
(618) 536-7791
www.imgip.siu.edu

Description: Fellowships for doctoral candidates in the life sciences, physical sciences, engineering, and mathematics.
Restrictions: U.S. citizenship or permanent resident status required. Limited to African American, Hispanic and Native American applicants. Must have been accepted to a doctoral program at one of the participating Illinois-based universities in fields where there is severe underrepresentation in their field.
$ Given: An unspecified number of fellowships awarded annually; each with a stipend of $13,500 plus full tuition and fees, an annual allowance of $1,500 for book, supplies, equipment and travel, for a maximum of three years.
Application Information: Write for details.
Deadline: February 1.
Contact: Jane Meuth.

U.S. Department of Energy Office of Biological and Environmental Research Alexander Hollaender Distinguished Postdoctoral Fellowship Program
Krell Institute
P.O. Box 511
Ames, IA 50010-9976
(515) 233-6867

Description: One-year fellowships for postdoctoral study tenable at DOE laboratories for the study of life, biomedical and environmental sciences, and other supporting scientific disciplines. Recipients chosen on the basis of academic achievement, recommendations, scientific interests, compatibility of applicant's background and interests with needs of host research laboratory.
Restrictions: U.S. citizenship or permanent resident status required. Must have received doctoral degree in appropriate discipline.
$ Given: An unspecified number of fellowships awarded annually; each with a stipend of $37,500 for the first year and $40,500 for the second year. Inbound travel and moving expenses up to $2,500 reimbursed. For one year, renewable for second year.
Application Information: Write for details.
Deadline: January 27.

Williams College Gaius Charles Bolin Fellowships for Minority Graduate Students
Hopkins Hall
Williamstown, MA 01267
(413) 597-4352
www.williams.edu

Description: One-year residential fellowships at Williams College for doctoral candidates at dissertation level in the humanities, natural sciences, social sciences, or behavioral sciences; fellowships tenure includes teaching responsibilities for only one semester course; recipients chosen on the basis of academic achievement and promise as college teachers.
Restrictions: Limited to minority group applicants.
$ Given: Two fellowships awarded annually; each for $25,000 plus up to $2,500 for research expenses.

Application Information: Write for details.
Deadline: January 15.
Contact: Peter Grudin, Dean of the Faculty.

Woodrow Wilson Johnson &
Johnson Dissertation Grants
in Children's Health
CN 5281
Princeton, NJ 08543-5281
(609) 452-7007
www.woodrow.org/womens-
studies/health

Description: Grants for dissertation research on issues related to children's health, specifically its significance for public policy or treatment. Recipients chosen on the basis of originality and significance, scholarly validity, commitment to women's health, academic achievement.
Restrictions: Applicants must have completed all pre-dissertation requirements at graduate schools in the United States.
$ Given: Five grants awarded annually, each for $2,000 to be used for expenses connected with dissertation.
Application Information: Write for details.
Deadline: November 8.

Woodrow Wilson Johnson &
Johnson Dissertation Grants
in Women's Health
CN 5281
Princeton, NJ 08543-5281
(609) 452-7007
www.woodrow.org/womens-
studies/health

Description: Grants for dissertation research on issues related to women's health, specifically its significance for public policy or treatment. Recipients chosen on the basis of originality and significance, scholarly validity, commitment to women's health, academic achievement.
Restrictions: Applicants must have completed all pre-dissertation requirements at graduate schools in the United States.
$ Given: Ten grants awarded annually, each for $2,000 to be used for expenses connected with dissertation.
Application Information: Write for details.
Deadline: November 8.

Wilson Ornithological Society
Louis Agassiz Fuertes and
Margaret Morse Nice
USGS-BRD
Midcontinent Ecological
Science Center
4512 McMurray Avenue
Ft. Collins, CO 80525-3400
(970) 226-9421

Description: Grants for graduate students in ornithology to conduct avian research; recipients chosen on the basis of financial need and proposed research.
Restrictions: Recipients must report their research results at society's annual meeting.
$ Given: One grant of $2,500 is awarded annually.
Application Information: Application form required.
Deadline: January 15.
Contact: Dr. Richard B. Stiehl.

Wilson Ornithological Society
Paul A. Stewart
Ornithological Research
Awards
USGS-BRD
Midcontinent Ecological
Science Center
4512 McMurray Avenue
Ft. Collins, CO 80525-3400
(970) 226-9421

Description: Grants for ornithologists to conduct avian research; recipients chosen on the basis of financial need and proposed research. Preference will be given to the study of bird movements.
Restrictions: Recipients must report their research at society's annual meeting.
$ Given: Up to four grants of $500 each are awarded annually.
Application Information: Application form required.
Deadline: January 15.
Contact: Dr. Richard B. Stiehl.

Physical Sciences and Mathematics

American Association of Petroleum Geologists AAPG Grants-in-Aid of Research
P.O. Box 979
Tulsa, OK 74101-0979
(918) 584-2555
www.aapg.org

Description: Grants for master's and doctoral candidates at thesis/dissertation level, for field work on research project leading to degree; relevant disciplines include sedimentology, stratigraphy, paleontology, mineralogy, structural geology, geochemistry, geophysics, environmental geology, and the search for hydrocarbons and economic sedimentary minerals; special named grants also available.
Restrictions: No funding for the purchase of capital equipment.
$ Given: An unspecified number of grants awarded annually; maximum $2,000.
Application Information: Write for application form.
Deadline: January 15.
Contact: W. A. Morgan, Chairman, Grants-in-Aid Committee.

American Association of University Women Educational Foundation AAUW Selected Professions Fellowships
1111 Sixteenth Street
Washington, DC 20036
(319) 337-1716
www.aauw.org

Description: Fellowships for graduate students entering their final year of study in fields with traditionally low female representation, including architecture, business administration, computer science, dentistry, engineering, law, mathematics/statistics, medicine, recipients chosen on the basis of academic achievement; tenable for full-time study at accredited United States institutions.
Restrictions: Limited to women who are members of minority groups in final years of study in law, medicine, or business. United States citizenship or permanent resident status required.
$ Given: Twenty-five fellowships of $5,000–$12,000 each are awarded annually.
Application Information: Application forms available August 1 through December 20.
Deadlines: January 10; postmark deadline November 15 for engineering.

**American Geological Institute
AGI Minority Geoscience
Scholarships**
4220 King Street
Alexandria, VA 22303
(703) 379-2480

Description: Scholarships for undergraduate and graduate students who are geoscience and geoscience education majors at accredited institutions; relevant disciplines include earth science geology, geophysics, geochemistry, hydrology, meteorology, physical oceanography, oceanography, planetary geology, and geoscience education; tenable in the United States; recipients chosen on the basis of academic achievement and financial need.
Restrictions: Limited to minority group applicants; United States citizenship required.
$ Given: An unspecified number of scholarships awarded annually; each for up to $4,000 at graduate level, up to $10,000 at undergraduate level; renewable.
Application Information: Application form required.
Deadline: February 1.
Contact: Marilyn J. Suiter, Administrator, Special Programs.

**American Geophysical Union
Horton Research Grant in
Hydrology and Water
Resources**
2000 Florida Avenue, N.W.
Washington, DC 20009
(202) 462-6900
www.agu.org

Description: Grants for doctoral candidates, to support research projects in hydrology and water resources; relevant disciplines include physical/chemical/biological aspects of hydrology, as well as water resources policy sciences (economic, sociology, and law).
Restrictions: Membership in American Geophysical Union required.
$ Given: One or more grants awarded annually; approximately $9,000 plus travel allowance to ensure attendance at awards luncheon.
Application Information: Proposal must be signed by faculty advisor; application forms required.
Deadline: March 1.
Contact: Winetta Singhateh.

**American Museum of Natural
History Fellowship Program**
Central Park West at 79th
Street
New York, NY 10024
(212) 769-5040
www.amnh.org

Description: Postdoctoral fellowship to support research in any of the following fields: anthropology, mineral sciences, vertebrate and invertebrate zoology, and paleontology.
Restrictions: None.
$ Given: Twelve fellowships awarded annually, each in the amount of $21,000.
Application Information: Write for details.
Deadline: January 15.

**American Philosophical
Society
John Clarke Slater
Fellowships**
104 South Fifth Street
Philadelphia, PA 19106
(215) 440-3403
www.amphilsoc.org

Description: Fellowships for doctoral candidates writing dissertations on the history of physical sciences in the twentieth century; recipients chosen on the basis of academic achievement and quality of proposed dissertation research.
Restrictions: Applicants must have completed all Ph.D. degree requirements except dissertation.
$ Given: An unspecified number of fellowships of $12,000 are awarded annually.
Application Information: Write for details.
Deadline: December 1.

**American Philosophical
Society Library
Mellon Resident Research
Fellowships**
104 South Fifth Street
Philadelphia, PA 19106
(215) 440-3400
www.amphilsoc.org

Description: One- to three-month residential fellowships for doctoral candidates at dissertation level and postdoctoral scholars studying the history of American science and technology, its European roots, and its relation to American history and culture; tenable at the Society Library for short-term research using the library's collections.
Restrictions: N/A.
$ Given: An unspecified number of fellowships awarded annually; each for $1,900/month; tenable at Society for one to three months.
Application Information: Write for details.
Deadline: March 1.
Contact: Associate Librarian for Research Programs.

**American Society for
Engineering Education
Natural Defense Science and
Engineering Fellowship
Office of Naval Research
Graduate Fellowships**
1818 N Street, N.W.
Suite 600
Washington, DC 20036
www.asee.org/ndseq

Description: Thirty-six-month fellowships (tenable over four years) for college seniors in engineering, mathematics, and science to support graduate work toward Ph.D. beginning the following September; fellowship includes summer work at Department of Defense Laboratories in freshman or sophomore year; relevant disciplines include biology/biomedical sciences, oceanography, mathematics, computer science, electrical engineering, material science, cognitive and neural sciences, naval architecture and ocean engineering, physics, chemistry, and aerospace/mechanical engineering; recipients chosen on the basis of academic achievement.
Restrictions: United States citizenship required; applicants already in graduate school ineligible.
$ Given: Up to 150 fellowships awarded annually; each for $18,500 for the first twelve months, $19,500 for the second twelve months, and $20,500 for the third twelve months, plus full tuition paid directly to the United States university.
Application Information: Write for details.
Deadline: January 14.
Contact: Projects Officer.

American Statistical Association
ASA/NSF/BLS Senior Research Fellow and Associate Program
1429 Duke Street
Alexandria, VA 22314
(703) 684-1221
www.amstat.org

Description: Fellowships/associateships for doctoral candidates and recent Ph.D.s in economics, business, and labor studies; for participation in research at the Bureau of Labor Statistics; recipients chosen on the basis of academic achievement and quality of proposed research.
Restrictions: Significant computer experience required.
$ Given: An unspecified number of associateships are awarded annually usually four to six months in duration stipend is commensurate with qualifications and experience; fringe benefits and travel allowance also included.
Application Information: Write for details.
Deadline: December 10.
Contact: Judy Dill, Director.

American Statistical Association
ASA/NSF Census Research Fellow and Associate Program
1429 Duke Street
Alexandria, VA 22314
(703) 684-1221
www.amstat.org

Description: Fellowships/associateship for doctoral candidates and recent Ph.D.s in demography and population studies; for participation in research at the United States bureau of Census; recipients chosen on the basis of academic achievement and quality of proposed research.
Restrictions: Significant computer experience required.
$ Given: An unspecified number of associateships are awarded annually; stipend is commensurate with qualifications and experience; fringe benefits and travel allowance also included.
Application Information: Write for details.
Deadline: December 10.
Contact: Judy Dill, Director.

American Statistical Association
ASA and USDA/NASS Research Fellow and Associate Program
1429 Duke Street
Alexandria, VA 22314
(703) 684-1221
www.amstat.org

Description: Nine- to twelve-month fellowships and associateships for doctoral candidates and postdoctoral researchers in agricultural statistics, for residential research/work at the National Agricultural Statistics Service; recipients chosen on the basis of academic achievement and proposed research.
Restrictions: N/A.
$ Given: An unspecified number of fellowships/associateship positions awarded annually; each with stipend.
Application Information: Write for details.
Deadline: March 1.
Contact: Carolyn Kessner.

American Water Works Association
LARS Scholarships
6666 West Quincy Avenue
Denver, CO 80235
(303) 794-7711
FAX (303) 794-6303
www.awwa.org

Description: Scholarships for outstanding graduate students in fields of water treatment, corrosion control, and aquatic/analytic/environmental chemistry.
Restrictions: Applicants must be graduate students at institutions in the United States, Canada, Guam, Puerto Rico, or Mexico who will complete their degree requirements after August 31 of the deadline year.

$ Given: Two scholarships awarded annually: $5,000 for M.S. candidate, $7,000 for Ph.D. candidate.
Application Information: Write for details.
Deadline: January 15.
Contact: Coordinator, Volunteer and Technical Support Group Scholarship.

American Water Works Association Abel Wolman Doctoral Fellowships
6666 West Quincy Avenue
Denver, CO 80235
(303) 794-7711
FAX (303) 794-6303
www.awwa.org

Description: Twelve-month fellowships for outstanding doctoral candidates, to support research and training in water supply and treatment.
Restrictions: Applicants must be within two years of completing Ph.D. requirements; United States, Canadian, or Mexican citizenship required.
$ Given: One fellowship awarded annually; $15,000 stipend plus $1,000 research supplies/equipment allowance and $4,000 for tuition and fees.
Application Information: Write for details.
Deadline: January 15.

American Water Works Association Abel Wolman Fellowship
6666 West Quincy Avenue
Denver, CO 80235
(303) 794-7711
www.awwa.org

Description: Up to two year fellowships for graduate students to support research in the U.S., Canada, or Mexico in the field of water supply and treatment.
Restrictions: U.S., Canadian, or Mexican citizenship or permanent resident status required.
$ Given: An unspecified number of fellowships awarded annually, each with an annual stipend of $15,000 plus $1,000 for research supplies and equipment, and an education allowance of up to $4,000.
Application Information: Write for details.
Deadline: January 15.
Contact: Scholarship Coordinator.

Association of American Geographers Dissertation Research Grants
1710 Sixteenth Street, N.W.
Washington, DC 20009-3198
(202) 234-1450

Description: Grants for doctoral candidates to pursue dissertation research in the field of geography.
Restrictions: Applicants must be members of AAG for at least one year and have completed all Ph.D. requirements except the dissertation to be eligible.
$ Given: Up to three grants awarded annually, each with a maximum stipend of $500.
Application Information: Write for details.
Deadline: December 31.
Contact: Ehsan Khater.

Association for Women in Science Educational Foundation
AWIS Predoctoral Award
1522 K Street, N.W.
Suite 820
Washington, DC 20005
(202) 326-8490
(800) 886-AWIS
FAX (202) 408-0742
www.awis.org

Description: Awards for doctoral candidates in life sciences, physical sciences, social sciences, engineering, mathematics, and behavioral sciences; recipients chosen on the basis of academic achievement and quality of proposed research.
Restrictions: Limited to women only; United States citizenship and enrollment in United States institution required.
$ Given: An unspecified number of grants of $1,000 each are awarded annually.
Application Information: Write for details.
Deadline: January 15.

AT&T Bell Laboratories Cooperative Research Fellowships for Minorities
600 Mountain Avenue
Murray Hill, NJ 07974
(201) 582-4822
www.att.com

Description: Fellowships for graduate study toward Ph.D. degree, for graduating college seniors with the potential to become professional research scientists or engineers; relevant disciplines include chemistry, communications science, computer science, engineering, information science, materials science, mathematics, operations research, physics, and statistics; fellowship tenure includes one summer of work at AT&T; recipients chosen on the basis of academic achievement and proposed research.
Restrictions: Limited to African-American, Hispanic, and Native American applicants only; GRE exam scores required; United States citizenship or permanent resident status required.
$ Given: An unspecified number of fellowships awarded annually for approved conferences; each for $1,400/month for the first two years and for ten months in ensuing years plus tuition and fees and expenses.
Application Information: Write for details.
Deadline: January 15.
Contact: Fellowship Manager.

AT&T Bell Laboratories Graduate Research Program for Women
600 Mountain Avenue
Murray Hill, NJ 07974
www.att.com

Description: Fellowships and grants for graduate study toward Ph.D. degree, for graduating college seniors with the potential to become professional research scientists or engineers; relevant disciplines include chemistry, chemical engineering, communications science, computer science, electrical engineering, information science, materials science, mathematics, operations research, physics, and statistics; fellowship tenure includes summer work at AT&T; recipients chosen on the basis of academic achievement and proposed research.
Restrictions: Limited to women applicants only; applicants must be admitted for full-time study in approved doctoral program; United States citizenship or permanent resident status required.

$ Given: An unspecified number of fellowships awarded annually; fellowships and grants are renewable annually.
Application Information: Application forms required; available on-line.
Deadline: January 15.
Contact: Fellowship or University Relations

AT&T Bell Laboratories
Ph.D. Scholarship Program
600 Mountain Avenue
Murray Hill, NJ 07974
www.att.com

Description: Fellowships for doctoral candidates in the fields of chemistry, communications science, manufactural engineering, electrical engineering, and materials science; recipients chosen on the basis of academic achievement and proposed research.
Restrictions: United States citizenship or permanent resident status required.
$ Given: An unspecified number of fellowships awarded annually; each for expenses and summer education/research expenses $1,400/month stipend plus travel support for conferences.
Application Information: Applicants must be nominated by faculty member or department chair.
Deadline: January 15.
Contact: University Relations or Fellowship Administrator.

Bunting Institute Science
Scholars Fellowship Program
34 Concord Avenue
Cambridge, MA 02138
(617) 495-8136
www.radcliffe.edu/bunting

Description: Postdoctoral fellowships to support women scientists in any level in any of the following fields: astronomy, molecular and cellular biology, biochemistry, chemistry, cognitive and neural sciences, mathematics, computer science, electrical, aerospace, and mechanical engineering, materials science, naval architecture, ocean engineering, oceanography, physics, and geology.
Restrictions: U.S. citizenship required. Limited to women applicants only who have received their doctorate at least two years prior to application.
$ Given: Eight fellowships awarded annually, each in the amount of $31,300.
Application Information: Write for details.
Deadline: Early October.

Canada Council Killam
Research Fellowships
99 Metcalfe Street
P.O. Box 1047
Ottawa, Ontario
Canada K1P 5V8

Description: Fellowships for senior scholars (eight to twelve years beyond the Ph.D.) to support research in any of the following fields: humanities, social sciences, natural sciences, health sciences, engineering, and studies linking disciplines within those fields.
Restrictions: Canadian citizenship or landed immigrant resident status required.
$ Given: Fifteen to eighteen fellowships awarded annually, each in the amount $53,000.

Application Information: Write for details.
Deadline: June 30.

Carnegie Institute of
Washington Fellowship in
Astronomy
Carnegie Observatories
813 Santa Barbara Street
Pasadena, CA 91101
www.carnegie-institute.com

Description: One- to two-year predoctoral and postdoctoral fellowships to support research in the field of astronomy.
Restrictions: None. Qualified women and minorities encouraged to apply.
$ Given: An unspecified number of fellowships of varying amounts awarded annually.
Application Information: Write for details.
Deadline: Varies.

Carnegie Institute of
Washington Fellowship in
Geophysics
Geophysical Laboratory
5251 Broad Branch Road N.W.
Washington, DC 20015
(202) 387-6400
www.carnegie-institute.com

Description: One- to two-year predoctoral and postdoctoral fellowships to support research of physicochemical studies of geological problems, with particular emphasis on the processes involved in the formation of the Earth's crust, mantle, and core.
Restrictions: None. Qualified women and minorities encouraged to apply.
$ Given: An unspecified number of fellowships of varying amounts awarded annually.
Application Information: Write for details.
Deadline: Varies.

Carnegie Institute of
Washington Fellowship in
Physics
Department of Terrestrial
Magnetism
5241 Broad Branch Road N.W.
Washington, DC 20015
(202) 387-6400
www.carnegie-institute.com

Description: One- to two-year predoctoral and postdoctoral fellowships to support research in the field of physics and related sciences, including astrophysics, geophysics and geochemistry, and planetary physics.
Restrictions: None. Qualified women and minorities encouraged to apply.
$ Given: An unspecified number of fellowships of varying amounts awarded annually.
Application Information: Write for details.
Deadline: Varies.

Center for the Advanced
Study in Behavioral Sciences
Postdoctoral Fellowships
202 Junipero Serra Blvd.
Stanford, CA 94305-6165
(650) 723-9626
www.stanford.edu/group/
CISAC

Description: Nine- to twelve month postdoctoral fellowships to support research in any of the following fields: anthropology, art history, biology, classics, economics, education, history, law, linguistics, literature, mathematical and statistical specialties, medicine, musicology, philosophy, political science, psychiatry, psychology, and sociology. Tenable at the Center for Advanced Study in Behavioral Sciences.
Restrictions: None.
$ Given: Approximately fifty fellowships of varying amounts awarded annually.
Application Information: Write for details.
Deadline: Ongoing.

**Winston Churchill
Foundation Scholarship**
P.O. Box 1240
Gracie Station
New York, NY 10028
TEL/FAX (212) 879-3480
http://members.aol.com/
churchillf/

Description: One-year scholarship for graduate students in the fields of engineering, mathematics, and sciences to study for one year at Churchill College in Cambridge, England.
Restrictions: U.S. citizenship required. Limited to applicants between the ages of 19 and 26. Must hold a bachelor's degree.
$ Given: One scholarship awarded annually; covers tuition and fees at Churchill College, plus a living allowance of $5,000–$6,000 and an additional $500 for travel expenses.
Application Information: Write for details.
Deadline: N/A.

**Council for the Advancement
of Science Writing
Fellowships in Science Writing**
P.O. Box 404
Greenlawn, NY 11740

Description: Fellowships for the study of science writing, available to B.S./B.A. holders in science of journalism, as well as to professional reporters and graduate students; recipients chosen on the basis of academic achievement, quality of writing, and commitment to writing career.
Restrictions: Preference to journalists with two years professional experience who want to specialize in science writing.
$ Given: An unspecified number of grants of up to $2,000 each are awarded annually.
Application Information: Write for details.
Deadline: June 1.
Contact: Diane McGurgan.

**Dibner Institute for the
History of Science and
Technology
Senior Fellows And
Postdoctoral Fellows Program**
Dibner Building, MIT E56-100
38 Memorial Drive
Cambridge, MA 02139
(617) 253-6989

Description: Six-month- to one-year fellowships for senior-level and postdoctoral research at the Bundy Library and the libraries of the consortium universities.
Restrictions: Senior Fellows applicants should have advanced degrees in disciplines relevant to their research and show evidence of substantial scholarly achievement and professional experience. Postdoctoral applicants should have been awarded their Ph.D. within the previous five years. Must reside in Cambridge/Boston area during the term of the grant.
$ Given: Approximately twenty fellowships awarded annually; fellowships provide office space, support facilities, and full privileges of the Bundy Library and consortium libraries. Funds are available for housing, living expenses and round-trip airfare for international fellows. Average stipend varies.
Application Information: Write for details.
Deadline: December 31.
Contact: Trudy Kontoff, Program Coordinator.

Albert Einstein Distinguished Educator Fellowship Program
Triangle Coalition for Science and Technology Foundation
1201 New York Avenue, N.W.
Suite 700
Washington, DC 20005
(202) 586-6549
(800) 582-0115

Description: Eight- to twelve-month fellowships for science, mathematics, or technology teachers to serve in professional staff positions in the U.S. Senate or House of Representatives, DOE, NASA, NSF, NIH, ED, or OSTP. Recipients chosen on the basis of their excellence in teaching science, mathematics, or technology, and experimental and innovative approach toward teaching, professional involvement and leadership, communication skills, and knowledge of national, state, and local policies that affect education.
Restrictions: U.S. citizenship required. Applicants must have a minimum of five years teaching experience.
$ Given: An unspecified number of fellowships awarded annually, each with a $4,500 monthly stipend, plus travel and moving expenses.
Application Information: Applications must be submitted online through the Department of Energy's Web page dedicated to the fellows program.
Deadline: February 25.
Contact: Peter Faletra or Cindy Musick.

Environmental Protection Agency STAR Graduate Fellowship
Office of Exploratory Research
Room 3102, NEM
401 M Street
Washington, DC 20460
(202) 564-6923
www.epa.gov

Description: One- to three year fellowships for graduate students in the fields of engineering, sciences, social sciences, or mathematics doing environmentally-oriented research.
Restrictions: U.S. citizenship required or permanent resident status required.
$ Given: One fellowship awarded annually; with a $17,000 stipend, up to $12,000 tuition support, and up to $5,000 expense allowance. Renewable.
Application Information: Write for details.
Deadline: Early November.
Contact: Virginia Broadway, Graduate Fellowship Office.

Florida Education Fund McKnight Doctoral Fellowships
201 East Kennedy Boulevard
Suite 1525
Tampa, FL 33602
www.fl-educ-fd.org/mdf.html

Description: Fellowships for graduate study at one of eleven participating doctoral-degree-granting universities in Florida in the fields of business, engineering, agriculture, biology, computer science, mathematics, physical science, and psychology; recipients chosen on the basis of academic achievement.
Restrictions: Limited to African-American applicants only; B.A./B.S. degree required; United States citizenship required.
$ Given: twenty-five fellowships awarded annually; each for a maximum of five years of study, with an annual $11,000 stipend plus up to $5,000 in tuition and fees.
Application Information: Write for details.
Deadline: January 15.
Contact: President.

French Embassy Scientific Services
Chateaubriand Research Scholarships for the Exact Sciences, Engineering, and Medicine
Department of Science and Technology
4101 Reservoir Road, N.W.
Washington, DC 20007
(202) 944-6246
www.info-france-usa.org

Description: Six- to twelve-month research scholarship for doctoral candidates at dissertation level, as well as postdoctoral scholars, to conduct research in France at French universities, engineering schools, and private laboratories; language training sessions provided; relevant disciplines include biological and agricultural sciences, physical sciences and mathematics, engineering and applied sciences, medicine, nutrition, optometry and vision sciences, pharmacy and pharmaceuticals sciences, and veterinary medicine and sciences; recipients chosen on the basis of proposed research.
Restrictions: Each applicant must be registered at United States university and already in contact with French host institution; United States citizenship required.
$ Given: Twenty to thirty scholarships awarded annually; each for 9,000 Francs per month plus airfare and health insurance.
Application Information: Application forms must be submitted with faculty recommendation.
Deadline: January 31.

Garden Club of America
Catherine H. Beattie Fellowship
Center for Plant Conservation
Missouri Botanical Garden
P.O. Box 299
St. Louis, MO 63166-0299
(314) 577-9503
www.mobot.org/cpc/beattie.html

Description: Graduate fellowships to promote conservation of rare and endangered flora in the U.S. through research in any of the following fields: Botany, horticulture, conservation, or ecology. Preference given to students whose projects focus on the endangered flora of the Carolinas and southeastern U.S.
Restrictions: None.
$ Given: One fellowship awarded annually in the amount of $4,000.
Application Information: Write for details.
Deadline: December 31.
Contact: Mary Yurlina, Conservation Programs Manager.

Geological Society of America
GSA Penrose Research Grants
P.O. Box 9140
Boulder, CO 80301
(303) 447-2020
www.geosociety.org

Description: Grants to support master's and doctoral candidates in thesis/dissertation research in geology; recipients chosen on the basis of academic achievement, financial need, and proposed research. Women, minorities, and people with disabilities are particularly encouraged to apply.
Restrictions: Enrollment at university in Canada, Mexico, or the United States required.
$ Given: An unspecified number of up to $2,000 grants awarded annually.
Application Information: Request current GSA application form from university geology department or write for application.
Deadline: February 1.
Contact: Research Grants and Awards Administrator.

Fannie and John Hertz Foundation
Fannie and John Hertz Foundation Graduate Fellowship Program
P.O. Box 5032
Livermore, CA 94551-5032
(925) 373-6329
www.hertzfoundation.org

Description: Fellowships to provide B.S./B.A. holders with support for academic study through graduate school in the applied physical sciences, including engineering, applied physics, mathematics, and chemistry; tenable at one of the participating schools; recipients chosen on the basis of outstanding academic achievement (minimum 3.5 GPA in last two years of undergraduate work. Lower average acceptable with other outstanding qualifications).
Restrictions: Applicants must have completed at least two years of college-level physics and college-level math courses, plus one year of college-level chemistry; recipients must agree to respond in time of national emergency; United States citizenship required.
$ Given: An unspecified number of fellowships awarded annually; each for $25,000 plus tuition and fees.
Application Information: Write for details.
Deadline: November 5.
Contact: Hertz Foundation Treasurer.

Hertz Foundation
Graduate Fellowship Awards
P.O. Box 5032
Livermore, CA 94551-5032
(925) 373-6329
www.hertzfndn.org

Description: Fellowships for graduate study in any discipline at one of several tenable schools. Recipients chosen on the basis of merit.
Restrictions: None.
$ Given: One fellowship awarded annually, annual stipend of $25,000 and tuition covered for a maximum tenure of five years.
Application Information: Write for details.
Deadline: N/A.

Hertz Foundation
Graduate Fellowship Awards
P.O. Box 5032
Livermore, CA 94551-5032
(925) 373-6329
www.hertzfoundation.org

Description: Fellowships for graduate study in any discipline at one of several tenable schools. Recipients chosen on the basis of merit.
Restrictions: None.
$ Given: One fellowship awarded annually, annual stipend of $25,000 and tuition covered for a maximum tenure of five years.
Application Information: Write for details.
Deadline: N/A.

Hudson River Foundation for Science and Environmental Research Graduate Fellowships
40 West 20th Street, 9th Floor
New York, NY 10011
(212) 924-8290
FAX (212) 924-8325
www.hudsonriver.org

Description: Graduate fellowships for research in the fields of the life sciences, environmental studies, or public policy, as they relate to the Hudson River System.
Restrictions: Applicants must be enrolled in an accredited doctoral or master's program, must have a research plan approved by their department.
$ Given: An unspecified number of fellowships awarded annually; doctoral in the amount of $15,000, with up to

$1,000 incidental research; master's in the amount of $11,000 with up to $1,000 incidental research.
Application Information: Write for details.
Deadline: March 6.
Contact: Science Director.

IBM Corporation
IBM Graduate Fellowships
Divisional University Relations
Room 22-130
T.J. Watson Research Center
P.O. Box 218
Yorktown Heights, NY 10598
(914) 945-3000

Description: Fellowships for graduate students in the fields of the physical sciences, mathematics, material sciences, mechanical engineering, electrical engineering, and computer science.
Restrictions: None.
$ Given: An unspecified number of fellowships awarded annually, each for $12,000 plus tuition for one year.
Application Information: Write for details.
Deadline: February 15.

Institute of International Education
Colombian Government Study and Research Grants
U.S. Student Programs Division
809 United Nations Plaza
New York, NY 10017-3580
(212) 984-5330
www.iie.org/fulbright

Description: Grants for B.S./B.A. holders to pursue up to two years of study/research at Colombian universities; relevant disciplines include agriculture, biology, business administration, economics, chemistry, engineering, education, health services administration, geography, history, Latin American literature, law, linguistics, political science, physics, regulatory development, public health, and remote sensing interpretation.
Restrictions: United States citizenship required.
$ Given: An unspecified number of grants awarded annually; each for modest monthly stipend, plus tuition and fees, health insurance, book/materials allowance, and one-way return airfare upon completion of study.
Application Information: Write for details.
Deadline: October 23.

Institute of International Education
Fulbright Fixed Sum—Bulgarian Government Grants
U.S. Student Programs Division
809 United Nations Plaza
New York, NY 10017-3580
(212) 984-5330
www.iie.org/fulbright

Description: Grants for B.A./B.S. holders in the humanities, physical sciences, and social sciences; for a six- to nine-month residency/exchange in Bulgaria (September–June).
Restrictions: Knowledge of Bulgarian language required; United States citizenship required; applicants must meet all Fulbright eligibility requirements.
$ Given: An unspecified number of grants awarded annually; Bulgarian government funds stipend, housing, and health/accident insurance; Fulbright provides fixed sum for round-trip transportation plus additional monthly stipend.
Application Information: Write for details.
Deadline: October 31.
Contact: U.S. Student Program Division.

Institute of International Education
Study and Research Grants for U.S. Citizens
U.S. Student Programs Division
809 United Nations Plaza
New York, NY 10017-3580
(212) 984-5330
www.iie.org/fulbright

Description: Grants to support study and research in all fields, as well as professional training in the creative and performing arts; tenable at institutions of higher learning outside of the United States for one year; list of participating countries in any given year may be obtained from IIE.
Restrictions: Open to United States citizens with B.A. or equivalent; acceptable plan of study and proficiency in host country's language required.
$ Given: A variable number of grants awarded annually; covers international transportation, language or orientation course (where appropriate), tuition, book and maintenance allowances, and health and accident insurance.
Application Information: If currently enrolled in a college or university, apply to the campus Fulbright Program Advisor; applications also available from IIE.
Deadline: October 31.

Iota Sigma Pi Agnes Fay Morgan Research Award
Chemistry and Physics Department
Radford University
Radford, VA 24142
(540) 831-5413
www.chem-faculty.ucsd.edu.sawrey/ISP

Description: Award to recognize research achievement by a woman chemist in the fields of chemistry or biochemistry.
Restrictions: Limited to women chemists forty years of age or under.
$ Given: One award of $400.
Application Information: Write for details.
Deadline: January 15.
Contact: Dr. Christine K. F. Hermann.

Japan Ministry of Education, Science, and Culture
Japanese Government (Monbusho) Scholarship Program
2-2 Kasumigaseki, 3-chome
Chiyoda-ku
Tokyo 100
Japan
03-581-4211

Description: Eighteen-month to two-year scholarships for non-Japanese graduate students to study at Japanese universities and research institutes; Research Students Program is specifically designed for graduate students (undergraduate program also available) in the humanities, social sciences, music, fine arts, and natural sciences; open to citizens of countries with educational exchange agreements with Japan.
Restrictions: Language proficiency required (twelve- to eighteen-month language training program required if language skills deemed insufficient); applicants must be under age thirty-five.
$ Given: An unspecified number of scholarships awarded annually; each to cover monthly stipend, airfare, tuition, and expense allowance.
Application Information: For further information, contact Japanese Embassy or Consulate.
Deadlines: June 15, September 30.
Contact: Student Exchange Division.

Kosciuszko Foundation
15 East 65th Street
New York, NY 10021-6595
(212) 734-2130
FAX (212) 628-4552
www.kosciuszkofoundation.
org

Description: One-year scholarships to U.S. citizens of Polish descent for graduate studies in any field at colleges and universities in the United States and to Americans of non-Polish descent whose studies at American universities are primarily focused on Polish subjects. Recipients chosen on the basis of academic achievement and financial need.
Restrictions: Must be enrolled in a graduate program at a U.S. university. Applicants must be U.S. citizens or of Polish descent.
$ Given: An unspecified number of scholarships of $1,000–$5,000 each are awarded annually.
Deadline: January 16.
Contact: Grants office.

The Library Company of Philadelphia
American History and Culture Research Fellowships
1314 Locust Street
Philadelphia, PA 19107
(215) 546-5167
www.librarycompany.org

Description: Residential research fellowships at the Library Company of Philadelphia for doctoral candidates and postdoctoral scholars in most disciplines as related to the history and culture of eighteenth- to nineteenth-century America; tenable for one or more months; recipients chosen on the basis of proposed research.
Restrictions: N/A.
$ Given: An unspecified number of fellowships awarded annually; each with $1,500/month stipend.
Application Information: Write for details.
Deadline: April 15.
Contact: James Green, Curator.

Marshall Scholarships
Marshall Aid Commemorating
Commission
Association of Commonwealth
Universities
36 Gordon Square
London WC1HOPF
(44) 1713878572
www.aca.ac.uk/marshall

Description: Two- to three-year scholarships for undergraduate or graduate level study at any university in the United Kingdom, in any discipline leading to the award of a British university degree.
Restrictions: U.S. citizenship required; limited to graduates of accredited four-year colleges and universities in the United States with at least a 3.75 GPA since freshman year.
$ Given: Up to forty scholarships awarded annually; each worth approximately $25,000 per year and comprising a personal allowance for cost of living and residence, tuition fees, books, travel in connection with studies, and to and from the United States.
Application Information: Write for details. Application forms also available from colleges and universities in the United States, British consulates in Atlanta, Boston, Chicago, Houston, and San Francisco, the British Council in Washington, DC, British Information Services in New York.
Deadline: N/A.

Monticello College Foundation and Washington University
Spencer T. Olin Fellowships for Women in Graduate Study
Graduate School of Arts and Sciences
Washington University
Campus Box 1187
One Brookings Drive
St. Louis, MO 63130-4899
(314) 935-6848

Description: Fellowships for graduate students to prepare for careers in higher education and professions in the fields of biological and biomedical sciences, humanities, physical sciences and mathematics, social and behavioral sciences, architecture, business administration, engineering, fine arts, law, medicine, and social work. Tenable at Washington University.
Restrictions: Limited to women applicants only.
$ Given: An unspecified number of fellowships awarded annually, each ranging from $20,000 to $33,000.
Application Information: Write for details.
Deadline: February 1.

NASA Graduate Student Researchers Program
NASA Headquarters
600 Independence Ave, S.W.
Washington, DC 20546
(202) 358-1531
(202) 358-1517
www.nasa.gov

Description: One-year scholarships for graduate students in fields related to NASA research areas, specifically engineering, science, and mathematics.
Restrictions: U.S. citizenship required.
$ Given: An unspecified number of scholarships awarded annually, each with a $22,000 stipend, plus departmental component. Renewable for total of three years.
Application Information: Write for details.
Deadline: February 1.
Contact: Ahmad Nurriddin.

NASA Fellowship in Aerospace History
American Historical Association
400 A Street, S.E.
Washington, DC 20003
(202) 358-1517
(202) 358-1110

Description: Six-month- to one-year postdoctoral fellowship to undertake a research project related to aerospace history, from the earliest human interest in flight to the present, including cultural and intellectual history, economic history, history of law and public policy, and the history of science, engineering, and management.
Restrictions: U.S. citizenship required. Applicants must possess a doctoral degree in history or a related field, or be enrolled as a student in a doctoral-degree-granting program.
$ Given: One fellowship awarded annually, with a maximum postdoctoral stipend of $30,000; maximum predoctoral stipend of $21,000.
Application Information: Write for details.
Deadline: February 1.

**National Aeronautics and
Space Administration
Space Science Dissertation
Research Fellowships**
University Programs Branch
Educational Affairs Division
NASA Headquarters
Code FEH
600 Independence Ave, S.W.
Washington, DC 20546
(202) 453-8344
www.nasa.gov

Description: One-year renewable fellowships for full-time graduate students in aeronautics and space science, for research using NASA facilities; recipients chosen on the basis of academic achievement, relevance of proposed research to NASA, ability to accomplish the defined research, and planned utilization of NASA facilities.
Restrictions: United States citizenship required. Women and minorities are strongly encouraged to apply.
$ Given: An unspecified number of fellowships awarded annually; maximum of $22,000 per year; renewable for up to three years.
Application Information: Write for details.
Deadline: February 1.

**National Air and Space
Museum
Guggenheim Fellowships**
Smithsonian Institution
Washington, DC 20560-0312
(202) 357-1529
www.nasm.edu

Description: Twelve-month- to three-year residential fellowships for doctoral candidates at dissertation level, as well as recent Ph.D.s (within past seven years), for historical/scientific research on aviation and space; relevant disciplines include history, aerospace, and engineering.
Restrictions: N/A.
$ Given: An unspecified number of fellowships awarded annually; $15,000 predoctoral stipend, $27,000 postdoctoral stipend.
Application Information: Write for details.
Deadline: January 15.
Contact: Fellowship Coordinator.

**National Air and Space
Museum
Verville Fellowships**
Smithsonian Institution
Washington, DC 20560-0312
(202) 357-1529
www.nasm.edu

Description: Nine- to twelve-month fellowships for analysis of major developments, trends, and accomplishments in history of aviation/space studies; relevant disciplines include history, aerospace, and engineering.
Restrictions: Applicants must demonstrate skills in research and writing.
$ Given: An unspecified number of fellowships for $35,000 each are awarded annually.
Application Information: Write for details.
Deadline: January 15.
Contact: Fellowship Coordinator.

National Center for Atmospheric Research NCAR Graduate Research Assistantships
Advanced Study Program
P.O. Box 3000
Boulder, CO 80307-3000
(303) 497-1601

Description: Research positions for doctoral candidates at dissertation level in the atmospheric sciences and related fields; recipients chosen on the basis of academic achievement, financial need, and proposed research.
Restrictions: Proposed thesis work must coincide with NCAR program.
$ Given: An unspecified number of positions available annually; $16,870 stipend plus up to $1,200 for travel expenses; renewable for one year.
Application Information: Proposals must be submitted jointly by university scientist and NCAR scientist; graduate student will work under supervision of both scientists.
Contact: Barbara Kansford, Coordinator, Advanced Study Program.

National Geographic Society Research Grants
Committee for Research and Exploration
1145 17th Street, N.W.
Washington, DC 20036
(202) 857-7439
www.nationalgeographic.com

Description: Grants for research in anthropology, archaeology, astronomy, biology, glaciology, botany, ecology, physical and human geography, mineralogy, geology, oceanology, paleontology, zoology, and other sciences pertinent to geography; funding primarily for postdoctoral researchers, but occasionally awarded to exceptional doctoral candidates; recipients chosen on the basis of proposed research.
Restrictions: Open to all nationalities.
$ Given: An unspecified number of grants of $15,000–$20,000 average each are awarded annually.
Application Information: Write for details.
Deadline: Applications accepted continuously.
Contact: Committee for Research and Exploration.

National Research Council Ford Foundation Predoctoral and Dissertation Fellowships
FF/TJ2041
2101 Constitution Avenue
Washington, DC 20418
(202) 334-2872
FAX (202) 334-3419

Description: Three-year predoctoral fellowships and nine- to twelve-month dissertation fellowships for study in selected disciplines (humanities, social sciences, sciences, mathematics, and engineering). Recipients chosen on the basis of academic achievement and commitment to scholarship, research, and careers in teaching.
Restrictions: Limited to U.S. citizens or nationals only. Limited to members of the following groups: Alaskan Natives, African Americans, Mexican Americans, Native American Indians, Native Pacific Islanders, Puerto Ricans. Applicants must be enrolled in or planning to enroll in a research-based Ph.D. or Sc.D. Program.
$ Given: Fifty predoctoral fellowships and twenty-nine dissertation fellowships awarded annually; predoctoral fellowships have annual stipend of $14,000 and institutional award of $7,500. Dissertation fellowships offer stipend of $21,500.

Application Information: Write for details.
Deadline: November 12.

National Research Council NRC/Ford Predoctoral and Dissertation Fellowships for Minorities
Fellowships Office
2101 Constitution Avenue, N.W.
Washington, DC 20418
(202) 334-2872
www.nas.edu

Description: Fellowships for graduate students in the humanities, social sciences, biological and agricultural sciences, physical sciences and mathematics, and engineering and applied sciences; recipients chosen on the basis of academic achievement and proposed research.
Restrictions: Limited to members of minority groups; United States citizenship or legal residency required.
$ Given: Fifty predoctoral fellowships awarded; $14,000 for fellow, $7,500 for Institution; twenty-nine dissertation fellowships available for $21,500.
Application Information: Write for details.
Deadline: November 24.

National Research Council Postdoctoral and Senior Research Associateship Awards
2101 Constitution Avenue, N.W.
Washington, DC 20418
FAX (202) 334-2759
www.nas.edu/rap/welcome/html

Description: Twelve-month awards for recent Ph.D. or M.D. Graduates for independent research in chemistry, earth and atmospheric sciences, engineering, mathematics, and applied sciences, life and medical sciences, space and planetary sciences, and physical sciences. Tenable at over 100 laboratories representing nearly all U.S. government agencies with research facilities.
Restrictions: None.
$ Given: Three hundred and fifty awards for $30,000 to $47,000 depending upon sponsoring laboratory. Renewable for up to three years. Support for relocation and professional travel.
Application Information: Write for details.
Deadlines: January 15, April 15, August 15.

National Physical Sciences Consortium Fellowship Program
New Mexico State University
Box 30001, Dept. 3NPS
Las Cruces, NM 88003-0001
(800) 952-4118
www.npsc.org

Description: Fellowships for graduate students in the fields of the physical sciences, mathematics, and computer sciences enrolled at or applying to one of approximately 62 participating institutions to pursue a Ph.D.
Restrictions: U.S. citizenship required. Recruiting Native American, African American, Hispanic American and/or women.
$ Given: One fellowship awarded annually; with an annual stipend of $12,000 plus tuition and fees. Renewable for a total of six years.
Application Information: Write for details.
Deadline: Early November.

National Science Foundation Graduate Research Fellowship Program
Oak Ridge Associated Universities
P.O. Box 3010
Oak Ridge, TN 37831-3010
(865) 241-4300

Description: Three-year fellowships for graduate study leading to research-based master's or doctoral degrees in the mathematical, physical, biological, engineering, and behavioral and social sciences.
Restrictions: U.S. citizenship or permanent resident status required.
$ Given: An unspecified number of fellowships awarded annually; each with an annual stipend of $15,000, and a cost-of-education allowance of $10,500 per tenure year.
Application Information: Write for details.
Deadline: November 4.

National Science Foundation Minority Graduate Research Fellowships
Directorate for Education and Human Resources
4201 Wilson Blvd
Arlington, VA 22230
(703) 306-1630
www.nsf.gov

Description: Fellowships to support master's and doctoral candidates for three years of full-time study (over a five-year period) in mathematics, engineering, physical, biological, and social sciences, and history/philosophy of science. Applicants should aspire to a teaching and/or research career.
Restrictions: Limited to members of ethnic minority groups; United States citizenship or residency required.
$ Given: One hundred and fifty fellowships awarded annually, ten of them for Women in Engineering; each for $12,900/year (renewable for up to three years), plus $10,500 institutional allowance in lieu of tuition and fees plus a one-time international research travel allowance of $1,000 is available.
Application Information: Write for details.
Deadline: November 4.
Contact: Division Director.

National Security Education Program Graduate International Fellowships
Academy for Educational Development
1825 Connecticut Avenue
Washington, DC 20009-5721
(800) 498-9360
www.aed.org/nsep

Description: One-to-six-semester (twenty-four-month) fellowships for graduate students to pursue specialization in area and language study in a diverse list of fields of study, specifically business, economics, history, international affairs, law, applied sciences and engineering, health and biomedical sciences, political science and other social sciences, which are connected to U.S. national security.
Restrictions: U.S. citizenship required. Application to or enrollment in a graduate program in an accredited U.S. college or university located within the United States. Must be willing to enter into service agreement to seek employment with an agency or office of the federal government involved in national security affairs. Recipients chosen on the basis of the relationship of the applicant's proposed study to U.S. national security and how the applicant proposes to use knowledge and experience gained from NSEP support to contribute to U.S. national security.

$ Given: An unspecified number of fellowships awarded annually; each for $2,000 per semester for language or area studies coursework at your home university and $10,000 per semester for two semesters of overseas study program expenses.
Application Information: Write for details.
Deadline: January 15.

National Speleological Society Ralph W. Stone Award in Speleology
Ames Research Center
MS 239-4
Moffet Field, CA 94035

Description: Grants to registered graduate students for research in geology, biology, speleology, geochemistry, hydrology, and other cave-related sciences; recipients chosen on the basis of financial need and proposed research.
Restrictions: NSS membership required.
$ Given: One grant for $1,500 is awarded annually.
Application Information: Write for details.
Deadline: May 1.
Contact: David Des Marais.

National Sciences and Engineering Research Council of Canada
NSERC Postgraduate Scholarships
350 Albert Street
Ottawa, Ontario K1A 1H5
(613) 995-5521
FAX (613) 992-5337
www.nserv.ca

Description: Up to twenty-four-month scholarships for highly qualified science or engineering students from a university approved by NSERC. Canadian citizenship or permanent resident status required.
$ Given: An unspecified number of scholarships awarded annually; each with stipend of $13,800 per year toward tuition.
Application Information: Write for details.
Deadline: December 1.
Contact: Information Officer.

Natural Sciences and Engineering Research Council of Canada
NSERC Postgraduate Scholarships in Science Librarianship and Documentation
200 Kent Street
Ottawa, Ontario K1A 1H5
Canada
(613) 992-8203
(613) 995-5521
www.nserc.ca

Description: One-year scholarships for first- and second-year study toward MLS degree in library science; recipients chosen on the basis of academic achievement, commitment to field, and relevant experience.
Restrictions: Applicants must have B.S. degree in science or engineering; Canadian citizenship or permanent resident status required.
$ Given: A few scholarships awarded annually; each for $13,500 Canadian plus travel allowance.
Application Information: Write for details.
Deadline: December 1.
Contact: Nadine Bohan; Information Officer.

Oak Ridge Institute for Science and Education Nuclear Engineering and Health Physics Fellowships
P.O. Box 117
Oak Ridge, TN 37831-0117
(865) 576-3146
www.ornl.gov

Description: One-year fellowship for graduate students studying nuclear science and engineering or health physics at participating Oak Ridge Associated Universities with practicum at various DOE facilities; recipients chosen on the basis of academic achievement, career goals, and interests.
Restrictions: N/A.
$ Given: An unspecified number of fellowships awarded annually; each with $14,400 stipend, plus $300/month during practicum, and travel, tuition, and fees; renewable for up to four years.
Application Information: Write for details.
Deadline: January 25.

Optical Society of America Newport Research Awards
2010 Massachusetts Avenue, N.W.
Washington, DC 20036
(202) 416-1960
FAX (202) 416-6134
www.osa.org

Description: Grants to doctoral candidates for one year of research on electro-optics and laser technology.
Restrictions: Applicants must be enrolled at United States universities. Must be nominated by an OSA member.
$ Given: Three new grants and three renewals awarded annually; each with up to $12,000 stipend plus $4,000 research expense allowance.
Application Information: Write for application forms.
Deadline: February 15.
Contact: Doreen Weinberger, Chair, Newport Research Award Committee.

President's Commission on White House Fellowships White House Fellowships
712 Jackson Place, N.W.
Washington, DC 20503
(202) 395-4522

Description: Twelve-month appointments as special assistants to the Vice President, Cabinet members, and the Presidential staff; fellowships include participation in educational program; positions available for students in public affairs, education, the sciences, business, and the professions; recipients chosen on the basis of leadership qualities, commitment to community service, and career/academic achievement.
Restrictions: Limited to young adults, ages 30–39; civilian federal employees are ineligible; recipients may not hold official state or local office while serving as White House fellows; United States citizenship required.
$ Given: Eleven to nineteen wage-earning fellowships for up to a maximum of $65,000 are awarded annually.
Application Information: Write for details.
Deadline: February 1.

Rockefeller University
Rockefeller Archive Center
Research Grants
15 Dayton Avenue
Pocantico Hills
North Tarrytown, NY 10591
(914) 631-4505
www.rockefeller.edu/archives.
ctr

Description: Residential research fellowships for graduate students and postdoctoral scholars pursuing research using Archive Center resources; relevant disciplines including philanthropy, education, science, medicine, black history, agriculture, labor, social welfare, social sciences, politics, religion, population, economic development, and the arts; recipients chosen on the basis of proposed research and necessity of using Archive Center resources.
Restrictions: N/A.
$ Given: An unspecified number of grants awarded annually; each for up to $2,500 for travel, lodging, and research expenses.
Application Information: Write for details.
Deadline: November 30.
Contact: Director.

Sigma Xi, The Scientific
Research Society
Grants-in-Aid of Research
P.O. Box 13975
Research Triangle Park, NC
27709
(800) 243-6534
(919) 549-4691
www.sigmaxi.org

Description: Research grants to graduate and undergraduate students in science and engineering, to support research projects; recipients chosen on the basis of proposed research.
Restrictions: Open to all nationalities.
$ Given: An unspecified number of grants awarded annually; each for up to $1,000 (average $500).
Application Information: Application forms required.
Deadlines: February 1, May 1, and November 1.
Contact: Committee on Grants-in-Aid of Research.

Smithsonian Institution
Graduate Student Research
Fellowships
Office of Fellowships and
Grants
955 L'Enfant Plaza
Suite 7300
Washington, DC 20560
(202) 287-3271
www.si.edu/research&study

Description: Ten-week residential fellowships for graduate students to pursue research at the Smithsonian; relevant disciplines include art history, anthropology, ecology, biology, environmental science, astrophysics, history of science, Oriental art, natural history, African art and culture, and American cultural/sociological history; recipients chosen on the basis of proposed research.
Restrictions: N/A.
$ Given: Approximately thirty-eight fellowships are awarded annually; each with maximum $5,000 stipend.
Application Information: Write for details.
Deadline: January 15.
Contact: Program Assistant.

**Smithsonian Institution
Minority Students Internships**
Office of Fellowships and
Grants
955 L'Enfant Plaza
Suite 7300
Washington, DC 20560
(202) 287-3271
www.si.edu/research&study

Description: Nine- to twelve-week internships for undergraduate upperclassmen and graduate students in the humanities, social sciences, natural sciences, and physical sciences; internship program includes participation in ongoing research or activities at the Museum plus supervised independent research in any bureau; recipients chosen on the basis of academic achievement and proposed research.
Restrictions: Limited to minority group applicants.
$ Given: An unspecified number of internship positions are awarded annually; $250/week undergraduate stipend, $300/week graduate stipend.
Application Information: Write for details.
Deadlines: January 15 and October 15.

**Smithsonian Institution
Predoctoral Research
Fellowships in Astrophysics
and Related Topics**
Smithsonian Astrophysical
Observatory
60 Garden Street
Mail Stop 47
Cambridge, MA 02138
(617) 495-7103
www.si.edu/research&study

Description: One-year fellowships for doctoral candidates in astrophysics and related topics to conduct independent dissertation research, working with Smithsonian staff and using Smithsonian resources; recipients chosen on the basis of academic achievement and proposed research.
Restrictions: Applicants must have completed all preliminary coursework and examinations.
$ Given: An unspecified number of fellowships awarded annually; each for $14,000/year; renewable for one year.
Application Information: Write for details.
Deadline: April 15.
Contact: Secretary, Predoctoral Fellowship Committee.

**Smithsonian Institution
Predoctoral Research
Fellowships in the History of
Science and Technology**
Office of Fellowships and
Grants
955 L'Enfant Plaza
Suite 7300
Washington, DC 20560
(202) 287-3271
www.si.edu/research&study

Description: Three- to twelve-month residential fellowships for doctoral candidates at dissertation level and postdoctoral students in the history of science and technology, to pursue independent research using the Smithsonian's collections, resources, and staff expertise; relevant disciplines include history of mathematics, physical sciences, pharmacy, medicine, civil and mechanical engineering, electrical technology, and history of American science; recipients chosen on the basis of proposed research.
Restrictions: Applicants must have completed all preliminary coursework and exams for degree.
$ Given: An unspecified number of fellowships are awarded annually; each with $14,000 stipend.
Application Information: Write for details.
Deadline: January 15.
Contact: Program Assistant.

**Smithsonian Institution
Libraries**
NHB 24
Washington, DC 20560-0154
(202) 357-2240
FAX (202) 786-2866

Description: Grants for doctoral candidates, postdoctoral scholars, and professionals studying the history of science and technology, to support one to three months of research/study at Dibner Library of the History of Science and Technology and other libraries of the Smithsonian.
Restrictions: N/A
$ Given: An unspecified number of grants awarded annually; each with $1,500/month stipend to cover expenses.
Application Information: Write for details.
Deadline: December 1.

**Social Science Research
Council
MacArthur Foundation
Fellowships on International
Peace and Security in a
Changing World**
www.ssrc.org

Description: Fellowship support for up to two years of research in the setting and nation of the recipient's choice; funding made available to doctoral candidates at dissertation level, postdoctoral scholars, and professionals studying international peace and security (in disciplines of humanities, social sciences, physical sciences, and natural sciences); recipients chosen on the basis of proposed research.
Restrictions: Open to all nationalities.
$ Given: N/A.
Application Information: Write for details.
Deadline: March 5.
Contact: Jessica Olsen.

**Society of Exploration
Geophysicists
SEG Foundation Scholarship
Program**
P.O. Box 702740
Tulsa, OK 74170
(918) 493-3516
www.seg.org

Description: One-year scholarships for undergraduate and graduate students in geophysics; recipients chosen on the basis of academic achievement and commitment to career in exploration geophysics.
Restrictions: N/A.
$ Given: An unspecified number of scholarships awarded annually; each for $500–$10,000; average grant is $1,200; renewable.
Application Information: Write for details.
Deadline: March 1.

**Paul and Daisy Soros
Fellowships for New
Americans**
400 West 59th Street
New York, NY 10019
(212) 547-6926
FAX (212) 548-4623
www.pdsoros.org

Description: Fellowships for up to two years of graduate study in the United States in any professional field or scholarly discipline in the Arts, Humanities, Social Sciences, and Sciences. Recipients chosen on the basis of the relevance of graduate school to their long-term career goals, their potential for enhancing their contributions to society, academic achievement, creativity, originality, and initiative.

Restrictions: Limited to applicants under 30 years of age. Applicants must either be a resident alien (holding a Green Card), naturalized as a U.S. citizen, or the child of two parents who are both naturalized citizens.
$ Given: Thirty fellowships awarded annually, each with a maintenance grant of $20,000 and a tuition grant of one-half the tuition costs of the graduate program.
Application Information: Write for details.
Deadline: November 30.

Southern Illinois University at Carbondale
Minority Doctoral Fellowships in Science and Engineering
Graduate School
Woody Hall, B-114
Carbondale, IL 62901
(618) 536-7791
www.sin.edu

Description: Three-year fellowships for doctoral candidates in the life sciences, physical sciences, and engineering; recipients chosen on the basis of GRE or other national standardized test scores.
Restrictions: Limited to minority group applicants; applicants of Mexican or Puerto Rican descent preferred; United States citizenship required.
$ Given: An unspecified number of fellowships awarded annually; each for $15,000/year plus full tuition and fees (for three years).
Application Information: Write for details.
Deadline: February 1.
Contact: Jane Meuth.

Southern Illinois University at Carbondale Minority Graduate Incentive Program
Woody Hall, B-114
Carbondale, IL 62901
(618) 453-4558
(618) 536-7791
www.imgip.siu.edu

Description: Fellowships for doctoral candidates in the life sciences, physical sciences, engineering, and mathematics.
Restrictions: U.S. citizenship or permanent resident status required. Limited to African American, Hispanic and Native American applicants. Must have been accepted to a doctoral program at one of the participating Illinois-based universities in fields where there is severe underrepresentation in their field.
$ Given: An unspecified number of fellowships awarded annually; each with a stipend of $13,500 plus full tuition and fees, and annual allowance of $1,500 for books, supplies, equipment, and travel, for a maximum of three years.
Application Information: Write for details.
Deadline: February 1.
Contact: Jane Meuth.

**U.S. Department of Energy
Office of Biological and
Environmental Research
Alexander Hollaender
Distinguished Postdoctoral
Fellowship Program**
Krell Institute
P.O. Box 511
Ames, IA 50010-9976
(515) 233-6867

Description: One-year fellowships for postdoctoral
study tenable at DOE laboratories for the study of life,
biomedical and environmental sciences, and other supporting scientific disciplines. Recipients chosen on the
basis of academic achievement, recommendations, scientific interests, compatibility of applicant's background and
interests with needs of host research laboratory.
Restrictions: U.S. citizenship or permanent resident status required. Must have received doctoral degree in appropriate discipline.
$ Given: An unspecified number of fellowships awarded
annually; each with a stipend of $37,500 for the first year
and $40,500 for the second year. Inbound travel and mov-
ing expenses up to $2,500 reimbursed. For one year,
renewable for second year.
Application Information: Write for details.
Deadline: January 27.

Engineering and Applied Sciences

American Association for the Advancement of Science Mass Media Science and Engineering Fellows Program
1333 H Street, N.W.
Washington, DC 20005
(202) 326-6760
www.aas.org

Description: Ten-week summer fellowships for science graduate students to work as journalists (print, radio, or television and internet sites) to increase their understanding of the news media; available to students at any graduate and postgraduate level of study in family policy, child and family development, physical sciences, and the natural and social sciences, as well as engineering; recipients chosen on the basis of academic achievement and demonstrated commitment of conveying to the public a better understanding and appreciation of science and technology.
Restrictions: No funding to non-technical applicants; United States citizenship required; no concurrent funding allowed.
$ Given: Twenty-five to thirty fellowships awarded annually; weekly living stipend for ten weeks plus travel costs.
Application Information: Write for details and application form; minorities and individuals with disabilities encouraged to apply.
Deadline: January 15.
Contact: Katrina Malloy, Program Manager.

American Association of University Women Educational Foundation AAUW Selected Professions Fellowships
1111 Sixteenth Street
Washington, DC 20036
(319) 337-1716
www.aauw.org

Description: Fellowships for graduate students entering their final year of study in fields with traditionally low female representation, including architecture, business administration, computer science, dentistry, engineering, law, mathematics/statistics, medicine, and veterinary medicine; recipients chosen on the basis of academic achievement; tenable for full-time study at accredited United States institutions.
Restrictions: Limited to women who are members of minority groups in final year of study in law, medicine, or business; United States citizenship or permanent resident status required.
$ Given: Twenty-five fellowships of $5,000–$12,000 each are awarded annually.
Application Information: Application forms available August 1 through December 20.
Deadlines: January 10 postmark deadline–November 15 for engineering.

**American Association of
University Women
Educational Foundation
AAUW Selected Professions
Program Dissertation
Fellowships in Engineering**
1111 Sixteenth Street
Washington, DC 20036
(319) 337-1716
www.aauw.org

Description: Fellowships for doctoral candidates in engineering; to support dissertation work.
Restrictions: Limited to women applicants; applicants must have completed all coursework and exams for Ph.D.; United States citizenship or permanent resident status required.
$ Given: An unspecified number of fellowships awarded annually.
Application Information: Application forms available August 1 through December 20.
Deadline: N/A.
Contact: Selected Professions Fellowship Program.

**American Indian Graduate
Center
Native American Graduate
Student Fellowships**
4520 Montgomery Boulevard, N.E.
Suite 1-B
Albuquerque, NM 87109
(505) 881-4584
www.aigc.com

Description: Fellowships for full-time graduate study in all fields; recipients chosen on the basis of financial need academic achievement, and desire to perform community service after graduation; preference for graduate studies in health, law, education, natural resources, and engineering.
Restrictions: Applicants must have 1/4 or more Indian blood from federally recognized Alaskan Native or Native American tribe; United States citizenship required.
$ Given: An unspecified number of fellowships awarded annually; each for $4,000–$6,000 renewable per year, average award $4,000.
Application Information: Write for details. One time, non-refundable $15 fee.
Deadline: June 2.
Contact: Oran LaPointe, Executive Director.

**American Philosophical
Society Library
Mellon Resident Research
Fellowships**
104 South Fifth Street
Philadelphia, PA 19106-3386
(215) 440-3400
www.amphilsoc.org

Description: One- to three-month residential fellowships for doctoral candidates at dissertation level and postdoctoral scholars studying the history of American science and technology, its European roots, and its relation to American history and culture; tenable at the Society Library for short-term research using the library's collections.
Restrictions: United States citizenship required.
$ Given: An unspecified number of fellowships awarded annually; each for $1,900/month; tenable at Society for one to three months.
Application Information: Write for details.
Deadline: March 1.
Contact: Associate Librarian for Research Programs.

American Society for Engineering Education Helen Carr Minority Fellowships
1818 North Street, N.W.
Suite 600
Washington, DC 20036
(202) 331-3525
www.asee.org

Description: One-year fellowships for doctoral candidates in engineering at the following schools: Hampton University, Morgan State University, Howard University, North Carolina A&T State University, Prairie View A&M University, Tennessee State University, Tuskegee University, and Southern University; recipients chosen on the basis of financial need.
Restrictions: Limited to African-American applicants only; applicants must intend to return to one of the historically black engineering colleges to teach; United States citizenship required.
$ Given: An unspecified number of fellowships awarded annually; each for up to $10,000/year; renewable.
Application Information: Write for details.
Deadlines: January 15 for fall, May 15 for following spring.

American Society for Engineering Education Natural Defense Science and Engineering Fellowships Office of Naval Research Graduate Fellowships
1818 North Street, N.W.
Suite 600
Washington, DC 20036
(202) 331-3525
www.asee.org/ndseq

Description: Thirty-six-month fellowships (tenable over four years) for college seniors in engineering, mathematics, and science to support graduate work toward Ph.D. beginning the following September; fellowship includes summer work at Department of Defense Laboratories in freshman or sophomore year; relevant disciplines include biology/biomedical sciences, oceanography, mathematics, computer science, electrical engineering, material science, cognitive and neural sciences, naval architecture and ocean engineering, physics, chemistry, and aerospace/mechanical engineering; recipients chosen on the basis of academic achievement.
Restrictions: United States citizenship required.
$ Given: Up to 150 fellowships awarded annually; each for $18,500 for the first twelve months, $19,500 for the second twelve months, and $20,500 for the third twelve.
Application Information: Write for details.
Deadline: January 14.
Contact: Projects Officer.

American Society of Heating, Refrigerating and Air Conditioning Engineers ASHRAE Graduate Student Grant-in-Aid Program
1791 Tullie Circle, N.E.
Atlanta, GA 30329
(404) 636-8400
www.ashrae.org

Description: Grants for full-time graduate students of technologies and environmental effects related to heating, refrigerating, and air-conditioning engineering.
Restrictions: N/A.
$ Given: Twelve to eighteen grants awarded annually; each for up to $7,500; non-renewable.
Application Information: Write for details.
Deadline: December 15.
Contact: Manager of Research.

American Water Works Association Academic Achievement Awards
6666 West Quincy Avenue
Denver, CO 80235
(303) 794-7711
www.awwa.org

Description: Awards for best master's theses and doctoral dissertations addressing potable water, in any discipline.
Restrictions: N/A.
$ Given: Four awards annually, 1st and 2nd in each category (thesis and dissertation); 1st place awards each $3,000; 2nd place awards each $1,500.
Application Information: Write for announcement and application form.
Deadline: October 1.
Contact: Scholarships Coordinator.

Association for Women in Science Educational Foundation AWIS Predoctoral Award
1522 K Street, N.W.
Suite 820
Washington, DC 20005
(202) 326-8490
or (800) 886-awis
FAX (202) 408-0742
www.awis.org

Description: Awards for doctoral candidates in life sciences, physical sciences, social sciences, engineering, mathematics, and behavioral sciences; recipients chosen on the basis of academic achievement and quality of proposed research.
Restrictions: Limited to women only; United States citizenship and enrollment in United States institution required.
$ Given: An unspecified number of grants of $1,000 each are awarded annually.
Application Information: Write for details.
Deadline: January 15.

AT&T Bell Laboratories Cooperative Research Fellowships for Minorities
600 Mountain Avenue
Murray Hill, NJ 07974
(201) 582-4822
www.att.com

Description: Fellowships for graduate study toward Ph.D. degree, for graduating college seniors with the potential to become professional research scientists or engineers; relevant disciplines include chemistry, communications science, computer science, engineering, information science, materials science, mathematics, operations research, physics, and statistics; fellowship tenure includes one summer of work at AT&T; recipients chosen on the basis of academic achievement and proposed research.
Restrictions: Limited to African-American, Hispanic, and Native American applicants only; GRE exam scores required; United States citizenship or permanent resident status required.
$ Given: An unspecified number of fellowships awarded annually; for approved conferences; each for $1,400/month for the first two years and for ten months in ensuing years plus tuition and fees and expenses.
Application Information: Write for details.
Deadline: January 15.
Contact: Fellowship Manager.

**AT&T Bell Laboratories
Graduate Research Program
for Women**
600 Mountain Avenue
Murray Hill, NJ 07974
www.att.com

Description: Fellowships and grants for graduate study toward Ph.D. degree, for graduating college seniors with the potential to become professional research scientists or engineers; relevant disciplines include chemistry, chemical engineering, communications science, computer science, electrical engineering, information science, materials science, mathematics, operations research, physics, and statistics; fellowship tenure includes summer work at AT&T; recipients chosen on the basis of academic achievement and proposed research.
Restrictions: Limited to women applicants only; applicants must be admitted for full-time study in approved doctoral program; United States citizenship or permanent resident status required.
$ Given: An unspecified number of fellowships awarded annually; fellowships and grants are renewable annually.
Application Information: Application forms required, available on-line.
Deadline: January 15.
Contact: Fellowship or University Relations.

**AT&T Bell Laboratories
Ph.D. Scholarship Program**
600 Mountain Avenue
Murray Hill, NJ 07974
www.att.com

Description: Fellowships for doctoral candidates in the fields of chemistry, communications science, manufactural engineering, electrical engineering, and materials science; recipients chosen on the basis of academic achievement and proposed research.
Restrictions: United States citizenship or permanent resident status required.
$ Given: An unspecified number of fellowships awarded annually; each for expenses and summer education/research expenses; $1,400/month stipend plus travel support for conferences.
Application Information: Applicants must be nominated by faculty member or department chair.
Deadline: January 15.
Contact: University Relations or Fellowship Administrator.

**Bunting Institute Science
Scholars Fellowship Program**
34 Concord Avenue
Cambridge, MA 02138
(617) 495-8136
www.radcliffe.edu/bunting

Description: Postdoctoral fellowships to support women scientists in any level in any of the following fields: astronomy, molecular and cellular biology, biochemistry, chemistry, cognitive and neural sciences, mathematics, computer science, electrical, aerospace, and mechanical engineering, materials science, naval architecture, ocean engineering, oceanography, physics, and geology.
Restrictions: U.S. citizenship required. Limited to women applicants only who have received their doctorate at least two years prior to application.

$ Given: Eight fellowships awarded annually, each in the amount of $31,300.
Application Information: Write for details.
Deadline: Early October.

Canada Council Killam
Research Fellowships
99 Metcalfe Street
P.O. Box 1047
Ottawa, Ontario
Canada K1P 5V8

Description: Fellowships for senior scholars (eight to twelve years beyond the Ph.D.) to support research in any of the following fields: humanities, social sciences, natural sciences, health sciences, engineering, and studies linking disciplines within those fields.
Restrictions: Canadian citizenship or landed immigrant resident status required.
$ Given: Fifteen to eighteen fellowships awarded annually, each in the amount $53,000.
Application Information: Write for details.
Deadline: June 30.

Center for the Advanced
Study in Behavioral Sciences
Postdoctoral Fellowships
202 Junipero Serra Blvd.
Sanford, CA 94305-6165
(650) 723-9626
www.stanford.edu/group/
CISAC

Description: Nine- to twelve-month postdoctoral fellowships to support research in any of the following fields: anthropology, art history, biology, classics, economics, education, history, law, linguistics, literature, mathematical and statistical specialties, medicine, musicology, philosophy, political science, psychiatry, psychology, and sociology. Tenable at the Center for Advanced Study in Behavioral Sciences.
Restrictions: None.
$ Given: Approximately fifty fellowships of varying amounts awarded annually.
Application Information: Write for details.
Deadline: Ongoing.

Winston Churchill
Foundation Scholarship
P.O. Box 1240
Gracie Station
New York, NY 10028
TEL/FAX (212) 879-3480
http://members.aol.com/
churchillf/

Description: One-year scholarship for graduate students in the fields of engineering, mathematics, and sciences to study for one year at Churchill College in Cambridge, England.
Restrictions: U.S. citizenship required. Limited to applicants between the ages of 19 and 26. Must hold a bachelor's degree.
$ Given: One scholarship awarded annually; covers tuition and fees at Churchill College, plus a living allowance of $5,000–$6,000 and an additional $500 for travel expenses.
Application Information: Write for details.
Deadline: N/A.

Dibner Institute for the History of Science and Technology
Senior Fellows and Postdoctoral Fellows Program
Dibner Building, MIT E56-100
38 Memorial Drive
Cambridge, MA 02139
(617) 253-6989

Description: Six-month- to one-year fellowships for senior-level and postdoctoral research at the Bundy Library and the libraries of the consortium universities.
Restrictions: Senior Fellows applicants should have advanced degrees in disciplines relevant to their research and show evidence of substantial scholarly achievement and professional experience. Postdoctoral applicants should have been awarded their Ph.D. within the previous five years. Must reside in Cambridge/Boston area during the term of the grant.
$ Given: Approximately twenty fellowships awarded annually; fellowships provide office space, support facilities, and full privileges of the Bundy Library and consortium libraries. Funds are available for housing, living expenses, and round-trip airfare for international fellows. Average stipend varies.
Application Information: Write for details.
Deadline: December 31.
Contact: Trudy Kontoff, Program Coordinator.

Electrical Women's Round Table, Inc.
Julia Kiene Fellowship
P.O. Box 292793
Nashville, TN 37229-2793
(615) 254-4479

Description: Fellowship for graduate students in the field of electrical engineering or physics.
Restrictions: Limited to women applicants only.
$ Given: One fellowship awarded annually for up to $1,000.
Application Information: Write for details.
Deadline: March.

Albert Einstein Distinguished Educator Fellowship Program
Triangle Coalition for Science and Technology Foundation
1201 New York Avenue, N.W., Suite 700
Washington, DC 20005
(202) 586-6549
(800) 582-0115

Description: Eight- to twelve-month fellowships for science, mathematics, or technology teachers to serve in professional staff positions in the U.S. Senate or House of Representatives, DOE, NASA, NSF, NIH, ED, or OSTP. Recipients chosen on the basis of their excellence in teaching science, mathematics, or technology, and experimental and innovative approach toward teaching, professional involvement and leadership, communication skills, and knowledge of national, state, and local policies that affect education.
Restrictions: U.S. citizenship required. Applicants must have a minimum of five years teaching experience.
$ Given: An unspecified number of fellowships awarded annually, each with a $4,500 monthly stipend, plus travel and moving expenses.
Application Information: Applications must be submitted online through the Department of Energy's Web page dedicated to the fellows program.
Deadline: February 25.
Contact: Peter Faletra or Cindy Musick.

Environmental Protection Agency STAR Graduate Fellowship Office of Exploratory Research
Room 3102, NEM
401 M Street
Washington, DC 20460
(202) 564-6923
www.epa.gov

Description: One- to three year fellowships for graduate students in the fields of engineering, sciences, social sciences, or mathematics doing environmentally-oriented research.
Restrictions: U.S. citizenship required or permanent resident status required.
$ Given: One fellowship awarded annually; with a $17,000 stipend, up to $12,000 tuition support, and up to $5,000 expense allowance. Renewable.
Application Information: Write for details.
Deadline: Early November.
Contact: Virginia Broadway, Graduate Fellowship Office.

Florida Education Fund McKnight Doctoral Fellowships
201 East Kennedy Blvd
Suite 1525
Tampa, FL 33602
www.fl-educ-fd.org

Description: Fellowships for graduate study at one of eleven participating doctoral-degree-granting universities in Florida in the fields of business, engineering, agriculture, biology, computer science, mathematics, physical science, and psychology, recipients chosen on the basis of academic achievement.
Restrictions: Limited to African-American applicants only; B.A./B.S. degree required; United States citizenship required.
$ Given: Twenty-five fellowships awarded annually; each for a maximum of five years of study, with an annual $11,000 stipend plus up to $5,000 in tuition and fees.
Application Information: Write for details.
Deadline: January 15.
Contact: President.

French Embassy Scientific Services
Chateaubriand Research Scholarships for the Exact Sciences, Engineering, and Medicine
Department of Science and Technology
4101 Reservoir Road, N.W.
Washington, DC 20007
(202) 944-6246
www.info.france-usa.org

Description: Six- to twelve-month research scholarships for doctoral candidates at dissertation level, as well as postdoctoral scholars, to conduct research in France at French universities, engineering schools, and private laboratories; language training sessions provided; relevant disciplines include biological and agricultural sciences, physical sciences and mathematics, engineering and applied sciences, medicine, nutrition, optometry and vision sciences, pharmacy and pharmaceutical sciences, and veterinary medicine and sciences; recipients chosen on the basis of proposed research.
Restrictions: Each applicant must be registered at United States university and already in contact with French host institution; United States citizenship required.
$ Given: Twenty to thirty scholarships awarded annually; each for F9,000 per month plus airfare and health insurance.

Application Information: Request application forms after September.
Deadline: January 31.
Contact: Anne Bartheleny.

Fannie and John Hertz Foundation
Fannie and John Hertz Foundation Graduate Fellowship Program
P.O. Box 5032
Livermore, CA 94551-5032
(925) 373-6329
www.hertz

Description: Fellowships to provide B.S./B.A. holders with support for academic study through graduate school in the applied physical sciences, including engineering, applied physics, mathematics, and chemistry; tenable at one of the twenty-six participating schools; recipients chosen on the basis of outstanding academic achievement (minimum 3.5 GPA in last two years of undergraduate work). Lower average acceptable with other outstanding qualifications.
Restrictions: Applicants must have completed at least two years of college-level physics and college-level math courses, plus one year of college-level chemistry; recipients must agree to respond in time of national emergency; United States citizenship required.
$ Given: An unspecified number of fellowships awarded annually; each for $25,000 tuition and fees.
Application Information: Write for details.
Deadline: November 5.
Contact: Hertz Foundation Treasurer.

Hertz Foundation
Graduate Fellowship Awards
P.O. Box 5032
Livermore, CA 94551-5032
(925) 373-6329
www.hertzfoundation.org

Description: Fellowships for graduate study in any discipline at one of several tenable schools. Recipients chosen on the basis of merit.
Restrictions: None.
$ Given: One fellowship awarded annually, annual stipend of $25,000 and tuition covered for a maximum tenure of five years.
Application Information: Write for details.
Deadline: N/A.

Hughes Aircraft Company
Doctoral Fellowships
7200 Hughes Terrace
Los Angeles, CA 90045
(213) 568-6711
www.hughes.com

Description: Fellowships for doctoral candidates and master's degree holders in aerospace, electrical/mechanical/system engineering, computer science, physics, and mathematics; work-study and full-study programs offered, with work-study involving twenty to thirty-six hours/week employment at Hughes facility; participation in both programs includes initial full-time summer (ten to thirteen weeks) employment at Hughes facility; most fellows attend UCLA, USC, CalTech, MIT, Cornell, Purdue, Stanford, Georgia Tech, University of Arizona, University of Illinois, etc.; recipients chosen on the basis of academic achievement (minimum 3.0 GPA).
Restrictions: United States citizenship and good health required.

$ Given: An unspecified number of fellowships awarded annually; each for tuition, stipend, academic expenses, relocation allowance, and salary/benefits during employment.

Application Information: Write for application packet; include university, field of interest, year of graduation, and GPA in query letter.

Deadline: February 1.

Contact: Kimberly J. Everett, Educational Coordinator.

Hughes Aircraft Company Engineering Fellowships
7200 Hughes Terrace
Los Angeles, CA 90045
(213) 568-6711
www.hughes.com

Description: Fellowships for doctoral candidates and master's degree holders aerospace or electrical/mechanical/systems engineering; work-study and full-study programs offered, with work-study involving twenty to thirty-six hours/week employment at Hughes facility (most fellows attend southern California schools as work-study participants); participation in both programs includes initial full-time summer (ten to thirteen weeks) employment at Hughes facility; most fellows attend UCLA, USC, CalTech, MIT, Cornell, Purdue, Stanford, Georgia Tech, University of Arizona, University of Illinois, etc.; recipients chosen on the basis of academic achievement (minimum 3.0 GPA).

Restrictions: United States citizenship and good health required.

$ Given: An unspecified number of fellowships awarded annually; each for tuition, stipend, academic expenses, relocation allowance, and salary/benefits during employment.

Application Information: Write for application packet; include university, field of interest, year of graduation, and GPA in query letter.

Deadline: March 15.

Contact: Kimberly J. Everett, Educational Coordinator.

Hughes Aircraft Company Master of Science Fellowships
7200 Hughes Terrace
Los Angeles, CA 90045
(213) 568-6711
www.hughes.com

Description: Fellowships for B.S. degree holders in aerospace, physics, computer science, mathematics, and electrical/mechanical/systems engineering; work-study and full-study programs offered, with work-study involving twenty to thirty-six hours/week employment at Hughes facility (80% of participants are work-study and attend southern California schools); participation in both programs includes initial full-time summer (ten to thirteen weeks) employment at Hughes facility; most fellows attend UCLA, USC, CalTech, MIT, Cornell, Purdue, Stanford, Georgia Tech, University of Arizona, University of Illinois, etc.; recipients chosen on the basis of academic achievement (minimum 3.0 GPA).

Restrictions: Applicants must have B.S. degree from institution accredited by the Accrediting Board of

Engineering Technology; United States citizenship and good health required.

$ Given: An unspecified number of fellowships awarded annually; each for tuition, stipend, academic expenses, relocation allowance, and salary/benefits during employment.

Application Information: Write for application packet; include university, field of interest, year of graduation, and GPA in query letter.

Deadline: March 15.

Contact: Kimberly J. Everett, Educational Coordinator.

IBM Corporation IBM Graduate Fellowships Divisional University Relations
Room 22-130
T. J. Watson Research Center
P.O. Box 218
Yorktown Heights, NY 10598
(914) 945-3000

Description: Fellowships for graduate students in the fields of the physical sciences, mathematics, material sciences, mechanical engineering, electrical engineering, and computer science.

Restrictions: None.

$ Given: An unspecified number of fellowships awarded annually, each for $12,000 plus tuition for one year.

Application Information: Write for details.

Deadline: February 15.

Institute of International Education Colombian Government Study and Research Grants
U.S. Student Programs Division
809 United Nations Plaza
New York, NY 10017-3580
(212) 984-5330
www.iie.org/fulbright

Description: Grants for B.S./B.A. holders to pursue up to two years of study/research at Colombian universities; relevant disciplines include agriculture, biology, business administration, economics, chemistry, engineering, education, health services administration, geography, history, Latin American literature, law, linguistics, political science, physics, regulatory development, public health, and remote sensing interpretation.

Restrictions: United States citizenship required.

$ Given: An unspecified number of grants awarded annually; each for modest monthly stipend, plus tuition and fees, health insurance, book/materials allowance, and one-way return airfare upon completion of study.

Application Information: Write for details.

Deadline: October 23.

Institute of International Education Study and Research Grants for U.S. Citizens
U.S. Student Programs Division
809 United Nations Plaza
New York, NY 10017-3580
(212) 984-5330
www.iie.org/fulbright

Description: Grants to support study and research in all fields, as well as professional training in the creative and performing arts; tenable at institutions of higher learning outside of the United States for one year; list of participating countries in any given year may be obtained from IIE.

Restrictions: Open to United States citizens with B.A. or equivalent; acceptable plan of study and proficiency in host country's language required.

$ Given: A variable number of grants awarded annually; covers international transportation, language or orienta-

tion course (where appropriate), tuition, book and mainte-
nance allowances, and health and accident insurance.
Application Information: If currently enrolled in a col-
lege or university, apply to the campus Fulbright Program
Advisor; applications also available from IIE.
Deadline: October 23.

Kosciuszko Foundation
15 East 65th Street
New York, NY 10021-6595
(212) 734-2130
FAX (212) 628-4552
www.kosciuszkofoundation.
org

Description: One-year scholarships to U.S. citizens of
Polish descent for graduate studies in any field at colleges
and universities in the United States and to Americans of
non-Polish descent whose studies at American universities
are primarily focused on Polish subjects. Recipients chosen on the basis of academic achievement and financial
need.
Restrictions: Must be enrolled in a graduate program at
a U.S. university. Applicants must be U.S. citizens or of
Polish descent.
$ Given: An unspecified number of scholarships of
$1,000–$5,000 each are awarded annually.
Deadline: January 16.
Contact: Grants office.

Marshall Scholarships
Marshall Aid
Commemorating Commission
Association of Commonwealth
Universities
36 Gordon Square
London WC1HOPF
(44) 1713878572
www.aca.ac.uk/marshall

Description: Two- to three-year scholarships for undergraduate or graduate level study at any university in the
United Kingdom, in any discipline leading to the award of
a British university degree.
Restrictions: U.S. citizenship required; limited to graduates of accredited four-year colleges and universities in
the United States with at least a 3.75 GPA since freshman
year.
$ Given: Up to forty scholarships awarded annually;
each worth approximately $25,000 per year and compris-
ing a personal allowance for cost of living and residence,
tuition fees, books, travel in connection with studies, and
to and from the United States.
Application Information: Write for details. Application
forms also available from colleges and universities in the
United States, British consulates in Atlanta, Boston,
Chicago, Houston, and San Francisco, the British Council
in Washington, DC, British Information Services in New
York.
Deadline: N/A.

**Monticello College
Foundation and Washington
University
Spencer T. Olin Fellowships
for Women in Graduate Study
Graduate Schools of Arts and
Sciences**
Washington University
Campus Box 1187
One Brookings Drive
St. Louis, MO 63130-4899
(314) 935-6848

Description: Fellowships for graduate students to prepare for careers in higher education and professions in the
fields of biological and biomedical sciences, humanities,
physical sciences and mathematics, social and behavioral
sciences, architecture, business administration, engineering, fine arts, law, medicine, and social work. Tenable at
Washington University.
Restrictions: Limited to women applicants only.
$ Given: An unspecified number of fellowships awarded
annually, each ranging from $20,000 to $33,000.
Application Information: Write for details.
Deadline: February 1.

**National Air and Space
Museum
Guggenheim Fellowships**
Smithsonian Institution
Washington, DC 20560-0312
(202) 357-1529
www.nasm.edu

Description: Twelve-month to three-year residential fellowships for doctoral candidates at dissertation level, as
well as recent Ph.D.s (within past seven years), for histori-
cal/scientific research an aviation and space; relevant disciplines include history, aerospace, and engineering.
Restrictions: N/A.
$ Given: An unspecified number of fellowships awarded
annually; $15,000 predoctoral stipend, $27,000 postdoctoral stipend.
Application Information: Write for details.
Deadline: January 15.
Contact: Fellowship Coordinator.

**National Air and Space
Museum
Verville Fellowships**
Smithsonian Institution
Washington, DC 20560-0312
(202) 357-1529
www.nasm.edu

Description: Nine- to twelve-month fellowships for
analysis of major developments, trends, and accomplishments in history of aviation/space studies; relevant disciplines include history, aerospace, and engineering.
Restrictions: Applicants must demonstrate skills in
research and writing.
$ Given: An unspecified number of fellowships for
$35,000 each are awarded annually.
Application Information: Write for details.
Deadline: January 15.
Contact: Fellowship Coordinator.

**National Association of
Purchasing Management
Doctoral Dissertation Grant**
Center for Advanced
Purchasing Studies
2055 East Centennial Circle
P.O. Box 22160
Tempe, AZ 85285-2160
(602) 752-2277

Description: Grants for doctoral candidates to conduct
dissertation research on purchasing and materials management; open to individuals seeking Ph.D. in business,
economics, industrial engineering, management, and purchasing logistics; tenable at accredited United States institutions; recipients chosen on the basis of proposed
research; preference for applicants planning careers in
college teaching and research.
Restrictions: Must be enrolled in an accredited
institution.

$ Given: Four grants awarded annually; each for $10,000 per academic year, paid in three equal installments.
Application Information: Write for details.
Deadline: January 31.
Contact: Assistant Director.

National Consortium for Graduate Degrees for Minorities in Engineering and Science, Inc.
Graduate Engineering for Minorities (GEM) Fellowships
P.O. Box 537
Notre Dame, IN 46556
(219) 287-1097

Description: Fellowships for master's candidates in engineering, physical and life sciences; recipients chosen on the basis of academic achievement.
Restrictions: Limited to African-American, Native American, Mexican-American, and Puerto Rican, or other Hispanic American applicants only; United States citizenship required.
$ Given: Two hundred and twenty-five master's, thirty Ph.D. (English) and thirty Ph.D. (science) fellowships awarded annually; each for tuition and fees at member institution plus $6,000/year living stipend. Ph.D.s receive $14,400 and an initial $5,500 for the first year.
Application Information: Write for details.
Deadline: December 1.

National Italian American Foundation Scholarship Program
Michael and Francesca Marinelli Scholarships
1860 19th Street, N.W.
Washington, DC 20009
www.niaf.org

Description: Scholarships for graduate students in the DC area and for undergraduates at Nova University in Florida; relevant disciplines limited to science and business; recipients chosen on the basis of academic achievement and financial need.
Restrictions: Applicants must be of Italian descent.
$ Given: Two scholarships of $2,000 each are awarded annually.
Application Information: Essay required.
Deadline: May 31.
Contact: Education Director.

National Research Council Postdoctoral and Senior Research Associateship Awards
2101 Constitution Avenue, N.W.
Washington, DC 20418
FAX (202) 334-2759
www.nas.edu/rap/welcome/html

Description: Twelve-month awards for recent Ph.D. or M.D. graduates for independent research in chemistry, earth and atmospheric sciences, engineering, mathematics, and applied sciences, life and medical sciences, space and planetary sciences, and physical sciences. Tenable at over 100 laboratories representing nearly all U.S. government agencies with research facilities.
Restrictions: None.
$ Given: Three hundred and fifty awards for $30,000 to $47,000 depending upon sponsoring laboratory. Renewable for up to three years. Support for relocation and professional travel.
Application Information: Write for details.
Deadlines: January 15, April 15, August 15.

National Research Council NRC/Ford Predoctoral and Dissertation Fellowships for Minorities
Fellowships Office
2101 Constitution Avenue, N.W.
Washington, DC 20418
(202) 334-2872

Description: Fellowships for graduate students enrolled or planning to enroll in a Ph.D. or Sc.D. program in the humanities, social sciences, biological and agricultural sciences, physical sciences and mathematics, and engineering and applied sciences; recipients chosen on the basis of academic achievement and proposed research.
Restrictions: Limited to members of the following groups: Alaskan natives, African Americans, Mexican Americans, Native Pacific Islanders, Puerto Ricans. GRE test scores required. United States citizenship or legal residency required.
$ Given: Approximately fifty fellowships awarded; $14,000 for fellow, $7,500 for institution; twenty dissertation fellowships available for $18,000. Duration of support is three years to be used over a five-year period plus travel and living expenses for three Ford conferences.
Application Information: Write for details.
Deadline: November 12 for information form, January 7 for supporting materials.

NASA Graduate Student Researchers Program
NASA Headquarters
600 Independence Avenue, S.W.
Washington, DC 20546
(202) 358-1531
(202) 358-1517
www.nasa.gov

Description: One-year scholarships for graduate students in fields related to NASA research areas, specifically engineering, science, and mathematics.
Restrictions: U.S. citizenship required.
$ Given: An unspecified number of scholarships awarded annually, each with a $22,000 stipend, plus department component. Renewable for total of three years.
Application Information: Write for details.
Deadline: February 1.
Contact: Ahmad Nurriddin.

National Science Foundation Graduate Research Fellowship Program
Oak Ridge Associated Universities
P.O. Box 3010
Oak Ridge, TN 37831-3010
(865) 241-4300

Description: Three-year fellowships for graduate study leading to research-based master's or doctoral degrees in the mathematical, physical, biological, engineering, and behavioral and social sciences.
Restrictions: U.S. citizenship or permanent resident status required.
$ Given: An unspecified number of fellowships awarded annually; each with an annual stipend of $15,000, and a cost-of-education allowance of $10,500 per tenure year.
Application Information: Write for details.
Deadline: November 4.

National Sciences and Engineering Research Council of Canada
NSERC Postgraduate Scholarships
350 Albert Street
Ottawa, Ontario K1A 1H5
(613) 995-5521
FAX (613) 992-5337
www.nserv.ca

Description: Up to twenty-four-month scholarships for highly qualified science or engineering students from a university approved by NSERC. Canadian citizenship or permanent resident status required.
$ Given: An unspecified number of scholarships awarded annually; each with stipend of $13,800 per year toward tuition.
Application Information: Write for details.
Deadline: December 1.
Contact: Information Officer.

National Security Education Program
Graduate International Fellowships
Academy for Educational Development
1825 Connecticut Avenue
Washington, DC 20009-5721
(800) 498-9360
www.aed.org/nsep

Description: One- to six-semester (twenty-four-month) fellowships for graduate students to pursue specialization in area and language study in a diverse list of fields of study, specifically business, economics, history, international affairs, law, applied sciences and engineering, health and biomedical sciences, political science, and other social sciences, which are connected to U.S. national security.
Restrictions: U.S. citizenship required. Application to or enrollment in a graduate program in an accredited U.S. college or university located within the United States. Must be willing to enter into service agreement to seek employment with an agency or office of the federal government involved in national security affairs. Recipients chosen on the basis of the relationship of the applicant's proposed study to U.S. national security and how the applicant proposes to use knowledge and experience gained from NSEP support to contribute to U.S. national security.
$ Given: An unspecified number of fellowships awarded annually; each for $2,000 per semester for language or area studies coursework at your home university and $10,000 per semester for two semesters of overseas study program expenses.
Application Information: Writes for details.
Deadline: January 15.

Natural Sciences and Engineering Research Council of Canada
NSERC Postgraduate Scholarships in Science Librarianship and Documentation
200 Kent Street
Ottawa, Ontario K1A 1H5
Canada
(613) 992-8203
(613) 995-5521
www.nserc.ca

Description: One-year scholarships for first- and second-year study toward M.L.S. degree in library science; recipients chosen on the basis of academic achievement, commitment to field, and relevant experience.
Restrictions: Applicants must have B.S. degree in science or engineering; Canadian citizenship or permanent resident status required.
$ Given: A few scholarships awarded annually; each for $13,500 Canadian plus travel allowance.
Application Information: Write for details.
Deadline: December 1.
Contact: Nadine Bohan; Information Officer.

Oak Ridge Institute for Science and Education
Nuclear Engineering and Health Physics Fellowships
P.O. Box 2008
Oak Ridge, TN 37831-0117
www.ornl.gov

Description: One-year fellowship for graduate students studying nuclear science and engineering or health physics at participating Oak Ridge Associated Universities with practicum at various DOE facilities; recipients chosen on the basis of academic achievement, career goals, and interests.
Restrictions: N/A.
$ Given: An unspecified number of fellowships awarded annually; each with $14,400 stipend, plus $300/month during practicum, and travel, tuition, and fees; renewable for up to four years.
Application Information: Write for details.
Deadline: January 25.

President's Commission on White House Fellowships
White House Fellowships
712 Jackson Place, N.W.
Washington, DC 20503
(202) 395-4522

Description: Twelve-month appointments as special assistants to the Vice President, Cabinet members, and the Presidential staff; fellowships include participation in educational program; positions available for students in public affairs, education, the sciences, business, and the professions; recipients chosen on the basis of leadership qualities, commitment to community service, and career/academic achievement.
Restrictions: Limited to young adults, ages 30–39; civilian federal employees are ineligible, recipients may not hold official state or local office while serving as White House fellows; United States citizenship required.
$ Given: Eleven to nineteen wage-earning fellowships for up to a maximum of $65,000 are awarded annually.
Application Information: Write for details.
Deadline: February 1.

Rockefeller University
Rockefeller Archive Center
Research Grants
15 Dayton Avenue
Pocantico Hills
North Tarrytown, NY
10591-1598
(914) 631-4505
www.rockefeller.edu/archives.
ctr

Description: Residential research fellowships for gradu-ate students and postdoctoral scholars pursuing research using Archive Center resources; relevant disciplines includ-ing philanthropy, education, science, medicine, black his-tory, agriculture, labor, social welfare, social sciences, politics, religion, population, economic development, and the arts; recipients chosen on the basis of proposed research and necessity of using Archive Center resources.
Restrictions: N/A.
$ Given: An unspecified number of grants awarded annually; each for up to $2,500 for travel, lodging, and research expenses.
Application Information: Write for details.
Deadline: November 30.
Contact: Director.

Sigma Xi, The Scientific
Research Society
Grants-in-Aid of Research
P.O. Box 13975
Research Triangle Park, NC
27709
(800) 243-6534 or
(919) 549-4691

Description: Research grants to graduate and under-graduate students in science and engineering, to support research projects; recipients chosen on the basis of pro-posed research.
Restrictions: Open to all nationalities.
$ Given: An unspecified number of grants awarded annually; each for up to $1,000 (average $500).
Application Information: Application forms required.
Deadlines: February 1, May 1, and November 1.
Contact: Committee on Grants-in-Aid of Research.

Smithsonian Institution
Predoctoral Research
Fellowships in Astrophysics
and Related Topics
Smithsonian Astrophysical
Observatory
60 Garden Street
Mail Stop 47
Cambridge, MA 02138
(617) 495-7103
www.si.edu/research+study/

Description: One-year fellowships for doctoral candi-dates in astrophysics and related topics to conduct inde-pendent dissertation research, working with Smithsonian staff and using Smithsonian resources; recipients chosen on the basis of academic achievement and proposed research.
Restrictions: Applicants must have completed all pre-liminary coursework and examinations.
$ Given: An unspecified number of fellowships awarded annually; each for $14,000/year; renewable for one year.
Application Information: Write for details.
Deadline: April 15.
Contact: Secretary, Predoctoral Fellowship Committee.

Smithsonian Institution Predoctoral Research Fellowships in the History of Science and Technology
Office of Fellowships and Grants
955 L'Enfant Plaza
Suite 7300
Washington, DC 20560
(202) 287-3271
www.si.edu/research+study/

Description: Three- to twelve-month residential fellowships for doctoral candidates at dissertation level and postdoctoral students in the history of science and technology, to pursue independent research using the Smithsonian's collections, resources, and staff expertise; relevant disciplines include history of mathematics, physical sciences, pharmacy, medicine, civil and mechanical engineering, electrical technology, and history of American science; recipients chosen on the basis of proposed research.
Restrictions: Applicants must have completed all preliminary coursework and exams for degree.
$ Given: An unspecified number of fellowships are awarded annually; each with $14,000 stipend.
Application Information: Write for details.
Deadline: January 15.
Contact: Program Assistant.

Southern Illinois University at Carbondale Minority Doctoral Fellowships in Science and Engineering
Graduate School
Woody Hall, B-114
Carbondale, IL 62901
(618) 536-7791
www.sin.edu

Description: Three-year fellowships for doctoral candidates in the life sciences, physical sciences, and engineering; recipients chosen on the basis of GRE or other national standardized test scores.
Restrictions: Limited to minority group applicants; applicants of Mexican or Puerto Rican descent preferred; United States citizenship required.
$ Given: An unspecified number of fellowships awarded annually; each for $15,000/year plus full tuition and fees (for three years).
Application Information: Write for details.
Deadline: February 1.
Contact: Jane Meuth.

Southern Illinois University at Carbondale Minority Graduate Incentive Program
Woody Hall, B-114
Carbondale, IL 62901
(618) 453-4558
(618) 536-7791
www.imgip.siu.edu

Description: Fellowships for doctoral candidates in the life sciences, physical sciences, engineering, and mathematics.
Restrictions: U.S. citizenship or permanent resident status required. Limited to African American, Hispanic and Native American applicants. Must have been accepted to a doctoral program at one of the participating Illinois-based universities in fields where there is severe underrepresentation in their field.
$ Given: An unspecified number of fellowships awarded annually; each with a stipend of $13,500 plus full tuition and fees, and annual allowance of $1,500 for book, supplies, equipment, and travel, for a maximum of three years.
Application Information: Write for details.
Deadline: February 1.
Contact: Jane Meuth.

**Paul and Daisy Soros
Fellowships for New
Americans**
400 West 59th Street
New York, NY 10019
(212) 547-6926
FAX (212) 548-4623
www.pdsoros.org

Description: Fellowships for up to two years of graduate study in the United States in any professional field or
scholarly discipline in the arts, humanities, social sciences, and sciences. Recipients chosen on the basis of the
relevance of graduate school to their long-term career
goals, their potential for enhancing their contributions to
society, academic achievement, creativity, originality, and
initiative.
Restrictions: Limited to applicants under 30 years of
age. Applicants must either be a resident alien (holding a
Green Card), naturalized as a U.S. citizen, or the child of
two parents who are both naturalized citizens.
$ Given: Thirty fellowships awarded annually, each with
a maintenance grant of $20,000 and a tuition grant of one-
half the tuition costs of the graduate program.
Application Information: Write for details.
Deadline: November 30.

**Transportation Research
Board
Graduate Research Award
Program on Public-Sector
Aviation Issues**
National Research Council
2101 Constitution Avenue,
N.W.
Washington, DC 20418
(202) 334-3206
www.nas.edu/trb

Description: Awards for gifted graduate students for
developing research papers on public sector aviation
issues; final selection by expert panel; intended to attract
students to policy and management positions.
Restrictions: N/A.
$ Given: Up to five awards made annually; each for
$6,000.
Application Information: Write for details.
Deadline: October 25.
Contact: Joseph Breen, Research Award Program, Air
Transport Section.

**Zonta International
Foundation
Amelia Earhart Fellowship
Awards**
557 West Randolph Street
Chicago, IL 60661-2206
(312) 930-5848
www.zonta.org

Description: Fellowships for women pursuing graduate
degrees in aerospace-related sciences and aerospace-
related engineering. Tenable at any university. Recipients
chosen on the basis of academic achievement, the relevance of applicant's research to aerospace-related sciences
or engineering, and career goals as they relate to advancing knowledge in these fields.
Restrictions: Limited to women applicants who have
completed one year of graduate school only.
$ Given: One fellowship awarded annually for $6,000.
Application Information: Write for details.
Deadline: November 1.

**Zonta International
Foundation
Michael J. Freeman
Scholarships for Irish Women**
557 West Randolph Street
Chicago, IL 60661-2206
(312) 930-5848
www.zonta.org

Description: Full-tuition scholarships to assist Irish women pursuing technical and scientific studies.
Restrictions: Limited to Irish women citizens only.
$ Given: An unspecified number of scholarships of varying amounts awarded annually.
Application Information: Write for details.
Deadline: N/A.

Business, Education, Health, and Law

Alcohol, Drug Abuse, and Mental Health Administration Predoctoral National Research Service Awards
5600 Fishers Lane
Rockville, MD 20857

Description: Predoctoral awards for students who are enrolled in an academic program which leads to a combined M.D./Ph.D. degree to pursue research as it relates to alcohol-derived, drug abuse, or mental health/mental illness and their basic processes, incidence and prevalence, etiology, description, diagnosis, and pathogenesis, treatment, development, assessment and evaluation, and prevention.
Restrictions: U.S. citizenship or permanent resident status required.
$ Given: An unspecified number of fellowships awarded annually, each with a stipend of $12,000.
Application Information: Write for details.
Deadline: September 10.

American Association for the Advancement of Science Mass Media Science and Engineering Fellows Program
1333 H Street, N.W.
Washington, DC 20005
(202) 326-6760
www.aas.org

Description: Ten-week summer fellowships for science graduate students to work as journalists (print, radio, or television and internet sites) to increase their understanding of the news media; available to students at any graduate level and postgraduate of study in family policy, child and family development, physical sciences, and the natural and social sciences, as well as engineering; recipients chosen on the basis of academic achievement and demonstrated commitment to conveying to the public a better understanding and appreciation of science and technology.
Restrictions: No funding to non-technical applicants; United States citizenship required; no concurrent funding allowed.
$ Given: Twenty-five to thirty fellowships awarded annually; weekly living stipend for ten weeks plus travel costs.
Application Information: Write for details and application form; minorities and individuals with disabilities encouraged to apply.
Deadline: January 15.
Contact: Katrina Malloy.

American Association of University Women Educational Foundation AAUW Selected Professions Fellowships
1111 Sixteenth Street
Washington, DC 20036
(319) 337-1716
www.aauw.org

Description: Fellowships for graduate students entering their final year of study in fields with traditionally low female representation, including architecture, business administration, computer science, dentistry, engineering, law, mathematics/statistics, medicine; recipients chosen on the basis of academic achievement; tenable for full-time study at accredited United States institutions.
Restrictions: Limited to women who are members of minority groups in final year of study in law, medicine, or business; United States citizenship or permanent resident status required.
$ Given: Twenty-five fellowships of $5,000–$12,000 each are awarded annually.
Application Information: Application forms available August 1 through December 20.
Deadline: January 10 postmark deadline, November 15 for engineering.

American Association of Women Dentists Colgate-Palmolive Award
401 N. Michigan Avenue
Chicago, IL 60611
(312) 280-9296

Description: Grants for dental school students, to support senior year of study; recipients chosen on the basis of financial need.
Restrictions: Limited to women dental students only.
$ Given: Ten awards made annually; each for $500.
Application Information: Ten dental schools participate annually; the ten schools are selected on a rotating basis; each school's dean chooses one student to receive the award.
Deadline: Varies.
Contact: Scholarship Director.

American Cancer Society Postdoctoral Fellowships
Research Department
1599 Clifton Road
Atlanta, GA 30329
(800) ACS-2345
www.cancer.org

Description: One- to three-year postdoctoral fellowships in the biomedical fields, as related to neoplasia.
Restrictions: U.S. citizenship or permanent resident status required.
$ Given: An unspecified number of fellowships awarded annually, each with an annual stipend ranging from $24,000 to $26,000.
Application Information: Write for details.
Deadlines: March 1 and October 1.

American Foundation for Pharmaceutical Education Graduate Fellowships
618 Somerset Street
P.O. Box 7126
North Plainfield, NJ 07060

Description: One-year graduate and postdoctoral fellowships to support research in the pharmaceutical sciences.
Restrictions: U.S. citizenship required.
$ Given: An unspecified number of fellowships awarded annually, each with a stipend ranging from $6,000 to $16,000.
Application Information: Write for details.
Deadline: March 1.

**American Dental Hygienists'
Association Institute for Oral
Health
ADHA Institute for Oral
Health Graduate Scholarships**
444 North Michigan Avenue
Suite 3400
Chicago, IL 60611
(312) 440-8900
www.adha.org

Description: Scholarships for full-time master's and doctoral candidates in dental hygiene studies; recipients chosen
on the basis of academic achievement (minimum 3.0 GPA
in dental hygiene curriculum) and financial need.
Restrictions: Applicants must be licensed dental
hygienists with at least B.S./B.A. degree; applicants must
be accepted by graduate program.
$ Given: Approximately twenty scholarships are
awarded annually; each for up to $1,500.
Application Information: Write for application packet.
Deadline: June 1.
Contact: Scholarship Director.

**American Dental Hygienists'
Association Institute for Oral
Health
ADHA Institute for Oral
Health Research Grants
Program**
444 North Michigan Avenue
Suite 3400
Chicago, IL 60611
(312) 440-8900
www.adha.org

Description: Research grants for dental hygienists pursuing associate, baccalaureate, master's or doctoral
degree, as well as for licensed dental hygienists, for conducting research related to dental hygiene.
Restrictions: Applicants must be licensed dental
hygienists or students pursing license; ADHA membership or student scholarship by ADHA member required.
$ Given: An unspecified number of scholarships are
awarded annually; each for $1,000–$5,000.
Application Information: Write for application packet.
Deadline: January 15.
Contact: Research Grants Program.

**American Foundation for
Aging Research AFAR Grants**
1414 Avenue of the Americas
New York, NY 10019
www.afar.org

Description: Grants for master's and doctoral candidates, to support biomedical or basic biological research
on aging or cancer.
Restrictions: Applicants must already be involved in
relevant research.
$ Given: Twenty-five grants awarded annually; up to
$50,000 for one to two years of research.
Application Information: Application must be submitted by United States university on behalf of student.
Deadline: December 15.
Contact: President.

**American Foundation for the
Blind
TSI/VTEK Scholarship**
11 Penn Plaza
Suite 300
New York, NY 10001
(212) 502-7661

Description: Scholarships for undergraduate and graduate
students studying rehabilitation and/or education of the
blind/visually impaired; tenable within the United States.
Restrictions: Limited to legally blind applicants; United
States citizenship required.
$ Given: An unspecified number of scholarships for
$1,000 each are awarded annually.
Application Information: Write for details.
Deadline: April 30.
Contact: Julie Tucker.

American Geophysical Union Horton Research Grant in Hydrology and Water Resources
2000 Florida Avenue, N.W.
Washington, DC 20009
(202) 462-6900
www.agu.org

Description: Grants for doctoral candidates, to support research projects in hydrology and water resources; relevant disciplines include physical/chemical/biological aspects of hydrology, as well as water resources policy sciences (economics, sociology, and law).
Restrictions: Membership in American Geophysical Union required.
$ Given: One or more grants awarded annually; each for $4,500–$9,500 plus travel allowance to ensure attendance at awards luncheon.
Application Information: Proposal must be signed by faculty advisor; application forms required.
Deadline: March 1.
Contact: Winetta Singhateh.

American Heart Association Postdoctoral Fellowships
Division of Research
Administration
7272 Greenville Avenue
Dallas, TX 75231-4596
(717) 393-0725

Description: Five-year postdoctoral fellowships to support research in the field of cardiovascular functions and disease, and stroke.
Restrictions: U.S. citizenship or permanent resident status required.
$ Given: A variable number of fellowships awarded annually, each in the amount of $45,000.
Application Information: Write for details.
Deadline: June 1.

American Indian Graduate Center
Native American Graduate Student Fellowships
4520 Montgomery Boulevard, N.E.
Suite 1-B
Albuquerque, NM 87109
(505) 881-4584
www.aigc.com

Description: Fellowships for full-time graduate study in all fields; recipients chosen on the basis of financial need, academic achievement, and desire to perform community service after graduation; preference for graduate studies in health, law, education, natural resources, and engineering.
Restrictions: Applicants must have 1/4 or more Indian blood from federally recognized Alaskan Native or Native American tribe; United States citizenship required.
$ Given: An unspecified number of fellowships awarded annually; each for $4,000–$6,000 renewable per year; average award $4,000; renewable.
Application Information: Write for details. One time, non-refundable $15 fee.
Deadline: June 2.
Contact: Oran LaPointe, Executive Director.

American Institute of Certified Public Accountants
AICPA Doctoral Fellowships
1211 Avenue of the Americas
New York, NY 10036-8775
(212) 596-6221
www.aicpa.org

Description: Fellowships for full-time students entering accredited doctoral degree programs in accounting.
Restrictions: Doctoral program must be accredited by the American Assembly of Collegiate Schools of Business; applicant must have CPA certificate; United States citizenship preferred.
$ Given: An unspecified number of fellowships awarded

annually; each for $5,000/year; renewable for up to three years.
Application Information: Request application forms from the Institute.
Deadline: April 1.
Contact: Leticia B. Romeo

American Institute of Certified Public Accountants John L. Carey Scholarships in Accounting
1211 Avenue of the Americas
New York, NY 10036-8775
(212) 596-6221
www.aicpa.org

Description: Scholarships for college liberal arts majors to study accounting on the graduate level; tenable at United States graduate schools.
Restrictions: Applicants must be college seniors who are liberal arts majors at Yale, University of Georgia, or University of Illinois; recipients must plan careers in accounting.
$ Given: An unspecified number of scholarships awarded annually; each for $5,000/year; renewable for second year.
Application Information: Request application forms from the Institute.
Deadline: April 1.

American Institute of Certified Public Accountants Minority Accounting Scholarships
1211 Avenue of the Americas
New York, NY 10036-8775
(212) 596-6223
www.aicpa.org

Description: Scholarships for undergraduate and graduate students majoring in accounting, recipients chosen on the basis of academic achievement.
Restrictions: Limited to minority group members only; United States citizenship or permanent resident status required.
$ Given: An unspecified number of scholarships awarded annually; varying amounts up to $5,000.
Application Information: Request application forms from the Institute.
Deadline: July 1.

American Institute of Certified Public Accountants Minority Scholarships
1211 Avenue of the Americas
New York, NY 10036-8775
(212) 596-6227
www.aicpa.org.

Description: Scholarships for full-time undergraduate and graduate students at accredited institutions pursuing degrees in accounting. Recipients chosen on the basis of financial need and potential to become CPAs.
Restrictions: U.S. citizenship required. Limited to minority applicants only.
$ Given: An unspecified number of scholarships awarded, each in the amount of $5,000.
Application Information: Write for details.
Deadline: July 1.

American Institute of Real Estate Appraisers Student Scholarships
875 North Michigan Avenue
Suite 2400
Chicago, IL 60611
(312) 335-4100

Description: Scholarships for undergraduate and graduate students in land economics, real estate, real estate appraising, and allied fields; recipients chosen on the basis of academic achievement.
Restrictions: N/A.
$ Given: Fifteen scholarships awarded annually; $2,000 per undergraduate fellowship; $3,000 per graduate fellowship; renewable.
Application Information: Application forms available. Online or write for details.
Deadline: February 1.
Contact: Education Department.

American Legion National Headquarters
Eight and Forty Nurses Scholarships
P.O. Box 1055
Indianapolis, IN 46206
(317) 634-1804

Description: One-year scholarships for registered nurses pursuing undergraduate or graduate study in lung and respiratory diseases; recipients chosen on the basis of academic achievement and leadership qualities.
Restrictions: Applicants must be employed full-time and attending courses full-time at an accredited nursing school; minimum age 22; United States citizenship required.
$ Given: An unspecified number of $2,500 scholarships awarded annually; renewable.
Application Information: Write for details.
Deadline: May 15.

American Nurses' Foundation Nursing Research Grants
600 Maryland Avenue, S.W.
Suite 100W
Washington, DC 20024
(202) 651-7231

Description: Grants for United States registered nurses to conduct research related to nursing; recipients chosen on the basis of proposed one-year research project.
Restrictions: N/A.
$ Given: An unspecified number of grants awarded annually; varying amounts.
Application Information: Write for details.
Deadline: May 3.
Contact: Grants Administrator.

American Psychological Association
APA Minority Fellowship Program in Neuroscience
1200 Seventeenth Street, N.W.
Washington, DC 20036
(202) 955-7761
www.apa.org

Description: Ten-month fellowships for doctoral candidates in neuroscience; recipients chosen on the basis of academic achievement, financial need, and commitment to future career in neuroscience research as well as researchers and teachers whose work focuses on minority and relevant issues.
Restrictions: African-American, Hispanic, Native American, Alaskan Native, Asian-American, and Pacific Islander applicants preferred; applicants must be planning careers in neuroscience; United States or Canadian citizenship or permanent resident status required.

$ Given: An unspecified number of fellowships awarded annually; $12,240 for ten months, $14,688 for twelve months; funding for postdoctorates varies; plus cost-sharing arrangement for full tuition scholarship; and travel funds depending on experience. Renewable for up to three years if recipient maintains good academic standing.
Application Information: Write for details.
Deadline: January 15.
Contact: Dr. James M. Jones, Director; or Ernesto Guerra, Minority Fellowship Program.

American Psychological Association
APA Minority Fellowship Program in Psychology
750 First Street, N.E.
Washington, DC 20002-4242
(202) 336-6127
www.apa.org

Description: Fellowship for doctoral candidates in psychology; one program to support the training of clinicians, another program to support the training of researchers; recipients chosen on the basis of academic achievement and financial need.
Restrictions: African-American, Hispanic, Native American, Alaskan Native, Asian-American, and Pacific Islander applicants preferred; United States citizenship or legal residency required; applicants must be planning careers in psychology.
$ Given: An unspecified number of fellowships awarded annually; $7,084 for ten months; renewable for up to three years.
Application Information: Write for details.
Deadline: January 15.
Contact: Dr. James M. Jones, Director; or Ernesto Guerra, Minority Fellowship Program.

American Psychological Association
Psychology Dissertation Research Awards
750 First Street, N.E.
Washington, DC 20002
(202) 336-6000

Description: Awards for doctoral candidates at dissertation level in psychology; to fund dissertation research.
Restrictions: Dissertation topics must be pre-approved; applicants must be APA-student affiliates enrolled in APA-approved psychology graduate programs.
$ Given: Fifty awards for $1,000 each are given annually.
Application Information: Write for details.
Deadlines: February 15; September 15.
Contact: APA, Science Directorate.

American Sociological Association Minority Fellowship Program
1807 New York Avenue, N.W.
Suite 700
Washington, DC 20005-4701

Description: One-year fellowships for graduate students entering a doctoral program in sociology for the first time or for those who are in the early stages of their graduate programs. Institutions in which applicants are enrolled or to which they are applying must have strong mental health research programs. Recipients chosen on the basis of their commitment to research in mental health and mental illness, academic achievement, scholarship, writing ability,

research potential, financial need, and racial/ethnic minority background.
Restrictions: U.S. citizenship or permanent resident status required. Limited to one of the following ethnic/racial backgrounds: African Americans, Latinos, American Indians or Alaska Natives, Asians, or Pacific Islanders.
$ Given: An unspecified number of fellowships awarded annually; each with a stipend of $14,688 plus tuition. Renewable for up to three years.
Application Information: Write for details.
Deadline: December 31.

American Statistical Association ASA/NSF/BLS Senior Research Fellow and Associate Program
1429 Duke Street
Alexandria, VA 22314
(703) 684-1221
www.amstat.org

Description: Fellowships/associateships for doctoral candidates and recent Ph.D.s in economics, business, and labor studies; for participation in research at the Bureau of Labor Statistics; recipients chosen on the basis of academic achievement and quality of proposed research.
Restrictions: Significant computer experience required.
$ Given: An unspecified number of associateships are awarded annually; stipend is commensurate with qualifications and experience; fringe benefits and travel allowance also included.
Application Information: Write for details.
Deadline: December 10.
Contact: Carolyn Kesner, Fellowship Program Director.

Armenian General Benevolent Union Graduate Program
55 East 59th Street
New York, NY 10022
(212) 319-6383
www.agbu.org

Description: Scholarships for graduate students in law, medicine, international relations, and Armenian studies; recipients chosen on the basis of academic achievement, financial need, and involvement in the Armenian community.
Restrictions: Limited to individuals of Armenian descent who are enrolled in accredited United States institutions.
$ Given: An unspecified number of grants of $3,000–$7,500 are awarded annually; renewable.
Application Information: Write for details.
Deadline: April 1.

Arthritis Foundation Doctoral Dissertation Awards for Nonphysician Health Professionals
1330 West Peachtree Street
Atlanta, GA 30309
(404) 872-7100
www.arthritis.org

Description: One to two years of grant support for doctoral candidates conducting dissertation-level research related to arthritis; recipients chosen on the basis of proposed research.
Restrictions: Applicants must be planning careers in arthritis research; membership in or eligibility for professional organization required.
$ Given: One grant awarded annually; for up to $10,000/year.

Application Information: Applicant's doctoral chair-person must approve the project.
Deadline: September 1.
Contact: Leigh Hoffner, Administrative Assistant, Research Administration.

Arthritis Foundation Medical Student Research Awards
1330 West Peachtree Street
Atlanta, GA 30309
(404) 872-7100
www.arthritis.org

Description: Two years of grant support for medical students in M.D. or M.D./Ph.D. programs at accredited United States medical schools, for arthritis-related research in the fields of biochemistry, microbiological science, immunology, and medicine; recipients chosen on the basis of proposed research and potential as biomedical investigators.
Restrictions: Applicants must be planning careers in medicine; applicants must have research advisors who agree to provide the necessary space, facilities, and guidance for the proposed research.
$ Given: One grant awarded annually. Stipend is $35,000 plus a $500 institutional grant; renewable for third year.
Application Information: Write for details.
Deadlines: March 1, November 1.
Contact: Leigh Hoffner, Administrative Assistant, Research Administration.

Association of School Administrators Graduate Scholarships
1801 N. Moore Street
Arlington, VA 22209-1813
(703) 875-0736

Description: Scholarships for graduate students who intend to pursue a career in public school superintendency.
Restrictions: None.
$ Given: Six scholarships awarded annually, each for $2,000.
Application Information: Write for details.
Deadline: September 1.
Contact: Darlene Pierce.

Atlantic Salmon Federation Bensinger-Liddle Salmon Fellowship
P.O. Box 5200
Saint Andrews,
New Brunswick
Canada
(506) 529-4581
www.asf.ca

Description: Fellowship to support individual research overseas on Atlantic salmon conservation and management; recipients chosen on the basis of research capability and benefit of proposed research.
Restrictions: United States or Canadian citizenship required in even-numbered years; United Kingdom citizenship required in odd-numbered years.
$ Given: One fellowship awarded annually.
Application Information: For application form, contact the United States office, Atlantic Salmon Federation, P.O. Box 807, Calais, ME 04619.
Deadline: March 1.
Contact: Muriel Ferguson.

Atlantic Salmon Federation
Olin Fellowships
P.O. Box 429
Saint Andrews, New
Brunswick
E0G 2X0
Canada
(506) 529-1033

Description: Fellowship to support research on Atlantic salmon conservation and management; tenable at any accredited university or research laboratory, recipients chosen on the basis of academic achievement and benefit of proposed research.
Restrictions: United States or Canadian residency required.
$ Given: Two to six fellowships awarded annually; each for $1,000–$3,000 Canadian.
Application Information: For application form, contact the United States office, Atlantic Salmon Federation, P.O. Box 807, Calais, ME 04619.
Deadline: March 15.
Contact: Muriel Ferguson.

Bunting Institute Fellowship
Program
34 Concord Avenue
Cambridge, MA 02138
(617) 495-8136
www.radcliffe.edu/bunting

Description: Postdoctoral fellowships for women to pursue research in all fields of scholarship, professions, creative writing, poetry, visual and performing arts, music, and sciences not included in the Science Scholars Fellowship.
Restrictions: U.S. citizenship required. Limited to women applicants only who have received their doctorate at least two years prior to application.
$ Given: Five to eight fellowships awarded annually, each in the amount $28,500.
Application Information: Write for details.
Deadline: Early October.

Business and Professional
Women's Clubs—New York
State
Grace LeGendre Fellowships
and Endowment Fund
7509 Route 5
Clinton, NY 13323

Description: Fellowships and grants for master's and doctoral candidates in all fields of study; tenable at accredited New York State institutions.
Restrictions: Limited to women applicants who are residents of New York State; United States citizenship or legal residency required.
$ Given: An unspecified number of $1,000 grants are awarded annually.
Application Information: Write for details.
Deadline: February 28.

Business and Professional
Women's Foundation
Education Program
New York Life Foundation for
Women in the Health
Professions
2012 Massachusetts Avenue,
N.W.
Washington, DC 20036
(202) 293-1200
www.bpwusa.org

Description: Fellowships to support women seeking entry or re-entry into the work force in the field of healthcare. Recipients chosen on the basis of financial need.
Restrictions: U.S. citizenship required. Limited to women 25 years of age or older.
$ Given: An unspecified number of fellowships awarded annually, each from $500 to $1,000.
Application Information: Send SASE.
Deadline: April 15.

Business and Professional Women's Foundation Education Program Wyeth-Ayerst Laboratories Scholarship for Women in Graduate Medical and Health Business Programs
2012 Massachusetts Avenue, N.W.
Washington, DC 20036
(202) 293-1200
www.bpwusa.org

Description: Fellowships to support women seeking entry into underrepresented and underutilized health-related occupations in the fields of biomedical engineering, biomedical research, medical technology, pharmaceutical marketing, public health, and public health policy. Recipients chosen on the basis of financial need.
Restrictions: U.S. citizenship required. Limited to women 25 years of age or older.
$ Given: An unspecified number of fellowships awarded annually, each for $2,000.
Application Information: Send SASE.
Deadline: April 15.

California Western School of Law
Trustees Scholars
225 Cedar Street
San Diego, CA 92101
(619) 239-0391
www.cwsl.edu

Description: Six-trimester scholarships to study law at California Western School of Law; recipients chosen on the basis of academic achievement, LSAT scores, and personal interview.
Restrictions: Applicants must have already been accepted by California Western School of Law.
$ Given: Four full-tuition scholarships are awarded annually.
Application Information: Contact Admissions Office for details.
Deadline: None.
Contact: Admissions Office.

Canada Council Killam Research Fellowships
99 Metcalfe Street
P.O. Box 1047
Ottawa, Ontario
Canada KIP 5V8

Description: Fellowships for senior scholars (eight to twelve years beyond the Ph.D.) to support research in any of the following fields: humanities, social sciences, natural sciences, health sciences, engineering, and studies linking disciplines within those fields.
Restrictions: Canadian citizenship or landed immigrant resident status required.
$ Given: Fifteen to eighteen fellowships awarded annually, each in the amount $53,000.
Application Information: Write for details.
Deadline: June 30.

Canadian Association of University Teachers
J.H. Stewart Reid Memorial Fellowship for Doctoral Studies
2675 Queensview Drive
Ottawa, Ontario K2B 8K2
Canada
(613) 820-2270
www.caut.ca

Description: Fellowship for doctoral candidates in all fields; tenable at Canadian institutions; recipients chosen on the basis of outstanding academic achievement.
Restrictions: Canadian citizenship or minimum one-year landed immigrant status required.
$ Given: One fellowship for $5,000 Canadian is awarded annually.
Application Information: Write for details.
Deadline: April 30.
Contact: Awards Officer.

Canadian Embassy
Canadian Studies Graduate
Student Fellowships
501 Pennsylvania Avenue,
N.W.
Washington, DC 20001
(202) 682-1740
www.cdnemb-washdc.org

Description: Fellowships for doctoral candidates in the humanities, social sciences, fine arts, business, law, or environmental studies who are working on dissertation topics related in substantial part to Canada; funding for dissertation research in Canada over a three- to nine-month fellowship period.
Restrictions: Applicants must be doctoral students at accredited institutions in Canada or the United States; applicants must have completed all degree requirements other than the dissertation; United States citizenship or permanent resident status required.
$ Given: An unspecified number of fellowships with $850/month stipends are awarded annually; non-renewable.
Application Information: Write for details.
Deadline: October 31.
Contact: Academic Relations Officer.

CDS International
Robert Bosch Foundation
Fellowships
871 United Nations Plaza
15th Floor
New York, NY 10017-1814
(212) 497-3500
FAX (212) 268-1288
www.cdsintl.org

Description: Nine-month internships at German government and business institutions (September–May) for master's degree holders and professionals in communications, journalism, economics, political science, public affairs, business administration, law, and German studies; German internships provided in a framework of government and commerce; recipients chosen on the basis of academic achievement, evidence of leadership, and community participation.
Restrictions: Recipients must be proficient in German by the start of the internship (fees for language courses reimbursed); United States citizenship required. Age range 23–34.
$ Given: Twenty fellowships awarded annually; each with DM3,500/month stipend plus travel expenses and possible spouse stipend.
Application Information: Write for details.
Deadline: October 15.
Contact: Program Officer.

Council for Advancement and
Support of Education
John Grenzebach
Outstanding Doctoral
Dissertation Award
1307 New York Avenue, N.W.
Suite 1000
Washington, DC 20005
(202) 328-5985
www.case.org

Description: Award for outstanding doctoral dissertation addressing philanthropy for education.
Restrictions: N/A.
$ Given: One award of $2,000 for the author, plus travel and lodging expenses for the author and a faculty member to attend the CASE annual assembly.
Application Information: Write for details.
Deadline: February 28.
Contact: Paul Chewing, Grenzebach Research Awards.

Cross-Cultural Institute
Kobe College
4-1 Okadayama
Nishinomiya 662
Japan
798 51 8557
FAX 798 51 8559

Description: One-year fellowships for graduate students for study in Japan. Preference will be given to applicants who have a documented interest in Japanese studies, such as the arts, culture, history, journalism, or business. Recipients chosen on the basis of academic achievement, quality of proposal, plan for teaching upon completion of degree, documented interest in women's education, feasibility of project and proposed schedule.
Restrictions: U.S. citizenship required. Must be enrolled in teaching/research master's or doctoral degree programs only. Two fellowships are restricted to women and one is open to both men and women.
$ Given: Three fellowships awarded annually, each for $24,000.
Application Information: Write for details.
Deadline: N/A.
Contact: Professor Terumasa Ueno, Chair of the Graduate School of Letters.

Deafness Research
Foundation Research Grants
575 Fifth Avenue
11th Floor
New York, NY 10017
(212) 599-0027
www.drf.org

Description: Grant for doctoral candidates, faculty, and staff members, to support research on any aspects of the ear—its function, physiology, biochemistry, genetics, anatomy, pathology, or rehabilitation; recipients chosen on the basis of proposed research.
Restrictions: Funding must be used at United States or Canadian facility; applicants must disclose any other sources of funding for the project.
$ Given: An unspecified number of grants of up to $20,000 are awarded annually; renewable for one to two additional years.
Application Information: Write for details.
Deadline: July 15.
Contact: Medical Director.

Educational Foundation of the
National Restaurant
Association
Heinz Graduate Degree
Fellowships
250 South Wacker Drive
Suite 1400
Chicago, IL 60606
(312) 715-1010
www.edfound.org

Description: Fellowships for master's and doctoral candidates in food service management and education; recipients chosen on the basis of academic achievement and ability to improve teaching/administration skills.
Restrictions: Applicants must be employed full-time as teachers or administrators of food service education, and must be pursuing full-time or part-time graduate study.
$ Given: Seven fellowships awarded annually; one for $2,000; one for $1,200; five for $1,000 each.
Application Information: Write for details.
Deadline: March 15.
Contact: Scholarship Services.

Educational Testing Service Second/Foreign Language Postdoctoral Fellowships
P.O. Box 6155
Princeton, NJ 08541
(609) 734-1806
www.ets.org

Description: Twelve-month awards for research on second/foreign language testing conducted as part of dissertation work for doctoral degree.
Restrictions: Applicants should hold a doctorate in second language testing or a related field.
$ Given: An unspecified number of grants of $35,000 each are awarded annually.
Application Information: Write for details.
Deadline: February 1.
Contact: Linda Dehauro, Director, TOEFL Research Program.

Albert Einstein Distinguished Educator Fellowship Program
Triangle Coalition for Science and Technology Foundation
1201 New York Avenue, N.W.
Suite 700
Washington, DC 20005
(202) 586-6549
(800) 582-0115

Description: Eight- to twelve-month fellowships for science, mathematics, or technology teachers to serve in professional staff positions in the U.S. Senate or House of Representatives, DOE, NASA, NSF, NIH, ED, or OSTP. Recipients chosen on the basis of their excellence in teaching science, mathematics, or technology, and experimental and innovative approach toward teaching, professional involvement and leadership, communication skills, and knowledge of national, state, and local policies that affect education.
Restrictions: U.S. citizenship required. Applicants must have a minimum of five years teaching experience.
$ Given: An unspecified number of fellowships awarded annually, each with a $4,500 monthly stipend, plus travel and moving expenses.
Application Information: Applications must be submitted online through the Department of Energy's Web page dedicated to the fellows program.
Deadline: February 25.
Contact: Peter Faletra or Cindy Musick.

Eisenhower World Affairs Institute Graduate Fellowships Program
Graduate Fellowship Office
Cornell University
155 Caldwell Hall
Ithaca, NY 14853
(607) 255-9110

Description: Fellowships for advanced doctoral candidates in the fields of history, government, economics, business administration, and international affairs to pursue research. Preference will be given to those applicants whose research relates directly to President Eisenhower, the Eisenhower administration, and issues of major concern to him.
Restrictions: None.
$ Given: An unspecified number of fellowships awarded annually, each ranging from $7,000 to $10,000.
Application Information: Write for details.
Deadline: February 6.

Electrical Women's Round Table, Inc.
Julia Kiene Fellowship
P.O. Box 292793
Nashville, TN 37229-2793
(615) 254-4479

Description: Fellowship for graduate students in the field of electrical engineering or physics.
Restrictions: Limited to women applicants only.
$ Given: One fellowship awarded annually for up to $1,000.
Application Information: Write for details.
Deadline: March.

Epilepsy Foundation of America
EFA Behavioral Sciences Student Research Fellowships
4351 Garden City Drive
Suite 406
Landover, MD 20785
(301) 459-3700
www.efa.org

Description: One-year research fellowship for graduate students interested in basic and clinical research in the biological, behavioral, and social sciences designed to advance the understanding, treatment, and prevention of epilepsy; tenable at United States institutions; recipients chosen on the basis of demonstrated competence in epilepsy research.
Restrictions: Funding must be used in the United States; no funding for capital equipment.
$ Given: One fellowships for $30,000 and various smaller fellowships awarded annually.
Application Information: Write for details.
Deadline: February 1.
Contact: Cathy Morris, Administrative Assistant, Research and Professional Education.

Epilepsy Foundation of America
Medical Student Fellowships
4351 Garden City Drive
Suite 406
Landover, MD 20785
(301) 459-3700
www.efa.org

Description: Short-term fellowships (three months) for medical students interested in careers in epilepsy research; tenable for research at United States institutions with ongoing epilepsy research/service projects; recipients chosen on the basis of submitted statement addressing relevant experiences and interest.
Restrictions: End-of-project report required.
$ Given: An unspecified number of fellowships for $2,000 each are awarded annually.
Application Information: Submit outline of proposed eight- to twelve-week program of research, plus personal statement addressing interest in epilepsy research.
Deadline: February 1.
Contact: Cathy Morris, Administrative Assistant, Research and Professional Education.

Florida Education Fund
McKnight Doctoral Fellowships
201 East Kennedy Boulevard
Suite 1525
Tampa, FL 33602

Description: Fellowships for graduate study at one of ten participating doctoral-degree-granting universities in Florida in the fields of business, engineering, agriculture, biology, computer science, mathematics, physical science, and psychology; recipients chosen on the basis of academic achievement.
Restrictions: Limited to African-American applicants only; B.A./B.S. degree required; United States citizenship required.

$ Given: Up to twenty-five fellowships awarded annually; each for a maximum of five years of study, with an annual $11,000 stipend plus up to $5,000 in tuition and fees.
Application Information: Write for details.
Deadline: January 15.
Contact: Dr. Israel Tribble, Jr.

Ford Foundation Predoctoral and Dissertation Fellowships
FF/TJ2041
National Research Council
2101 Constitution Avenue
Washington, DC 20418
(202) 334-2872
FAX (202) 334-3419

Description: Three-year predoctoral fellowships and nine- to twelve-month dissertation fellowships for study in selected disciplines (humanities, social sciences, sciences, mathematics, and engineering). Recipients chosen on the basis of academic achievement and commitment to scholarship, research, and careers in teaching.
Restrictions: Limited to U.S. citizens or nationals only. Limited to members of the following groups: Alaskan Natives, African Americans, Mexican Americans, Native American Indians, Native Pacific Islanders, or Puerto Ricans. Applicants must be enrolled in or planning to enroll in a research-based Ph.D. or Sc.D. Program.
$ Given: Fifty predoctoral fellowships and twenty-nine dissertation fellowships awarded annually; predoctoral fellowships have annual stipend of $14,000 and institutional award of $7,500. Dissertation fellowships offer stipend of $21,500.
Application Information: Write for details.
Deadline: November 12.

French Embassy Scientific Services
Chateaubriand Research Scholarships for the Exact Sciences, Engineering, and Medicine
Department of Science and Technology
4101 Reservoir Road, N.W.
Washington, DC 20007
(202) 944-6241
www.info.france-usa.org

Description: Six- to twelve-month research scholarships for doctoral candidates at dissertation level, as well as postdoctoral scholars, to conduct research in France at French universities, engineering schools, and private laboratories; language training sessions provided; relevant disciplines include biological and agricultural sciences, physical sciences and mathematics, engineering and applied sciences, medicine, nutrition, optometry and vision sciences, pharmacy and pharmaceutical sciences, and veterinary medicine and sciences; recipients chosen on the basis of proposed research.
Restrictions: Each applicant must be registered at United States university and already in contact with French host institution; United States citizenship required.
$ Given: Twenty to thirty scholarships awarded annually; each for F9,000 per month plus airfare and health insurance.
Application Information: Request application forms after September.
Deadline: January 31.
Contact: Anne Bartheleny.

**Hagley Museum and Library
Grants-in-Aid**
P.O. Box 3630
Wilmington, DE 19807
(302) 658-2400 ext 243

Description: Grants for two- to eight-week short-term research work conducted at the Hagley Museum and Library, using the imprint, manuscript, pictorial, and artifact collections; grants made available to degree candidates, advanced scholars, independent scholars, and professionals for study of American economic and technological history and French eighteenth-century history; recipients chosen on the basis of proposed research.
Restrictions: N/A.
$ Given: Several grants of up to $1,200/month each are awarded quarterly.
Application Information: Write for details.
Deadline: Applications accepted continuously.
Contact: Dr. Philip B. Scranton.

**Hagley Museum and Library
Hagley-Winterthur Research
Fellowships in Arts and
Industries**
P.O. Box 3630
Wilmington, DE 19807
(302) 658-2400 ext 243

Description: One- to six-month short-term research fellowships for work using both the Hagley and the Winterthur collections and resources; fellowships made available to master's and doctoral candidates, as well as to independent scholars studying historical and cultural relationships of economic life and the arts, including design, architecture, crafts, and the fine arts; recipients chosen on the basis of research abilities and project relevance to both libraries' holdings.
Restrictions: N/A.
$ Given: Six fellowships awarded annually; each with $1,200/month stipend, plus seminar participation and use of both research collections.
Application Information: Write for details.
Deadline: December 1.

**Harvard University Center for
International and Area
Studies Fellowships Program**
Center for International Affairs
420 Coolidge Hall
1737 Cambridge Street
Cambridge, MA 02138
(617) 495-2137
www.cfia.harvard.edu

Description: Grants for doctoral candidates at dissertation level and recent Ph.D.s to conduct research in several fields, including area and cultural studies, demography and population studies, economics, geography, history, languages, literatures and linguistics, political science and public policy, psychology, sociology, anthropology, archaeology, law, international affairs, and interdisciplinary programs in the humanities and social sciences; recipients chosen on the basis of academic achievement and proposed research.
Restrictions: Young applicants preferred; preference to individuals pursuing careers involving social science disciplines as relevant to specific geographic areas.
$ Given: A few grants are awarded annually; $22,000–$25,000 stipend for two years of predoctoral research, $32,000–$35,000 stipend for two years of postdoctoral research, plus travel and research allowance.

Application Information: Write for details.
Deadline: October 9.
Contact: Clare Putnam, Fellowship Coordinator.

**Herb Society of America
Research and Education
Grants**
9019 Kirtland Chardon Road
Kirtland, OH 44094
(440) 256-0514
www.herbsociety.org

Description: Grants to graduate students for study/research in horticulture, science, literature, art, and economics—as related to herbs; recipients chosen on the basis of proposed research, which may be scientific or academic; research period may be up to one year.
Restrictions: N/A.
$ Given: One to two grants totaling $5,000 are awarded annually.
Application Information: Write for details.
Deadline: January 31.
Contact: Grants Administrator.

**Hertz Foundation
Graduate Fellowship Awards**
P.O. Box 5032
Livermore, CA 94551-5032
(925) 373-6329
www.hertzfoundation.org

Description: Fellowships for graduate study in any discipline at one of several tenable schools. Recipients chosen on the basis of merit.
Restrictions: None.
$ Given: One fellowship awarded annually, annual stipend of $25,000 and tuition covered for a maximum tenure of five years.
Application Information: Write for details.
Deadline: N/A.

**Horticultural Research
Institute
HRI Grants**
12501 Street, N.W.
Suite 500
Washington, DC 20005
(202) 789-2900
www.amla.org

Description: Research grants to support work on improving the efficiency of the landscape/nursery trade; recipients chosen on the basis of proposed research.
Restrictions: N/A.
$ Given: Fifteen to twenty grants for $500–$10,000 each are awarded annually.
Application Information: Write for details.
Deadline: May 1.
Contact: Marpesa Heath.

**Hudson Institute
Herman Kahn Fellowship**
5395 Emerson Way
P.O. Box 26919
Indianapolis, IN 46226
(317) 545-1000
www.hudson.org

Description: Fellowships for one year of research/study in Indianapolis, for doctoral candidates at dissertation level; relevant topics include education, economics, political economy, national security, policy issues, and political theory; recipients chosen on the basis of academic achievement, proposed research, and faculty recommendation.
Restrictions: N/A.
$ Given: Up to three fellowships awarded annually; each for $18,000 plus travel expenses.
Application Information: Write for details.
Deadline: April 15.
Contact: Director of Programs.

**Howard Hughes Medical
Institute
Doctoral Fellowships in
Biological Sciences**
Grants and Special Programs
4000 Jones Bridge Road
Chevy Chase, MD 20815
(301) 215-8500
www.hhmi.org

Description: Three-year international fellowships to
support full-time study toward Ph.D. or Sc.D. degree in
biological sciences; intended for students at or near the
beginning of graduate studies; relevant fields include biochemistry, biophysics, biostatistics, mathematical biology,
cell biology, developmental biology, epidemiology, genetics immunology, microbiology, molecular biology, neuroscience, pharomacology, physiology, structural biology,
and virology; tenable at United States institutions; recipients chosen on the basis of academic achievement and
future promise in biomedical research; women and
minorities encouraged to apply.
Restrictions: Open to all nationalities.
$ Given: Sixty-six fellowships awarded annually; each
with $16,000/year stipend and $15,000 annual cost-of-
education allowance in lieu of tuition and fees; renewable
for two additional years.
Application Information: Write for details.
Deadline: November 9.
Contact: Fellowship Office, National Research Council.

**Howard Hughes Medical
Institute
HHMI-NIH Research
Scholars Awards**
One Cloister Court
Bethesda, MD 20814-1460
(301) 951-6710
(800) 424-9924
www.hhmi.org

Description: One-year research scholar position for
medical students to participate in laboratory research at
the National Institutes of Health in Bethesda, Maryland;
sponsored by HHMI and NIH.
Restrictions: Applicants must be attending medical
school (usually in second year) in the United States or
Puerto Rico; United States citizenship or permanent resident status required.
$ Given: An unspecified number of awards of $17,800.
Application Information: Kits and brochures available
from medical school deans' offices.
Deadline: January 10.
Contact: Senior Scientific Officer and Director,
Research Scholars Program.

**Howard Hughes Medical
Institute
Research Training Fellowships
for Medical Students**
Grants and Special Programs
4000 Jones Bridge Road
Chevy Chase, MD 20815
(301) 215-8500
www.hhmi.org

Description: Fellowships for medical students to participate in a one-year program of intensive, fundamental,
full-time research in the biomedical sciences at an academic or research institution in the United States; recipients
chosen on the basis of academic achievement, quality of
proposed research, and future research potential.
Restrictions: Applicants must be enrolled at United
States medical schools; Ph.D. and M.D./Ph.D. candidates
are ineligible.
$ Given: Up to sixty fellowships for $20,000 each are
awarded annually.
Application Information: Write for details.
Deadline: December 2.

**Institute of International
Education
Colombian Government Study
and Research Grants**
U.S. Student Programs
Division
809 United Nations Plaza
New York, NY 10017-3580
(212) 984-5330
www.iie.org

Description: Grants for B.S./B.A. holders to pursue up to two years of study/research at Colombian universities; relevant disciplines include agriculture, biology, business administration, economics, chemistry, engineering, education, health services administration, geography, history, Latin American literature, law, linguistics, political science, physics, regulatory development, public health, and remote sensing interpretation.
Restrictions: United States citizenship required.
$ Given: An unspecified number of grants awarded annually; each for modest monthly stipend, plus tuition and fees, health insurance, book/materials allowance, and one-way return airfare upon completion of study.
Application Information: Write for details.
Deadline: October 25.

**Institute of International
Education
Fulbright–Spanish
Government Grants**
U.S. Student Programs
Division
809 United Nations Plaza
New York, NY 10017
(212) 984-5330
www.iie.org

Description: Grants for B.A./B.S. holders studying anthropology, archaeology, art history, ceramics, philosophy, economics, Hispano-American studies, history, law, Mediterranean studies, musicology, philosophy, political science, sociology, and Spanish language and literature; for study at a Spanish university.
Restrictions: Fluency in Spanish (written and spoken) required; United States citizenship required; applicants must meet all Fulbright eligibility requirements.
$ Given: Thirty-four grants awarded annually; Spanish government funds tuition and stipend; Fulbright funds round-trip transportation, and expense allowance.
Application Information: Write for details.
Deadline: October 25.

**Institute of International
Education
Germanistic Society of
America Fellowships**
U.S. Student Programs
Division
809 United Nations Plaza
New York, NY 10017-3580
(212) 984-5330
www.iie.org

Description: Fellowships for master's degree holders and some B.A./B.S. holders studying German language and literature, art history, history, economics, philosophy, international law, political science, and public affairs; for one academic year of study in Germany.
Restrictions: United States citizenship required; applicants must meet all Fulbright eligibility requirements.
$ Given: Four fellowships awarded annually; each for $11,000 plus consideration for a Fulbright Travel Grant.
Application Information: Write for details.
Deadline: October 25.

Institute of International Education Study and Research Grants for U.S. Citizens
U.S. Student Programs Division
809 United Nations Plaza
New York, NY 10017-3580
(212) 984-5330
www.iie.org

Description: Grants to support study and research in all fields, as well as professional training in the creative and performing arts; tenable at institutions of higher learning outside of the United States for one year; list of participating countries in any given year may be obtained from IIE.
Restrictions: Open to United States citizens with B.A. or equivalent; acceptable plan of study and proficiency in host country's language required.
$ Given: A variable number of grants awarded annually; covers international transportation, language or orientation course (where appropriate), tuition, book and maintenance allowances, and health and accident insurance.
Application Information: If currently enrolled in a college or university, apply to the campus Fulbright Program Advisor; applications also available from IIE.
Deadline: October 25.

International Foundation of Employee Benefit Systems Graduate Research Grants
18700 W. Bluemound Road
P.O. Box 69
Brookfield, WI 53008
(262) 786-6710
www.ifebp.org

Description: Grants to support doctoral candidates conducting research on labor studies and employee benefit topics, such as health-care benefits, retirement, and income security; recipients chosen on the basis of proposed original research.
Restrictions: United States or Canadian citizens with thesis/dissertation topics approved by advisor.
$ Given: Five to seven grants of up to $5,000 each are awarded annually.
Application Information: Include twenty-page proposal (or shorter), curriculum vitae, and two letters of recommendation (one from thesis/dissertation advisor).
Deadline: Applications accepted continuously.
Contact: Director of Research.

International Research and Exchanges Board
1616 H Street, N.W.
Washington, DC 20006
(202) 628-8188
www.irex.org

Description: Individually designed fellowships for doctoral scholars to study within the United States in preparation for eventual field research in Eastern Europe; relevant disciplines include musicology, demography, economics, geography, political science, psychology, sociology, anthropology, archaeology, business, law, and international affairs; recipients chosen on the basis of proposed research.
Restrictions: United States citizenship required. Command of host language. Two to twelve months for pre- and postdoctoral scholars.
$ Given: An unspecified number of fellowships awarded annually; each for academic tuition, language training, stipend, or research allowance, travel.
Application Information: Write for details.
Deadline: November 1.
Contact: Elizabeth Sirk, Program Officer.

Japan Foundation
Dissertation Fellowships
152 West 57th Street
39th Floor
New York, NY 10019
(212) 489-0299
www.ipf.go.jp

Description: Fellowships for two to fourteen months of dissertation research in Japan; funding made available to doctoral candidates at dissertation level in the humanities and social sciences, with emphasis on political science, law, economics, business, and journalism—as related to Japan; recipients chosen on the basis of academic achievement and quality of proposed research.
Restrictions: Applicants must be proficient in Japanese; no funding for Japanese language study; recipients may not hold other fellowships concurrently.
$ Given: Thirteen fellowships awarded annually; each for ¥310,000 plus further allowances including one round-trip air ticket.
Application Information: Write for details.
Deadline: December 1.

Kaiser Media Fellowships in Health
Henry J. Kaiser Family Foundation
2400 Sand Hill Road
Menlo Park, CA 94025
(650) 854-9400

Description: One-year fellowships for journalists, editors, and producers who cover health issues to research specific topics in the field of health policy, health financing, or public health issues.
Restrictions: U.S. citizenship or employment by an accredited U.S. media organization required.
$ Given: Up to six fellowships awarded annually, each with a basic annual stipend of $45,000.
Application Information: Write for details.
Deadline: March 12.
Contact: Penny Duckham, Executive Director, Fellowships Program.

Kaiser Media Mini-Fellowships in Health
Henry J. Kaiser Family Foundation
2400 Sand Hill Road
Menlo Park, CA 94025
(650) 854-9400

Description: Limited grants for journalists, editors, and producers who cover health issues to undertake a specific research project in the field of health policy, health financing, or public health issues.
Restrictions: U.S. citizenship or employment by an accredited U.S. media organization required.
$ Given: An unspecified number of fellowships awarded annually, each for an average of $5,000 for project-related travel and expenses.
Application Information: Write for details.
Deadline: March 12.
Contact: Penny Duckham, Executive Director, Fellowships Program.

Kosciuszko Foundation
15 East 65th Street
New York, NY 10021-6595
(212) 734-2130
FAX (212) 628-4552
www.kosciuszkofoundation.org

Description: One-year scholarships to U.S. citizens of Polish descent for graduate studies in any field at colleges and universities in the United States and to Americans of non-Polish descent whose studies at American universities are primarily focused on Polish subjects. Recipients chosen on the basis of academic achievement and financial need.
Restrictions: Must be enrolled in a graduate program at a U.S. university. Applicants must be U.S. citizens or of Polish descent.
$ Given: An unspecified number of scholarships of $1,000–$5,000 each are awarded annually.
Deadline: January 16.
Contact: Grants office.

**Lyndon Baines Johnson
Foundation
Grants-in-Aid of Research**
2313 Red River Street
Austin, TX 78705
(512) 478-7829
www.lbjib.utexas.edu

Description: Grants for individuals to conduct research at the LBJ Library; relevant fields include communications, economics, environmental policy and resource management, history, political science, and public policy; recipients chosen on the proposed research.
Restrictions: N/A.
$ Given: A few grants awarded annually to help defray the costs of living, travel, and related expenses; grants normally range from $300–$1,400.
Application Information: Contact the Chief Archivist regarding the availability of proposed material before applying.
Deadlines: January 31, July 31.
Contact: Assistant Executive Director.

**James Madison Foundation
Fellowships**
P.O. Box 4030
Iowa City, IA 52243-4030
(800) 525-6928
www.jamesmadison.com

Description: Fellowships for graduate study leading to a master's degree in American history or political science; a master's of Arts in Teaching or a master's of Education degree concentrating in constitutional history or American government or political theory. Fellowship includes the four-week Summer Institute on the Constitution at Georgetown University.
Restrictions: None.
$ Given: Up to $24,000 annually for tuition, fees, books, room, board.
Application Information: Write for details.
Deadline: March 1.

Marshall Scholarships
Marshall Aid Commemorating
Commission
Association of Commonwealth
Universities
36 Gordon Square
London WC1H0PF
(44) 1713878572
www.aca.ac.uk/marshall

Description: Two- to three-year scholarships for undergraduate or graduate level study at any university in the
United Kingdom, in any discipline leading to the award of
a British university degree.
Restrictions: U.S. citizenship required; limited to graduates of accredited four-year colleges and universities in
the United States with at least a 3.75 GPA since freshman
year.
$ Given: Up to forty scholarships awarded annually;
each worth approximately $25,000 per year and compris-
ing a personal allowance for cost of living and residence,
tuition fees, books, travel in connection with studies, and
to and from the United States.
Application Information: Write for details. Application
forms also available from colleges and universities in the
United States, British consulates in Atlanta, Boston,
Chicago, Houston, and San Francisco, the British Council
in Washington, DC, British Information Services in New
York.
Deadline: N/A.

Medical Library Association
MLA Doctoral Fellowships
65 East Wacker Place
Suite 1900
Chicago, IL 60601
(312) 419-9094
www2.mc.duke.edu/misc
MLA/HHSS/hhss.htm

Description: One-year fellowships for doctoral candidates in health sciences librarianship, with emphasis on
biomedical and health-related information science; funding intended to support research or travel, not tuition;
recipients chosen on the basis of academic achievement.
Restrictions: Applicants must hold master's degrees
from ALA-accredited schools; United States or Canadian
citizenship required.
$ Given: One fellowship of $2,000 is awarded biannu-
ally; non-renewable.
Application Information: Write for details.
Deadline: December 1.
Contact: Coordinator of Research and Professional
Recognition.

Medical Library Association
MLA Graduate Scholarships
65 East Wacker Place
Suite 1900
Chicago, IL 60601
www2.mc.duke.edu/misc
MLA/HHSS/hhss.htm

Description: Scholarships for master's candidates in
medical librarianship; recipients chosen on the basis of
academic achievement and professional potential.
Restrictions: Applicants must be entering an ALA-
accredited school or have at least one-half the academic
requirements yet to complete during the scholarship year;
United States or Canadian citizenship required.
$ Given: One scholarship for $2,000 is awarded annu-
ally.
Application Information: Write for details.
Deadline: December 1.
Contact: Coordinator of Research and Professional
Recognition.

Medical Library Association
MLA Graduate Scholarships
for Minority Students
65 East Wacker Place
Suite 1900
Chicago, IL 60601
www2.mc.duke.edu/misc
MLA/HHSS/hhss.htm

Description: Scholarships for master's candidates in health sciences librarianship; recipients chosen on the basis of academic achievement and professional potential.
Restrictions: Limited to minority group applicants only applicants must be entering an ALA-accredited school or have at least one-half the academic requirements yet to complete during the scholarship year; United States or Canadian citizenship required.
$ Given: One scholarship for $2,000 is awarded annually.
Application Information: Write for details.
Deadline: December 1.
Contact: Coordinator of Research and Professional Recognition.

Mexican American Legal
Defense and Educational
Fund
Law School Scholarships for
Hispanics
634 South Spring Street
11th Floor
Los Angeles, CA 90014
(213) 629-2512

Description: One-year scholarships tenable at any accredited law school; recipients chosen on the basis of academic achievement and financial need.
Restrictions: Limited to Hispanic American applicants only; applicants must be enrolled full-time in law school; United States citizenship required.
$ Given: Twenty scholarships awarded annually; nineteen for $1,000 each, one for $2,000; non-renewable but re-application is allowed.
Application Information: Application form required.
Deadline: May 30.

Monticello College
Foundation and Washington
University
Spencer T. Olin Fellowships
for Women in Graduate Study
Graduate School of Arts and
Sciences
Washington University
Campus Box 1187
One Brookings Drive
St. Louis, MO 63130-4899
(314) 935-6848

Description: Fellowships for graduate students to prepare for careers in higher education and professions in the fields of biological and biomedical sciences, humanities, physical sciences and mathematics, social and behavioral sciences, architecture, business administration, engineering, fine arts, law, medicine, and social work. Tenable at Washington University.
Restrictions: Limited to women applicants only.
$ Given: An unspecified number of fellowships awarded annually, each ranging from $20,000 to $33,000.
Application Information: Write for details.
Deadline: February 1.

Myasthenia Gravis
Foundation
Viets Medical Student
Myasthenia Gravis Research
Fellowships
123 West Madison Street
Suite 800
Chicago, IL 60602
(312) 853-0522
(800) 541-5454
www.myasthenia

Description: Fellowships for medical students, for training in myasthenia gravis research; recipients chosen on the basis of proposed research.
Restrictions: Applicants must find scientist with established research program to supervise fellowship training and research.
$ Given: A few fellowships awarded annually; of $3,000.
Application Information: Application materials include personal background, program of study, research description, and sponsor endorsement.
Deadline: March 15.
Contact: Anna El-Oudsi, Executive Administrator.

National Association of
Purchasing Management
Doctoral Dissertation Grant
Center for Advanced
Purchasing Studies
2055 East Centennial Circle
P.O. Box 22160
Tempe, AZ 85285-2160
(800) 888-6276
www.napm.org

Description: Grants for doctoral candidates to conduct dissertation research on purchasing and materials management; open to individuals seeking Ph.D. or D.B.A. in business, economics, industrial engineering, management, and purchasing logistics; tenable at accredited United States institutions; recipients chosen on the basis of proposed research; preference for applicants planning careers in college teaching and research.
Restrictions: United States citizenship or permanent resident status required.
$ Given: Four grants awarded annually; each for $10,000 per academic year, paid in three equal installments.
Application Information: Write for details.
Deadline: January 31.
Contact: Holly LaCroix Johnson.

National Italian American
Foundation Scholarship
Program
Oresto A. and Maddalena
Giargiari Endowment
Medical Scholarships
1860 19th Street, N.W.
Washington, DC 20009
www.niaf.org

Description: Scholarships for second-, third-, and fourth-year medical students at approved United States medical schools; recipients chosen on the basis of academic achievement and financial need.
Restrictions: Applicants must be of Italian descent.
$ Given: An unspecified number of scholarships for $5,000 each are awarded annually.
Application Information: Application materials must be submitted in triplicate.
Deadline: May 31.
Contact: Dr. Maria Lombardo, Education Director.

National Italian American Foundation Scholarship Program
Michael and Francesca Marinelli Scholarships
1860 19th Street, N.W.
Washington, DC 20009
www.niaf.org

Description: Scholarships for graduate students in the DC area and for undergraduates at Nova University in Florida; relevant disciplines limited to science and business; recipients chosen on the basis of academic achievement and financial need.
Restrictions: Applicants must be of Italian descent.
$ Given: Two scholarships for $2,000 each are awarded annually.
Application Information: Essay required.
Deadline: May 31.
Contact: Dr. Maria Lombardo, Education Director.

National Italian American Foundation Scholarship Program
Regional Scholarships
1860 19th Street, N.W.
Washington, DC 20009
www.niaf.org

Description: Fellowships for undergraduate and graduate law students; recipients chosen on the basis of 750-word essay describing the contributions of Italian-Americans to the American judicial system.
Restrictions: N/A.
$ Given: Twenty-four fellowships for $5,000 each are awarded annually.
Application Information: Send SASE for details.
Deadline: May 31.
Contact: Dr. Maria Lombardo, Education Director.

National Italian American Foundation Scholarship Program
Stella Business Scholarship
1860 19th Street, N.W.
Washington, DC 20009
www.niaf.org

Description: Scholarship for undergraduate and graduate students in business; recipients chosen on the basis of academic achievement and financial need.
Restrictions: Applicants must be of Italian descent.
$ Given: One scholarship for $2,000 is awarded annually.
Application Information: Send SASE for details.
Deadline: May 31.
Contact: Dr. Maria Lombardo, Education Director.

National Medical Fellowships, Inc.
William and Charlotte Cadbury Award
254 West 31st Street
7th Floor
New York, NY 10001
www.nmf-online.org

Description: Award for senior medical student; recipients chosen on the basis of academic achievement, leadership, and community service.
Restrictions: Limited to minority group members only; applicants must attend United States medical schools.
$ Given: One award made annually; for $2,000 plus certificate of merit.
Application Information: Applicants must be nominated by medical school deans; medical schools must provide letters of recommendation and transcripts for nominees.
Deadline: July 31 for nomination.
Contact: Programs Department.

National Medical Fellowships, Inc.
The Commonwealth Fund Medical Fellowships for Minorities
254 West 31st Street
7th Floor
New York, NY 10001
www.nmf-online.org

Description: Eight- to twelve-week fellowships for second- and third-year medical students to work in major research laboratories under the supervision/tutelage of prominent biomedical scientists; recipients chosen on the basis of academic achievement.
Restrictions: Limited to minority group members only; applicants must attend accredited United States medical schools and must be interested in careers in research/academic medicine.
$ Given: Thirty-five fellowships awarded annually; each for $6,000.
Application Information: Applicants must be nominated by medical school deans.
Deadline: September for nomination; application deadline follows.
Contact: Programs Department.

National Medical Fellowships, Inc.
Irving Graef Memorial Scholarship
254 West 31st Street
7th Floor
New York, NY 10001
www.nmf-online.org

Description: Two-year scholarship for rising third-year medical students; recipients chosen on the basis of academic achievement, leadership, and community service.
Restrictions: Limited to minority group members only; applicants must have received NMF assistance during second year of medical school.
$ Given: One scholarship for $2,000 is awarded annually. Renewable.
Application Information: Applicants must be nominated by medical school deans.
Deadline: September 7 for nomination.
Contact: Programs Department.

National Medical Fellowships, Inc.
Hugh Andersen Memorial Scholarships
254 West 31st Street
7th Floor
New York, NY 10001
www.nmf-online.org

Description: Awards for medical students beyond their first year of medical school for Minnesota residents attending any accredited U.S. medical school or students attending Minnesota medical schools.
Restrictions: Limited to minority applicants only; applicants must be accepted at accredited United States medical schools.
$ Given: Two awards for $2,500 each are awarded annually.
Application Information: Recipients chosen from General Scholarship applicants.
Deadline: June 30.
Contact: Programs Department.

National Medical Fellowships, Inc.
George Hill Memorial Scholarship
254 West 31st Street
7th Floor
New York, NY 10001
www.nmf-online.org

Description: Scholarship for senior medical students pursuing careers in cardiology or urology; recipients chosen on the basis of financial need, academic achievement, leadership, and community service.
Restrictions: Limited to minorities only; and must be accepted at accredited United States medical schools.
$ Given: One scholarship for $5,000 is awarded annually.
Application Information: Application forms included with General Scholarship application forms.
Deadline: February 15.
Contact: Programs Department.

National Medical Fellowships, Inc.
Franklin C. McLean Award
254 West 31st Street
7th Floor
New York, NY 10001
www.nmf-online.org

Description: Award for senior medical students; recipients chosen on the basis of academic achievement, leadership, and community service.
Restrictions: Limited to minority group members only; applicants must be enrolled in accredited United States medical schools.
$ Given: One award for $3,000 is made annually.
Application Information: Applicants must be nominated by medical school deans; medical schools must provide letters of recommendation and transcripts for nominees.
Deadline: July 31 for nomination.
Contact: Programs Department.

National Medical Fellowships, Inc.
Metropolitan Life Foundation Awards Program for Academic Excellence in Medicine
254 West 31st Street
7th Floor
New York, NY 10001
www.nmf-online.org

Description: Awards for second- and third-year medical students; recipients chosen on the basis of academic achievement, leadership, financial need, and potential for contribution to the field of medicine.
Restrictions: Limited to minority group members only; applicants must attend medical schools in or be residents of the following areas: San Francisco, CA; Tampa, FL; Atlanta, GA; Aurora, IL; Wichita, KS; New York, NY; Tulsa, OK; Pittsburgh, PA; Scranton, PA; Warwick; RI; Greenville, SC; and San Antonio, TX.
$ Given: Up to nine awards made annually; each for $3,500.
Application Information: Applicants must be nominated by medical school deans.
Deadline: September 29.
Contact: Programs Department.

National Medical Fellowships, Inc.
National General Medical Scholarships for Minorities
254 West 31st Street
7th Floor
New York, NY 10001
www.nmf-online.org

Description: Scholarships for second- and third-year medical students in M.D. programs at accredited United States medical schools.
Restrictions: Limited to minority group members only; must be interested in community-based primary care.
$ Given: Fifteen fellowships of $10,000 awarded annually.
Application Information: Write for details.
Deadline: October 30.
Contact: Scholarships Department.

National Medical Fellowships, Inc.
National Medical Association Special Awards Program
254 West 31st Street
7th Floor
New York, NY 10001
www.nmf-online.org

Description: Need-based awards for medical students; recipients chosen on the basis of academic achievement, leadership, and potential for contribution to the field of medicine, as well as financial need; NMA Merit Scholarship (four per year), Slack Award for Medical Journalism (one per year), Beecham/NMA Scholarship (one per year), and Ford/NMA Scholarship (one per year).
Restrictions: Limited to African-American applicants only; applicants must attend accredited M.D. or D.O. degree-granting United States medical schools.
$ Given: Seven awards made annually; each for $2,250–$4,000.
Application Information: Applicants must be nominated by medical school deans.
Deadline: May for nomination.
Contact: NMA Special Awards Program.

National Medical Fellowships, Inc.
Wyeth-Ayerst Laboratories Prize in Women's Health
254 West 31st Street
7th Floor
New York, NY 10001
www.nmf-online.org

Description: Prizes to graduating medical students who will practice or conduct research in the field of women's health.
Restrictions: Limited to minority fourth-year women; applicants must attend accredited United States medical schools; good academic standing required.
$ Given: One prize of $5,000 awarded annually.
Application Information: Applicants must be nominated by medical school deans and chairs of departments of surgery.
Deadline: February 15.
Contact: Programs Department.

**National Science Foundation
Behavioral and Neural
Sciences Research Grants**
4201 Wilson Boulevard
Arlington, VA 22230
(703) 306-1234
www.nsf.gov

Description: Grants to support research on nervous systems and human/animal behavior; awarded in the following subprogram categories: cultural/physical anthropology, archaeology, animal behavior, behavioral neuroendocrinology, cellular neuroscience, developmental neuroscience, human cognition/perception, linguistics, neural mechanisms of behavior, neurobiology of learning/memory, sensory system, and social psychology; recipients chosen on the basis of proposed research.
Restrictions: N/A.
$ Given: An unspecified number of grants awarded annually; varying amounts.
Application Information: Write for subprogram details.
Deadline: Applications accepted continuously; January 15, July 15.
Contact: Dr. Christopher Comer, Division of Integrative Biology and Neuroscience.

**National Security Education
Program Graduate
International Fellowships**
Academy for Educational
Development
1825 Connecticut Avenue
Washington, DC 20009-5721
(800) 498-9360
www.aed.org/nsep

Description: One- to six-semester (twenty-four-month) fellowships for graduate students to pursue specialization in area and language study in a diverse list of fields of study, specifically business, economics, history, international affairs, law, applied sciences and engineering, health and biomedical sciences, political science and other social sciences, which are connected to U.S. national security.
Restrictions: U.S. citizenship required. Application to or enrollment in a graduate program in an accredited U.S. college or university located within the United States. Must be willing to enter into service agreement to seek employment with an agency or office of the federal government involved in national security affairs. Recipients chosen on the basis of the relationship of the applicant's proposed study to U.S. national security and how the applicant proposes to use knowledge and experience gained from NSEP support to contribute to U.S. national security.
$ Given: An unspecified number of fellowships awarded annually; each for $2,000 per semester for language or area studies coursework at your home university and $10,000 per semester for two semesters of overseas study program expenses.
Application Information: Write for details.
Deadline: January 15.

New York State Senate Graduate/Post-Graduate Fellowship Program Richard J. Roth Journalism Fellowship
Room 416
90 South Swan Street
Albany, NY 12247
(518) 455-2611

Description: Graduate fellowships to support one year of working as a full-time staff member in the Senate Press Office. Preference will be given to those candidates pursing careers in journalism or public relations.
Restrictions: U.S. citizenship required. Applicants must be residents of New York or enrolled in a New York state graduate school who have completed at least two semesters of graduate study.
$ Given: One fellowship in the amount of $25,000 awarded annually.
Application Information: Write for details.
Deadline: May 1.
Contact: Dr. Russell J. Williams, Director.

New York University Publishing Studies Fellowships
11 West 42nd Street
Room 400
New York, NY 10036
(212) 790-3232

Description: Fellowships sponsored by North American publishing houses to train graduate students in book/magazine publishing; participation requires enrollment in two-year M.A. program (first year, full-time coursework; second year; paid internship in New York City). Must be accepted and attend one semester at NYU Center for Publishing before applying for fellowship.
Restrictions: Applicants must be college graduates with minimum 3.0 GPA.
$ Given: Nine fellowships for $5,500 each are awarded annually.
Application Information: Application requires college transcripts, two letters of recommendation, and interview.
Deadline: March 1.
Contact: Mary Witty, Publishing Studies Program Coordinator, Gallatin Division.

New York University Student Affairs and Services Graduate Assistantships and Internships
239 Greene Street
New York, NY 10003
(212) 998-5656

Description: Graduate internships and assistantships for master's and doctoral candidates in higher education who are planning careers in student affairs and services.
Restrictions: N/A.
$ Given: An unspecified number of positions filled annually; varying amount.
Application Information: Write for details.
Deadline: February 1.
Contact: Judith Casey, Coordinator of Internship Program.

Oak Ridge Institute for Science and Education Nuclear Regulatory Commission Engineering and Health Physics Graduate Fellowships
P.O. Box 117
Oak Ridge, TN 37831-0117
(865) 576-3146
www.oriu.gov/orise.htm

Description: Fellowships for master's candidates studying nuclear engineering and health physics; participation includes work/orientation prefellowship; recipients chosen on the basis of academic achievement.
Restrictions: United States citizenship or permanent resident status required.
$ Given: An unspecified number of fellowships awarded annually; each for cost-of-education (paid directly to university) plus $1,500/month stipend.
Application Information: Write for details.
Deadline: January 27.

Parenteral Drug Association Foundation for Pharmaceutical Sciences Nina Dale Demuth Research Grant
7500 Old Georgetown Road
Suite 260
Bethesda, MD 20814
(301) 986-0293
www.pda.org

Description: Research grant for master's and doctoral candidates who are parenteral nutrition majors; recipients chosen on the basis of proposed research.
Restrictions: No geographical restrictions.
$ Given: One grant of $15,000 is awarded annually.
Application Information: Application form and eight copies of proposal required.
Deadline: June 15.
Contact: Grants Administrator.

Parenteral Drug Association Foundation for Pharmaceutical Sciences Parenteral Drug Association Foundation Research Grants
7500 Old Georgetown Road
Suite 260
Bethesda, MD 20814
(301) 986-0293
www.pda.org

Description: Grants to support research in parenteral technology and related fields; recipients chosen on the basis of proposed research.
Restrictions: United States citizenship required.
$ Given: Two grants of $15,000 each are awarded annually; renewable once.
Application Information: Write for details.
Deadline: June 15.
Contact: Nina L. Demuth.

Parenteral Drug Association Foundation for Pharmaceutical Sciences Charles P. Schaufus Parenteral Processing Technology Research Grant
7500 Old Georgetown Road
Suite 260
Bethesda, MD 20814
(301) 986-0293
www.pda.org

Description: Grants to support parenteral processing technology research; recipients chosen on the basis of proposed research.
Restrictions: United States citizenship required.
$ Given: One grant of $10,000 is awarded annually; renewable.
Application Information: Write for details.
Deadline: June 15.
Contact: Nina L. Demuth.

President's Commission on White House Fellowships
White House Fellowships
712 Jackson Place, N.W.
Washington, DC 20503
(202) 395-4522
www.whitehouse.gov/WH-fellows/index.html

Description: Twelve-month appointments as special assistants to the Vice President, Cabinet members, and the Presidential staff; fellowships include participation in educational program; positions available for students in public affairs, education, the sciences, business, and the professions; recipients chosen on the basis of leadership qualities, commitment to community service, and career/academic achievement.
Restrictions: Limited to young adults, ages 30–39; civilian federal employees are ineligible; recipients may not hold official state or local office while serving as White House fellows; United States citizenship required.
$ Given: Eleven to nineteen wage-earning fellowships for up to a maximum of $70,500 are awarded annually.
Application Information: Write for details.
Deadline: February 1.

Purina Mills Company
Purina Mills Research Fellowships
Purina Research Awards Committee
P.O. Box 66812
St. Louis, MO 63166-6812
www.purina-mills.com

Description: Fellowships for graduate students at agriculture colleges, for nutrition and physiology research as related to dairy, poultry, and animal sciences, recipients chosen on the basis of academic achievement and proposed research.
Restrictions: N/A.
$ Given: Five fellowships awarded annually, at least one in each of these categories; dairy science, animal science, poultry science; each for $10,000 per academic year; renewable for one additional year.
Application Information: Write for guidelines.
Deadline: February 5.
Contact: Dolores M. Adams–1E.

Rockefeller University
Rockefeller Archive Center Research Grants
15 Dayton Avenue
Pocantico Hills
North Tarrytown, NY
10591-1598
(914) 631-4505
www.rockefeller.edu/archives.ctr

Description: Residential research fellowships for graduate students and postdoctoral scholars pursuing research using Archive Center resources; relevant disciplines including philanthropy, education, science, medicine, black history, agriculture, labor, social welfare, social sciences, politics, religion, population, economic development, and the arts; recipients chosen on the basis of proposed research and necessity of using Archive Center resources.
Restrictions: N/A.
$ Given: An unspecified number of grants awarded annually; each for up to $2,500 for travel, lodging, and research expenses.
Application Information: Write for details.
Deadline: November 30.
Contact: Pamela Harris, Director.

Smithsonian Institution Predoctoral Research Fellowships in the History of Science and Technology
Office of Fellowships and Grants
955 L'Enfant Plaza
Suite 7300
Washington, DC 20560
(202) 287-3271
www.si.edu

Description: Three- to twelve-month residential fellowships for doctoral candidates at dissertation level in the history of science and technology, to pursue independent research using the Smithsonian's collections, resources, and staff expertise; relevant disciplines include history of mathematics, physical sciences, pharmacy, medicine, civil and mechanical engineering, electrical technology, and history of American science; recipients chosen on the basis of proposed research.
Restrictions: Applicants must have completed all preliminary coursework and exams for degree.
$ Given: An unspecified number of fellowships are awarded annually; each with $15,000 stipend.
Application Information: Write for details.
Deadline: January 15.
Contact: Program Assistant.

The Spencer Foundation Spencer Dissertation Fellowships for Research Related to Education
875 North Michigan Avenue
Suite 3930
Chicago, IL 60611-1803
(312) 337-7000
www.spencer.org

Description: Fellowships for doctoral candidates at dissertation level in education, to support final year of dissertation research and writing; preference for candidates interested in careers in education research.
Restrictions: Applicants must be enrolled in United States graduate schools and must have completed all coursework and field work for dissertation.
$ Given: Thirty fellowships for $20,000 awarded annually.
Application Information: Write for details.
Deadline: October 20.

Social Science Research Council
South Asia Doctoral Dissertation and Advanced Research Fellowships
810 Seventh Avenue
New York, NY 10019
(212) 377-2700
www.ssic.org

Description: Nine- to eighteen-month fellowships for doctoral candidates to conduct dissertation-related or advanced field research in Bangladesh, Nepal, Sri Lanka, Pakistan, Bhutan, or Maldives for dissertation work in the humanities and social sciences, business administration, and management; recipients chosen on the basis of academic achievement, proposed research, and proficiency in a major South Asian language.
Restrictions: N/A.
$ Given: Up to 15 fellowships awarded annually; varying amounts.
Application Information: Write for details.
Deadline: November 15.

Social Science Research Council
Southeast Asia Doctoral Dissertation and Advanced Research Fellowships
810 Seventh Avenue
New York, NY 10019
(212) 377-2700
www.ssic.org

Description: Nine- to 18-month fellowships for doctoral candidates to conduct dissertation-related or advanced field research in Brunei, Burma, Indonesia, Laos, Kampuchea, Malaysia, Thailand, Singapore, the Philippines, or Vietnam; for dissertation work in the humanities and social sciences, including law, public health, and public planning; recipients chosen on the basis of academic achievement, proposed research, and proficiency in a major Southeast Asian language.
Restrictions: N/A.
$ Given: An unspecified number of fellowships awarded annually; varying amounts.
Application Information: Write for details.
Deadline: November 15.

SUNY Albany Fellowship on Women and Public Policy
Center for Women in Government
University at Albany
State University of New York
Draper Hall, Rm 302
135 Western Avenue
Albany, NY 12222
(518) 442-3877

Description: Seven-month fellowship for graduate students in all fields of study pursuing careers in public policy. Fellows are assigned to a non-profit organization or legislator of a state agency for thirty hours per week.
Restrictions: Applicants must be matriculated graduate students in N.Y. State program. Background in research, employment, or volunteer activities designed to improve status of women and underrepresented populations preferred.
$ Given: One fellowship awarded annually with $9,000 stipend.
Application Information: Write for details.
Deadline: March 15.
Contact: Dorothy Hogan.

Truman Foundation
Truman Scholarships
712 Jackson Place, N.W.
Washington, DC 20006
(202) 395-4831

Description: Scholarships for undergraduate and graduate studies in any discipline; preference given to candidates proposing to enroll in professional programs oriented to careers in public service, including public administration, public policy analysis, public health, international relations, government, economics, social services, education and human resource development, and conservation and environmental protection. Recipients chosen on the basis of public and community service, commitment to careers in government and public service, leadership potential and communication skills.
Restrictions: U.S. citizenship required.
$ Given: Seventy-five to eighty scholarships awarded annually for varying amounts; up to $27,000 for graduate studies.
Application Information: Write for details.
Deadline: February 1.

U.S. Arms Control and Disarmament Agency Hubert H. Humphrey Doctoral Fellowships in Arms Control and Disarmament
Office of Public Affairs
The State Department
320 21st Street
Washington, DC 20451
(202) 647-4153
www.acda.gov

Description: Fellowship for doctoral candidates at dissertation level, as well as third-year law students; to support up to twelve months of research on arms control and disarmament; recipients chosen on the basis of academic achievement and proposed research.
Restrictions: United States citizenship or legal residency required.
$ Given: An unspecified number of fellowships awarded annually; each with $8,000 stipend, plus up to $6,000 paid to institution to cover tuition and fees.
Application Information: Write for details.
Deadline: March 31.

Wellesley College M.A. Carland Shackford Medical Fellowship
106 Central Street
Office of Financial Aid
Wellesley, MA 02181
www.wellesley.edu

Description: Fellowship for medical students pursuing general medical practice (not psychiatry); recipients chosen on the basis of academic achievement and financial need.
Restrictions: Limited to women only; applicants may be graduates of any United States undergraduate academic institution.
$ Given: One fellowship for a minimum of $7,000 awarded annually.
Application Information: Application forms available after November 20.
Deadline: January 3.
Contact: Secretary to the Committee on Graduate Fellowships.

Woodrow Wilson National Fellowship Foundation Charlotte W. Newcombe Doctoral Dissertation Fellowships
CN 5281
Princeton, NJ 08543
(609) 452-7007
www.woodrow.org

Description: Twelve-month research fellowships for doctoral candidates at dissertation level, for dissertation research on ethical or religious values in all fields of social sciences, humanities, and education.
Restrictions: Applicants must be enrolled in United States graduate schools.
$ Given: Forty fellowships for $15,000 each are awarded annually.
Application Information: Write for details.
Deadline: Early December.
Contact: Program Officer.

Woodrow Wilson Johnson & Johnson Dissertation Grants in Children's Health
CN 5281
Princeton, NJ 08543-5281
(609) 452-7007
www.woodrow.org/womens-studies/health

Description: Grants for dissertation research on issues related to children's health, specifically its significance for public policy or treatment. Recipients chosen on the basis of originality and significance, scholarly validity, commitment to women's health, academic achievement.
Restrictions: Applicants must have completed all pre-dissertation requirements at graduate schools in the United States.

$ Given: Five grants awarded annually, each for $2,000 to be used for expenses connected with dissertation.
Application Information: Write for details.
Deadline: November 8.

**Woodrow Wilson Johnson &
Johnson Dissertation Grants
in Women's Health**
CN 5281
Princeton, NJ 08543-5281
(609) 452-7007
www.woodrow.org/womens-
studies/health

Description: Grants for dissertation research on issues related to women's health, specifically its significance for public policy or treatment. Recipients chosen on the basis of originality and significance, scholarly validity, commitment to women's health, academic achievement.
Restrictions: Applicants must have completed all pre-dissertation requirements at graduate schools in the United States.
$ Given: Ten grants awarded annually, each for $2,000 to be used for expenses connected with dissertation.
Application Information: Write for details.
Deadline: November 8.

**Woodrow Wilson Postdoctoral
Fellowships in the Humanities**
5 Vaugh Drive, Suite 300
Princeton, NJ 08540-6313
(609) 452-7007
www.woodrow.org

Description: Two-year fellowships to enable young teachers and scholars to remain in academia, providing fellows the time and resources necessary to continue their research, turn a dissertation into a publication, and broaden their teaching experience. Recipients chosen on the basis of teaching experience.
Restrictions: U.S. citizenship or permanent resident status required. Applicants must have completed their Ph.D. requirements.
$ Given: Host institutions are to provide a minimum salary of $30,000 and benefits (with partial support from WWNFF), office space, and research and library support.
Application Information: Write for details.
Deadline: November 19.

**Women's Research and
Education Institute
Congressional Fellowships on
Women and Public Policy**
1750 New York Avenue, N.W.
Suite 350
Washington, DC 20006
(202) 328-7070
www.wrei.org

Description: Congressional fellowship program designed to train women as potential public policy leaders; fellowship runs January through September and involves thirty hours/week work in a United States Congress office as a legislative aide on policy issues affecting women; open to master's and doctoral candidates at United States institutions; relevant disciplines include humanities, social sciences, biology and biomedical sciences, engineering and applied sciences, biomedical engineering, technology management and policy, business administration and management, health services management and hospital administration, education, allied health professionals, medicine, nursing, public and community health, and law; recipients chosen on the basis of political/civic activity and interest in women's issues.

Restrictions: Limited to women applicants; nine hours previous graduate coursework preferred; United States citizenship preferred.
$ Given: Eight to fifteen fellowships awarded annually; each with $1,150 stipend per month for nine months plus $500 for health insurance and up to $1,500 toward three hours tuition at home institution.
Application Information: Request application after November 1.
Deadline: June 15.
Contact: Susan Scanlan, Fellowship Director.

World Health Organization
WHO Fellowships
1775 K Street, N.W.
Suite 430
Washington, DC 20006
(202) 331-9081
www.who.int

Description: One-year or shorter fellowships for individual or group health training/study in another country; intended for training/study not available in recipient's own country; relevant disciplines include public health administration, environmental health, medical social work, maternal and child health, communicable diseases, laboratory services, clinical medicine, basic medical sciences, and medical/allied education; recipients chosen on the basis of academic achievement and proposed study/training.
Restrictions: Applicants must be planning careers in public health; language proficiency required, as appropriate.
$ Given: An unspecified number of fellowships awarded annually; each to cover monthly stipend, tuition, and books.
Application Information: Contact WHO for detailed information booklet; application forms are available from national health administrations.
Deadline: At least six months prior to study.

Yale Law School Fellowships
for Journalists
401A Yale Station
New Haven, CT 06520
(203) 432-1696

Description: One-year fellowships for experienced professional journalists to participate in intensive program leading to Master of Studies in Law degree.
Restrictions: N/A.
$ Given: Three fellowships awarded annually; each for $22,500 stipend plus tuition.
Application Information: Write for details.
Deadline: January 3.
Contact: Elizabeth Stauderman, Director of Public Affairs.

Zonta International Foundation
Jane M. Kausman Women in Business Scholarships
557 West Randolph Street
Chicago, IL 60661-2206
(312) 930-5848
www.zonta.org

Description: Scholarships for undergraduate women pursuing careers and leadership positions in business-related fields.
Restrictions: Limited to women applicants in their second or third year of a business-related program only.
$ Given: An unspecified number of scholarships of varying amounts awarded annually.
Application Information: Write for details.
Deadline: N/A.

Women Only, Women Preferred, Women's Studies

**American Association of
University Women
Educational Foundation
AAUW American Fellowships**
Department 60
2201 No. Dodge Street
Iowa City, IA 52243-4030
(319) 337-1716
www.aauw.org

Description: Fellowships for full-time doctoral students and postdoctoral scholars, for research in all disciplines; recipients chosen on the basis of academic achievement and commitment to women's issues in professional career.
Restrictions: Limited to women applicants; United States citizenship or permanent resident status required.
$ Given: Eight fellowships awarded annually, one for a senior fellow and seven for less experienced researchers; each for $115–$27,000.
Application Information: Write for details.
Deadline: November 15.
Contact: American Fellowship Program.

**American Association of
University Women
Educational Foundation
AAUW Dissertation
Fellowships**
Department 60
2201 No. Dodge Street
Iowa City, IA 52243-4030
(319) 337-1716
www.aauw.org

Description: Fellowships to support doctoral candidates in full-time dissertation work for at least twelve months in any field.
Restrictions: Limited to women applicants; applicants must have completed all coursework and exams for Ph.D. by November; United States citizenship required.
$ Given: Fifty of fellowships awarded annually; each for $13,500 which may not be used for tuition or loan repayment.
Application Information: Application forms must be requested in writing.
Deadline: November 15.
Contact: Dissertation Fellowship Program.

**American Association of
University Women
Educational Foundation
AAUW International
Fellowships**
Department 60
2201 No. Dodge Street
Iowa City, IA 52243-4030
(319) 337-1716
www.aauw.org

Description: Fellowships for one year of graduate study/research at an approved institution in the United States; recipients chosen on the basis of professional potential and importance of project to home country.
Restrictions: Limited to women applicants; applicants must be citizens of countries other than the United States; applicants must hold B.A./B.S. or equivalent; proficiency in English required; recipients must return to home countries to work after fellowships are completed.
$ Given: An unspecified number of fellowships awarded annually; each for $16,500.

Application Information: Write for details.
Deadline: Postmark December 15.
Contact: International Fellowship Program.

American Association of University Women Educational Foundation AAUW Selected Professions Fellowships
Department 60
2201 No. Dodge Street
Iowa City, IA 52243-4030
(319) 337-1716
www.aauw.org

Description: Fellowships for graduate students entering their final year of study in fields with traditionally low female representation, including architecture, business administration, computer science, dentistry, engineering, law, mathematics/statistics, medicine, and veterinary medicine; recipients chosen on the basis of academic achievement; tenable for full-time study at accredited United States institutions.
Restrictions: Limited to women who are members of minority groups; United States citizenship or permanent resident status required.
$ Given: An unspecified number of fellowships of $5,000–$12,000 each are awarded annually.
Application Information: Application forms available August 1 through November 1.
Deadline: November 15.

American Association of University Women Educational Foundation AAUW Selected Professions Program Dissertation Fellowships in Engineering
Department 60
2201 No. Dodge Street
Iowa City, IA 52243-4030
(319) 337-1716
www.aauw.org

Description: Fellowships for doctoral candidates in engineering; to support dissertation work.
Restrictions: Limited to women applicants; applicants must have completed all coursework and exams for Ph.D.; United States citizenship or permanent resident status required.
$ Given: An unspecified number of fellowships awarded annually; each for $15,000.
Application Information: Application forms available August 1 through November 1.
Deadline: November 15.
Contact: Selected Professions Fellowship Program.

American Association of Women Dentists Colgate-Palmolive Award
401 N. Michigan Avenue
Chicago, IL 60611
(800) 920-2293
www.aawd.org

Description: Grants for dental school students, to support senior year of study; recipients chosen on the basis of financial need.
Restrictions: Limited to women dental students only.
$ Given: Ten awards made annually; each for $500.
Application Information: Ten dental schools participate annually; the ten schools are selected on a rotating basis; each school's dean chooses one student to receive the award.
Deadline: Varies.
Contact: Deene Alongi.

Association for Women in Science Educational Foundation
AWIS Predoctoral Award
1200 New York Avenue, N.W.
Suite 650
Washington, DC 20005
(202) 326-8940
www.awis.org

Description: Awards for doctoral candidates in life sciences, physical sciences, social sciences, engineering, mathematics, and behavioral sciences; recipients chosen on the basis of academic achievement and quality of proposed research.
Restrictions: Limited to women only; United States citizenship or enrollment in United States institution required.
$ Given: An unspecified number of grants of $1,000 each are awarded annually.
Application Information: Write for details.
Deadline: January 15.

AT&T Bell Laboratories Graduate Research Program for Women
1505 Riverview Road
P.O. Box 297
St. Peter, MN 56082
www.bell-labs.com

Description: Fellowships and grants for graduate study toward Ph.D. degree, for graduating college seniors with the potential to become professional research scientists or engineers; relevant disciplines include chemistry, chemical engineering, communication science, computer science, electrical engineering, information science, materials science, mathematics, operations research, physics, and statistics; fellowship tenure includes summer work at AT&T; recipients chosen on the basis of academic achievement and proposed research.
Restrictions: Limited to women applicants only; applicants must be admitted for full-time study in approved doctoral program; United States citizenship or permanent resident status required.
$ Given: An unspecified number of fellowships awarded annually; fellowships and grants are renewable annually. Living stipend of $17,000 plus tuition and fees. An additional $2,000 is available the following year to benefit professional development.
Application Information: Application forms required.
Deadline: December 20.
Contact: Special Programs Manager, GRPW.

Bunting Institute Fellowship Program
34 Concord Avenue
Cambridge, MA 02138
(617) 495-8136
www.radcliffe.edu/bunting

Description: Postdoctoral fellowships for women to pursue research in all fields of scholarship, professions, creative writing, poetry, visual and performing arts, music, and sciences not included in the Science Scholars Fellowship.
Restrictions: U.S. citizenship required. Limited to women applicants only who have received their doctorate at least two years prior to application.
$ Given: Five to eight fellowships awarded annually, each in the amount $28,500.
Application Information: Write for details.
Deadline: Early October.

Bunting Institute Fellowship Program
34 Concord Avenue
Cambridge, MA 02138
(617) 495-8136
www.radcliffe.edu/bunting

Description: Fellowships to support women actively involved in finding peaceful solutions to conflict or potential conflict among groups of nations.
Restrictions: Limited to women applicants only.
$ Given: One fellowship awarded annually in the amount of $25,000.
Application Information: Write for details.
Deadline: January.

Bunting Institute Science Scholars Fellowship Program
34 Concord Avenue
Cambridge, MA 02138
(617) 495-8136
www.radcliffe.edu/bunting

Description: Postdoctoral fellowships to support women scientists in any level in any of the following fields: astronomy, molecular and cellular biology, biochemistry, chemistry, cognitive and neural sciences, mathematics, computer science, electrical, aerospace, and mechanical engineering, materials science, naval architecture, ocean engineering, oceanography, physics, and geology.
Restrictions: U.S. citizenship required. Limited to women applicants only who have received their doctorate at least two years prior to application.
$ Given: Eight fellowships awarded annually, each in the amount of $31,300.
Application Information: Write for details.
Deadline: Early October.

Business and Professional Women's Foundation BPW Career Advancement Scholarships
2012 Massachusetts Avenue, N.W.
Washington, DC 20036
(202) 293-1100
www.bpwusa.org

Description: One-year scholarships for undergraduate and graduate study in all disciplines, with emphasis on computer science, education, science, mathematics, business, humanities, and paralegal training; scholarships are awarded within twenty-four months of the applicant's completing an undergraduate or graduate program in the United States; recipients chosen on the basis of financial need; funding designed to improve recipients' chances for career advancement/success.
Restrictions: Limited to women only; applicants must be at least 25 years old; no funding for Ph.D. studies, study abroad, or correspondence courses; United States citizenship and affiliation with United States institution required.
$ Given: Approximately 150 scholarships of up to $1,000 each are awarded annually.
Application Information: Request application materials between October 1 and April 1.
Deadline: April 15.
Contact: Assistant Director, Education and Training.

Business and Professional Women's Foundation BPW/Sears-Roebuck Loan Fund for Women in Graduate Business Studies
2012 Massachusetts Avenue, N.W.
Washington, DC 20036
(202) 293-1100
www.bpwusa.org

Description: Loans for master's degree candidates studying business administration at accredited institutions.
Restrictions: Limited to women only; BPW and Sears Foundation employees ineligible; United States citizenship required.
$ Given: An unspecified number of loans of up to $2,500 each are awarded annually.
Application Information: Request application materials between October 1 and April 1.
Deadline: May 1.
Contact: Education Department.

Business and Professional Women's Foundation Education Program
New York Life Foundation for Women in the Health Professions
2012 Massachusetts Avenue, N.W.
Washington, DC 20036
(202) 296-9118

Description: Fellowships to support women seeking entry or re-entry into the work force in the field of healthcare. Recipients chosen on the basis of financial need.
Restrictions: U.S. citizenship required. Limited to women 25 years of age or older.
$ Given: An unspecified number of fellowships awarded annually, each from $500 to $1,000.
Application Information: Send SASE.
Deadline: April 15.

Canadian Federation of University Women Georgette LeMoyne
251 Bank Street
Suite 600
Ottawa, Ontario K2P 1X3
Canada
(613) 234-2732
www.cfuw.ca

Description: Award for graduate studies in any field; intended for women taking refresher studies at universities where instruction is in French.
Restrictions: Limited to women only; applicant must hold B.S./B.A. degree and have been accepted to proposed program of graduate study; Canadian citizenship or minimum landed immigrant status required.
$ Given: One award for $1,000 Canadian made annually.
Application Information: Write for details.
Deadline: November 15.
Contact: Chair, Fellowships Committee.

Canadian Federation of University Women CFUW Memorial Grant
251 Bank Street
Suite 600
Ottawa, Ontario K2P 1X3
Canada
(613) 234-2732
www.cfuw.ca

Description: Grant for B.S./B.A. holders, to support graduate study in science and technology; recipients chosen on the basis of academic achievement, personal qualities, and potential.
Restrictions: Limited to women only; applicants must be accepted at intended places of study; Canadian citizenship or one-year landed immigrant status required.
$ Given: One grant of $1,000 Canadian awarded annually.
Application Information: Request application between July 1 and November 13.
Deadline: November 15.
Contact: Chair, Fellowships Committee.

Canadian Federation of University Women CFUW Polytechnique Commemorative Awards
251 Bank Street
Suite 600
Ottawa, Ontario K2P 1X3
Canada
(613) 234-2732
www.cfuw.ca

Description: Awards for graduate studies in any field, with preference for studies related to women's issues.
Restrictions: Applicant must hold B.S./B.A. degree and have been accepted to proposed program of graduate study; Canadian citizenship or minimum one-year landed immigrant status required.
$ Given: One grant of $1,400 Canadian awarded annually.
Application Information: Write for details.
Deadline: November 15.
Contact: Fellowships Committee.

Canadian Federation of University Women Beverly Jackson Fellowship
251 Bank Street
Suite 600
Ottawa, Ontario K2P 1X3
Canada
(613) 234-2732
www.cfuw.ca

Description: Fellowship for B.S./B.A. holders to pursue graduate work in any discipline; tenable at Ontario universities; recipients chosen on the basis of academic achievement, personal qualities, and potential.
Restrictions: Limited to women only; minimum age 35; applicants must hold B.S./B.A. from recognized university and be accepted into proposed place of study; Canadian citizenship or minimum one-year landed immigrant status required.
$ Given: One fellowship for $3,500 Canadian is awarded annually.
Application Information: Application forms are available July 1 through November 13.
Deadline: November 15.
Contact: Chair, Fellowships Committee.

Canadian Federation of University Women Margaret McWilliams Predoctoral Fellowship
251 Bank Street
Suite 600
Ottawa, Ontario K2P 1X3
Canada
(613) 234-2732
www.cfuw.ca

Description: Fellowship for doctoral candidates in any discipline who hold master's degrees and are at least one year into doctoral program; recipients chosen on the basis of academic achievement, personal qualities, and potential.
Restrictions: Limited to women only; Canadian citizenship or minimum one-year landed immigrant status required.
$ Given: One fellowship of $8,000 Canadian is awarded annually.
Application Information: Application forms are available July 1 through November 13.
Deadline: November 15.
Contact: Chair, Fellowships Committee.

**Canadian Federation of
University Women
Margaret Dale Philip Award**
251 Bank Street
Suite 600
Ottawa, Ontario K2P 1X3
Canada
(613) 234-2732
www.cfuw.ca

Description: Award to graduate students in the humanities and social sciences, with preference to applicants studying Canadian history; recipients chosen on the basis of academic achievement in college, personal qualities, and potential.
Restrictions: Limited to women only; applicants must hold B.S./B.A. degree and have been accepted to proposed program of graduate study; Canadian citizenship or minimum one-year landed immigrant status required.
$ Given: One grant of $1,000 Canadian is awarded annually.
Application Information: Write for details.
Deadline: November 15.
Contact: Fellowships Committee.

**Canadian Federation of
University Women
Professional Fellowship**
251 Bank Street
Suite 600
Ottawa, Ontario K2P 1X3
Canada
(613) 234-2732
www.cfuw.ca

Description: Fellowship for graduate work below Ph.D. level; recipients chosen on the basis of academic, personal qualities, and potential.
Restrictions: Limited to women only; applicants must hold B.S./B.A. degree and have been accepted to proposed program of graduate study; Canadian citizenship or minimum one-year landed immigrant status required.
$ Given: Two fellowships for $5,000 Canadian each are awarded annually.
Application Information: Application forms available July 1 through November 13.
Deadline: November 15.
Contact: Chair, Fellowships Committee.

**Canadian Federation of
University Women
Alice E. Wilson Grants**
251 Bank Street
Suite 600
Ottawa, Ontario K2P 1X3
Canada
(613) 234-2732
www.cfuw.ca

Description: Grants for women pursuing graduate refresher work in any field; recipients chosen on the basis of academic achievement, personal qualities, and potential; special consideration given to applicants returning to academic study after several years.
Restrictions: Limited to women only; applicants must hold B.S./B.A. degree and have been accepted to proposed program of graduate study; Canadian citizenship or minimum one-year landed immigrant status required.
$ Given: At least five grants for $1,000 Canadian each are awarded annually.
Application Information: Application forms available July 1 through November 13.
Deadline: November 15.
Contact: Chair, Fellowships Committee.

Carnegie Institute of Washington Fellowship in Astronomy
Carnegie Observatories
813 Santa Barbara Street
Pasadena, CA 91101
www.carnegie-institute.com

Description: One- to two-year predoctoral and postdoctoral fellowships to support research in the field of astronomy.
Restrictions: None. Qualified women and minorities encouraged to apply.
$ Given: An unspecified number of fellowships of varying amounts awarded annually.
Application Information: Write for details.
Deadline: Varies.

Carnegie Institute of Washington Fellowship in Embryology
Department of Embryology
115 West University Parkway
Baltimore, MD 21210
(202) 387-6400
www.carnegie-institute.com

Description: One- to two-year predoctoral and postdoctoral fellowships to support research in the field of embryology.
Restrictions: None. Qualified women and minorities encouraged to apply.
$ Given: An unspecified number of fellowships of varying amounts awarded annually.
Application Information: Write for details.
Deadline: Varies.

Carnegie Institute of Washington Fellowship in Geophysics
Geophysical Laboratory
5251 Broad Branch Road, N.W.
Washington, DC 20015
(202) 387-6400
www.carnegie-institute.com

Description: One- to two-year predoctoral and postdoctoral fellowships to support research of physicochemical studies of geological problems, with particular emphasis on the process involved in the formation of the Earth's crust, mantle, and core.
Restrictions: None. Qualified women and minorities encouraged to apply.
$ Given: An unspecified number of fellowships of varying amounts awarded annually.
Application Information: Write for details.
Deadline: Varies.

Carnegie Institute of Washington Fellowship in Physics
Department of Terrestrial Magnetism
5241 Broad Branch Road, N.W.
Washington, DC 20015
(202) 387-6400
www.carnegie-institute.com

Description: One- to two-year predoctoral and postdoctoral fellowships to support research in the field of physics and related sciences, including astrophysics, geophysics and geochemistry, and planetary physics.
Restrictions: None. Qualified women and minorities encouraged to apply.
$ Given: An unspecified number of fellowships of varying amounts awarded annually.
Application Information: Write for details.
Deadline: Varies.

Carnegie Institute of Washington Fellowship in Plant Biology
Department of Plant Biology
290 Panama Street
Stanford, CA 94305
www.carnegie-institute.com

Description: One- to two-year predoctoral and postdoctoral fellowships to support research in the field of photosynthesis and the physiological and biochemical mechanisms that underlie the financial diversity and adaptations of plants.
Restrictions: None. Qualified women and minorities encouraged to apply.
$ Given: An unspecified number of fellowships of varying amounts awarded annually.
Application Information: Write for details.
Deadline: Varies.

Electrical Women's Round Table, Inc.
Julia Kiene Fellowship
P.O. Box 292793
Nashville, TN 37229-2793
(615) 254-4479

Description: Fellowship for graduate students in the field of electrical engineering or physics.
Restrictions: Limited to women applicants only.
$ Given: One fellowship awarded annually for up to $1,000.
Application Information: Write for details.
Deadline: March.

French Association of University Women
Dorothy Leet Fellowships
4, rue de Chevreuse
75006 Paris
France

Description: Fellowships for American women who are doctoral candidates or postdoctoral scholars who wish to pursue research in France.
Restrictions: Limited to women applicants. U.S. citizenship required.
$ Given: An unspecified number of fellowships awarded annually, each for $500 to $2,000.
Application Information: Write for details.
Deadline: March 31.
Contact: Danielle Gondard-Cozette, President, Fellowship Committee.

Iota Sigma Pi Agnes Fay Morgan Research Award
Chemistry and Physics Department
Radford University
Radford, VA 24142
(540) 831-5413
www.chem-faculty.ucsd.edu.sawrey/ISP

Description: Award to recognize research achievement by a woman chemist in the fields of chemistry or biochemistry.
Restrictions: Limited to women chemists 40 years of age or under.
$ Given: One award of $400.
Application Information: Write for details.
Deadline: January 15.
Contact: Dr. Christine K. F. Hermann.

**Institute of International
Education
Fulbright Internships in India
U.S. Student Programs
Division**
809 United Nations Plaza
New York, NY 10017-3580
(212) 984-5330
www.iie.org

Description: Internships for master's candidates in child care, crafts, marketing, special education for the handicapped, sports education, and women's issues; for up to nine months of study in India for academic credit (June/July–March/April).
Restrictions: Knowledge of Indian language (esp. Hindi) useful but not required; applicants must be unmarried and at least 24 years old; United States citizenship required.
$ Given: An unspecified number of grants awarded annually; partial scholarship.
Application Information: Write for details.
Deadline: N/A.

**Monticello College
Foundation and Washington
University
Spencer T. Olin Fellowships
for Women in Graduate Study**
Graduate School of Arts and
Sciences
Washington University
Campus Box 1187
One Brookings Drive
St. Louis, MO 63130-4899
(314) 935-6848

Description: Fellowships for graduate students to prepare for careers in higher education and professions in the fields of biological and biomedical sciences, humanities, physical sciences and mathematics, social and behavioral sciences, architecture, business administration, engineering, fine arts, law, medicine, and social work. Tenable at Washington University.
Restrictions: Limited to women applicants only.
$ Given: An unspecified number of fellowships awarded annually, each ranging from $20,000 to $33,000.
Application Information: Write for details.
Deadline: February 1.

**National Physical Sciences
Consortium Fellowship
Program**
New Mexico State University
Box 30001, Dept. 3NPS
Las Cruces, NM 88003-0001
(800) 952-4118
www.npsc.org

Description: Fellowships for graduate students in the fields of the physical sciences, mathematics, and computer sciences enrolled at or applying to one of approximately sixty-two participating institutions to pursue a Ph.D.
Restrictions: U.S. citizenship required. Recruiting Native American, African American, Hispanic American, and/or women.
$ Given: One fellowship awarded annually; with an annual stipend of $12,000 plus tuition and fees. Renewable for a total of six years.
Application Information: Write for details.
Deadline: Early November.

National Women's Studies Association
NAIAD-NWSA Graduate Scholarships in Lesbian Studies
7100 Baltimore Avenue
Suite 500
College Park, MD 20740
(301) 403-0525
www.nws.org

Description: Scholarships for master's and doctoral candidates in lesbian studies; recipient chosen on the basis of financial need and thesis/dissertation topic.
Restrictions: Membership in NWSA preferred.
$ Given: One scholarship for $500 awarded annually.
Application Information: Write for details.
Deadline: February 15.
Contact: Loretta Younger, Office Manager.

National Women's Studies Association
NWSA Scholarship in Jewish Women's Studies
7100 Baltimore Avenue
Suite 500
College Park, MD 20740
(301) 403-0525

Description: Scholarship for graduate students in Jewish women's studies; recipients chosen on the basis of financial need and academic achievement.
Restrictions: N/A.
$ Given: One scholarship for $500 awarded annually.
Application Information: Write for details.
Deadline: February 15.
Contact: Loretta Younger, Office Manager.

National Women's Studies Association
Pergamon-NWSA Graduate Scholarships in Women's Studies
7100 Baltimore Avenue
Suite 500
College Park, MD 20740
(301) 403-0525

Description: Scholarship for master's and doctoral candidates in women's studies; recipients chosen on the basis of financial need and proposed research; preference for research project on women of color, Third World women, or women and class.
Restrictions: Membership in NWSA preferred. Minority applicants only.
$ Given: Two scholarships awarded annually; for $800.
Application Information: Write for details.
Deadline: February 1.
Contact: Loretta Younger, Office Manager.

Newberry Library
Frances C. Allen Fellowships
Committee on Awards
60 West Walton Street
Chicago, IL 60610-3380
(312) 943-9090
www.newberry.org

Description: One-month to one-year research fellowships for master's and doctoral candidates in the humanities and social sciences; tenable primarily at the D'Arcy McNickle Center for the History of the American Indian.
Restrictions: Limited to female Native American applicants.
$ Given: $30,000.
Application Information: Write for details.
Deadline: January 20.

Newberry Library Monticello College Foundation Fellowship for Women
60 West Walton Street
Chicago, IL 60610-3380
(312) 255-3595
www.newberry.org

Description: Six-month fellowships for women at the early stages of their professional careers to pursue six months of research and writing in any field appropriate to the Newberry's Collections, specifically American and European history and literature or women's studies.
Restrictions: U.S. citizenship or permanent resident status required. Limited to women applicants possessing a Ph.D.
$ Given: One fellowship awarded annually, with a $12,000 stipend.
Application Information: Write for details.
Deadline: January 20.

Organization of American States Julia Maclean Vinas Fellowship
89 F Street
Washington, DC 20006-4499
(202) 458-6208

Description: Fellowship for undergraduate or graduate students who are completing at least the last two years of their degree.
Restrictions: Limited to Peruvian women studying in the Washington, DC area.
$ Given: One to two fellowships awarded annually of unspecified amounts.
Application Information: Write for details.
Deadline: N/A.

Phi Beta Kappa Society Mary Isabel Sibley Fellowship
1785 Massachusetts Avenue, N.W.
4th Floor
Washington, DC 20036
(202) 265-3808
www.pbk.org

Description: One-year fellowship for postdoctoral scholars and doctoral candidates at dissertation level for research on French language and literature or Greek language, literature, history and archaeology; recipients chosen on the basis of academic achievement and quality of proposed research.
Restrictions: Limited to unmarried women ages 25–35 only; recipients must devote full-time efforts to research.
$ Given: One fellowship for $20,000 is awarded annually; non-renewable.
Application Information: French fellowship awarded in even-numbered years; Greek fellowship awarded in odd numbered years.
Deadline: January 15.
Contact: Linda D. Surles, Program Officer.

The Radcliffe Research Support Program
Henry A. Murray Research Center
10 Garden Street
Cambridge, MA 02138
(617) 495-8140
FAX (617) 495-8422
www.radcliffe.edu/murray/grants/rrsprog.htm

Description: Grants for post-doctoral scholars for research drawing on the Henry A. Murray Research Center's data resources. The Research Center is a repository for social science data on human development and social change, particularly the changing life experiences of American women. Recipients chosen on the basis of scientific merit of proposed research, potential contribution to the relevant field of study, the extent to which the project takes advantage of data in the Murray Center archive, and the adequacy of the budget for proposed work.

Restrictions: None.
$ Given: An unspecified number of grants awarded annually, each for up to $5,000.
Application Information: Write for details.
Deadline: January 15.
Contact: Grants Administrator.

**Sigma Delta Epsilon/
Graduate Women in Science
Eloise Gerry Fellowships**
P.O. Box 19947
San Diego, CA 92159
(619) 583-4856

Description: One-year research fellowships for graduate students and postdoctoral scholars in the biological and chemical sciences; recipients chosen on the basis of academic achievement, financial need, and proposed research.
Restrictions: Limited to women applicants only; funding may not be used for tuition; applicants may not apply simultaneously for other SDE fellowships.
$ Given: Three to six fellowships awarded annually; each for $1,200–$3,000.
Application Information: Write for details.
Deadline: December 1.
Contact: Doris Brown, Secretary.

**SUNY Albany Fellowship on
Women and Public Policy**
Center for Women in
Government
University at Albany
State University of New York
Draper Hall, Rm 302
135 Western Avenue
Albany, NY 12222
(518) 442-3877

Description: Seven-month fellowship for graduate students in all fields of study pursuing careers in public policy. Fellows are assigned to a non-profit organization or legislator of a state agency for thirty hours per week.
Restrictions: Applicants must be matriculated graduate students in N.Y. state program. Background in research, employment, or volunteer activities designed to improve status of women and underrepresented populations preferred.
$ Given: One fellowship awarded annually with $9,000 stipend.
Application Information: Write for details.
Deadline: March 15.
Contact: Dorothy Hogan.

**Wellesley College
Anne Louise Barett
Fellowship**
Office of Financial Aid
106 Central Street
Wellesley, MA 02181
(781) 283-3525
www.wellesley.edu

Description: Fellowship for B.S./B.A. holders and graduating college seniors in the fields of music theory, composition and history; tenable for full-time graduate study in the United States or abroad at institutions other than Wellesley; recipients chosen on the basis of merit and financial need.
Restrictions: Limited to women graduates of Wellesley.
$ Given: One fellowship of up to $4,000 is awarded annually.
Application Information: Request application form before November 25.
Deadline: January 3.
Contact: Secretary to the Committee on Graduate Fellowships.

Wellesley College
Ruth Ingersoll Goldmark
Fellowship
Office of Financial Aid
106 Central Street
Wellesley, MA 02181
(781) 283-3525
www.wellesley.edu

Description: Fellowship for B.S./B.A. holders and graduating college seniors in the fields of English literature, composition, and the classics; tenable for full-time graduate study in the United States or abroad at institutions other than Wellesley; recipients chosen on the basis of merit and financial need.
Restrictions: Limited to women graduates of Wellesley.
$ Given: One fellowship of up to $1,500 is awarded annually.
Application Information: Request application form before November 25.
Deadline: January 3.
Contact: Secretary to the Committee on Graduate Fellowships.

Wellesley College
Edna V. Moffett Fellowship
Office of Financial Aid
106 Central Street
Wellesley, MA 02181
(781) 283-3525
www.wellesley.edu

Description: Fellowship for B.S./B.A. holders and graduating college seniors in the field of history; tenable for full-time graduate study in the United States or abroad at institutions other than Wellesley; preference for individuals entering their first year of graduate study; recipients chosen on the basis of merit and financial need.
Restrictions: Limited to women graduates of Wellesley.
$ Given: One fellowship of up to $4,000 is awarded annually.
Application Information: Request application form before November 25.
Deadline: January 3.
Contact: Secretary to the Committee on Graduate Fellowships.

Wellesley College
Mary McEwin Schimke
Scholarships
Office of Financial Aid
Box GR
106 Central Street
Wellesley, MA 02181
(781) 283-3525
www.wellesley.edu

Description: Scholarships for B.S./B.A. in the fields of literature, history, and American studies; recipients chosen on the basis of merit and financial need; tenable for graduate study at institutions other than Wellesley; intended to afford relief from costs of household and child care during graduate study.
Restrictions: Limited to women applicants; minimum age 30; applicants must have received their bachelor's degrees from United States institutions.
$ Given: An unspecified number of scholarships of up to $1,000 each are awarded annually.
Application Information: Request application form before November 25.
Deadline: January 3.
Contact: Secretary to the Committee on Graduate Fellowships.

Wellesley College
Vida Dutton Scudder
Fellowship
Office of Financial Aid
106 Central Street
Wellesley, MA 02181
(781) 283-3525
www.wellesley.edu

Description: Fellowship for B.S./B.A. holders and graduating college seniors in the fields of literature, political
science, and the social sciences; tenable for full-time
graduate study in the United States or abroad at institutions other than Wellesley; recipients chosen on the basis
of merit and financial need.
Restrictions: Limited to women graduates of Wellesley.
$ Given: One fellowship of up to $4,000 is awarded
annually.
Application Information: Request application form
before November 25.
Deadline: January 3.
Contact: Secretary to the Committee on Graduate
Fellowships.

Wellesley College
M.A. Carland Shackford
Medical Fellowship
Office of Financial Aid
106 Central Street
Wellesley, MA 02181
(781) 283-3525
www.wellesley.edu

Description: Fellowship for medical students pursuing
general medical practice (not psychiatry); recipients chosen on the basis of academic achievement and financial
need.
Restrictions: Limited to women only; applicants may be
graduates of any United States undergraduate academic
institution.
$ Given: One fellowship with a minimum of $7,000
awarded annually.
Application Information: Application forms available
after November 20.
Deadline: January 3.
Contact: Secretary to the Committee on Graduate
Fellowships.

Wellesley College
Harriet A. Shaw Fellowship
Office of Financial Aid
106 Central Street
Wellesley, MA 02181
(781) 283-3525
www.wellesley.edu

Description: Fellowship for B.S./B.A. in the fields of
music and allied arts; tenable for full-time graduate study
in the United States or abroad; recipients chosen on the
basis of academic achievement and financial need.
Restrictions: Limited to women graduates of Wellesley.
$ Given: One fellowship of up to $4,000 is awarded
annually.
Application Information: Request application form
before November 25.
Deadline: January 3.
Contact: Secretary to the Committee on Graduate
Fellowships.

Woodrow Wilson Johnson & Johnson Dissertation Grants in Children's Health
CN 5281
Princeton, NJ 08543-5281
(609) 452-7007
www.woodrow.org/womens-studies/health

Description: Grants for dissertation research on issues related to children's health, specifically its significance for public policy or treatment. Recipients chosen on the basis of originality and significance, scholarly validity, commitment to women's health, academic achievement.
Restrictions: Applicants must have completed all pre-dissertation requirements at graduate schools in the United States.
$ Given: Five grants awarded annually, each for $2,000 to be used for expenses connected with dissertation.
Application Information: Write for details.
Deadline: November 8.

Woodrow Wilson Johnson & Johnson Dissertation Grants in Women's Health
CN 5281
Princeton, NJ 08543-5281
(609) 452-7007
www.woodrow.org/womens-studies/health

Description: Grants for dissertation research on issues related to women's health, specifically its significance for public policy or treatment. Recipients chosen on the basis of originality and significance, scholarly validity, commitment to women's health, academic achievement.
Restrictions: Applicants must have completed all pre-dissertation requirements at graduate schools in the United States.
$ Given: Ten grants awarded annually, each for $2,000 to be used for expenses connected with dissertation.
Application Information: Write for details.
Deadline: November 8.

Woodrow Wilson National Fellowship Foundation Women's Studies Doctoral Research Grants
CN 5281
Princeton, NJ 08543
(609) 452-7007
www.woodrow.org

Description: Research grants for doctoral candidates at dissertation level in women's studies; recipients chosen on the basis of proposed dissertation research.
Restrictions: Applicants should have completed all Ph.D. requirements except dissertation at United States graduate schools.
$ Given: Fifteen research grants for $1,500 each are awarded annually.
Application Information: Write for details.
Deadline: November 8.
Contact: Director, Women's Studies Program.

State Historical Society of Wisconsin
Alice E. Smith Fellowship
816 State Street
Madison, WI 53706
(608) 264-6464
www.shsw.wisc.edu

Description: Research fellowships for master's and doctoral candidates studying American history, especially that of Wisconsin or the Midwest; recipients chosen on the basis of proposed research.
Restrictions: Limited to women only.
$ Given: One fellowship for $2,000 is awarded annually.
Application Information: Write for details.
Deadline: July 15.
Contact: Michael E. Stevens, State Historian.

Women's Research and Education Institute Congressional Fellowships on Women and Public Policy
1750 New York Avenue, N.W.
Suite 350
Washington, DC 20006
(202) 328-7070
www.wrei.org

Description: Congressional fellowship program designed to train women as potential public policy leaders; fellowship runs January through September and involves thirty hours/week work in a United States Congress office as a legislative aide on policy issues affecting women; open to master's and doctoral candidates at United States institutions; relevant disciplines include humanities, social sciences, biology and biomedical sciences, engineering and applied sciences, biomedical engineering, technology management and policy, business administration and management, health services management and hospital administration, education, allied health professionals, medicine, nursing, public and community health, and law; recipients chosen on the basis of political/civic activity and interest in women's issues.
Restrictions: Limited to women applicants; nine hours previous graduate coursework preferred; United States citizenship preferred.
$ Given: Eight to fifteen fellowships awarded annually; each with $9,500 stipend plus $500 for health insurance and up to $1,500 toward six hours tuition at home institution.
Application Information: Request application after November 1.
Deadline: February 14.
Contact: Alison Dineen, Fellowship Director.

Zonta International Foundation Amelia Earhart Fellowship Awards
557 West Randolph Street
Chicago, IL 60661-2206
(312) 930-5848
www.zonta.org

Description: Fellowships for women pursuing graduate degrees in aerospace-related sciences and aerospace-related engineering. Tenable at any university. Recipients chosen on the basis of academic achievement, the relevance of applicant's research to aerospace-related sciences or engineering, and career goals as they relate to advancing knowledge in these fields.
Restrictions: Limited to women applicants who have completed one year of graduate school only.
$ Given: One fellowship awarded annually for $6,000.
Application Information: Write for details.
Deadline: November 1.

Zonta International Foundation Jane M. Kausman Women in Business Scholarships
557 West Randolph Street
Chicago, IL 60661-2206
(312) 930-5848
www.zonta.org

Description: Scholarships for undergraduate women pursuing careers and leadership positions in business-related fields.
Restrictions: Limited to women applicants in their second or third year of a business-related program only.
$ Given: An unspecified number of scholarships of varying amounts awarded annually.
Application Information: Write for details.
Deadline: N/A.

Zonta International Foundation Michael J. Freeman Scholarships for Irish Women
557 West Randolph Street
Chicago, IL 60661-2206
(312) 930-5848
www.zonta.org

Description: Full-tuition scholarships to assist Irish women pursuing technical and scientific studies.
Restrictions: Limited to Irish women citizens only.
$ Given: An unspecified number of scholarships of varying amounts awarded annually.
Application Information: Write for details.
Deadline: N/A.

Ethnic Only, Ethnic Preferred, Foreign Nationals

American Association of University Women Educational Foundation AAUW International Fellowships
Department 60
2201 No. Dodge Street
Iowa City, IA 52243-4030
(319) 337-1716
www.aauw.org

Description: Fellowships for one year of graduate study/research at an approved institution in the United States; recipients chosen on the basis of professional potential and importance of project to home country.
Restrictions: Limited to women applicants; applicants must be citizens of countries other than the United States; applicants must hold B.A./B.S. or equivalent; proficiency in English required; recipients must return to home countries to work after fellowships are completed.
$ Given: An unspecified number of fellowships awarded annually; each for $16,500.
Application Information: Write for details.
Deadline: December 1.
Contact: International Fellowship Program.

American Association of University Women Educational Foundation AAUW Selected Professions Fellowships
Department 60
2201 No. Dodge Street
Iowa City, IA 52243-4030
(319) 337-1716
www.aauw.org

Description: Fellowships for graduate students entering their final year of study in fields with traditionally low female representation, including architecture, business administration, computer science, dentistry, engineering, law, mathematics/statistics, medicine, and veterinary medicine; recipients chosen on the basis of academic achievement; tenable for full-time study at accredited United States institutions.
Restrictions: Limited to women who are members of minority groups; United States citizenship or permanent resident status required.
$ Given: An unspecified number of fellowships of $5,000–$12,000 each are awarded annually.
Application Information: Application forms available August 1 through November 1.
Deadline: November 15.

American Institute of Certified Public Accountants Minority Accounting Scholarships
1211 Avenue of the Americas
New York, NY 10036-8775
(212) 596-6223
www.aicpa.org

Description: Scholarships for undergraduate and graduate students majoring in accounting; recipients chosen on the basis of academic achievement.
Restrictions: Limited to minority group members only; United States citizenship or permanent resident status required.
$ Given: An unspecified number of scholarships awarded annually; varying amounts up to $5,000.

Application Information: Request application forms from the Institute.
Deadline: July 1.

**American Institute of
Certified Public Accountants
Minority Scholarships**
1211 Avenue of the Americas
New York, NY 10036-8775
(212) 596-6227
www.aicpa.org

Description: Scholarships for full-time undergraduate and graduate students at accredited institutions pursuing degrees in accounting. Recipients chosen on the basis of financial need and potential to become CPAs.
Restrictions: U.S. citizenship required. Limited to minority applicants only.
$ Given: An unspecified number of scholarships awarded, each in the amount of $5,000.
Application Information: Write for details.
Deadline: July 1.

**American Indian Graduate
Center Graduate Fellowships**
4520 Montgomery Boulevard,
N.E.
Suite 1-B
Albuquerque, NM 87109
(505) 881-4584
www.aigc.com

Description: Multi-year fellowships for graduate students in all fields of study offering a master's or doctoral degree. Recipients chosen on the basis of financial need.
Restrictions: U.S. citizenship required. Limited to American Indian and Alaska Native applicants.
$ Given: An unspecified number of fellowships for varying amounts awarded annually.
Application Information: Write for details.
Deadlines: April 15, June 1.

**American Planning
Association
Planning Fellowships**
122 South Michigan Avenue,
Suite 1600
Chicago, IL 60603
(312) 431-9100

Description: Fellowships for students enrolled in planning or closely related field at an APA approved college or university.
Restrictions: U.S. citizenship required; limited to African American, Hispanic, and Native American applicants only enrolled in an approved graduate planning program.
$ Given: An unspecified number of fellowships awarded annually; each ranging from $2,000 to $4,000.
Application Information: Write for details.
Deadline: N/A.
Contact: Margot Morrison.

**American Psychological
Association
APA Minority Fellowship
Program in Neuroscience**
Washington, DC 20002
(202) 336-5500
www.apa.org

Description: Ten-month fellowships for doctoral candidates in neuroscience; recipients chosen on the basis of academic achievement, financial need, and commitment to future career in neuroscience research.
Restrictions: African-American, Hispanic, Native American, Alaskan Native, Asian-American, and Pacific Islander applicants preferred; applicants must be planning careers in neuroscience; United States or Canadian citizenship or permanent resident status required.
$ Given: An unspecified number of fellowships awarded

annually; each for $7,084 plus cost-sharing arrangement for full tuition scholarship; renewable for up to three years if recipient maintains good academic standing.
Application Information: Write for details.
Deadline: January 15.
Contact: Dr. James M. Jones, Director; or Ernesto Guerra, Minority Fellowship Program.

American Psychological Association
APA Minority Fellowship Program in Psychology
750 First Street, NE
Washington, DC 20002-4242
(202) 336-0127
www.apa.org

Description: Fellowship for doctoral candidates in psychology; one program to support the training of clinicians, another program to support the training of researchers; recipients chosen on the basis of academic achievement and financial need.
Restrictions: African-American, Hispanic, Native American, Alaskan Native, Asian-American, and Pacific Islander applicants preferred; United States citizenship or legal residency required; applicants must be planning careers in psychology.
$ Given: An unspecified number of fellowships awarded annually; $7,084 for ten months; renewable for up to three years.
Application Information: Write for details.
Deadline: January 15.
Contact: Dr. James M. Jones, Director; or Ernesto Guerra, Minority Fellowship Program.

American Society for Engineering Education
Helen Carr Minority Fellowships
1818 North Street, N.W.
Suite 600
Washington, DC 20036
(202) 331-3525
www.asee.org

Description: One-year fellowships for doctoral candidates in engineering at the following schools: Hampton University, Morgan State University, Howard University, North Carolina A&T State University, Prairie View A&M University, Tennessee State University, Tuskegee University, and Southern University; recipients chosen on the basis of financial need.
Restrictions: Limited to African-American applicants only; applicants must intend to return to one of the historically black engineering colleges to teach; United States citizenship required.
$ Given: An unspecified number of fellowships awarded annually; each for up to $10,000/year; renewable.
Application Information: Write for details.
Deadline: May 1.

American Sociological Association Minority Fellowship Program
1807 New York Avenue, N.W.
Suite 700
Washington, DC 20005-4701

Description: One-year fellowships for graduate students entering a doctoral program in sociology for the first time or for those who are in the early stages of their graduate programs. Institutions in which applicants are enrolled or to which they are applying must have strong mental health research programs. Recipients chosen on the basis of their

commitment to research in mental health and mental illness, academic achievement, scholarship, writing ability, research potential, financial need, and racial/ethnic minority background.
Restrictions: U.S. citizenship or permanent resident status required. Limited to one of the following ethnic/racial backgrounds: African Americans, Latinos, American Indians or Alaska Natives, Asians, or Pacific Islanders.
$ Given: An unspecified number of fellowships awarded annually; each with a stipend of $14,688 plus tuition. Renewable for up to three years.
Application Information: Write for details.
Deadline: December 31.

Armenian General Benevolent Union Graduate Loan Program
55 East 59th Street
New York, NY 10022
(212) 319-6383
www.ugbu.org

Description: Scholarships for graduate students in law, medicine, international relations, and Armenian studies; recipients chosen on the basis of academic achievement, financial need, and involvement in the Armenian community.
Restrictions: Limited to individuals of Armenian descent who are enrolled in accredited United States institutions.
$ Given: Seventy grants of $1,000 are awarded annually; renewable.
Application Information: Write for details.
Deadline: April 30.

Asian Cultural Council
Asian Cultural Council
Fellowship Grants
437 Madison Avenue
37th Floor
New York, NY 10022
(212) 812-4300
www.asianculturalcouncil.org

Description: Grants for doctoral candidates and postdoctoral scholars in the visual and performing arts, archaeology, printmaking, architecture, art history, conservation, crafts, dance, design, film, musicology, music, painting, photography, sculpture, and theater; funding primarily for Asian scholars to visit the United States (and some support for United States citizens to visit Asia) for three- to twelve-month fellowship periods.
Restrictions: N/A.
$ Given: An unspecified number of grants are awarded annually; each grant covers airfare, per diem, maintenance stipend, health insurance, and expenses.
Application Information: Write for details.
Deadlines: February 1 and August 1.

**AT&T Bell Laboratories
Cooperative Research
Fellowships for Minorities**
1505 River View Road
P.O. Box 297
St. Peter, MN 56082
(201) 582-4822

Description: Fellowships for graduate study toward
Ph.D. degree, for graduating college seniors with the
potential to become professional research scientists or
engineers; relevant disciplines include chemistry, communications science, computer science, engineering, information science, materials science, mathematics,
operations research, physics, and statistics; fellowship
tenure includes one summer of work at AT&T; recipients
chosen on the basis of academic achievement and proposed research.
Restrictions: Limited to African-American, Hispanic,
and Native American applicants only; GRE exam scored
required; United States citizenship or permanent resident
status required.
$ Given: An unspecified number of fellowships awarded
annually; each for $17,000/year plus tuition and fees and
expenses.
Application Information: Write for details.
Deadline: December 20.
Contact: Special Programs Manager, CRFP.

**Canadian Association of
University Teachers
J. H. Stewart Reid Memorial
Fellowship for Doctoral
Studies**
2675 Queensview Drive
Ottawa, Ontario K2B 8K2
Canada
(613) 820-2270
www.caut.ca

Description: Fellowship for doctoral candidates in all
fields; tenable at Canadian institutions; recipients chosen
on the basis of outstanding academic achievement.
Restrictions: Canadian citizenship or minimum one-
year landed immigrant status required.
$ Given: One fellowship for $5,000 Canadian is
awarded annually.
Application Information: Write for details.
Deadline: April 30.
Contact: Awards Officer.

**Canadian Federation of
University Women
Georgette LeMoyne Award**
251 Bank Street
Suite 600
Ottawa, Ontario K2P 1X3
Canada
(613) 234-2732
www.cfuw.ca

Description: Award for graduate studies in any field
intended for women taking refresher studies at universities where instruction is in French.
Restrictions: Limited to women only; applicant must
hold B.S./B.A. degree and have been accepted to proposed program of graduate study; Canadian citizenship or
minimum landed immigrant status required.
$ Given: One award for $1,000 Canadian made annu-
ally.
Application Information: Write for details.
Deadline: November 15.
Contact: Chair, Fellowships Committee.

Canadian Federation of University Women
CFUW Memorial Grant
251 Bank Street
Suite 600
Ottawa, Ontario K2P 1X3
Canada
(613) 234-2732
www.cfuw.ca

Description: Grant for B.S./B.A. holders, to support graduate study in science and technology; recipients chosen on the basis of academic achievement, personal qualities, and potential.
Restrictions: Limited to women only; applicants must be accepted at intended places of study; Canadian citizenship or one-year landed immigrant status required.
$ Given: One grant of $1,000 Canadian awarded annually.
Application Information: Request application between July 1 and November 13.
Deadline: November 15.
Contact: Chair, Fellowships Committee.

Canadian Federation of University Women
CFUW Polytechnique Commemorative Awards
251 Bank Street
Suite 600
Ottawa, Ontario K2P 1X3
Canada
(613) 234-2732
www.cfuw.ca

Description: Awards for graduate studies in any field, with preference for studies related to women's issues.
Restrictions: Applicant must hold B.S./B.A. degree and have been accepted to proposed program of graduate study; Canadian citizenship or minimum one-year landed immigrant status required.
$ Given: One grant of $1,400 Canadian awarded annually.
Application Information: Write for details.
Deadline: November 15.
Contact: Fellowships Committee.

Canadian Federation of University Women
Beverly Jackson Fellowship
251 Bank Street
Suite 600
Ottawa, Ontario K2P 1X3
Canada
(613) 234-2732
www.cfuw.ca

Description: Fellowship for B.S./B.A. holders to pursue graduate work in any discipline; tenable at Ontario universities; recipients chosen on the basis of academic achievement, personal qualities, and potential.
Restrictions: Limited to women only; minimum age 35; applicants must hold B.S./B.A. from recognized university and be accepted into proposed place of study; Canadian citizenship or minimum one-year landed immigrant status required.
$ Given: One fellowship for $3,500 Canadian is awarded annually.
Application Information: Application forms are available July 1 through November 13.
Deadline: November 15.
Contact: Chair, Fellowships Committee.

Canadian Federation of University Women Margaret McWilliams Predoctoral Fellowship
251 Bank Street
Suite 600
Ottawa, Ontario K2P 1X3
Canada
(613) 234-2732
www.cfuw.ca

Description: Fellowship for doctoral candidates in any discipline who hold master's degree and are at least one year into doctoral program; recipients chosen on the basis of academic achievement, personal qualities, and potential.
Restrictions: Limited to women only; Canadian citizenship or minimum one-year landed immigrant status required.
$ Given: One fellowship of $8,000 Canadian is awarded annually.
Application Information: Application forms are available July 1 through November 13.
Deadline: November 15.
Contact: Chair, Fellowships Committee.

Canadian Federation of University Women Margaret Dale Philip Award
251 Bank Street
Suite 600
Ottawa, Ontario K2P 1X3
Canada
(613) 234-2732
www.cfuw.ca

Description: Award to graduate students in the humanities and social sciences, with preference to applicants studying Canadian history; recipients chosen on the basis of academic achievement in college, personal qualities, and potential.
Restrictions: Limited to women only; applicants must hold B.S./B.A. degree and have been accepted to proposed program of graduate study; Canadian citizenship or minimum one-year landed immigrant status required.
$ Given: One grant of $1,000 Canadian is awarded annually.
Application Information: Write for details.
Deadline: November 15.
Contact: Fellowships Committee.

Canadian Federation of University Women Professional Fellowship
251 Bank Street
Suite 600
Ottawa, Ontario K2P 1X3
Canada
(613) 234-2732
www.cfuw.ca

Description: Fellowship for graduate work below Ph.D. level; recipients chosen on the basis of academic, personal qualities, and potential.
Restrictions: Limited to women only; applicants must hold B.S./B.A. degree and have been accepted to proposed program of graduate study; Canadian citizenship or minimum one-year landed immigrant status required.
$ Given: Two fellowships for $5,000 Canadian each are awarded annually.
Application Information: Application forms available July 1 through November 13.
Deadline: November 15.
Contact: Chair, Fellowships Committee.

Canadian Federation of University Women Alice E. Wilson Grants
251 Bank Street
Suite 600
Ottawa, Ontario K2P 1X3
Canada
(613) 234-2732
www.cfuw.ca

Description: Grants for women pursuing graduate refresher work in any field; recipients chosen on the basis of academic achievement, personal qualities, and potential; special consideration given to applicants returning to academic study after several years.
Restrictions: Limited to women only; applicants must hold B.S./B.A. degree and have been accepted to proposed program of graduate study; Canadian citizenship or minimum one-year landed immigrant status required.
$ Given: At least five grants for $1,000 Canadian each are awarded annually.
Application Information: Application forms available July 1 through November 13.
Deadline: November 15.
Contact: Chair, Fellowships Committee.

Carnegie Institute of Washington Fellowship in Astronomy
Carnegie Observatories
813 Santa Barbara Street
Pasadena, CA 91101
www.carnegie-institute.com

Description: One- to two-year predoctoral and postdoctoral fellowships to support research in the field of astronomy.
Restrictions: None. Qualified women and minorities encouraged to apply.
$ Given: An unspecified number of fellowships of varying amounts awarded annually.
Application Information: Write for details.
Deadline: Varies.

Carnegie Institute of Washington Fellowship in Embryology
Department of Embryology
115 West University Parkway
Baltimore, MD 21210
(202) 387-6400
www.carnegie-institute.com

Description: One- to two-year predoctoral and postdoctoral fellowships to support research in the field of embryology.
Restrictions: None. Qualified women and minorities encouraged to apply.
$ Given: An unspecified number of fellowships of varying amounts awarded annually.
Application Information: Write for details.
Deadline: Varies.

Carnegie Institute of Washington Fellowship in Geophysics
Geophysical Laboratory
5251 Broad Branch Road N.W.
Washington, DC 20015
(202) 387-6400
www.carnegie-institute.com

Description: One- to two-year predoctoral and postdoctoral fellowships to support research of physicochemical studies of geological problems, with particular emphasis on the processes involved in the formation of the Earth's crust, mantle, and core.
Restrictions: None. Qualified women and minorities encouraged to apply.
$ Given: An unspecified number of fellowships of varying amounts awarded annually.
Application Information: Write for details.
Deadline: Varies.

Carnegie Institute of Washington Fellowship in Plant Biology
Department of Plant Biology
290 Panama Street
Stanford, CA 94305
www.carnegie-institute.com

Description: One- to two-year predoctoral and postdoctoral fellowships to support research in the field of photosynthesis and the physiological and biochemical mechanisms that underlie the financial diversity and adaptations of plants.
Restrictions: None. Qualified women and minorities encouraged to apply.
$ Given: An unspecified number of fellowships of varying amounts awarded annually.
Application Information: Write for details.
Deadline: Varies.

Carnegie Institute of Washington Fellowship in Physics
Department of Terrestrial Magnetism
5241 Broad Branch Road N.W.
Washington, DC 20015
(202) 387-6400
www.carnegie-institute.com

Description: One- to two-year predoctoral and postdoctoral fellowships to support research in the field of physics and related sciences, including astrophysics, geophysics and geochemistry, and planetary physics.
Restrictions: None. Qualified women and minorities encouraged to apply.
$ Given: An unspecified number of fellowships of varying amounts awarded annually.
Application Information: Write for details.
Deadline: Varies.

Committee of Vice-Chancellors and Principals Overseas Research Student Awards
29 Tavistock Square
London WC1H 9HQ
United Kingdom
(44) 171-383-4573
www.cvcp.ac.uk

Description: Grants to full-time graduate students/researchers in all fields attending colleges and universities in the United Kingdom; recipients chosen on the basis of academic achievement and proposed research.
Restrictions: For overseas students only; applicants may not be citizens of the European Union.
$ Given: An unspecified number of grants awarded annually; each for partial remission of tuition fees.
Application Information: Application form available from U.K. university registrars in December.
Deadline: April 30.

Council on Social Work Education CSWE Doctoral Fellowships in Social Work
Minority Fellowship Program
1725 Duke Street
Suite 500
Alexandria, VA 22314
(703) 683-8080
www.cswe.org

Description: One-year fellowships for doctoral candidates to conduct mental health research relevant to ethnic minorities; recipients chosen on the basis of academic achievement, financial need, and quality of proposed research; preference for applicants planning careers in social work specializing in ethnic minority issues of mental health.
Restrictions: Preference for African-American, Hispanic, Native American, and Asian-American applicants, as well as applicants of other ethnic minority groups; M.S.W. degree required; applicants must be full-time doctoral students; United States citizenship or permanent resident status required.
Given: An unspecified number of one-year fellowships are awarded annually; each carries a $708/month stipend

plus tuition support, as negotiated with recipient's university; renewable.
Application Information: Write for details.
Deadline: February 28.
Contact: Dr. E. Aracelis Francis, Director.

Dartmouth College
Thurgood Marshall
Dissertation Fellowships for
African-American Scholars
6062 Wentworth Hall
Room 304
Hanover, NH 03755
(603) 646-2107
www.dartmouth.edu

Description: One-year residential fellowships for doctoral candidates at dissertation level in any discipline taught in the Dartmouth undergraduate curriculum; intended to allow completion of dissertation during fellowship tenure; participation includes ten-week undergraduate course instruction.
Restrictions: Limited to African-American scholars only; applicants must have completed all Ph.D. requirements except dissertation.
$ Given: An unspecified number of fellowships awarded annually; each with $25,000 stipend plus office space, library privileges, housing allowance, and $2,500 research assistance fund.
Application Information: Write for details.
Deadline: February 1.
Contact: Dorothea French, Assistant Dean.

East-West Center
East-West Center Scholarship
and Fellowship Program
1601 East-West Road
Honolulu, HI 96848
(808) 944-7111
www.ewc.hawaii.ed

Description: Funding for graduate students for program work at the University of Hawaii; for students taking a multidisciplinary approach to problems of international concern in areas of population, resource systems, environment, culture, and communication; recipients chosen on the basis of academic achievement and proposed course of study.
Restrictions: United States, Asian country, or Pacific Island citizenship required.
$ Given: An unspecified number of grants awarded annually; each grant covers stipend, housing, medical insurance, travel, and university fees; supports up to twenty-four months of M.A. study, up to forty-eight months of Ph.D. study.
Application Information: Write for details.
Deadline: October 5.
Contact: Award Services Officer.

Five Colleges, Inc.
Five Colleges Fellowships
Program for Minority
Scholars
97 Spring Street
Amherst, MA 01002
(413) 256-8316
www.fivecolleges.edu

Description: Residential fellowships for doctoral candidates at dissertation level in all disciplines, to allow completion of dissertation and contact with faculty and students on host campus; tenable at Amherst, Hampshire, Mount Holyoke, Smith College, or University of Massachusetts.
Restrictions: Limited to minority group members only; applicants must have completed all Ph.D. requirements except dissertation.

$ Given: An unspecified number of fellowships awarded annually; each for $25,000 plus housing or housing assistance, office space, library privileges, and departmental affiliation at host college.
Application Information: Write for details.
Deadline: January 15.
Contact: Carol Angus, Fellowship Program Committee.

Florida Education Fund McKnight Doctoral Fellowships
201 East Kennedy Boulevard
Suite 1525
Tampa, FL 33602

Description: Fellowships for graduate study at one of ten participating doctoral-degree-granting universities in Florida in the fields of business, engineering, agriculture, biology, computer science, mathematics, physical science, and psychology; recipients chosen on the basis of academic achievement.
Restrictions: Limited to African-American applicants only; B.A./B.S. degree required; United States citizenship required.
$ Given: Up to twenty-five fellowships awarded annually; each for a maximum of five years of study, with an annual $11,000 stipend plus up to $5,000 in tuition and fees.
Application Information: Write for details.
Deadline: January 15.
Contact: Dr. Israel Tribble, Jr.

Ford Foundation Predoctoral and Dissertation Fellowships
FF/TJ2041
National Research Council
2101 Constitution Avenue
Washington, DC 20418
(202) 334-2872
FAX (202) 334-3419
www.fordfound.org

Description: Three-year predoctoral fellowships and nine- to twelve-month dissertation fellowships for study in selected disciplines (humanities, social sciences, sciences, mathematics, and engineering). Recipients chosen on the basis of academic achievement and commitment to scholarship, research, and careers in teaching.
Restrictions: Limited to U.S. citizens or nationals only. Limited to members of the following groups: Alaskan Natives, African Americans, Mexican Americans, Native American Indians, Native Pacific Islanders, Puerto Ricans. Applicants must be enrolled in or planning to enroll in a research-based Ph.D or Sc.D. Program.
$ Given: Fifty predoctoral fellowships and twenty-nine dissertation fellowships awarded annually; predoctoral fellowships have annual stipend of $14,000 and institutional award of $7,500. Dissertation fellowships offer stipend of $21,500.
Application Information: Write for details.
Deadline: November 12.

International Reading Association Reading/Literacy Research Fellowship
Research and Policy Division
800 Barksdale Road
P.O. Box 8139
Newark, DE 19714-8139
(302) 731-1600

Description: Fellowship for a postdoctoral researcher with exceptional promise in reading research.
Restrictions: Non-U.S. and Canadian citizens only. Limited to Association members. Candidates must have completed their doctorate within the last five years.
$ Given: One fellowship awarded annually for $1,000.
Application Information: Write for details.
Deadline: October 15.

Japanese American Citizens League National Scholarship and Student Aid Program
1765 Sutter Street
San Francisco, CA 94115
(415) 921-5225
www.jael.org

Description: Scholarships for undergraduate and graduate students, as well as for individuals involved in performing and creative arts projects reflecting the Japanese American experience and culture.
Restrictions: Membership in Japanese American Citizens League (or having parent who is member) preferred; United States citizenship required.
$ Given: An unspecified number of scholarships awarded annually; varying amounts.
Application Information: Application forms are available from local JACL chapters in September; write national office for list of local and regional chapters.
Deadline: March 1 for undergraduates, April for all others.

Kosciuszko Foundation
15 East 65th Street
New York, NY 10021-6595
(212) 734-2130
FAX (212) 628-4552
www.kosciuszkofoundation.
org

Description: One-year scholarship to U.S. citizens of Polish descent for graduate studies in any field at colleges and universities in the United States and to Americans of non-Polish descent whose studies at American universities are primarily focused on Polish subjects. Recipients chosen on the basis of academic achievement and financial need.
Restrictions: Must be enrolled in a graduate program at a U.S. university. Applicants must be U.S. citizens or of Polish descent.
$ Given: An unspecified number of scholarships of $1,000–$5,000 each are awarded annually.
Deadline: January 16.
Contact: Grants office.

Kosciuszko Foundation Year Abroad at the University of Cracow Program
15 East 65th Street
New York, NY 10021-6595
(212) 734-2130
FAX (212) 628-4552
www.kosciuszkofoundation.
org

Description: Grants to support participation in one-year program of academic study at the University of Cracow (Jagiellonian University) in Poland; funding made available to undergraduate upperclassmen and graduate students in the fields of Polish language, literature, history, and culture.
Restrictions: Applicants must have Polish background; United States or Canadian citizenship required.
$ Given: An unspecified number of grants awarded

annually; each for tuition, housing, and monthly food/expense allowance; round-trip travel not covered.
Application Information: Write for details.
Deadline: January 16.
Contact: Grants Office.

L.S.B. Leakey Foundation Franklin Mosher Baldwin Memorial Fellowships
P.O. Box 29346
Presidio Building 10024
O'Reilly Avenue
San Francisco, CA 94129-0346
www.leakeyfoundation.org

Description: Fellowship for master's candidates in anthropology; tenable at any qualified institution in the world.
Restrictions: Limited to citizens of African nations.
$ Given: One fellowship of up to $12,000 awarded annually for nontuition expenses.
Application Information: Write for details.
Deadline: February 15.
Contact: D. Karla Savage, Ph.D., Program and Grants Officer.

Medical Library Association MLA Graduate Scholarships for Minority Students
65 East Wacker Place
Suite 1900
Chicago, IL 60601
www2.me.duke.edu/mise MLA/HHSS/hhss.htm

Description: Scholarships for master's candidates in health sciences librarianship; recipients chosen on the basis of academic achievement and professional potential.
Restrictions: Limited to minority group applicants only applicants must be entering an ALA-accredited school or have at least one-half the academic requirements yet to complete during the scholarship year; United States or Canadian citizenship required.
$ Given: One scholarship for $2,000 is awarded annually.
Application Information: Write for details.
Deadline: December 1.
Contact: Coordinator of Research and Professional Recognition.

Mexican American Legal Defense and Educational Fund Law School Scholarships for Hispanics
634 South Spring Street
11th Floor
Los Angeles, CA 90014
(213) 629-2512

Description: One-year scholarships tenable at any accredited law school; recipients chosen on the basis of academic achievement and financial need.
Restrictions: Limited to Hispanic-American applicants only; applicants must be enrolled full-time in law school; United States citizenship required.
$ Given: Twenty scholarships awarded annually; nineteen for $1,000 each, one for $2,000; nonrenewable but re-application is allowed.
Application Information: Application form required.
Deadline: May 30.

National Consortium for Graduate Degrees for Minorities in Engineering and Science, Inc.
Graduate Engineering for Minorities (GEM) Fellowships
P.O. Box 537
Notre Dame, IN 46556
(219) 287-1097

Description: Fellowships for master's candidates in engineering, physical and life sciences; recipients chosen on the basis of academic achievement.
Restrictions: Limited to African-American, Native American, Mexican American, and Puerto Rican or other Hispanic American applicants only; United States citizenship required.
$ Given: Two hundred and twenty-five Masters, thirty Ph.D. (English) and thirty Ph.D. (Science) fellowships awarded annually; each for tuition and fees at member institution plus $6,000/year living stipend. Ph.Ds receive $14,400 and an initial $5,500 for the first year.
Application Information: Write for details.
Deadline: December 1.

National Foundation for Jewish Culture
Maurice and Marilyn Cohen Fund for Doctoral Dissertations in Jewish Studies
330 Seventh Avenue
21st Floor
New York, NY 10001
(212) 629-0500

Description: Fellowships for doctoral candidates to write their dissertations in Jewish studies.
Restrictions: U.S. citizenship or permanent resident status required. Applicants must have completed all requirements for the Ph.D. except the dissertation. Applicants must have proficiency in a Jewish language adequate for pursuing an academic career in their chosen field.
$ Given: Approximately twelve fellowships awarded annually for an average award of $10,000 apiece.
Application Information: Write for details.
Deadline: January 3.
Contact: Kim Bistrong.

National Italian American Foundation Scholarship Program
Doctoral Research in Italy Fellowship
1860 19th Street, N.W.
Washington, DC 20009
(202) 638-2137
FAX (202) 638-0002

Description: Scholarship for Ph.D. candidates for doctoral research in Italy in modern history, politics, or economics.
Restrictions: Applicants must be of Italian descent. Must provide letter of support from advisor.
$ Given: One scholarship awarded annually for $5,000.
Application Information: Send SASE for details.
Deadline: May 31.
Contact: Maria Lombardo, Education Director.

National Italian American Foundation Scholarship Program
Silvio Conte Internship
1860 19th Street, N.W.
Washington, DC 20009
www.niaf.org

Description: Internship for undergraduate and graduate students to work for one semester in Congressman Conte's Washington, DC office.
Restrictions: Applicants must be of Italian descent; recipient must write paper about the internship experience and its expected benefit to recipient's future career.
$ Given: One internship paying $2,000 is awarded annually.

Application Information: Send SASE for details.
Deadline: May 31.
Contact: Dr. Maria Lombardo, Education Director.

National Italian American Foundation Scholarship Program NIAF/NOIAW Cornaro Scholarship
1860 19th Street, N.W.
Washington, DC 20009
(202) 638-2137
FAX (202) 638-0002

Description: Scholarships for Italian-American undergraduate and graduate women.
Restrictions: Applicants must be of Italian descent.
$ Given: Two scholarships awarded annually; each for $2,000.
Application Information: Send SASE for details.
Deadline: May 31.
Contact: Maria Lombardo, Education Director.

National Italian American Foundation Scholarship Program Oresto A. and Maddalena Giargiari Endowment Medical Scholarships
1860 19th Street, N.W.
Washington, DC 20009
www.niaf.org

Description: Scholarships for second-, third-, and fourth-year medical students at approved United States medical schools; recipients chosen on the basis of academic achievement and financial need.
Restrictions: Applicants must be of Italian descent.
$ Given: An unspecified number of scholarships for $5,000 each are awarded annually.
Application Information: Application materials must be submitted in triplicate.
Deadline: May 31.
Contact: Dr. Maria Lombardo, Education Director.

National Italian American Foundation Scholarship Program Italian American Regional Scholarships
1860 19th Street, N.W.
Washington, DC 20009
www.niaf.com

Description: Scholarships for high school, undergraduate, and graduate students in all fields; regions are East Coast, Midwest, Southwest, and Mid-Atlantic; recipients chosen on the basis of academic achievement and financial need.
Restrictions: Applicants must be of Italian descent.
$ Given: Twenty scholarships awarded annually; each for $5,000.
Application Information: Send SASE for details.
Deadline: May 31.
Contact: Dr. Maria Lombardo, Education Director.

National Italian American Foundation Scholarship Program Michael and Francesca Marinelli Scholarships
1860 19th Street, N.W.
Washington, DC 20009
www.niaf.com

Description: Scholarships for graduate students in the DC area and for undergraduates at Nova University in Florida; relevant disciplines limited to science and business; recipients chosen on the basis of academic achievement and financial need.
Restrictions: Applicants must be of Italian descent.
$ Given: Two scholarships for $2,000 each are awarded annually.
Application Information: Essay required.
Deadline: May 31.
Contact: Dr. Maria Lombardo, Education Director.

National Italian American Foundation Scholarship Program Regional Scholarships
1860 19th Street, N.W.
Washington, DC 20009
www.niaf.org

Description: Fellowships for undergraduate and graduate students; recipients chosen on the basis of 750-word essay describing the contributions of Italian-Americans to the American judicial system.
Restrictions: N/A.
$ Given: Twenty-four fellowships for $5,000 each are awarded annually.
Application Information: Send SASE for details.
Deadline: May 31.
Contact: Dr. Maria Lombardo, Education Director.

National Italian American Foundation Scholarship Program Stella Business Scholarship
1860 19th Street, N.W.
Washington, DC 20009
www.niaf.org

Description: Scholarship for undergraduate and graduate students in business; recipients chosen on the basis of academic achievement and financial need.
Restrictions: Applicants must be of Italian descent.
$ Given: One scholarship for $2,000 is awarded annually.
Application Information: Send SASE for details.
Deadline: May 31.
Contact: Dr. Maria Lombardo, Education Director.

National Italian American Foundation Scholarship Program Study Abroad Scholarships
1860 19th Street, N.W.
Washington, DC 20009
(202) 638-2137
FAX (202) 638-0002

Description: Scholarship for any undergraduate and graduate student wishing to study in Italy.
Restrictions: Applicants must be of Italian descent. Must show letter of acceptance from an accredited school.
$ Given: Five scholarships awarded annually; each for $2,000.
Application Information: Send SASE for details.
Deadline: May 31.
Contact: Dr. Maria Lombardo, Education Director.

National Italian American Foundation Scholarship Program Vincent Visceglia General Graduate Scholarships
1860 19th Street, N.W.
Washington, DC 20009
www.niaf.org

Description: Scholarships for master's and doctoral candidates in Italian studies; recipients chosen on the basis of academic achievement and financial need.
Restrictions: Applicants must be of Italian descent or be working on M.A. or Ph.D. in Italian studies.
$ Given: An unspecified number of scholarships for $2,000 each are awarded annually.
Application Information: Application must be filled in triplicate; write for details.
Deadline: May 31.
Contact: Dr. Maria Lombardo, Education Director.

National Medical Fellowships, Inc.
William and Charlotte Cadbury Award
254 West 31st Street
7th Floor
New York, NY 10001
www.nmf.online.org

Description: Award for senior medical student; recipients chosen on the basis of academic achievement, leadership, and community service.
Restrictions: Limited to minority group members only; applicants must attend United States medical schools.
$ Given: One award made annually; for $2,000 plus certificate of merit.
Application Information: Applicants must be nominated by medical school deans; medical schools must provide letters of recommendation and transcripts for nominees.
Deadline: July 31 for nomination.
Contact: Programs Department.

National Medical Fellowships, Inc.
The Commonwealth Fund Medical Fellowships for Minorities
254 West 31st Street
7th Floor
New York, NY 10001
www.nmf-online.org

Description: Eight- to twelve-week fellowships for second- and third-year medical students to work in major research laboratories under the supervision/tutelage of prominent biomedical scientists; recipients chosen on the basis of academic achievement.
Restrictions: Limited to minority group members only; applicants must attend accredited United States medical schools and must be interested in careers in research/academic medicine.
$ Given: Thirty-five fellowships awarded annually; each for $6,000.
Application Information: Applicants must be nominated by medical school deans.
Deadline: September for nomination; application deadline follows.
Contact: Programs Department.

National Medical Fellowships, Inc.
Irving Graef Memorial Scholarship
254 West 31st Street
7th Floor
New York, NY 10001
www.nmf-online.org

Description: Two-year scholarship for rising third-year medical students; recipients chosen on the basis of academic achievement, leadership, and community service.
Restrictions: Limited to minority group members only; applicants must have received NMF assistance during second year of medical school.
$ Given: One scholarship for $2,000 is awarded annually. Renewable.
Application Information: Applicants must be nominated by medical school deans.
Deadline: September 7 for nomination.
Contact: Programs Department.

National Medical Fellowships, Inc.
Hugh Anderson Memorial Scholarships
254 West 31st Street
7th Floor
New York, NY 10001
www.nmf-online.org

Description: Supplemental scholarships for individuals accepted into the first year of medical school despite significant obstacles; recipients chosen on the basis of recommendations, personal statement, and financial need. Awards for medical students beyond their first year of medical school to Minnesota residents attending any accredited U.S. medical school or students attending Minnesota medical schools.
Restrictions: Limited to minority applicants only; applicants must be accepted at accredited United States medical schools.
$ Given: Two scholarships for $2,500 each are awarded annually.
Application Information: Recipients chosen from General Scholarship applicants.
Deadline: June 30.
Contact: Programs Department.

National Medical Fellowships, Inc.
C.R. Bard Foundation Prize
254 West 31st Street
7th Floor
New York, NY 10001
www.nmf-online.org

Description: Scholarship for senior medical students; recipients chosen on the basis of financial need, academic achievement, leadership, and community service.
Restrictions: Limited to minorities only; and must be accepted at accredited United States medical schools.
$ Given: One scholarship for $5,000/year is awarded annually.
Application Information: Application forms included with General Scholarship application forms.
Deadline: February 15.
Contact: Programs Department.

National Medical Fellowships, Inc.
Franklin C. McLean Award
254 West 31st Street
7th Floor
New York, NY 10001
www.nmf.online.org

Description: Award for senior medical students; recipients chosen on the basis of academic achievement, leadership, and community service.
Restrictions: Limited to minority group members only; applicants must be enrolled in accredited United States medical schools.
$ Given: One award for $3,000 is made annually.
Application Information: Applicants must be nominated by medical school deans; medical schools must provide letters of recommendation and transcripts for nominees.
Deadline: July 31 for nomination.
Contact: Programs Department.

National Medical Fellowships, Inc.
Metropolitan Life Foundation Awards Program for Academic Excellence in Medicine
254 West 31st Street
7th Floor
New York, NY 10001
www.nmf-online.org

Description: Awards for second- and third-year medical students; recipients chosen on the basis of academic achievement, leadership, financial need, and potential for contribution to the field of medicine.
Restrictions: Limited to minority group members only; applicants must attend medical schools in or be residents of the following areas: San Francisco, CA; Tampa, FL; Atlanta, GA; Aurora, IL; Wichita, KS; New York, NY; Tulsa, OK; Pittsburgh, PA; Scranton, PA; Warwick, RI; Greenville, SC; and San Antonio, TX.
$ Given: Up to fourteen awards made annually; each for $3,500.
Application Information: Applicants must be nominated by medical school deans.
Deadline: September 29.
Contact: Programs Department.

National Medical Fellowships, Inc.
The W.K. Kellogg Community Medicine Training Fellowship Program for Minority Students
254 West 31st Street
7th Floor
New York, NY 10001
www.nmf-online.org

Description: Scholarships for second- and third-year medical students in M.D. programs at accredited United States medical schools; must be interested in community-based primary care.
Restrictions: Limited to minority group members only.
$ Given: Fifteen $10,000 fellowships annually.
Application Information: Write for details.
Deadline: October 30.
Contact: Scholarships Department.

National Medical Fellowships, Inc.
Special Awards Program
254 West 31st Street
7th Floor
New York, NY 10001
www.nmf-online.org

Description: Need-based awards for medical students; recipients chosen on the basis of academic achievement, leadership, and potential for contribution to the field of medicine, as well as financial need; NMA Merit Scholarship (four per year), Slack Award for Medical Journalism (one per year), Beecham/NMA Scholarship (one per year), and Ford/NMA Scholarship (one per year).
Restrictions: Limited to African-American applicants only; applicants must attend accredited M.D. or D.O. degree-granting United States medical schools.
$ Given: Seven awards made annually; each for $2,250–$4,000.
Application Information: Applicants must be nominated by medical school deans.
Deadline: May for nomination.
Contact: NMA Special Awards Program.

National Medical Fellowships, Inc.
James H. Robinson Memorial Prizes in Surgery
Wyeth-Aycest
Laboratories Prize
in Women's Health

Description: Prizes to graduating medical students who will practice or conduct research in the field of women's health.
Restrictions: Limited to minority fourth-year women. Applicants must attend accredited United States medical schools; good academic standing required.
$ Given: One prize of $5,000 awarded annually.
Application Information: Applicants must be nominated by medical school deans and chairs of departments of surgery.
Deadline: February 15.
Contact: Programs Department.

National Physical Sciences Consortium Fellowship Program
New Mexico State University
Box 30001, Dept. 3NPS
Las Cruces, NM 88003-0001
(800) 952-4118
www.npsc.org

Description: Fellowships for graduate students in the fields of the physical sciences, mathematics, and computer sciences enrolled at or applying to one of approximately sixty-two participating institutions to pursue a Ph.D.
Restrictions: U.S. citizenship required. Recruiting Native American, African American, Hispanic American, and/or women.
$ Given: One fellowship awarded annually; with an annual stipend of $12,000 plus tuition and fees. Renewable for a total of six years.
Application Information: Write for details.
Deadline: Early November.
Contact: Gene Baily.

National Research Council
NRC/Ford Predoctoral and Dissertation Fellowships for Minorities
Fellowships Office
2101 Constitution Avenue, N.W.
Washington, DC 20418
(202) 334-2872
www.nas.edu/nre

Description: Fellowships for graduate students in the humanities, social sciences, biological and agricultural sciences, physical sciences and mathematics, and engineering and applied sciences; recipients chosen on the basis of academic achievement and proposed research.
Restrictions: Limited to members of minority groups; United States citizenship required.
$ Given: Fifty-three predoctoral fellowships awarded; $14,000 for fellow, $7,500 to institution in fellow's name; twenty-five dissertation fellowships of $21,500 for a one-year period.
Application Information: Write for details.
Deadline: November 5.

Natural Sciences and Engineering Research Council of Canada NSERC Postgraduate Scholarships in Science Librarianship and Documentation
350 Albert Street
Ottawa, Ontario K1A 1H5
Canada
(613) 995-5992
www.nserc.ca

Description: One-year scholarships for first- and second-year study toward M.L.S. degree in library science; recipients chosen on the basis of academic achievement, commitment to field, and relevant experience.
Restrictions: Applicants must have B.S. degree in science or engineering; Canadian citizenship or permanent resident status required.
$ Given: A few scholarships awarded annually; each for $13,500 Canadian plus travel allowance.
Application Information: Write for details.
Deadline: December 1.
Contact: Information Officer.

National Sciences and Engineering Research Council of Canada NSERC Postgraduate Scholarships
350 Albert Street
Ottawa, Ontario K1A 1H5
(613) 995-5521
FAX (613) 992-5337
www.nserc.ca

Description: Up to twenty-four-month scholarships for highly qualified science or engineering students from a university approved by NSERC. Canadian citizenship or permanent resident status required.
$ Given: An unspecified number of scholarships awarded annually; each with stipend of $13,800 per year toward tuition.
Application Information: Write for details.
Deadline: December 1.
Contact: Information Officer.

New York University AEJMC Summer Internship for Minorities in Journalism
269 Mercer Street
Suite 601
New York, NY 10003
(212) 998-2130
www.nyu.edu

Description: Summer internships for college upperclassmen and graduate students; participation includes actual work, journalism courses, workshops, and onsite visits; media worksites include *TV Guide*, *New York Times*, radio stations, public relations companies, advertising firms, and broadcasting companies.
Restrictions: Limited to minority group members only, especially African-American, Hispanic, Native American, Eskimo, and Asian-American applicants.
$ Given: An unspecified number of internships awarded annually; each pays at least $200/week.
Application Information: Request application form by December 3.
Deadline: December 11.
Contact: Glenda Noel-Doyle, AEJMC Internship Coordinator, Institute of Afro-American Affairs.

Newberry Library Frances C. Allen Fellowships
Committee on Awards
60 West Walton Street
Chicago, IL 60610-3380
(312) 943-9090
www.newberry.org

Description: One-month to one-year research fellowships for master's and doctoral candidates in the humanities and social sciences; tenable primarily at the D'Arcy McNickle Center for the History of the American Indian.
Restrictions: Limited to female Native American applicants.
$ Given: $30,000.

Application Information: Write for details.
Deadline: January 20.

Oak Ridge Institute for Science and Education Nuclear Engineering and Health Physics Fellowships
P.O. Box 117
Oak Ridge, TN 37831-0117
(865) 576-3146
www.ornl.gov

Description: One-year fellowship for graduate students studying nuclear science and engineering or health physics at participating Oak Ridge Associated Universities with practicum at various DOE facilities; recipients chosen on the basis of academic achievement, career goals, and interests.
Restrictions: N/A.
$ Given: An unspecified number of fellowships awarded annually; each with $14,400 stipend, plus $300/month during practicum, and travel, tuition, and fees; renewable for up to four years.
Application Information: Write for details.
Deadline: January 25.

Organization of American States OAS Regular Training Program Fellowships Department of Fellowships and Training
17th Street and Constitution Avenue, N.W.
Washington, DC 20006
(202) 458-3760
www.oas.org

Description: Three-month to two-year fellowships for graduate students in all fields except medicine to pursue advanced study or research in other countries; tenable at OAS member countries; fellowships intended to contribute to host country on economic, social, technical, and cultural levels; recipients chosen on the basis of academic achievement and financial need.
Restrictions: Applicants must be citizens of OAS member countries; applicants must hold B.S./B.A. or equivalent and must be accepted at university or research facility for proposed work; language proficiency required.
$ Given: An unspecified number of fellowships awarded annually; each to cover expenses, tuition, and stipend, varying by country.
Application Information: Write for details.
Deadline: March 31.

Population Council Population Council Fellowships in the Social Sciences
1 Dag Hammarskjold Plaza
New York, NY 10017
(212) 339-0671
www.popcouncil.org

Description: Fellowships for doctoral candidates at dissertation level and mid-career professionals seeking master's degrees; for study/research combining population studies and such other social science disciplines as anthropology, sociology, economics, geography, public health, and public administration; recipients chosen on the basis of academic achievement and proposed research.
Restrictions: Research/study must be carried out at institution with strong program in population studies; preference to applicants with employment experience in population studies or family planning; strong preference for nationals of developing countries who are committed to returning to their home countries in population-related careers. Monies available for partial tuition payments, transportation, and health insurance.

$ Given: An unspecified number of fellowships awarded annually; monthly stipend based on place of study and other factors.
Application Information: Women encouraged to apply.
Deadline: December 15.
Contact: Manager, Fellowships Program.

REFORMA, The National Association to Promote Library Services to the Spanish Speaking
REFORMA Scholarships in Library and Information Science
Auroria Library
Lawrence at 11th Street
Denver, CO 80204-2096
(303) 556-3526
www.clnet.ucr.edu/library/reforma

Description: Scholarships for individuals studying library and information science; recipients chosen on the basis of academic achievement and financial need.
Restrictions: Applicants must speak Spanish and must demonstrate a desire to serve the Spanish-speaking community; must be U.S. citizen or resident.
$ Given: An unspecified number of $1,000 minimum scholarships are awarded annually.
Application Information: Write for details.
Deadline: May 15.
Contact: Ninfa Trejo, Chair, REFORMA Scholarship, University of Arizona Library, P.O. Box 210005, Tucson, AZ 85721-0055, (520) 621-4868.

School of American Research Katrin H. Lamon Resident Scholar Program for Native Americans
P.O. Box 2188
Santa Fe, NM 87504
www.sarweb.org

Description: Nine-month residential fellowship for postdoctoral scholars and doctoral candidates at dissertation level in anthropology and related social sciences; intended to provide recipients with intellectual stimulation of campus life plus time to write up results of compiled field work/research.
Restrictions: Limited to Native American applicants.
$ Given: One fellowship awarded annually; maximum $29,000 stipend plus housing and office; nonrenewable.
Application Information: Write for details.
Deadline: December 1.
Contact: Resident Scholar Coordinator.

Smithsonian Institution Minority Students Internships
Office of Fellowships and Grants
955 L'Enfant Plaza
Suite 7000
Washington, DC 20560
(202) 287-3271

Description: Ten-week internships for undergraduate upperclassmen and graduate students in the humanities, social sciences, natural sciences, and physical sciences; internship program includes participation in ongoing research or activities at the Museum plus supervised independent research in any bureau; recipients chosen on the basis of academic achievement and proposed research.
Restrictions: Limited to minority group applicants.
$ Given: An unspecified number of internship positions are awarded annually; $300/week undergraduate stipend, $300/week graduate stipend.

Application Information: Write for details.
Deadlines: January 15 and October 15.

Social Sciences and Humanities Research Council of Canada
Jules and Gabrielle Leger Fellowships
Fellowships Division
350 Albert Street
Box 1610
Ottawa, Ontario K1P 6G4
Canada
(613) 943-7777
www.sshrc.ca

Description: One-year fellowships for university-affiliated and private scholars at graduate level in the humanities and social sciences, to support research and writing on the historical/contemporary contribution of the Crown and its representatives; tenable at recognized university/institution for at least eight months of full-time work; recipients chosen on the basis of academic achievement.
Restrictions: Canadian citizenship required.
$ Given: An unspecified number of fellowships awarded in alternate years; each for $40,000 Canadian plus $10,000 Canadian for research/travel expenses.
Application Information: Fellowships offered in odd-numbered years.
Deadline: October 1.

Social Sciences and Humanities Research Council of Canada
SSHRC Doctoral Fellowships
Fellowships Division
350 Albert Street
Box 1610
Ottawa, Ontario K1P 6G4
Canada
(613) 943-7777
www.sshrc.ca

Description: Six- to forty-eight-month renewable fellowships for doctoral candidates in the humanities, and social sciences; tenable in Canada or abroad; recipients chosen on the basis of academic achievement and proposed research.
Restrictions: Applicants must have completed one year of doctoral study; Canadian citizenship or permanent resident status required.
$ Given: Six hundred fellowships awarded annually, plus 600 annual renewables; each for up to $16,620 Canadian per year plus relocation costs.
Application Information: Write for details.
Deadline: November 15.

Social Sciences and Humanities Research Council of Canada
SSHRC Queen's Fellowships
Fellowships Division
350 Albert Street
Box 1610
Ottawa, Ontario K1P 6G4
Canada
(613) 943-7777
www.sshrc.ca

Description: One-year fellowships for graduate students in social sciences and humanities, to support study toward Ph.D. in Canadian studies at Canadian institutions.
Restrictions: Canadian citizenship required; must have completed one year of graduate study.
$ Given: One to two fellowships awarded annually; each for up to $16,620 Canadian plus tuition and travel allowance; nonrenewable.
Application Information: Applicants automatically eligible if currently studying Canadian studies at Canadian University; no application.
Deadline: October 15.

Southern Illinois University at Carbondale
Minority Doctoral Fellowships in Science and Engineering
Graduate School
Woody Hall, B-114
Carbondale, IL 62901
(618) 536-7791
www.siuc.edu

Description: Three-year fellowships for doctoral candidates in the life sciences, physical sciences, and engineering; recipients chosen on the basis of GRE or other national standardized test scores.
Restrictions: Limited to minority group applicants; applicants of Mexican or Puerto Rican descent preferred; United States citizenship required.
$ Given: Ten to twenty fellowships awarded annually; each for $15,000/year plus full tuition and fees (for three years).
Application Information: Write for details.
Deadline: February 2.
Contact: Dr. Harry Daniels, Associate Dean.

Southern Illinois University at Carbondale
Minority Graduate Incentive Program
Woody Hall, B-114
Carbondale, IL 62901
(618) 453-4558
(618) 536-7791
www.imgip.siu.edu

Description: Fellowships for doctoral candidates in the life sciences, physical sciences, engineering, and mathematics.
Restrictions: U.S. citizenship or permanent resident status required. Limited to African American, Hispanic, and Native American applicants. Must have been accepted to a doctoral program at one of the participating Illinois-based universities in fields where there is severe underrepresentation in their field.
$ Given: An unspecified number of fellowships awarded annually; each with a stipend of $13,500 plus full tuition and fees, and annual allowance of $1,500 for book, supplies, equipment, and travel, for a maximum of three years.
Application Information: Write for details.
Deadline: February 1.
Contact: Jane Meuth.

Special Libraries Association Affirmative Action Scholarship
1700 Eighteenth Street, N.W.
Washington, DC 20009
(202) 234-4700
www.sla.org

Description: Scholarship for master's candidates and graduating college; tenable at United States or Canadian institution of library and information science; preference to students with interest in special librarianship; recipients chosen on the basis of academic achievement and financial need.
Restrictions: Limited to minority group applicants only; United States or Canadian citizenship required.
$ Given: One scholarship for $6,000 each is awarded annually.
Application Information: Write for details.
Deadline: October 31.
Contact: Laura Devlin.

Williams College Committee on Institutional Cooperation
Hopkins Hall
Williamstown, MA 01267
(413) 597-4352
www.williams.edu

Description: One-year residential fellowships at Williams College for doctoral candidates at dissertation level in the engineering, humanities, mathematics, and social sciences.
Restrictions: Limited to minority group applicants. U.S. citizenship required. Tenable at any Big Ten University or the University of Chicago.
$ Given: Full tuition plus $8,000 stipend.
Application Information: Write for details.
Deadline: January 15.
Contact: Peter Grudin, Dean of the Faculty.

Zonta International Foundation
Michael J. Freeman
Scholarships for Irish Women
557 West Randolph Street
Chicago, IL 60661-2206
(312) 930-5848
www.zonta.org

Description: Full-tuition scholarships to assist Irish women pursuing technical and scientific studies.
Restrictions: Limited to Irish women citizens only.
$ Given: An unspecified number of scholarships of varying amounts awarded annually.
Application Information: Write for details.
Deadline: N/A.

Study/Research Abroad

American Academy in Rome
Samuel H. Kress Foundation
Predoctoral Fellowships
7 East 60th Street
New York, NY 10022-1001
(212) 751-7200
www.aarome.org
www.shkf.org

Description: Two two-year fellowships for independent study and research; one fellowship in classical art history, one fellowship in Italian art history; tenable at the American Academy in Rome; awarded to doctoral candidates who have completed coursework and are beginning the second year of dissertation work; recipients chosen on the basis of proposed research.
Restrictions: United States citizenship required.
$ Given: Two fellowships awarded annually; amount varies; travel allowance included.
Application Information: Write for details.
Deadline: November 30.
Contact: Fellowship Coordinator.

American Academy in Rome
Rome Prize Fellowships
School of Classical Studies
7 East 60th Street
New York, NY 10022-1001
(212) 751-7200
www.aarome.org

Description: One-year residential fellowships for doctoral candidates in classical studies, archaeology, classical art, history of art, postclassical humanistic studies, and medieval and Renaissance studies; tenable at the American Academy in Rome.
Restrictions: Applicants must have completed all doctoral coursework and one year of dissertation work; recipients may not hold job or travel extensively during fellowship year. U.S. citizenship or three-year residency in U.S. required.
$ Given: An unspecified number of fellowships of $15,000–$17,000 are awarded annually; each with $7,500 stipend plus $800 travel allowance.
Application Information: Write for details.
Deadline: November 15.
Contact: Fellowships Coordinator.

American Academy in Rome
Rome Prize Fellowships
School of Fine Arts
7 East 60th Street
New York, NY 10022-1001
(212) 751-7200

Description: Several six-month to one-year fellowships in architecture, historical preservation and conservation, landscape architecture, design art, painting, sculpture, visual arts, and musical compositions; tenable at the American Academy in Rome.
Restrictions: Painting, sculpture, and visual arts candidates need not hold a degree but must have three years

professional commitment, clear ability, and current studio work; architecture and landscape architecture candidates need appropriate degree; other applicants need B.A. degree; recipients may not hold job or travel extensively during fellowship year. U.S. citizenship required.
$ Given: Fourteen fellowships, $9,000–$15,000 awarded annually.
Application Information: Write for details.
Deadline: November 15.
Contact: Fellowships Coordinator.

American Architectural Foundation
RTKL Traveling Fellowship
129 Sibley Dome
Cornell University
Ithaca, NY 14853
(607) 255-9110

Description: Fellowship for student in second-to-last year of a bachelor or master of architecture program planning to travel outside the U.S. in an established program or accepted in a professional degree program and planning foreign travel that will have a beneficial and direct relationship to educational goals.
Restrictions: None.
$ Given: One fellowship awarded annually for $2,500.
Application Information: Write for details.
Deadline: N/A.
Contact: Director, AIA Scholarship and Career Programs.

American Council of Learned Societies
Eastern European Dissertation Fellowships
Office of Fellowships and Grants
228 East 45th Street
New York, NY 10017-3398
(212) 697-1505
www.acls.org

Description: Fellowships for doctoral dissertation research related to Eastern Europe (Albania, Bulgaria, Czech Republic, Germany, Hungary, Poland, Romania, Slovakia, and (former) Yugoslavia); for research-related study at a university abroad, but not within Eastern Europe; for doctoral candidates in the humanities and social sciences; recipients chosen on the basis of academic achievement, financial need, and quality of proposed research.
Restrictions: United States citizenship or legal residency required.
$ Given: An unspecified number of fellowships awarded annually; each carries an annual stipend of up to $25,000; renewable for second year.
Application Information: Write for details.
Deadline: November 1.
Contact: Ruth Waters.

American Council of Learned Societies
Fellowships for Dissertation Research Abroad Related to China
Office of Fellowships and Grants
228 East 45th Street
New York, NY 10017-3398
(212) 697-1505
www.acls.org

Description: Fellowships for doctoral dissertation research related to China; for research-related travel within the People's Republic of China; for doctoral candidates in the humanities and social sciences; recipients chosen on the basis of academic achievement, financial need, and quality of proposed research.
Restrictions: Foreign national applicants must be enrolled as full-time Ph.D. candidates at United States universities.
$ Given: An unspecified number of fellowships awarded annually; each carries an annual stipend of up to $15,000.
Application Information: Write for details.
Deadline: December 1.

American Council of Learned Societies
International and Area Studies Fellowships
Office of Fellowships and Grants
228 East 45th Street
New York, NY 10017-3398
(212) 697-1505
www.acsl.org

Description: Six- to twelve-month fellowships for post-doctoral research in all disciplines of the humanities and humanities-related social sciences on the societies and cultures of Asia, Africa, the Near and Middle East, Latin America, East Europe, and the former Soviet Union.
Restrictions: U.S. citizenship or permanent resident status required.
$ Given: Approximately eight fellowships awarded annually, each for $25,000 (Junior Fellowships); to $40,000 (Senior Fellowships).
Application Information: Write for details.
Deadline: October 1.

American Institute of Indian Studies
1130 East 59th Street
Chicago, IL 60637
(773) 702-8638

Description: Postdoctoral and graduate fellowships to support research in all fields related to India.
Restrictions: U.S. citizenship or resident alien status required.
$ Given: A varying number of fellowships of varying amounts awarded annually.
Application Information: Write for details.
Deadline: July 1.

American Institute of Pakistan Studies
American Institute of Pakistan Studies Fellowships
P.O. Box 7568
Wake Forest University
Winston-Salem, NC 27109
(919) 759-5453

Description: Fellowships for doctoral candidates, post-doctoral scholars, and professional researchers to undertake study/research in Pakistan; for students of humanities and social sciences, especially rural development, agriculture, local government, economics, demography, history, and culture; recipients chosen on the basis of proposed research.
Restrictions: Doctoral candidates must have completed all preliminary Ph.D. requirements; United States citizenship required.
$ Given: An unspecified number of fellowships awarded annually; each to cover air travel, maintenance, rental allowance, research allowance, internal travel, and excess baggage allowance.

Application Information: Write for details.
Deadline: January 1.
Contact: Dr. Charles H. Kennedy, Director.

American Research Center in Egypt
Fellowships for Research in Egypt
30 East 20th Street
Suite 401
New York, NY 10003
(212) 529-6661

Description: Fellowships for doctoral candidates and postdoctoral scholars in archaeology, art, humanities, and social sciences in Egypt; recipients chosen on the basis of quality of proposed research; intended as maintenance support for research conducted in Egypt for three- to twelve-month period.
Restrictions: Proficiency in Arabic required; recipients may not hold outside employment during fellowship period; United States and Egyptian citizens only.
$ Given: Up to twenty fellowships awarded annually; each with stipend of $1,000/month plus round-trip airfare and dependents' stipends, if needed.
Application Information: Write for details.
Deadline: October 1.
Contact: Dr. Terence Walz, United States Director.

American Research Institute in Turkey
ARIT Fellowships
University Museum
33rd and Spruce Streets
Philadelphia, PA 19104-6324
(215) 898-3474

Description: Fellowships for doctoral candidates to conduct research concerning Turkey in ancient, medieval, and modern times in any field of the humanities or social sciences; recipients chosen on the basis of quality of proposed research; intended as maintenance support for dissertation research in Turkey over one- to twelve-month fellowship period.
Restrictions: Applicants must have satisfied all doctoral requirements except dissertation; recipients must obtain research permission from the Turkish government; applicants must be affiliated with United States or Canadian institutions.
$ Given: Six to ten fellowships for $3,000–$10,000 per year are awarded annually.
Application Information: Write for details.
Deadline: November 15.
Contact: Nancy Leinwand.

American Research Institute in Turkey
Bosphorus University
Summer Turkish Language Program
University Museum
33rd and Spruce Streets
Philadelphia, PA 19104-6324
(215) 898-3474

Description: Fellowships for college graduates through doctoral candidates; for the study of Turkish language in an eight-week summer program at Bosphorus University in Istanbul; recipients chosen on the basis of academic achievement (minimum 3.0 GPA).
Restrictions: Preference for individuals planning career in Turkish studies; two years of college-level Turkish language courses or equivalent required (written and oral exam required); United States citizenship or permanent resident status required.

$ Given: Ten to fifteen grants are awarded annually; grant covers tuition, maintenance stipend, and roundtrip travel; non-renewable.
Application Information: Write for details. ARIT Summer Fellowship Program, Center for the Study of Islamic Societies and Civilizations, Washington University, Campus Box 1230, One Brookline Drive, St. Louis, MO 63130-4899.
Deadline: February 15.
Contact: Shelia Andrew at (314) 935-5166.

American-Scandinavian Foundation Fellowships
725 Park Avenue
New York, NY 10021
(212) 879-9779
www.amscan.org

Description: Grants and fellowships for graduate students at dissertation level for study or research in Denmark, Finland, Iceland, Norway, or Sweden in all fields.
Restrictions: U.S. citizenship or permanent resident status required.
$ Given: An unspecified number of grants and fellowships awarded annually; grants are for $3,000 for visits of one to three months; fellowships are for $15,000 in support of full year of study or research.
Application Information: Write for details.
Deadlines: September 1, October 15, January 15, April 1.

American School of Classical Studies at Athens Fellowships
6-8 Charlton Street
Princeton, NJ 08540-5232
(609) 683-0800
www.ascsa.org

Description: Fellowships for graduate students to engage in study/research in Greece for one academic year; intended for students of archaeology, classical studies, classical art history, and ancient Greece; named fellowships include Thomas Day Seymour Fellowship, John Williams White Fellowship, Samuel H. Kress Fellowship, and James Rignall Wheeler Fellowship.
Restrictions: Applicants must be affiliated with United States or Canadian institution; United States or Canadian citizenship required; B.A. major in classics or classical archaeology required.
$ Given: Four fellowships awarded annually; each for $8,840 plus fees, room, and partial board.
Application Information: Write for details. ASCSA Committee on Admissions and Fellowships, State University of New York at Buffalo, Department of Classics, 338 Millard Filmore Academic Center, Buffalo, NY 14261.
Deadline: January 7.
Contact: Professor Carolyn Higbie, Chair.

American School of Classical Studies at Athens
Gennadeion Fellowship
6-8 Charlton Street
Princeton, NJ
08540-5232
(609) 683-0800
www.ascsa.org

Description: Fellowship for doctoral candidates at dissertation level to engage in study/research at the Gennadius Library in Athens for one academic year; intended for students of Byzantine and Greek studies; recipients chosen on the basis of academic achievement and quality of proposed research.
Restrictions: Applicants must be affiliated with a United States or Canadian institution; United States or Canadian citizenship required.
$ Given: One fellowship awarded annually for $8,840 plus fees, room, and partial board.
Application Information: Write for details.
Deadline: January 7.
Contact: Professor James McCredie.

American School of Classical Studies at Athens
Jacob Hirsch Fellowship
6-8 Charlton Street
Princeton, NJ
08540-5232
(609) 683-0800
www.ascsa.org

Description: Fellowship for doctoral candidates at dissertation level to engage in study/research in Greece; intended for students of archaeology; recipients chosen on the basis of academic achievement and quality of proposed research.
Restrictions: United States or Israeli citizenship required.
$ Given: One fellowship awarded annually for $8,840 plus room and partial board; non-renewable.
Application Information: Write for details. ASCSA Committee on Admissions and Fellowships, State University of New York at Buffalo, Department of Classics, 338 Millard Filmore Academic Center, Buffalo, NY 14261.
Deadline: January 7.
Contact: Professor Carolyn Higbie, Chair.

American School of Classical Studies at Athens
Solow Art and Architecture Foundation
9 West 57th Street
Suite 4500
New York, NY 10019
www.asor.org

Description: Postdoctoral scholars working toward publication of material from the school's excavations at the Athenian Agora or Ancient Corinth.
Restrictions: N/A.
$ Given: Several fellowships with maximum of $1,500/month.
Application Information: Write for details.
Deadline: January 7.
Contact: Rosalie Wolff.

American Schools of Oriental Research
George A. Barton Fellowship at the Albright Institute for Archaeological Research, Jerusalem
656 Beacon Street
5th Floor
Boston, MA 02215-2010
(617) 353-6570
www.asor.org

Description: Residential fellowships for doctoral study in Near Eastern archaeology, geography, history, and biblical studies, for one to five months of study/research at the Albright Institute in Jerusalem; recipients chosen on the basis of proposed research.
Restrictions: Fellowship may not be used for summer study.
$ Given: Award of $6,000 plus $2,650 stipend.
Application Information: Write for details.
Deadlines: September 15, October 15.
Contact: Dr. Rudolph H. Dornemann, Executive Director.

American Schools of Oriental Research
Samuel H. Kress Foundation Fellowship at the Albright Institute for Archaeological Research, Jerusalem
656 Beacon Street
5th Floor
Boston, MA 02215-2010
(617) 353-6570
www.asor.org

Description: Residential fellowships for doctoral candidates at dissertation level in art history, archaeology, and architecture; for nine to ten months of dissertation research at the Albright Institute in Jerusalem; recipients chosen on the basis of proposed research.
Restrictions: N/A.
$ Given: An unspecified number of fellowships of $16,500 awarded annually; each with $9,800 stipend plus room and half-board.
Application Information: Write for details.
Deadline: October 15.
Contact: Dr. Rudolph H. Dornemann, Executive Director.

Archaeological Institute of America
Anna C. and Oliver C. Colburn Fellowship
656 Beacon Street
Boston, MA 02215-2010
(617) 353-9361
www.archaeological.org

Description: One-year fellowship for doctoral candidates and postdoctoral scholars, for study/research in classical studies; tenable at the American School of Classical Studies in Athens.
Restrictions: United States or Canadian citizenship or legal residency required.
$ Given: One fellowship of $14,000 is awarded annually.
Application Information: Write for details.
Deadline: January 31.
Contact: Colburn Fellowship.

Archaeological Institute of America
Olivia James Traveling Fellowships
656 Beacon Street
Boston, MA 02215-2010
(617) 353-9361
www.archaeological.org

Description: Fellowships for doctoral candidates at dissertation level in architecture; for travel to Greece, the Aegean islands, Sicily, southern Italy, Asia Minor, and/or Mesopotamia; recipients chosen on the basis of proposed research/study.
Restrictions: Preference to project of at least six months duration; no funding for field excavation; United States citizenship or legal residency required.
$ Given: One fellowship of up to $22,000 is awarded annually.

Application Information: Write for details.
Deadline: November 1.
Contact: Olivia James Traveling Fellowship.

Archaeological Institute of America
Harriet and Leon Pomerance Fellowship
656 Beacon Street
Boston, MA 02215-2010
(617) 353-9361
www.bu.edu
www.archaeological.org

Description: Fellowship for doctoral candidates studying Aegean Bronze Age archaeology; for travel to the Mediterranean; recipients chosen on the basis of proposed research/study.
Restrictions: United States or Canadian citizenship required.
$ Given: One fellowship of $4,000 is awarded annually; non-renewable.
Application Information: Write for details.
Deadline: November 1.
Contact: Harriet Pomerance Fellowship.

Association of College and Research Libraries
Martinus Nijhoff International West European Specialist Study Grant
50 East Huron Street
Chicago, IL 60611
(312) 280-2510
(800) 545-2433

Description: Grant for scholars in library science to travel for up to fourteen days to study West European professional librarianship; recipients chosen on the basis of proposed research.
Restrictions: Personal membership in ALA required.
$ Given: An unspecified number of grants are awarded annually; award covers air travel, surface travel, expenses, room, and board.
Application Information: Write for details.
Deadline: December 1.
Contact: Melani Marques Pedarsoli.

Canada Council Killam Research Fellowships
99 Metcalfe Street
P.O. Box 1047
Ottawa, Ontario
Canada K1P 5V8

Description: Fellowships for senior scholars (eight to twelve years beyond the Ph.D.) to support research in any of the following fields: humanities, social sciences, natural sciences, health sciences, engineering, and studies linking disciplines within those fields.
Restrictions: Canadian citizenship or landed immigrant resident status required.
$ Given: Fifteen to eighteen fellowships awarded annually, each in the amount $53,000.
Application Information: Write for details.
Deadline: June 30.

Canadian Embassy
Canadian Studies Graduate Student Fellowships
510 Pennsylvania Avenue, N.W.
Washington, DC 20001
(202) 682-1740
www.cdnemb-washdc.org/

Description: Fellowships for doctoral candidates in the humanities, social sciences, fine arts, business, law, or environmental studies who are working on dissertation topics related in substantial part to Canada; funding for dissertation research in Canada over a three- to nine-month fellowship period.
Restrictions: Applicants must be doctoral students at accredited institutions in Canada or the United States;

applicants must have completed all degree requirements other than the dissertation; United States citizenship or permanent resident status required.

$ Given: An unspecified number of fellowships with a maximum of $850/month stipends are awarded annually; for a period of up to nine months; non-renewable.

Application Information: Write for details.

Deadline: October 30.

Contact: Daniel Abele, Academic Relations Officer.

CDS International Robert Bosch Foundation Fellowships
871 United Nations Plaza
15th Floor
New York, NY 10017-1814
(212) 497-3500
www.cdsintl.org

Description: Nine-month internships at German government and business institutions (September-May) for master's degree holders and professionals in communications, journalism, economics, political science, public affairs, business administration, law, and German studies; German internships provided in a framework of government and commerce; recipients chosen on the basis of academic achievement, evidence of leadership, and community participation.

Restrictions: Recipients must be proficient in German by the start of the internship (fees for language courses reimbursed); United States citizenship required, ages 23 to 34.

$ Given: Twenty fellowships awarded annually; each with DM3,500/month stipend plus travel expenses and possible spouse stipend.

Application Information: Write for details.

Deadline: October 15.

Winston Churchill Foundation Scholarship
P.O. Box 1240
Gracie Station
New York, NY 10028
(212) 879-3480
FAX (212) 879-3480
www.members.aol.com/churchillf/

Description: One-year scholarship for graduate students in the fields of engineering, mathematics, and sciences to study for one year at Churchill College in Cambridge, England.

Restrictions: U.S. citizenship required. Limited to applicants between the ages of 19 and 26. Must hold a bachelor's degree.

$ Given: One scholarship awarded annually; covers tuition and fees at Churchill College, plus a living allowance of $5,000–$6,000 and an additional $500 for travel expenses.

Application Information: Write for details.

Deadline: N/A.

**Committee of Vice-
Chancellors and Principals
Overseas Research Student
Awards**
29 Tavistock Square
London WC1H 9HQ
United Kingdom
(44) 171 383 4573
www.cvcp.ac.uk

Description: Grants to full-time graduate students/researchers in all fields attending colleges and universities in the United Kingdom; recipients chosen on the basis of academic achievement and proposed research.
Restrictions: For overseas students only; applicants may not be citizens of the European Union.
$ Given: An unspecified number of grants awarded annually; each for partial remission of tuition fees.
Application Information: Application form available from U.K. university registrars in December.
Deadline: April 30.

**Committee on Scholarly
Communication with the
People's Republic of China
National Program for
Advanced Study and Research
in China—Graduate Program**
1055 Thomas Jefferson Street,
N.W.
Suite 2013
Washington, DC 20007
(202) 337-1250
www.acls.org/csnatgd.htm

Description: Funding for one academic year of advanced study/research in China; for master's and doctoral candidates in the humanities and social sciences; recipients chosen on the basis of academic achievement and proposed research; tenable at university or research institute in China.
Restrictions: Three years of Chinese language training; United States citizenship required.
$ Given: N/A.
Application Information: Write for details.
Deadline: December 1.
Contact: Program Officer.

**Dr. M. Aylwin Cotton
Foundation Fellowship Awards**
c/o Albany Trustee Company,
Limited
P.O. Box 232 Pollet House
The Pollet, St. Peter Port
Guerney, Channel Islands
England
(44) 1481 724 136
FAX (44) 1481 710 478

Description: One-year fellowships for post-doctoral studies in archaeology, architecture, history, language, and art of the Mediterranean.
Restrictions: None.
$ Given: An unspecified number of fellowships awarded annually; each with a maximum stipend of 10,000 British pounds.
Application Information: Write for details.
Deadline: February 28.

**Council of American Overseas
Research Centers
Fellowships for Advanced
Multi-Country Research**
1100 Jefferson Drive, S.W.
IC 3123, MRC 705
Washington, DC
20560-0705
www.caorc.org

Description: Fellowships for U.S. doctoral candidates who have already earned their Ph.D. in the fields of the humanities, social sciences, or allied natural sciences to conduct research of regional significance in more than one country, at least one of which hosts a participating OARC. Recipients will be chosen on the basis of their intellectual capacity, maturity, and fitness for field work, and proposal's significance, relevance, and potential contribution to regional scholarly research. Scholars may apply individually or in teams.

Restrictions: U.S. citizenship required.
$ Given: Eight fellowships awarded annually, each in the amount of up to $6,000 with up to an additional $3,000 for travel.
Application Information: Write for details.
Deadline: December 31.

Council for European Studies Pre-Dissertation Fellowship Program
Box 44
Schermerhorn Hall
Columbia University
New York, NY 10027
(212) 854-4172
www.europanet.org

Description: Two- to three-month research fellowships in European Union countries for doctoral candidates in European history, sociology, political science, anthropology, and economics.
Restrictions: Applicants must have completed at least two years of graduate study; language proficiency required; United States or Canadian citizenship or permanent resident status required.
$ Given: Three grants of $4,000 each are awarded annually.
Application Information: Write for details.
Deadline: February 1.

Cross-Cultural Institute
Kobe College
4 - 1 Okadayama
Nishinomiya 662
Japan
798 51 8557
FAX 798 51 8559

Description: One-year fellowships for graduate students for study in Japan. Preference will be given to applicants who have a documented interest in Japanese studies, such as the arts, culture, history, journalism, or business. Recipients chosen on the basis of academic achievement, quality of proposal, plan for teaching upon completion of degree, documented interest in women's education, feasibility of project and proposed schedule.
Restrictions: U.S. citizenship required. Must be enrolled in teaching/research master's or doctoral degree programs only. Two fellowships are restricted to women and one is open to both men and women.
$ Given: Three fellowships awarded annually, each for $24,000.
Application Information: Write for details.
Deadline: N/A.
Contact: Professor Terumasa Ueno, Chair of the Graduate School of Letters.

Friedrich Ebert Foundation Doctoral Research Fellowships
342 Madison Avenue
New York, NY 10173
(212) 687-0208
FAX (212) 687-0261

Description: Five- to twelve-month residential study/research fellowships in Germany for doctoral candidates at dissertation level in political science, sociology, history, or economics as related to German/European affairs or German-American relations.
Restrictions: Applicants must have completed all degree requirements except dissertation; affiliation with American university required; knowledge of German adequate for research required; United States citizenship required.

$ Given: An unspecified number of fellowships awarded annually; each with DM1,390/month stipend plus airfare, domestic travel allowance, tuition and fees, luggage/books allowance, and dependents' allowance (if needed).
Application Information: Write for details.
Deadline: February 28.
Additional Addresses: 1155 Fifteenth Street, N.W., Suite 1100, Washington, DC 20005, (202) 331-1819; and Godesberger Allee 149, Bonn 2, D 53170, Germany.

Friedrich Ebert Foundation Pre-Dissertation/Advanced Graduate Fellowships
342 Madison Avenue
New York, NY 10173
(212) 687-0208
FAX (212) 687-0261

Description: Five- to twelve-month independent study/research fellowships in Germany for doctoral candidates in political science, sociology, history, or economics as related to German/European affairs or German-American relations.
Restrictions: Applicants must have completed as least two years of graduate study at an American university; knowledge of German adequate for research required; United States citizenship required.
$ Given: An unspecified number of fellowships awarded annually; each with DM1,250/month stipend plus airfare, domestic travel allowance, tuition and fees, luggage/books allowance, and dependents' allowance (if needed).
Application Information: Write for details.
Deadline: February 28.
Addition Addresses: 806 Fifteenth Street, N.W., Suite 230, Washington, DC 20005, (202) 331-1819; and Godesberger Allee 149, Bonn 2, D-53170, Germany.

Eta Sigma Phi National Classics Honor Society Eta Sigma Phi Summer Scholarships
University of South Dakota
Box 171
Vermillion, SD 57069
www.monm.edu

Description: Summer scholarships for study at the American Academy in Rome or the American School of Classical Studies in Athens; for recent graduates who majored in Latin, Greek, or the classics; recipients can earn six semester hours of graduate-level credit during summer session.
Restrictions: Preference for students planning to teach classics; membership in Eta Sigma Phi required; Ph.D. candidates ineligible; applicants must have graduated college within the past five years.
$ Given: Two scholarships awarded annually; $2,400 to attend the American Academy in Rome, $2,600 to attend the American School of Classical Studies in Athens.
Application Information: Request application forms from Professor Thomas Sienkewicz, Department of Classics, Monmouth College, Monmouth, IL 61462, (309) 457-2371.

Deadline: December 5.
Contact: Brent M. Froberg, Executive Secretary,
Department of Classics.

**Foundation for European
Language and Educational
Centers
Intensive European Language
Courses Scholarships**
Scholarship Department
Eurocentres
Seestrasse 247
Zurich CH-8038
Switzerland
(01) 485-5251

Description: Partial scholarships for three-month foreign language courses in English, French, German,
Italian, and Spanish; each course held in country where
language is spoken; recipients chosen on the basis of
financial need and prior knowledge of language to be
studied.
Restrictions: Applicants must be ages 18 to 30 and
must have at least two years of professional experience in
any field.
$ Given: An unspecified number of scholarships are
awarded annually; each for between $250 and $750,
which covers only part of the course tuition.
Application Information: Write for details.
Deadline: January 15, March 31, June 15, and
October 15.
Contact: Eric Steenbergen, Students' Assistance
Department.

**French Association of
University Women
Dorothy Leet Fellowships**
4, rue de Chevreuse
75006 Paris
France

Description: Fellowships for American women who are
doctoral candidates or postdoctoral scholars who wish to
pursue research in France.
Restrictions: Limited to women applicants. U.S. citi-
zenship required.
$ Given: An unspecified number of fellowships awarded
annually, each for $500 to $2,000.
Application Information: Write for details.
Deadline: March 31.
Contact: Danielle Gondard-Cozette, President,
Fellowship Committee.

**French Embassy Scientific
Services
Chateaubriand Research
Scholarships for the Exact
Sciences,
Engineering, and Medicine**
Department of Science and
Technology
4101 Reservoir Road, N.W.
Washington, DC 20007
(202) 944-6241
www.info-france-USA.org

Description: Six- to twelve-month research scholarship
for doctoral candidates at dissertation level, as well as
postdoctoral scholars, to conduct research in France at
French universities, engineering schools, and private laboratories; language training sessions provided; relevant disciplines include biological and agricultural sciences,
physical sciences and mathematics, engineering and
applied sciences, medicine, nutrition, optometry and
vision sciences, pharmacy and pharmaceuticals sciences,
and veterinary medicine and sciences; recipients chosen
on the basis of proposed research.
Restrictions: Each applicant must be registered at
United States university and already in contact with
French host institution; United States citizenship required.

$ Given: Twenty to thirty scholarships awarded annually; each for 9,000 francs per month plus airfare and health insurance.
Application Information: Application forms must be submitted with faculty recommendation.
Deadline: January 31.

German Academic Exchange Service
German Studies Summer Seminar Grants for Graduate Students and Ph.D. Candidates
950 Third Avenue
19th Floor
New York, NY 10022
(212) 758-3223
FAX (212) 755-5780
www.daad.org

Description: Six-week interdisciplinary seminars at the University of Chicago, for advanced graduate students and doctoral candidates in the humanities and social sciences, including students of German intellectual and social history; for the study of Germany after World War II; recipients chosen on the basis of academic achievement; participants eligible for academic credit.
Restrictions: Working knowledge of German required; U.S. or Canadian citizens.
$ Given: An unspecified number of grants are awarded annually; each with a $3,000 stipend.
Application Information: Write for details.
Deadline: March 1.

German Academic Exchange Service
Short Term Visits to Germany Research Grants for Ph.D. Candidates and Recent Ph.D.s
950 Third Avenue
19th Floor
New York, NY 10022
(212) 758-3223
FAX (212) 755-5780
www.daad.org

Description: One to six months of grant funding for doctoral candidates and recent Ph.D.s to conduct research/study in Germany; for work in all fields; recipients chosen on the basis of academic achievement.
Restrictions: Maximum eligible age range of 32 to 35; working knowledge of German required; United States or Canadian citizenship required; affiliation with United States university required.
$ Given: An unspecified number of grants are awarded annually; each with monthly stipend, travel allowance, and health insurance.
Application Information: Write for details.
Deadlines: February 1, August 1.

German Academic Exchange Service
Summer Language Study Grants at Goethe Institutes for Undergraduate and Graduate Students
950 Third Avenue
19th Floor
New York, NY 10022
(212) 758-3223
FAX (212) 755-5780
www.daad.org

Description: Grants for two-month intensive German language course at the Goethe Institutes in Germany for undergraduate upperclassmen and graduate students; recipients chosen on the basis of academic achievement.
Restrictions: Basic knowledge of German required, three semesters of college-level German preferred; applicants must be between the ages of 18 and 32; United States or Canadian citizenship required; full-time enrollment in United States university required; individuals with previous study experience in Germany ineligible; previous language scholarship recipients ineligible; majors in modern languages and literatures ineligible.

$ Given: An unspecified number of grants are awarded annually; each for tuition and fees, plus room and partial board; no travel allowance.
Application Information: Write for details.
Deadline: January 31.

Florence Gould Foundation Pre-Dissertation Fellowships for Research in France
Council for European Studies
Columbia University
807-807a IAB
New York, NY 10027
(212) 854-4172

Description: Three-month pre-dissertation fellowships for research in France to determine the viability of a projected doctoral dissertation in modern history and the social sciences. Recipients will test the research design of their dissertation, determine availability of archival materials, and contact French scholars in the relevant field. Does not support language training or tuition for courses at a French university.
Restrictions: U.S. citizenship or permanent resident status required. Completion of at least two, but no more than three, years of full-time graduate study required.
$ Given: Six fellowships awarded annually; each with a maximum stipend of $4,000.
Application Information: Write for details.
Deadline: February 1.
Contact: Ionnis Sinanoglou, is8@columbia.edu.

Ed A. Hewett Policy Fellowship Program
National Council for Eurasian and East European Research
910 17th Street, N.W.
Suite 300
Washington, DC 20006
(202) 822-6950

Description: Fellowship for U.S. based scholars or researchers to study the countries of the Newly Independent States of the Former Soviet Union (NIS) and/or Central and Eastern Europe (CEE), conducted under the auspices of and placement in a U.S. government agency with responsibility for the administration of some aspect of U.S. Foreign policy toward the NIS and CEE.
$ Given: One fellowship awarded annually with a maximum stipend of $60,900.
Application Information: Write for details.
Deadline: March 15.
Contact: Robert T. Huber, President, NCEEER.

Institute for European History Research Fellowships
Alte Universitaetsstrasse 19
Mainz 1
D-6500
Germany
(061) 31 39 93 60

Description: Residential fellowships at the Institute for doctoral candidates and postdoctoral scholars studying the history of Europe and European religion from the sixteenth to the twentieth century; recipients chosen on the basis of academic achievement and proposed research.
Restrictions: Open to all nationalities; applicants must have thorough command of German.
$ Given: Twenty fellowships of DM13,080–DM17,280 each are awarded annually.
Application Information: Write for details.
Deadline: February, June, October.

Contact: For European History program, contact Professor Dr. Karl Otmar Freiherr von Aretin, (06131) 226143; for History of European Religion program, contact Professor Dr. Peter Manns, (06131) 224870.

Institute of International Education
Colombian Government Study and Research Grants
U.S. Student Programs Division
809 United Nations Plaza
New York, NY 10017-3580
(212) 984-5330
www.iie.org

Description: Grants for B.S./B.A. holders to pursue up to two years of study/research at Colombian universities; relevant disciplines include agriculture, biology, business administration, economics, chemistry, engineering, education, health services administration, geography, history, Latin American literature, law, linguistics, political science, physics, regulatory development, public health, and remote sensing interpretation.
Restrictions: United States citizenship required.
$ Given: An unspecified number of grants awarded annually; each for a modest monthly stipend, plus tuition and fees, health insurance, book/materials allowance, and one-way return airfare upon completion of study.
Application Information: Write for details.
Deadline: October 25.

Institute of International Education
Fulbright Fixed Sum–Bulgarian Government Grants
U.S. Student Programs Division
809 United Nations Plaza
New York, NY 10017-3580
(212) 984-5330
www.iie.org

Description: Grants for B.A./B.S. holders in the humanities, physical sciences, and social sciences; for a six- to nine-month residency/exchange in Bulgaria (October–June).
Restrictions: Proficiency in Bulgarian language is desirable; United States citizenships required; applicants must meet all Fulbright eligibility requirements.
$ Given: Five grants awarded annually; Bulgarian government funds stipend, housing, and health/accident insurance; Fulbright provides fixed sum for round-trip transportation plus additional monthly stipend.
Application Information: Write for details.
Deadline: October 25.
Contact: United States Student Program Division.

Institute of International Education
Fulbright Fixed Sum–Syrian Government Grants
U.S. Student Programs Division
809 United Nations Plaza
New York, NY 10017-3580
(212) 984-5330
www.iie.org

Description: Grants for degree holders in Arabic language and culture, history, and geography preference for Ph.D. candidates for study at the University of Damascus.
Restrictions: Applicants studying modern social sciences not eligible; minimum two years of Arabic language study or demonstrated proficiency required; United States citizenship required; applicants must meet all Fulbright funding.
$ Given: An unspecified number of grants awarded annually; monthly stipend, tuition, and health insurance, supplemented by Fulbright funding.

Application Information: Write for details.
Deadline: October 25.
Contact: Campus Fulbright program advisor.

Institute of International Education
Fulbright–Spanish Government Grants
U.S. Student Programs Division
809 United Nations Plaza
New York, NY 10017-3580
(212) 984-5330
www.iie.org

Description: Grants for B.A./B.S. holders in all fields for study at a Spanish university. Of particular interest are projects dealing with contemporary issues.
Restrictions: Proficiency in Spanish (written and spoken) required; United States citizenship required; applicants must meet all Fulbright eligibility requirements.
$ Given: Thirty-four grants awarded annually; Spanish government funds tuition and stipend; Fulbright funds round-trip transportation, and expense allowance.
Application Information: Write for details.
Deadline: October 25.

Institute of International Education
Fulbright Travel–Iceland Government Grants
U.S. Student Programs Division
809 United Nations Plaza
New York, NY 10017-3580
(212) 984-5330
www.iie.org

Description: Grants for B.A./B.S. holders studying Icelandic language, literature, and history; for eight months of advanced study at the University of Iceland in Reykjavik.
Restrictions: Knowledge of Icelandic, Old Norse, or other Scandinavian language required for language/literature study; United States citizenship required; applicants must meet all Fulbright eligibility requirements.
$ Given: Five grants awarded annually; cash stipend plus tuition.
Application Information: Write for details.
Deadline: October 25.

Institute of International Education
Germanistic Society of America Fellowships
U.S. Student Programs Division
809 United Nations Plaza
New York, NY 10017-3580
(212) 984-5330
www.iie.org

Description: Fellowships for master's degree holders and some B.A./B.S. holders studying German language and literature, art history, history, economics, philosophy, international law, political science, and public affairs; for one academic year of study in Germany.
Restrictions: United States citizenship required; applicants must meet all Fulbright eligibility requirements.
$ Given: Four fellowships awarded annually; each for $11,000 plus consideration for a Fulbright Travel Grant.
Application Information: Write for details.
Deadline: October 25.

Institute of International Education
Study and Research Grants for U.S. Citizens
U.S. Student Programs Division
809 United Nations Plaza
New York, NY 10017-3580
(212) 984-5330
www.iie.org

Description: Grants to support study and research in all fields, as well as professional training in the creative and performing arts; tenable at institutions of higher learning outside of the United States for one year; list of participating countries in any given year may be obtained from IIE.
Restrictions: Open to United States citizens with B.A. or equivalent; acceptable plan of study and proficiency in host country's language required.
$ Given: A variable number of grants awarded annually; covers international transportation, language or orientation course (where appropriate), tuition, book and maintenance allowances, and health and accident insurance.
Application Information: If currently enrolled in a college or university, apply to the campus Fulbright Program Advisor; applications also available from IIE.
Deadline: October 25.

Institute of International Education
Lusk Memorial Fellowships
U.S. Student Programs Division
809 United Nations Plaza
New York, NY 10017-3580
(212) 984-5330
www.iie.org

Description: Grants for individuals in the creative and performing arts; for one academic year of study in the United Kingdom and Italy.
Restrictions: Written and spoken proficiency in Italian required for study in Italy; applicants must have completed at least four years of professional study; United States citizenship required.
$ Given: An unspecified number of grants awarded annually; maintenance allowance, health/accident insurance, and round-trip travel allowance.
Application Information: Write for details.
Deadline: October 25.

Inter-American Foundation
Doctoral Field Research Fellowships
IAF Fellowship Program
Department 111
901 N. Stuart Street
Arlington, VA 22203
(703) 306-4301
www.iaf.gov

Description: Up to eighteen-month fellowships for doctoral candidates to support field research in independent Latin American and Caribbean countries (except Cuba) through a substantive collaboration with an affiliated development or applied research institution in the chosen country.
Restrictions: U.S., Latin American, or Caribbean citizenship required. Applicants must be enrolled in a U.S. university and must speak and write the local language.
$ Given: An unspecified number of fellowships awarded annually, each with a modest monthly living stipend, health insurance, and round-trip international transportation to the field research site.
Application Information: Write for details.
Deadline: N/A.

International Research and Exchanges Board
IREX Research Exchange Program with Mongolia
1616 H Street, N.W.
Washington, DC 20006
(202) 628-8188
www.irex.org

Description: One- to four-month exchange program for doctoral candidates to study in Mongolia; relevant disciplines include the humanities, social sciences, and natural sciences; recipients chosen on the basis of proposed research.
Restrictions: Command of host country's language required; United States citizenship required.
$ Given: Three fellowships awarded annually; varying amounts.
Application Information: Write for details.
Deadline: December 15.
Contact: Emili Dickson, Program Officer.

Japan Foundation
Dissertation Fellowships
152 West 57th Street
39th Floor
New York, NY 10019
(212) 489-0299
www.ipf.go.jp

Description: Fellowships for two to fourteen months of dissertation research in Japan; funding made available to doctoral candidates at dissertation level in the humanities and social sciences, with emphasis on political science, law, economics, business, and journalism—as related to Japan; recipients chosen on the basis of academic achievement and quality of proposed research.
Restrictions: Applicants must be proficient in Japanese; no funding for Japanese language study; recipients may not hold other fellowships concurrently.
$ Given: Thirteen fellowships awarded annually; each for ¥310,000 plus further allowances including one round trip air ticket.
Application Information: Write for details.
Deadline: December 1.

Japan Ministry of Education, Science, and Culture
Japanese Government (Monbusho) Scholarship Program
2-2 Kasumigaseki, 3-chome
Chiyoda-ku
Tokyo 100
Japan
03-581-4211
www.embjapan.org

Description: Eighteen-month to two-year scholarships for non-Japanese graduate students to study at Japanese universities and research institutes; Research Students Program is specifically designed for graduate students (undergraduate program also available) in the humanities, social sciences, music, fine arts, and natural sciences; open to citizens of countries with educational exchange agreements with Japan.
Restrictions: Language proficiency required (twelve- to eighteen-month language training program required if language skills deemed insufficient); applicants must be under age 35.
$ Given: An unspecified number of scholarships awarded annually; each to cover monthly stipend, airfare, tuition, and expense allowance.
Application Information: For further information, contact Japanese Embassy or Consulate.
Deadline: August 14.

Contact: Student Exchange Division. Leslie Fedsta, Japan Information Center, Consulate General of Japan, 100 Colony Square, Suite 2000, Atlanta, GA 30361, (404) 892-2700.

Kosciuszko Foundation Graduate Studies and Research in Poland Program
15 East 65th Street
New York, NY 10021-6595
(212) 734-2130
FAX (212) 628-4552

Description: Grants to allow Americans to pursue graduate and postgraduate studies in Poland in any subject.
Restrictions: Applicants must have strong command of Polish language; United States citizenship or permanent resident of Polish descent; Polish studies background required.
$ Given: An unspecified number of grants of $1,000–$5,000 awarded annually; each for tuition, room, board, and monthly stipend for living expenses.
Application Information: Write for details.
Deadline: January 16.
Contact: Grants Office.

Kosciuszko Foundation Year Abroad at the University of Cracow Program
15 East 65th Street
New York, NY 10021-6595
(212) 734-2130
FAX (212) 628-4552

Description: Grants to support participation in one-year program of academic study at the University of Cracow (Jagiellonian University) in Poland; funding made available to undergraduate upperclassmen and graduate students in the fields of Polish language, literature, history, and culture.
Restrictions: Applicants must have Polish background; United States citizenship or permanent resident.
$ Given: An unspecified number of grants awarded annually; each for tuition, housing, and monthly food/expense allowance; round-trip travel not covered.
Application Information: Write for details.
Deadline: November 15.
Contact: Grants Office.

Samuel H. Kress Foundation Art History Travel Fellowships
174 East 80th Street
New York, NY 10021
(212) 861-4993
www.shkf.org

Description: Fellowships for doctoral candidates at dissertation level in art history to travel for the purpose of viewing original materials/works; recipients chosen on the basis of academic achievement, financial need, and necessity of travel.
Restrictions: United States citizenship or enrollment in United States university required.
$ Given: Fifteen to twenty fellowships of $1,000–$5,000 awarded annually.
Application Information: Applicants must be nominated by their art history departments.
Deadline: November 30.
Contact: Lisa Ackerman, Chief Administrative Officer.

L.S.B. Leakey Foundation
Franklin Mosher Baldwin
Memorial Fellowships
P.O. Box 29346
Presidio Building 1002A
O'Reilly Avenue
San Francisco, CA 94129-0346
www.leakeyfoundation.org

Description: Fellowship for master's candidates in anthropology; tenable at any qualified institution in the world.
Restrictions: Limited to citizens of African nations.
$ Given: One fellowship of up to $12,000 awarded annually for expenses.
Application Information: Write for details.
Deadline: February 15.
Contact: D. Karla Savage, Ph.D., Program and Grants Officer.

L.S.B. Leakey Foundation
Foraging Peoples Study
Fellowships
P.O. Box 29346
Presidio Building 1002A
O'Reilly Avenue
San Francisco, CA 94129-0346
www.leakeyfoundation.org

Description: Fellowship for doctoral candidates study-ing contemporary foraging peoples; recipients chosen on the basis of proposed research; preference for urgent research projects that might not ordinarily be funded by other agencies.
Restrictions: N/A.
$ Given: One occasional fellowship of up to $40,000 awarded for one to two years of field expenses.
Application Information: Write for details.
Deadlines: Preapplication and curriculum vitae due October 15; formal application due January 2.
Contact: D. Karla Savage, Ph.D., Program and Grants Officer.

Marshall Scholarships
Marshall Aid Commemorating
Commission
Association of Commonwealth
Universities
36 Gordon Square
London WC1H0PF
(44) 1713878572
www.aca.ac.uk/marshall

Description: Two- to three-year scholarships for under-graduate or graduate level study at any university in the United Kingdom, in any discipline leading to the award of a British university degree.
Restrictions: U.S. citizenship required; limited to grad-uates of accredited four-year colleges and universities in the United States with at least a 3.75 GPA since freshman year.
$ Given: Up to forty scholarships awarded annually; each worth approximately $25,000 per year and compris-ing a personal allowance for cost of living and residence, tuition fees, books, travel in connection with studies, and to and from the United States.
Application Information: Write for details. Application forms also available from colleges and universities in the United States, British consulates in Atlanta, Boston, Chicago, Houston, and San Francisco, the British Council in Washington, DC, British Information Services in New York.
Deadline: N/A.

Metropolitan Museum of Art
Theodore Rousseau
Scholarships
Office of Academic Programs
Fifth Avenue and 82nd Street
New York, NY 10028
(212) 570-3874
www.metmuseum.org

Description: Fellowships for master's and doctoral candidates in art history, for study in Europe; intended to allow recipients first-hand examination of painting in major European collections.
Restrictions: Applicants must have completed at least one year of graduate training; applicants should be planning careers as museum curators of painting.
$ Given: An unspecified number of fellowships awarded annually.
Application Information: Write for details.
Deadline: November 5.
Contact: Marcie Karp, Fellowships Coordinator.

National Italian American
Foundation Scholarship
Program
Doctoral Research in Italy
Fellowship
1860 19th Street, N.W.
Washington, DC 20009
(202) 638-2137
FAX (202) 638-0002

Description: Scholarship for Ph.D. candidates for doctoral research in Italy in modern history, politics, or economics.
Restrictions: Applicants must be of Italian descent. Must provide letter of support from advisor.
$ Given: One scholarship awarded annually for $5,000.
Application Information: Send SASE for details.
Deadline: May 31.
Contact: Maria Lombardo, Education Director.

National Italian American
Foundation Scholarship
Program
Study Abroad Scholarships
1860 19th Street, N.W.
Washington, DC 20009
(202) 638-2137
FAX (202) 638-0002

Description: Scholarship for any undergraduate and graduate student wishing to study in Italy.
Restrictions: Applicants must be of Italian descent. Must show letter of acceptance from an accredited school.
$ Given: Five scholarships awarded annually; each for $2,000.
Application Information: Send SASE for details.
Deadline: May 31.
Contact: Maria Lombardo, Education Director.

National Science Foundation
Postdoctoral Research
Fellowships in Biological
Informatics
P.O. Box 218
Jessup, MD 20794-0218
(301) 947-2722
www.nsf.gov

Description: Fellowships for postdoctoral-level research and training at the intersection of biology and the informational, computational, mathematical, and statistical sciences. Research may be conducted at any appropriate U.S. or foreign host institution. Recipients chosen on the basis of their ability, accomplishments, and potential, the research and training plan's scientific merit, feasibility, significance in generating new biological knowledge, and impact on the career development of the applicant.
Restrictions: U.S. citizenship or permanent resident status required. Fellows must affiliate with a host institution during the entire tenure of the fellowship.
$ Given: Approximately twenty fellowships awarded annually, each for $50,000 per year for two or three years.
Application Information: Write for details.
Deadline: First Monday in November.

Norwegian Information Service in the United States Norwegian Emigration Fund of 1975 Scholarships and Grants for Americans
825 Third Avenue
38th Floor
New York, NY 10022
(212) 421-7333
www.norway.org

Description: Grants for American master's and doctoral candidates to visit Norway to study history and relations between the United States and Norway.
Restrictions: United States citizenship or permanent resident status required.
$ Given: An unspecified number of grants of NKr5,000–NKr40,000 each are awarded annually.
Application Information: Write for details.
Deadline: July 1.
Contact: Grants and Scholarships Section.

Norwegian Information Service in the United States Norwegian Marshall Fund Grants
825 Third Avenue
38th Floor
New York, NY 10022
(212) 421-7333
www.norway.org

Description: Grants for American master's and doctoral candidates in science and the humanities to conduct research abroad.
Restrictions: United States citizenship required.
$ Given: An unspecified number of grants of up to $5,000 each are awarded annually.
Application Information: Request application forms from Norway-American Association, Drammensveien 20 C, Oslo 2, 0255, Norway, (02) 44.76.83.
Deadline: March 15.
Contact: Grants and Scholarships Section.

Norwegian Information Service in the United States SASS Travel Grants
825 Third Avenue
38th Floor
New York, NY 10022
(212) 421-7333
www.norway.org

Description: Grants for master's and doctoral candidates who have passed preliminary exams, as well as for Norwegian language/culture teachers, for study/research in Norway.
Restrictions: United States citizenship or permanent resident status required; membership in SASS (Society for the Advancement of Scandinavian Study) required.
$ Given: An unspecified number of grants of $750–$1,500 each are awarded annually.
Application Information: Write for details.
Deadline: April 15.
Contact: Grants and Scholarships Section.

Organization of American States OAS Regular Training Program Fellowships
Department of Fellowships and Training
17th Street and Constitution Avenue, N.W.
Washington, DC 20006
(202) 458-3000
www.oas.org

Description: Three-month to two-year fellowships for graduate students in all fields except medicine to pursue advanced study or research in other countries; tenable at OAS member countries; fellowships intended to contribute to host country on economic, social, technical, and cultural levels; recipients chosen on the basis of academic achievement and financial need.
Restrictions: Applicants must be citizens of OAS member countries; applicants must hold B.S./B.A. or equivalent and must be accepted at university or research facility for proposed work; language proficiency required.

$ Given: An unspecified number of fellowships awarded annually; each to cover expenses, tuition, and stipend, varying by country.
Application Information: Write for details.
Deadline: March 31.

Pacific Cultural Foundation Grants for Chinese Studies
Palace Office Building
Suite 807
Taipei, Taiwan 10567
Republic of China
(02) 752-7424 through -7429
(six phone lines)

Description: Grants for master's degree holders for research in Chinese studies; four types of studies grants: research, writing, publication, and seminar; recipients chosen on the basis of proposed work/research.
Restrictions: Applicants must be residents of the free world.
$ Given: Approximately eighty grants of $2,000–$5,000 each are awarded annually.
Application Information: Separate application for travel grant available.
Deadlines: March 1, September 1.

Pitt Rivers Museum
James A. Swan Fund
Oxford University
South Parks Road
Oxford, England OX1 3PP
0865-270927
www.prm.ox.ac.UK

Description: Grants for individuals to travel to Africa to pursue study/research on the hunter-gatherer peoples of Africa; recipients chosen on the basis of proposed research.
Restrictions: N/A.
$ Given: Ten grants of 1,000 pounds–2,000 pounds each are awarded annually; renewable.
Application Information: No application form; submit research proposal and proposed budget.
Deadline: Applications accepted continuously.
Contact: Dr. Schuyler Jones, Curator.

Rotary Foundation of Rotary International
Rotary Foundation Ambassadorial Scholarships
1560 Sherman Avenue
Evanston, IL 60201
(708) 866-3000
www.rotary.org

Description: Scholarships for graduate students with B.A./B.S. degree in any discipline; for one academic year in another country with Rotary club.
Restrictions: Applicants must be ages 18 to 30; members of Rotary clubs, as well as spouses and lineal descendants of members and employees of Rotary clubs, are ineligible; language proficiency test required in host country's language; open to citizens of all countries with Rotary clubs.
$ Given: An unspecified number of scholarships are awarded annually; each to cover transportation, academic fees, educational supplies, room and board, and additional expenses.
Application Information: By nomination from local Rotary club, each of which designs its own selection criteria.
Deadline: July 15.
Contact: Local Rotary club.

Social Science Research Council
Advanced German and European Studies Doctoral Dissertation Fellowships
810 Seventh Avenue
New York, NY 10019
(212) 377-2700
www.ssrc.org

Description: Nine- to twelve-month residential fellowships for doctoral candidates at dissertation level to study at the Free University of Berlin; for dissertation work addressing the economic, political, and social aspects of modern and contemporary German and European affairs; recipients chosen on the basis of academic achievement and proposed research.
Restrictions: Good command of German required; United States citizenship or permanent resident status required.
$ Given: An unspecified number of fellowships awarded annually; each covers monthly stipend and travel expenses.
Application Information: Write for details.
Deadline: February 1.

Social Science Research Council
International Predissertation Research Fellowships
Contact individual universities for details and deadline information

Description: Fellowships for doctoral candidates in the early stages of Ph.D. programs in the social sciences, to promote internationalization of graduate training and to focus research on the developing world; relevant disciplines include political science, economics, and sociology; tenable for twelve months of support over two-year period, for domestic and overseas study.
Restrictions: Applicants must be full-time students in Ph.D. degree-granting programs at the following schools; University of California at Berkeley, UCLA, University of California at San Diego, University of Chicago, Columbia, Cornell, Duke, Harvard, University of Illinois, Indiana University at Bloomington, Massachusetts Institute of Technology, University of Michigan, Michigan State University, University of Minnesota at Twin Cities, University of North Carolina Northwestern, University of Pennsylvania, Princeton, Stanford, University of Texas at Austin, University of Washington, University of Wisconsin at Madison, and Yale; no funding for dissertation research.
$ Given: An unspecified number of fellowships awarded annually; each for $1,500 for domestic study plus allowance for overseas expenses.
Application Information: Write for details.
Deadline: N/A.
Contact: Dr. Ellen Perecman, Program Director.

Social Sciences and Humanities Research Council of Canada
SSHRC Doctoral Fellowships
Fellowships Division
350 Albert Street
Box 1610
Ottawa, Ontario K1P 6G4
Canada
(613) 943-7777
www.sshrc.ca

Description: Six- to forty-eight-month fellowships for doctoral candidates in the humanities, and social sciences; tenable in Canada or abroad; recipients chosen on the basis of academic achievement and proposed research.
Restrictions: Applicants must have completed one year of doctoral study; Canadian citizenship or permanent resident status required.
$ Given: Six hundred fellowships awarded annually, plus 600 annual renewables; each for up to $16,620 Canadian per year plus relocation costs.
Application Information: Write for details.
Deadline: November 15.

Donald E. Stokes Dissertation Research Fellowship of the British Politics Group
West Virginia University
Eberly College of Arts and Sciences
P.O. Box 6317
Morgantown, WV 26506-6317
(304) 293-3811, ext: 5269
FAX (304) 293-8644

Description: Fellowship for a North American graduate student doing Ph.D. dissertation research on British politics to conduct research in the United Kingdom, including comparative and historical work as well as contemporary British politics.
Restrictions: None.
$ Given: One fellowship awarded annually for $500 U.S. or 300 pounds sterling (choice of recipient).
Application Information: Write for details.
Deadline: March 15.
Contact: Donly T. Studlar, Ph.D.

Swedish Institute International Summer Courses Scholarships
P.O. Box 7434
Stockholm S-103 91
Sweden
46-8-789 20 00

Description: Scholarship for four-week summer courses (July–August) at Swedish folk high schools throughout Sweden, for study in Swedish language, culture, and literature; instruction in Swedish; classes six hours/day, five days/week.
Restrictions: Minimum age 18; language proficiency requirement, dependent on level of study.
$ Given: A few scholarships awarded annually; varying amounts.
Application Information: Write for details.
Deadline: March 31.
Contact: Brita Holm, Course Director; or Pernilla Eldblom, Course Secretary.

University of North Carolina at Chapel Hill
Gilbert Chinard French History and Literature Research Grants
Romance Languages
Department
CB3170
Chapel Hill, NC 27599
(919) 962-2062
www.unc.edu

Description: Grants for doctoral candidates at dissertation level and recent Ph.D.s (within past six years) for two months' study of French history and literature in France; recipients chosen on the basis of academic achievement and proposed work.
Restrictions: Applicants must be affiliated with United States universities; United States citizenship or permanent resident status required.
$ Given: Two to three grants for $1,000 each are awarded annually.
Application Information: Write for details.
Deadline: January 15.
Contact: Catherine Maley, President, Institut Français de Washington.

Wellesley College
Anne Louise Barett Fellowship
Office of Financial Aid
106 Central Street
Wellesley, MA 02181
(781) 283-3525
www.wellesley.edu

Description: Fellowship for B.S./B.A. holders and graduating college seniors in the fields of music theory, composition and history; tenable for full-time graduate study in the United States or abroad at institutions other than Wellesley; recipients chosen on the basis of merit and financial need.
Restrictions: Limited to Wellesley graduates.
$ Given: One fellowship of up to $4,000 is awarded annually.
Application Information: Request application form before November 25.
Deadline: January 3.
Contact: Secretary to the Committee on Graduate Fellowships.

Wellesley College
Ruth Ingersoll Goldmark Fellowship
Office of Financial Aid
106 Central Street
Wellesley, MA 02181
(781) 283-3525
www.wellesley.edu

Description: Fellowship for B.S./B.A. holders and graduating college seniors in the fields of English literature, composition, and the classics; tenable for full-time graduate study in the United States or abroad at institutions other than Wellesley; recipients chosen on the basis of merit and financial need.
Restrictions: Limited to women graduates of Wellesley.
$ Given: One fellowship of up to $1,500 is awarded annually.
Application Information: Request application form before November 25.
Deadline: January 3.
Contact: Secretary to the Committee on Graduate Fellowships.

Wellesley College
Edna V. Moffett Fellowship
Office of Financial Aid
106 Central Street
Wellesley, MA 02181
(781) 283-3525
www.wellesley.edu

Description: Fellowship for B.S./B.A. holders and graduating college seniors in the field of history; tenable for full-time graduate study in the United States or abroad at institutions other than Wellesley; preference for individuals entering their first year of graduate study; recipients chosen on the basis of merit and financial need.
Restrictions: Limited to women graduates of Wellesley.
$ Given: One fellowship of up to $4,000 is awarded annually.
Application Information: Request application form before November 25.
Deadline: January 3.
Contact: Secretary to the Committee on Graduate Fellowships.

Wellesley College
Mary McEwin Schimke
Scholarships
Office of Financial Aid
Box GR
106 Central Street
Wellesley, MA 02181
(781) 283-3525

Description: Scholarships for B.S./B.A. holders in the fields of literature, history, and American studies; recipients chosen on the basis of merit and financial need; tenable for graduate study at institutions other than Wellesley; intended to afford relief from costs of household and child care during graduate study.
Restrictions: Limited to women applicants; minimum age 30; applicants must have received their bachelor's degrees from United States institutions.
$ Given: An unspecified number of scholarships of up to $1,000 each are awarded annually.
Application Information: Request application form before November 25.
Deadline: January 3.
Contact: Secretary to the Committee on Graduate Fellowships.

Wellesley College
Vida Dutton Scudder
Fellowship
Office of Financial Aid
106 Central Street
Wellesley, MA 02181
(781) 283-3525
www.wellesley.edu

Description: Fellowship for B.S./B.A. holders and graduating college seniors in the fields of literature, political science, and the social sciences; tenable for full-time graduate study in the United States or abroad at institutions other than Wellesley; recipients chosen on the basis of merit and financial need.
Restrictions: Limited to Wellesley graduates.
$ Given: One fellowship of up to $4,000 is awarded annually.
Application Information: Request application form before November 25.
Deadline: January 3.
Contact: Secretary to the Committee on Graduate Fellowships.

World Health Organization
WHO Fellowships
1775 K Street, N.W.
Suite 430
Washington, DC 20006
(202) 331-9081
www.who.int

Description: One-year or shorter fellowships for individual or group health training/study in another country; intended for training/study not available in recipient's own country; relevant disciplines include public health administration, environmental health, medical social work, maternal and child health, communicable diseases, laboratory services, clinical medicine, basic medical sciences, and medical/allied education; recipients chosen on the basis of academic achievement and proposed study/training.

Restrictions: Applicants must be planning careers in public health; language proficiency required, as appropriate.

$ Given: An unspecified number of fellowships awarded annually; each to cover monthly stipend, tuition, and books.

Application Information: Contact WHO for detailed information booklet; application forms are available from national health administrations.

Deadline: At least six months prior to study.

All Areas of Study

American Association of University Women Educational Foundation AAUW American Fellowships
Dept. 60
2201 No. Dodge Street
Iowa City, IA 52243-4030
(319) 337-1716
www.aauw.org

Description: Fellowships for full-time doctoral students and postdoctoral scholars, for research in all disciplines; recipients chosen on the basis of academic achievement and commitment to women's issues in professional career.
Restrictions: Limited to women applicants; United States citizenship or permanent resident status required.
$ Given: Eight fellowships awarded annually, one for a senior fellow and seven for less experienced researchers each for $115–$27,000.
Application Information: Write for details.
Deadline: November 15.
Contact: American Fellowship Program.

American Association of University Women Educational Foundation AAUW Dissertation Fellowships
Dept. 60
2201 No. Dodge Street
Iowa City, IA 52243-4030
(319) 337-1716
www.aauw.org

Description: Fellowships to support doctoral candidates in full-time dissertation work for at least twelve months in any field.
Restrictions: Limited to women applicants; applicants must have completed all coursework and exams for Ph.D. by November; United States citizenship required.
$ Given: Fifty fellowships awarded annually; each for $13,500 which may not be used for tuition or loan repayment.
Application Information: Application forms must be requested in writing.
Deadline: November 15.
Contact: Dissertation Fellowship Program.

American Association of University Women Educational Foundation AAUW International Fellowships
Dept. 60
2201 No. Dodge Street
Iowa City, IA 52243-4030
(319) 337-1716
www.aauw.org

Description: Fellowships for one year of graduate study/research at an approved institution in the United States; recipients chosen on the basis of professional potential and importance of project to home country.
Restrictions: Limited to women applicants; applicants must be citizens of countries other than the United States; applicants must hold B.A./B.S. or equivalent; proficiency in English required; recipients must return to home countries to work after fellowships are completed.
$ Given: An unspecified number of fellowships awarded annually; each for $16,500.

Application Information: Write for details.
Deadline: December 1.
Contact: International Fellowship Program.

American Foundation for the Blind
Delta Gamma Foundation Memorial Scholarship
11 Penn Plaza, Suite 300
New York, NY 10001
(212) 502-7661

Description: Scholarship for an undergraduate or graduate student who is legally blind who is studying in the field of rehabilitation and/or education of persons who are blind or visually impaired. Recipients chosen on the basis of academic achievement and good character.
Restrictions: Applicants must be legally blind. U.S. citizenship required.
$ Given: One scholarship awarded annually for $1,000.
Application Information: Write for details.
Deadline: N/A.

American Foundation for the Blind
Ferdinand Torres Scholarship
11 Penn Plaza, Suite 300
New York, NY 10001
(212) 502-7661

Description: Scholarship for a full-time post-secondary student in any field who is legally blind and who presents evidence of economic need.
Restrictions: Applicants must be legally blind, and reside in the United States but need not be a citizen of the United States. Preference given to applicants residing in New York City and new immigrants to the United States.
$ Given: One scholarship awarded annually for $1,000.
Application Information: Write for details.
Deadline: N/A.

American Foundation for the Blind
Karen D. Carsel Memorial Scholarship
11 Penn Plaza, Suite 300
New York, NY 10001
(212) 502-7661
www.afb.org

Description: Funding to support full-time graduate studies; recipients chosen on the basis of financial need.
Restrictions: Limited to legally blind applicants only; United States citizenship required.
$ Given: One grant for $500 is awarded annually.
Application Information: Applications must include proof of legal blindness, proof of graduate school acceptance, evidence of financial need, personal statement, and letters of recommendation.
Deadline: April 1.
Contact: Julie Tucker, National Consultant in Low Vision.

Armenian Students' Association of America
Armenian Students' Association Scholarship
395 Concord Avenue
Belmont, MA 02478
(617) 484-9548
www.asainc.org

Description: Scholarships for undergraduate (sophomore, junior, senior) and graduate students in all disciplines; recipients chosen on the basis of financial need, academic achievement, self-help, and extracurricular involvement.
Restrictions: Limited to individuals of Armenian descent.
$ Given: Fifty-five scholarships awarded annually; each for $500–$1,500.
Application Information: Write for details.

Deadlines: January 15, March 15.
Contact: Christine Williamson, Scholarship Administrator.

Business and Professional Women's Clubs—New York State
Grace LeGendre Fellowships and Endowment Fund
7509 Route 5
Clinton, NY 13323

Description: Fellowships and grants for graduate students in all fields of study; tenable at accredited New York State institutions.
Restrictions: Limited to women applicants who are residents of New York State; United States citizenship or legal residency required.
$ Given: An unspecified number of $1,000 grants are awarded annually.
Application Information: Write for details.
Deadline: February 28.

Canadian Association of University Teachers
J. H. Stewart Reid Memorial Fellowship for Doctoral Studies
2675 Queensview Drive
Ottawa, Ontario K2B 8K2
Canada
(613) 820-2270
www.caut.ca

Description: Fellowship for doctoral candidates in all fields; tenable at Canadian institutions; recipients chosen on the basis of outstanding academic achievement.
Restrictions: Canadian citizenship or minimum one-year landed immigrant status required.
$ Given: One fellowship for $5,000 Canadian is awarded annually.
Application Information: Write for details.
Deadline: April 30.
Contact: Awards Officer.

Canadian Federation of University Women
Georgette LeMoyne Award
251 Bank Street
Suite 600
Ottawa, Ontario K2P 1X3
Canada
www.cfuw.ca

Description: Award for graduate studies in any field; intended for women taking refresher studies at universities where instruction is in French.
Restrictions: Limited to women only; applicant must hold B.S./B.A. degree and have been accepted to proposed program of graduate study; Canadian citizenship or minimum landed immigrant status required.
$ Given: One award for $1,000 Canadian made annually.
Application Information: Write for details.
Deadline: November 30.
Contact: Chair, Fellowships Committee.

Canadian Federation of University Women
CFUW Polytechnique Commemorative Awards
251 Bank Street
Suite 600
Ottawa, Ontario K2 P 1X3
Canada
www.cfuw.ca

Description: Awards for graduate studies in any field, with preference for studies related to women's issues.
Restrictions: Applicant must hold B.S./B.A. degree and have been accepted to proposed program of graduate study; Canadian citizenship or minimum one-year landed immigrant status required.
$ Given: One grant of $1,400 Canadian awarded annually.
Application Information: Write for details.
Deadline: November 30.
Contact: Fellowships Committee.

**Canadian Federation of
University Women
Beverly Jackson Fellowship**
251 Bank Street
Suite 600
Ottawa, Ontario K2P 1X3
Canada
www.cfuw.ca

Description: Fellowship for B.S./B.A. holders to pursue graduate work in any discipline; tenable at Ontario universities; recipients chosen on the basis of academic achievement, personal qualities, and potential.
Restrictions: Limited to women only; minimum age 35; applicants must hold B.S./B.A. from recognized university and be accepted into proposed place of study; Canadian citizenship or minimum one-year landed immigrant status required.
$ Given: One fellowship for $3,500 Canadian is awarded annually.
Application Information: Application forms are available July 1 through November 13.
Deadline: November 30.
Contact: Chair, Fellowships Committee.

**Canadian Federation of
University Women
Margaret McWilliams
Predoctoral Fellowship**
251 Bank Street
Suite 600
Ottawa, Ontario K2P 1X3
Canada
www.cfuw.ca

Description: Fellowship for doctoral candidates in any discipline who hold master's degree and are at least one year into doctoral program; recipients chosen on the basis of academic achievement, personal qualities, and potential.
Restrictions: Limited to women only; Canadian citizenship or minimum one-year landed immigrant status required.
$ Given: One fellowship of $8,000 Canadian is awarded annually.
Application Information: Application forms are available July 1 through November 13.
Deadline: November 30.
Contact: Chair, Fellowships Committee.

**Canadian Federation of
University Women
Professional Fellowship**
251 Bank Street
Suite 600
Ottawa, Ontario K2P 1X3
Canada
www.cfuw.ca

Description: Fellowship for graduate work below Ph.D. level; recipients chosen on the basis of academic, personal qualities, and potential.
Restrictions: Limited to women only; applicants must hold B.S./B.A. degree and have been accepted to proposed program of graduate study; Canadian citizenship or minimum one-year landed immigrant status required.
$ Given: Two fellowships for $5,000 Canadian each are awarded annually.
Application Information: Application forms available July 1 through November 13.
Deadline: November 30.
Contact: Chair, Fellowships Committee.

Canadian Federation of University Women Alice E. Wilson Grants
251 Bank Street
Suite 600
Ottawa, Ontario K2P 1X3
Canada
www.cfuw.ca

Description: Grants for women pursuing graduate refresher work in any field; recipients chosen on the basis of academic achievement, personal qualities, and potential; special consideration given to applicants returning to academic study after several years.
Restrictions: Limited to women only; applicants must hold B.S./B.A. degree and have been accepted to proposed program of graduate study; Canadian citizenship or minimum one-year landed immigrant status required.
$ Given: At least five grants for $1,000 Canadian each are awarded annually.
Application Information: Application forms available July 1 through November 13.
Deadline: November 30.
Contact: Chair, Fellowships Committee.

Committee of Vice-Chancellors and Principals Overseas Research Student Awards
29 Tavistock Square
London WC1H 9HQ
United Kingdom
44-171-383-4573
www.cvcp.ac.uk

Description: Grants to full-time graduate students/researchers in all fields attending colleges and universities in the United Kingdom; recipients chosen on the basis of academic achievement and proposed research.
Restrictions: For overseas students only; applicants may not be citizens of the European Union.
$ Given: An unspecified number of grants awarded annually; each for partial remission of tuition fees.
Application Information: Application form available from U.K. university registrars in December.
Deadline: April 30.

Dartmouth College Thurgood Marshall Dissertation Fellowships for African-American Scholars
6062 Wentworth Hall
Room 304
Hanover, NH 03755
(603) 646-2107
www.dartmouth.edu

Description: One-year residential fellowships for doctoral candidates at dissertation level in any discipline taught in the Dartmouth undergraduate curriculum; intended to allow completion of dissertation during fellowship tenure; participation includes ten-week undergraduate course instruction.
Restrictions: Limited to African-American scholars only; applicants must have completed all Ph.D. requirements except dissertation.
$ Given: An unspecified number of fellowships awarded annually; each with $25,000 stipend plus office space, library privileges, housing allowance, and $2,500 research assistance fund.
Application Information: Write for details.
Deadline: February 1.
Contact: Dorothea French, Assistant Dean.

Five Colleges, Inc.
Five Colleges Fellowships
Program for Minority
Scholars
97 Spring Street
Amherst, MA 01002
(413) 256-8316
www.fivecolleges.edu

Description: Residential fellowships for doctoral candidates at dissertation level in all disciplines, to allow completion of dissertation and contact with faculty and students on host campus; tenable at Amherst, Hampshire, Mount Holyoke, Smith College, or University of Massachusetts.
Restrictions: Limited to minority group members only; applicants must have completed all Ph.D. requirements except dissertation.
$ Given: An unspecified number of fellowships awarded annually; each for $25,000 plus housing or housing assistance, office space, library privileges, and departmental affiliation at host college.
Application Information: Write for details.
Deadline: January 15.
Contact: Carol Angus, Fellowship Program Committee.

German Academic Exchange
Service
Short Term Visits to Germany
Research Grants for Ph.D.
Candidates and Recent Ph.D.s
950 Third Avenue
19th Floor
New York, NY 10022
(212) 758-3223
FAX (212) 755-5780
www.daad.org

Description: One month to six months of grant funding for doctoral candidates and recent Ph.D.s to conduct research/study in Germany; for work in all fields; recipients chosen on the basis of academic achievement.
Restrictions: Maximum eligible age range of 32 to 35; working knowledge of German required; United States or Canadian citizenship required; affiliation with United States university required.
$ Given: An unspecified number of grants are awarded annually; each with monthly stipend, travel allowance, and health insurance.
Application Information: Write for details.
Deadline: February 1, August 1.
Contact: Barbara Motyka.

Institute of International
Education
Colombian Government Study
and Research Grants
U.S. Student Program Division
809 United Nations Plaza
New York, NY 10017-3580
(212) 984-5330
www.iie.org

Description: Grants for B.S./B.A. holders to pursue up to two years of study/research at Colombian Universities; relevant disciplines include agriculture, biology, business administration, economics, chemistry, engineering, education, health services administration, geography, history, Latin American literature, law, linguistics, political science, physics, regulatory development, public health, and remote sensing interpretation.
Restrictions: United States citizenship required.
$ Given: An unspecified number of grants awarded annually; each for modest monthly stipend, plus tuition and fees, health insurance, book/materials allowance, and one-way return airfare upon completion of study.
Application Information: Write for details.
Deadline: October 31.

Institute of International Education
Fulbright Fixed Sum-Bulgarian Government Grants
U.S. Student Program Division
809 United Nations Plaza
New York, NY 10017-3580
(212) 984-5330
www.iie.org

Description: Grants for B.A./B.S. holders in the humanities, physical sciences, and social sciences; for a six- to nine-month residency/exchange in Bulgaria (October-June).
Restrictions: Proficiency in Bulgarian language desirable; United States citizenship required; applicants must meet all Fulbright eligibility requirements.
$ Given: Five grants awarded annually; Bulgarian government funds stipend, housing, and health/accident insurance; Fulbright provides fixed sum for round-trip transportation plus additional monthly stipend.
Application Information: Write for details.
Deadline: October 25.
Contact: United States Student Programs Division.

Institute of International Education
Fulbright-Spanish Government Grants
U.S. Student Program Division
809 United Nations Plaza
New York, NY 10017-3580
(212) 984-5330
www.iie.org

Description: Grants for B.A./B.S. holders studying in all fields for study at a Spanish university. Of particular interest are projects dealing with contemporary issues.
Restrictions: Proficiency in Spanish (written and spoken) required; United States citizenship required; applicants must meet all Fulbright eligibility requirements.
$ Given: Thirty-five grants awarded annually; Spanish government funds tuition and stipend; Fulbright funds round-trip transportation, and expense allowance.
Application Information: Write for details.
Deadline: October 25.

Institute of International Education
Germanistic Society of America Fellowships
U.S. Student Program Division
809 United Nations Plaza
New York, NY 10017
(212) 984-5330
www.iie.org

Description: Fellowships for master's degree holders and some B.A./B.S. holders studying German language and literature, art history, history, economics, philosophy, international law, political science, and public affairs; for one academic year of study in Germany.
Restrictions: United States citizenship required; applicants must meet all Fulbright eligibility requirements.
$ Given: Four fellowships awarded annually; each for $11,000 plus consideration for a Fulbright Travel Grant.
Application Information: Write for details.
Deadline: October 25.

Institute of International Education
Study and Research Grants for United States Citizens
U.S. Student Program Division
809 United Nations Plaza
New York, NY 10017-3580
(212) 984-5330
www.iie.org

Description: Grants to support study and research in all fields, as well as professional training in the creative and performing arts; tenable at institutions of higher learning outside of the United States for one year; list of participating countries in any given year may be obtained from IIE.
Restrictions: Open to United States citizens with B.A. or equivalent; acceptable plan of study and proficiency in host country's language required.
$ Given: A variable number of grants awarded annually; covers international transportation, language or orienta-

tion course (where appropriate), tuition, book and mainte-
nance allowances, and health and accident insurance.
Application Information: If currently enrolled in a col-
lege or university, apply to the campus Fulbright Program
Advisor; applications also available from IIE.
Deadline: October 25.

Japan Ministry of Education, Science, and Culture Japanese Government (Monbusho) Scholarship Program
2-2 Kasumigaseki, 3-chome
Chiyoda-ku
Tokyo 100
Japan
03-581-4211
www.embjapan.org

Description: Eighteen-month to two-year scholarships
for non-Japanese graduate students to study at Japanese
universities and research institutes; Research Students
Program is specifically designed for graduate students
(undergraduate program also available) in the humanities,
social sciences, music, fine arts, and natural sciences;
open to citizens of countries with educational exchange
agreements with Japan.
Restrictions: Language proficiency required (twelve- to
eighteen-month language training program required if
language skills deemed insufficient); applicants must be
under age 35.
$ Given: An unspecified number of scholarships
awarded annually; each to cover monthly stipend, airfare,
tuition, and expense allowance.
Application Information: For further information, contact Japanese Embassy or Consulate.
Deadline: August 4.
Contact: Student Exchange Division, Leslie Fedsta,
Japan Information Center, Consulate General of Japan,
100 Colony Square, Suite 2000, Atlanta, GA 30361,
(404) 892-2700.

Japanese American Citizens League National Scholarship and Student Aid Program
1765 Sutter Street
San Francisco, CA 94115
(415) 921-5225
www.jacl.org

Description: Scholarships for undergraduate and graduate students, as well as for individuals involved in performing and creative arts projects reflecting the Japanese
American experience and culture.
Restrictions: Membership in Japanese American
Citizens League (or having parent who is member) preferred; United States citizenship required.
$ Given: An unspecified number of scholarships
awarded annually; varying amounts.
Application Information: Application forms are available from local JACL chapters in September; write
national office for list of local and regional chapters.
Deadline: March 1 for undergraduates, April for all
others.

National Collegiate Athletic Association
NCAA Postgraduate Scholarships
6201 College Boulevard
Overland Park, KS 66211
(913) 339-1906
www.ncaa.org

Description: Scholarships for varsity college athletes in sports which NCAA conducts national championships; for full-time graduate study in any field; recipients chosen on the basis of academic achievement (minimum 3.0 GPA), athletic achievement, and capability for graduate study.
Restrictions: N/A.
$ Given: One hundred and twenty-five scholarships are awarded annually: thirty-five in football, thirty-two in basketball (sixteen to men, sixteen to women), and one hundred and seven other varsity sports (thirty-six to men, seventy-one to women); $5,000.
Application Information: Applicants must be nominated by college director of athletics during final season of NCAA eligibility; maximum two football, two basketball (one man, one woman), and four other sports (two men, two women) nominations per NCAA member school per year.
Deadlines: October 2 for football; March 4 for basketball; April 14 for other varsity sports.
Contact: Fannie B. Vaughan, Executive Assistant.

National Italian American Foundation Scholarship Program
Silvio Conte Internship
1860 19th Street, N.W.
Washington, DC 20009

Description: Internship for undergraduate and graduate students to work for one semester in Congressman Conte's Washington, DC office.
Restrictions: Applicants must be of Italian descent; recipient must write paper about the internship experience and its expected benefit to recipient's future career.
$ Given: One internship paying $2,000 is awarded annually.
Application Information: Send SASE for details.
Deadline: May 31.
Contact: Dr. Maria Lombardo, Education Director.

National Italian American Foundation Scholarship Program
Italian American Regional Scholarships
1860 19th Street, N.W.
Washington, DC 20009

Description: Scholarships for high school, undergraduate, and graduate students in all fields; regions are East Coast, Midwest, Southwest, and Mid-Atlantic; recipients chosen on the basis of academic achievement and financial need.
Restrictions: Applicants must be of Italian descent.
$ Given: Twenty scholarships awarded annually; each for $5,000.
Application Information: Send SASE for details.
Deadline: May 31.
Contact: Dr. Maria Lombardo, Education Director.

**National Research Council
NRC/Ford Predoctoral and
Dissertation Fellowships for
Minorities**
Fellowships Office
2101 Constitution Avenue,
N.W.
Washington, DC 20418
(202) 334-2872
www.nas.edu/nrc

Description: Fellowships for graduate students in the humanities, social sciences, biological and agricultural sciences, physical sciences and mathematics, and engineering and applied sciences; recipients chosen on the basis of academic achievement and proposed research.
Restrictions: Limited to members of minority groups; United States citizenship or legal residency required.
$ Given: Fifty-five fellowships awarded; $11,500 for fellow, $6,000 for Institution; twenty dissertation fellowships available for $21,500.
Application Information: Write for details.
Deadline: November 5.

**Norwood University
Alden B. Dow Creativity
Center
Summer Residency Program**
Alden B. Dow Creativity
Center
2600 N. Military Trail
West Palm Beach, FL 33409
(561) 478-5526

Description: Ten-week residency program (June-August), held at the Institute, for individuals to conduct independent research to develop innovative projects in all fields; projects should hold promise of impact on their respective fields; recipients chosen on the basis of proposed project.
Restrictions: Open to all nationalities; applicants must speak English.
$ Given: An unspecified number of grants are awarded annually; each to cover travel within the United States, room, board, stipend, and project costs.
Application Information: Write for details.
Deadline: December 31.
Contact: Gail Ross-Edwards.

**Organization of American
States
OAS Regular Training
Program Fellowships**
Department of Fellowships and
Training
17th Street and Constitution
Avenue, N.W.
Washington, DC 20006
(202) 458-3760
www.ornl.gov

Description: Three-month to two-year fellowships for graduate students in all fields except medicine to pursue advanced study or research in other countries; tenable at OAS member countries; fellowships intended to contribute to host country on economic, social, technical, and cultural levels; recipients chosen on the basis of academic achievement and financial need.
Restrictions: Applicants must be citizens of OAS member countries; applicants must hold B.S./B.A. or equivalent and must be accepted at university or research facility for proposed work; language proficiency required.
$ Given: An unspecified number of fellowships awarded annually; each to cover expenses, tuition, and stipend, varying by country.
Application Information: Write for details.
Deadline: March 31.

Phi Eta Sigma
National Honor Society
Phi Eta Sigma Scholarships
228 Foy Union Building
Auburn University, AL 36849

Description: Scholarships for B.S./B.A. holders to support first year of graduate study in any field; recipients chosen on the basis of academic achievement.
Restrictions: Membership in Phi Eta Sigma required.
$ Given: Fifty fellowships are awarded annually (ten for graduate students, forty for undergraduates); each for $1,000–$2,000.
Application Information: Write for details.
Deadline: March 1.
Contact: Local chapter advisor.

Phi Kappa Phi Foundation
Phi Kappa Phi Graduate
Fellowships
Louisiana State University
P.O. Box 16000
Baton Rouge, LA 70893

Description: Fellowships for B.S./B.A. holders to support the first year of graduate study; recipients chosen on the basis of academic achievement.
Restrictions: Active membership in Phi Kappa Phi required.
$ Given: Fifty fellowships for $7,000 each are awarded annually; thirty honorable mentions for $500 each are also awarded annually.
Application Information: Applicants must be nominated by the university's chapter of Phi Kappa Phi.
Deadline: March 1.
Contact: Local chapter secretary.

President's Commission on
White House Fellowships
White House Fellowships
712 Jackson Place, N.W.
Washington, DC 20503
(202) 395-4522
WH-fellows/index.html
www2.whitehouse.gov

Description: Twelve-month appointments as special assistants to the Vice President, Cabinet members, and the Presidential staff; fellowships include participation in educational program; positions available for students in public affairs, education, the sciences, business, and the professions; recipients chosen on the basis of leadership qualities, commitment to community service, and career/academic achievement.
Restrictions: Limited to young adults, ages 30 to 39; civilian federal employees are ineligible; recipients may not hold official state or local office while serving as White House fellows; United States citizenship required.
$ Given: Eleven to nineteen wage-earning fellowships for up to a maximum of $70,500 are awarded annually.
Application Information: Write for details.
Deadline: February 1.

Rotary Foundation of Rotary
International
Rotary Foundation
Ambassadorial Scholarships
1560 Sherman Avenue
Evanston, IL 60201
(708) 866-3000
www.rotary.org

Description: Scholarships for graduate students with B.A./B.S. degree in any discipline; for one academic year in another country with Rotary club.
Restrictions: Applicants must be ages 18–30; members of Rotary clubs, as well as spouses and lineal descendants of members and employees of Rotary clubs, are ineligible; language proficiency test required in host country's language; open to citizens of all countries with Rotary clubs.

$ Given: An unspecified number of scholarships are awarded annually; each to cover transportation, academic fees, educational supplies, room and board, and additional expenses.
Application Information: By nomination from local Rotary club, each of which designs its own selection criteria.
Deadline: July 15.
Contact: Local Rotary club.

Winterthur Museum, Garden, and Library
Winterthur Museum Visiting Research Scholars
Office of Advanced Studies
Winterthur, DE 19735
(302) 888-4649

Description: One-month to one-year residential fellowships for doctoral candidates in all disciplines related to the Winterthur collections; intended for scholars who have been granted awards from other institutions but need a place to work/research; fellowship tenure features full access to museum resources and rental housing on Winterthur grounds; recipients chosen on the basis of proposed research.
Restrictions: N/A.
$ Given: Short term grants of $1,500/month.
Application Information: Write for details.
Deadline: January 15.
Contact: Research Fellowship Program.

Women's Research and Education Institute
Congressional Fellowships on Women and Public Policy
1750 New York Avenue, N.W.
Suite 350
Washington, DC 20006
(202) 328-7070
www.wrei.org

Description: Congressional fellowship program designed to train women as potential public policy leaders; fellowship runs January through September and involves thirty hours/week work in a United States Congress office as a legislative aide on policy issues affecting women; open to master's and doctoral candidates at United States institutions; relevant disciplines include humanities, social sciences, biology and biomedical sciences, engineering and applied sciences, biomedical engineering, technology management and policy, business administration and management, health services management and hospital administration, education, allied health professionals, medicine, nursing, public and community health, and law; recipients chosen on the basis of political/civic activity and interest in women's issues.
Restrictions: Limited to women applicants; nine hours previous graduate coursework preferred; United States citizenship preferred.
$ Given: Eight to fifteen fellowships awarded annually; each with $9,500 stipend plus $500 for health insurance and up to $1,500 toward six hours tuition at home institution.
Application Information: Request application after November 1.
Deadline: February 14.
Contact: Alison Dineen, Fellowship Director.

Bibliography: Graduate, Postgraduate, and Research

The Directory of Grants in the Humanities. Phoenix: Oryx Press, 1998–99.
Free Money® for Graduate School. New York: Facts On File, 2000.
Money for Graduate Research and Study in the Social Sciences. El Dorado Hills, Calif.: Reference Service Press, 1998–2000.
Peterson's Grants for Graduate and Postdoctoral Study. Lawrenceville, N.J.: Petersons Guides, 1998.

Index